New Testament Commentary

Hebrews to Revelation

F B Hole

Scripture Truth Publications

HEBREWS TO REVELATION

First published as articles in the magazines "Edification" 1929-33 and "Scripture Truth" 1945-47.

Hardback edition first published in May 1983 as "Epistles (Volume Three): Hebrews - Revelation" by Central Bible Hammond Trust Limited, Wooler.

Transferred to Digital Printing 2007

ISBN: 978-0-901860-45-3 (paperback)

ISBN: 978-0-901860-49-1 (hardback)

© Copyright 1983 Central Bible Hammond Trust

A publication of Scripture Truth

All rights reserved. No part of this publication may be reproduced, stored in a retrieval system, or transmitted, in any form or by any means, electronic, mechanical, photocopying, recording or otherwise without prior permission of Scripture Truth Publications.

Scripture quotations, unless otherwise indicated, are taken from The Authorized (King James) Version. Rights in the Authorized Version are vested in the Crown. Reproduced by permission of the Crown's patentee, Cambridge University Press.

Cover photograph ©iStockphoto.com/ofbeautifulthings (Tim Robbins)

Published by Scripture Truth Publications
Coopies Way, Coopies Lane,
Morpeth, Northumberland, NE61 6JN

Scripture Truth is an imprint of Central Bible Hammond Trust, a charitable trust

Printed and bound by Lightning Source

CONTENTS

Hebrews	pages 1-65
James	pages 67-95
1 Peter	pages 97-122
2 Peter	pages 123-141
1 John	pages 143-184
2 John	pages 185-190
3 John	pages 191-196
Jude	pages 197-207
Revelation	pages 209-297

HEBREWS

INTRODUCTION

A FEW PRELIMINARY words may be useful, before we consider the chapter in its details.

Although in our Bibles the title of this wonderful treatise always appears as, "The Epistle of Paul to the Hebrews," yet the author of it was led by the inspiring Spirit to suppress both his own name and the name of those to whom he wrote it. Almost every line of it however bears witness that it was addressed to Hebrew believers, and there are in it a number of small allusions which make it pretty certain that it was written by Paul. If so, we have in it that epistle to Jewish believers which Peter, in his second epistle, mentions as having been written by "our beloved brother Paul" (iii. 15).

As we go through it we shall see that the occasion of it was that a certain weariness had come over these saints, their hands were drooping and their knees feeble in the Christian race, and these disquieting symptoms raised fears lest this backsliding tendency might mean some of them falling into open apostasy.

We shall also see that the main burden of it is the immeasurable superiority of Christianity to Judaism, although the latter appealed to sight and the former to faith only. Incidentally also it called upon them to cut their last links with the worn out Jewish system, to which they had such a tendency to cling, as the Acts of the Apostles shows us. It must have been written only a few years before the imposing ritual of Judaism ceased in the destruction of Jerusalem.

The importance of this epistle for the present hour cannot be exaggerated. Multitudes of believers today, though Gentiles and hence in no way connected with Judaism, are yet entangled in perverted forms of Christianity, which consist very largely in forms and ceremonies and ritual, which in their turn are largely an imitation of that Jewish ritual, once ordained of God to fill up the time until Christ came. It may be that most of our readers are, through God's mercy, free of these systems today, yet most of us have had something to do with them, and almost insensibly the influence of them clings to us.

If our faith is stirred up as we read it; if our spiritual eyes get a fresh sight of the immeasurable glories of Christ, and of the reality of all those spiritual verities which are established in Him, we shall find ourselves thoroughly braced up to "run with patience the race that is set before us."

CHAPTER 1

THE EPISTLE OPENS in the most majestic manner. Hebrews is the only book in the Bible which begins with the word, GOD. We are at once brought face to face with the tremendous fact that God, who had spoken to the fathers of Israel by prophets in former days, had now spoken in divine

HEBREWS

fulness and with finality in His Son. Just notice in passing that this first verse witnesses that the epistle is to the Hebrews, for the expression, "the fathers," would have no meaning for a Gentile.

God being the *living* God, it is only to be expected that He would *speak*. Before sin came in He spoke freely to Adam, and face to face; afterwards He only addressed Himself to chosen men, who became thereby His mouthpieces. The prophets had to speak just what He gave them, and often they uttered words, the full meaning of which was hidden from them, as we are told in 1 Peter i. 10-12. When the Lord Jesus came to accomplish redemption God told out all His mind. He spoke not merely *by* Him as His mouthpiece, but *in* Him. The distinction, is not made in our Authorized version, but it should be, for the preposition in verse 2 is not "by" but "in." It is an important distinction, for it at once preserves the unique character of our Lord. When the Son spoke it was God speaking, for the simple reason that the Son was God.

Having mentioned the Son, the Holy Spirit proceeds to unfold His glory, not only that glory which is His essentially as God and Creator, but also that which is His by reason of His redemption work. This leads to a long but very necessary digression, which lasts until the end of the chapter; so much so that all these verses might be placed within brackets. We should then read straight from the word "Son" to the beginning of chapter ii. and find the sense complete. "God ... hath ... spoken unto us in His Son ... therefore we ought to give the more earnest heed." Indeed it is not until we arrive at verse 3 of chapter ii. that we discover what is the main drift and theme of this Divine speaking. It was "*so great salvation* which first began to be *spoken by the Lord.*" When God formulated His demands upon men it was sufficient that angels should serve Him, and that a man such as Moses should be His mouthpiece. Now that His great salvation is the theme the Son Himself comes forth and speaks.

However the immediate theme before us in chapter i. is the unique glory of the Son. Immediately He is mentioned our thoughts are swept forward to the moment when His glory shall be fully manifested, and then back to the moment when first it appeared, as far as all created beings are concerned. On the one hand He is the Heir not merely to David's throne but of "all things," and this expression covers things in the heavens and not only things on earth. On the other hand when the worlds were made He was the Maker of them. God created indeed, as we are told in Genesis i. 1, but when the Persons are distinguished, as in this Scripture, creation is attributed not to the Father but to the Son. The Son—whom we know as our blessed Lord Jesus—was the mighty Actor in those creatorial scenes of inconceivable splendour.

Verse 3 brings before us three great things concerning Him. First, we have *what He is*, as the outshining of the glory of God and the exact expression of all that God is. Secondly, we are told *what He has done*. By

HEBREWS

Himself He has done the work which purges sins away. How He did it we are not told for the moment, but we know it was by the death of the cross. Thirdly, *where He is* comes before us. He has taken His seat at the right hand of the Majesty in the heavens; that is, He sits in the place of supreme power, from whence everything shall in due season be administrated. How wonderfully these three things go together! The efficacy of the work that He did was dependent upon the fact of who and what He was; whilst the proof and demonstration of the efficacy of His work is found in where He is, in the fact that He is seated in the place of supreme power. If any believer in Jesus is still plagued with doubts and misgivings as to whether his sins are really and effectively purged away, let him look by faith to that seat on high where Jesus sits, and doubt no more!

In verse 3 we also find the wonderful fact that the Son is the Upholder of all things. The previous verse has set Him before us as the Creator of all, and as the One who shall inherit all things, now we discover that all things are upheld and hang together by the word of His power. We may talk sometimes about the laws of the universe. We may observe the working of the law of gravitation, though the real why and wherefore of it is unknown to us. We *may* even, before we are much older, have to listen to fickle "science" altering or overturning all that she had previously asserted as to these laws. Well, so be it! We know that THE LAW of the universe is the word of His power, and this is all that really matters. Any laws which we may observe, or think we observe, are very secondary, and should the leaders of scientific speculation suddenly reverse their pronouncements we shall not turn a hair.

Let us put this together then in brief fashion. The Son is the Creator, the Upholder and the Heir of all things. He is moreover the exact Expression of all that God is, being God Himself, and being that exact Expression He has come forth to be the Divine Spokesman on the one hand, and the Redeemer on the other. Had He spoken only we should all have been terrified; but as He has made purification for sins as well as speaking, we can receive with joy the revelation which He has made.

In verse 4 He is contrasted with angles, and this contrast is not merely mentioned and then dismissed; the theme is elaborated at considerable length, and continues to the end of the chapter. It is very definitely CONTRAST. In saying this we are pointing out one of the characteristic features of this epistle. As we proceed we shall find continued references to the old order of things, established when the law was given by Moses. These old and material things bore a certain resemblance to the new and spiritual things established and introduced by the Lord Jesus, and hence they were designed to act as patterns or types. Yet when these types are put alongside the realities which they typified an immense contrast is seen. As the heavens are high above the earth so the antitype exceeds the type. In

HEBREWS

our epistle the *resemblance* is taken for granted, and it is the *contrast* which is stressed.

It may be asked however, Why is the contrast with *angels* so elaborated, and even carried on into the next chapter? What is the point of it? Well, every Jew knew that angels played a very large part in connection with the giving of the law by Moses, though but little is said of them in Exodus. The words of Stephen, recorded in Acts. vii. 53 show this, as also the second verse of our second chapter. This display of angelic might gave a very powerful sanction to Moses and the law he brought them, in the minds of the people. And now there appears amongst men the Divine Spokesman, yet to them He is but Jesus of Nazareth, a humble and despised Man. There is no beauty about Him that they should desire Him or His words, nor is there any display of angels to accredit Him. It became therefore of the utmost importance to insist on the true glory of His person as being immeasurably above all angels. Had He been visibly attended by ten thousand times ten thousand, it would have added nothing to Him!

Two things are said in verse 4. First, He has a more excellent name than angels *by inheritance;* second, He has been *made* better than they. The words, "Being made," may also be translated, "Having become," or, "Taking a place." The first refers to His superiority by reason of His Godhead glory; the second to the place He now occupies in Manhood, as the Accomplisher of redemption. And notice that His superiority is equally pronounced in both, as evidenced by these little words in the sentence, "SO . . . AS." Read the verse again for yourself, and see.

These facts, as stated in verse 4, are supported and proved by a remarkable series of quotations from the Old Testament, extending from verse 5 to the end of the chapter. Let us just notice how the argument runs.

Verses 5 and 6 contain three quotations giving the pronouncements of God when introducing the Lord Jesus to men. They very definitely support what is said in verse 4, especially the statement as to His being better than angels by *inheritance.*

In verse 7 we have a quotation which plainly states the nature of angels and the reason why they exist. They are spirits in their nature and they exist as ministers to serve the Divine will. This is in contrast to what goes before and also to that which follows.

In verses 8 to 12 we get two quotations giving us utternaces of God to Christ, in both of which He is addressed as Man and yet He is saluted as God and as the Creator.

In verse 13 comes the quotation giving the decree which has exalted Him to the right hand of the Majesty on high, and this, we are assured, is something which never was said to angels. They are but spirits who are glad to serve, according to the Divine will, such humble creatures as those who once were fallen sinners, but who shall be heirs of salvation. All this, and

HEBREWS

particularly verses 9 and 13, show us that He is better than angels, inasmuch as He has *taken a place* which is so much higher than theirs.

There are seven quotations in all from the Old Testament in these verses: one in regard to angels and six in regard to Christ. These latter come from Psalm ii. 7; 2 Samuel vii. 14; Psalm xcvii. 7; xlv. 6, 7; cii. 25-27; cx. 1., and each deserves to be separately studied.

The first is deeply interesting for it shows that even as a Man born in time He is the Son of God. These words from Psalm ii. anticipate the virgin birth, and their fulfilment is announced in Luke i. 35. We may say they give us God's utterance to Christ at His incarnation.

The second is remarkable as showing how the Holy Ghost always has Christ in view. Reading Samuel we might think that the words only referred to Solomon. *Immediately*, Solomon was in view, as the words following those quoted show; but *ultimately*, Christ was in view.

The third gives us the decree concerning Christ at the moment of His reintroduction into the world in power and glory; not His first coming, but His second. We read the Psalm and the "Him" is clearly Jehovah. We read Hebrews and the "Him" is clearly Christ. What does that teach us? Notice also that the term "gods" may be used of any who represent God, whether angels as here, or men as in Psalm lxxxii. 6,—the passage which the Lord Jesus quoted in John x. 34.

The fourth is what is said to the Son by God at the opening of the Millenial kingdom. He is a Man, for God is His God, yet He is addressed as God. As Man He has His fellows, or companions, yet He possesses a gladness which is above them—and how glad we are that He does!

The fifth gives us the divine word addressed to Him in the moments of His deepest humiliation and sorrow—we might almost say, in the garden of Gethsemane. He who is being cut off in the midst of His days is declared to be the mighty Creator, who shall ultimately consume or change all in creation which needs changing, and yet Himself remain eternally the same.

The sixth turns our thoughts to Christ as the risen One and gives us God's utterance to Him as He ascended into the heavens. Thus we are conducted to the place where Christ is; and we are prepared to see Him there and to learn the meaning of His session in glory when we come to chapter ii.

All this wonderful unfolding of the excellence of our blessed Saviour is in order that we may be impressed with the greatness of the One in whom God has spoken to us. He is, as chapter iii. 1 puts it, "the *Apostle* ... of our profession." An apostle is a "sent one," one who comes forth from God to us, bringing the divine message. Our Lord Jesus has thus come forth, bringing us the complete divine revelation; only He is Himself God. This

HEBREWS

fact at once lifts all that He has said to us on to a plane far above all that went before. The prophets of old were fully inspired of God, and consequently all that they said was reliable and comes to pass, but they could never convey to us the revelation which we have in Christ.

Into the marvellous light of that revelation the Hebrews had been brought. And so have we, thanks be to God!

CHAPTER 2

SEEING THAT GOD has addressed Himself to us in Christ, who is far superior, not only to Moses but also to those angels through whose hands Moses received the law, we ought to give more abundant heed to all that has been said. With this the second chapter opens, and it is impossible to evade the solemn force of it. God's word spoken by angels was by no means to be trifled with, as Israel discovered before they had gone very far on their wilderness journey; what then shall be said as to the word that has now reached us in and through the Son of God?

A better rendering of the first verse is perhaps, "lest at any time we should slip away." To let slip the things heard would mean forgetfulness, but to slip away oneself from them might even mean apostasy. So also in verse 3 the word "neglect" carries the thought of not caring for God's great salvation when they were inside the Christian company as having professed faith, and not merely neglecting the Gospel when it was preached to them. In these words then we have the first of the solemn warnings against apostasy that we find repeated through the epistle; but this being so, the common use of these words in connection with the Gospel is fully justified. If the professor of Christianity who neglects the great salvation will by no means escape, even less will they escape who pay no attention to it when they hear it.

However the point in verses 2 and 3 is that it is more serious to trifle with God's salvation than to transgress His law, for there is no greater sin than that of despising the grace of God. Of old Moses had been the sent one, and had been commissioned to announce salvation out of Egypt to their fathers, and then through Moses that salvation had duly been carried out. The greatness of our salvation may be seen in the fact that He who has announced it is the Lord, whose glory has been set before us in chapter i., and from the fact that the apostles, who confirmed His message after His exaltation into the heavens, were themselves accredited by ample displays of divine power in the energy of the Holy Spirit who had been given to them. Further on we shall find that not only did the Lord Jesus act as the Apostle in announcing the great salvation, but that all is carried out through Him as Surety, Mediator and Sacrifice.

In our chapter we shall find that it is His priesthood that is emphasized. Presently a new order of things is to be established, spoken of in verse 5 as "the world to come." Every Jew expected that new order to be introduced by the advent of the Messiah. Now in that world to come angels will not be the supreme authority, though they will have certain services to render in it, as other scriptures show. It is in its entirety subject to Christ as the Son of Man, as the eighth Psalm had predicted, and when the Lord takes up His great authority "He shall be a Priest upon His throne" (Zech. vi. 13).

The quotation from the eighth Psalm covers not only verse 7 but also the first sentence of verse 8. In the rest of verse 8 and in verse 9 we have an inspired explanation of how the Psalm applies at the present moment. The quotation begins at the point where David, having surveyed the wonders of the universe, asks what man is worth. He used a Hebrew word which has the sense of "frail man" or "mortal man." Well, what is he worth? Evidently he is worth nothing. What then shall be said of the Son of Man? Ah! now we have a very different story. Even in the psalm David changed the word for man, and wrote "the Son of Adam"; and this we know our Lord was, as seen in Luke iii. 38. He is worth everything. Though once made a little lower than the angels He is to be crowned with splendour and be set in absolute dominion, with all things under His feet.

It is very noticeable that the quotation stops just at the point where, in the psalm, words are added which seem to confine the "all things" set under His feet to all things on earth and in the sea. The Old Testament view of things did not for the moment go beyond that. In our chapter however the moment we turn from the quotation to the explanation a far larger range of things comes before us. We are assured that the little word "all" is to be given its full value, without the least shadow of qualification. Search through the universe and there is to be found nothing which is not put under Him. In that world to come man, in the person of the Son of Man, is to be absolutely supreme.

This is a most wonderful and glorious fact, and it illustrates for us how God always sees the end from the beginning, and is never defeated nor turned aside from His purpose in anything to which He sets His hand. God never made angels to rule: He made them to serve. The only creature, of which we have any knowledge, that was made to rule was man. Only of man was it said, "Let us make . . . and let them have *dominion* . . . So God created *man*" (Gen. i. 26, 27). Man fell: he ceased to rule the lower creation in any proper sense; he ceased indeed to properly rule himself. What then? Has God's purpose failed? Not only has it not failed but, when the SON OF MAN comes forth in His glory, the Divine purpose will be seen established with an extended fulness and glory undreamed of when Adam was created, by any save God Himself. Instead of failing God has triumphed most gloriously.

Some may say to themselves—That may be, but there are no very obvious signs of it in the world at the present moment. That is so. We do

HEBREWS

not yet see all things put under Christ. Even those who profess to be His followers show very little sign of being really subject to Him. The fact is that we are living in a time during which there is very little to see except we possess that kind of telescopic sight that faith gives.

Faith it is that sees. This we shall find elaborated when we come to chapter xi, especially verses 8 to 22, and verse 27. These great men of old penetrated by faith into the unseen world, yet they never saw the sight that shines before us—if we really possess faith's keen vision. We see the once humbled Jesus crowned with glory and honour in the highest heaven. Did the Hebrews possess faith's telescopic powers of sight, penetrating to the glory-crowned Jesus, and to the things which are above the sun? *Do we?* If we do we shall not be neglecting the great salvation; we shall not be letting go nor slipping into apostasy. Looking unto Jesus we shall be running the Christian race with energy divinely given.

But what means this statement in Psalm viii., that the Son of Man is made "a little lower than the angels"? Have we not read in chapter i. that He is "made so much better than the angels"? There is an apparent contradiction here!

These passages where verbal contradictions appear upon the surface do us a good service if they cause us to pause, *and think*. Viewing them in their context and meditating upon them, we discover harmonies and teaching which otherwise we had passed over. See how it is in the case before us. In chapter i. the Deity of our Lord is the great point, connected with His Apostleship. Yet He has become a Man, so that God is His God. Seeing however that it is GOD who has become Man, He is of necessity "made so much better than the angels."

In chapter ii. the emphasis lies upon the Manhood of the Lord Jesus. He became a Man with a view to the suffering of death. Man was so created—spirit, soul and body—that he could die, by the spiritual part of him being separated from the body. In this respect man was made a little lower than the angels. Now the Son of God has become the Son of Man in so real a sense that as a Man He has taken up the death penalty and died for men. From this standpoint He has been made a little lower than the angels, for angels never die.

In these wonderful verses one expression is repeated six times: thrice in verse 8, once in verse 9 and twice in verse 10. It is the word for all or all things, and only at the end of verse 9 is it otherwise translated. The Lord Jesus has tasted death for "all" and not merely for the Jew. At the present moment "all" is made subject to Him, and in the age to come we shall see it to be so.

In verse 10 we find a second object that was in view in the sufferings and death of Christ. Not only did He accomplish propitiation for all, but He thereby qualified Himself—if we may so put it—for the position He was to take up according to the purpose of God. God has instituted a new pilgrimage. Of old He used Moses and Joshua to bring a nation from Egypt to Canaan. Now He has set His hand to the mighty task of bringing many sons, gathered out from all the nations, to glory. He will not fail in this glorious enterprise for, firstly, He who has initiated it has all things at His disposal, and secondly, the One to whom it is entrusted as Leader is the risen Christ. He went through all possible sufferings here in order that He might have full experimental knowledge of all the sorrows under which lay those who are now the sons on the way to glory.

Is it not a wonderful thing that the Lord Jesus should have condescended to become the Leader of our salvation? Wonderful as it is, it is a fact. Having died and risen again, He has placed Himself at the head of the great redeemed family that is being gathered out of the nations and led to glory. They are the sanctified ones of whom verse 11 speaks—that is, those set apart for God—but He is the Sanctifier. They are set apart for God by virtue of their connection with Him.

Our connection with Him is of a very close and intimate order, so much so that it can be said of Sanctifier and sanctified that they are "all of one." Of one what?—we may ask. Well, we are not told. But inasmuch as it goes on to say, *"for this cause* He is not ashamed to call them brethren," it would seem that the thought must be that He and they are of one lineage, of one life and nature. The day is now arrived in which we know, according to the Lord's own words in John xiv. 20, that He is in the Father, that *we are in Him*, and He in us; as also the day in which, according to John xvii. 19, He has set Himself apart in heaven in order that we may be set apart through the truth.

Three Old Testament Scriptures are quoted in verses 12 and 13 in order to show how thoroughly we are identified with Him and He with us, and also that this immense privilege was foreseen, though not realized, in the days before His advent. The first of the three is especially remarkable. It comes from the latter part of Psalm xxii., just at that point where the prophecy passes from His death to His resurrection, and the word "congregation" is translated into "church." The church (that is, the *ecclesia*, the *called out ones*) is that to which we all belong, and here it is quite definitely identified with the "many sons" and the "sanctified" of the earlier verses.

But if we were in this marvellous way to be identified with Him, it was necessary first that He should in His grace identify Himself with us in our need, and this He did in everything, apart from sin. He did not come to save angels but men. Consequently He did not take on Him the nature of angels but of men; and in particular of the seed of Abraham, for, as we know, our Lord sprang out of Judah. The word used here means, "to take hold of," and it has been stated that, "it is constantly used for 'taking up a person to help him,' though in other senses as well." Amazing grace this, when we see that it involved His taking a part in flesh and blood, which is the common lot of mankind; and that this He took in order that He might die.

Verse 14 is as clear on this as verse 9 had been before. Only death could meet the tragic situation in which we were found. Death is possible for man since he is a partaker of flesh and blood. His blood may be shed, his flesh go to corruption, his spirit depart to God who gave it—and all this is impossible to angels. Death is actually passed as the Divine sentence upon all men because of sin, and Satan who at the outset manoeuvred man into disobedience, now wields the power of death in the consciences of men, making them afraid and thereby holding them in bondage. What could destroy (that is, annul or bring to nothing, make of no effect) the devil and the power he wields? One thing only. Nothing but DEATH could annul *death*. And it must be the death of a MAN to annul death for *men*. All this was fulfilled. The Captain of our salvation, by taking part in flesh and blood, became a true Man, and for us He died.

Flesh and blood is a term which describes the state and condition of manhood, without reference to the question of sin. When Adam came forth fresh from God's creating hands he was a partaker of flesh and blood, but his humanity was *innocent*. He fell, and he and his posterity remained partakers of flesh and blood, but theirs is a *fallen* humanity. Our blessed Lord Jesus took part in flesh and blood and His humanity is the very essence of *holiness*.

Yet in all things it befitted Him to be made like to those whose cause He had taken up, as verse 17 declares. A very strong statement this, and the reality that it presents will be a theme of wonder and worship to us throughout eternity. Just think of how it might have pleased Him to stoop and rescue His sinful and degraded creatures without being made like them at all. That however would not have fitted His love, even if it could have been done in conformity with His righteousness. Having taken part in flesh and blood He would be made like them *in all things*. He would be tempted and suffer, as verse 18 says, and thus enter into all their experiences save those that involved sin; and this in view of becoming the High Priest of His people.

All through the latter part of this chapter the Lord is presented in the same light. Whether as Captain of our salvation, or Sanctifier, or High Priest, He is seen as standing on our behalf before God, and not as standing on God's behalf before us; as He is when His Apostleship is in question. As High Priest He acts in things relating to God, as also He is able to succour us in our temptations. Towards us He is ever merciful, while always maintaining the purposes and glory of God with the utmost faithfulness. But while this is so His personal glory and pre-eminence is fully established. He is not ashamed to call us brethren, but nowhere are

HEBREWS

we encouraged to turn round and use that same term towards Him, as sometimes is done.

Before we leave the chapter notice how everything is cast in a mould suited to Jewish minds. Each point is supported by quotations from the Old Testament, showing how that which is now established in Christ had been foreseen and indicated. This might mean nothing to a Gentile, but it would be very significant to a Jew. Moreover the truth is stated in terms which would instantly remind them of the way in which their ancient religion had foreshadowed these good things to come. The end of verse 17 is an illustration of what we mean, where the work of the Lord Jesus is spoken of as making "reconciliation" (or "propitiation," as it really is) "for the sins of the people." Why put it thus? Why not say, "for our sins," or, "for the sins of men"? Because then the truth would not have been nearly so striking to Jewish minds. As it stands it would at once turn their thoughts to the well known work of Aaron, and their subsequent high priests, on the great day of atonement; of which we read in Leviticus xvi, and which was a striking type of the work of Christ.

No new Testament book throws greater light on the Old Testament than Hebrews; and none shows more clearly how needful it is for us to read and understand the Old Testament. If we read Hebrews apart from this it is very easy to run away with mistaken notions.

CHAPTER 3

THE FIRST CHAPTER has presented to us the Lord Jesus as the Apostle, that is, as the Sent One, who came forth from God to us, bringing us the Divine revelation. The second set Him before us as the High Priest, who has gone in from us to God, representing us and maintaining our cause in His presence. Now we are bidden to consider Him very thoroughly in both these characters. We are to set our minds to it as those who aim at discovering all that is involved.

These Hebrews had taken up a new profession, or, we had better say, they had entered upon the confession of the name of Jesus, who had been rejected by their nation. The national attitude towards Him was summed up in these words, "We know that God spake unto Moses: as for this fellow, we know not from whence He is" (John ix. 29). The more these converted Hebrews considered JESUS and studied Him the more certainly would they know from whence He was: they would perceive that truly "He was come from God, and went to God" (John xiii. 3).

The Jews made their boast in Moses and in Aaron. God had indeed spoken to the one and made him His spokesman, and He had established the other in the priestly office; nevertheless both were dead. The Christian, and the Christian alone, has an Apostle and High Priest who lives, to be

HEBREWS

known and contemplated and loved: One who is God and yet Man, endowed with all the attributes and glory enumerated in chapters i. and ii.

He is worthy of our eternal study. Let us consider Him well, for as we do so we shall the more clearly see how rich is the place we have as set in relation to Him, and how high is the calling in which we partake. Both these things are mentioned in the first verse. Do not pass them over lightly. They are worthy of serious attention.

We are addressed as "holy brethren." This is tremendously significant. It does not merely mean that all Christians are brethren and all set apart for God. The expression must be understood in relation to its context, that is, in relation to what has gone before, and particularly to verses 10 and 11 of chapter ii. In the latter of these two verses we have "sanctifieth" and "sanctified," and in our verse "holy." These are all different forms of the same word. We are holy inasmuch as we have come into the wonderful sanctification of being "all of one" with the great Captain of our salvation. For the same reason are we "brethren," since He is not ashamed to call us that. In addressing us as "holy brethren" the Spirit of God is reminding us of the place of extraordinary nearness and honour in which we are set.

As holy brethren we partake in the heavenly calling. We all know how God called Israel out of Egypt and into the land which He had purposed for them. Theirs was an earthly calling, though by no means to be despised. We are not called to any particular place on the earth, but to a place in the heavens.

In the gospels we see how the Lord was preparing the minds of His disciples for this immense change. At one point in the midst of His ministry He bade them not rejoice so much in the possession of miraculous powers: "but rather rejoice," He said, "because your names are written in heaven" (Luke x. 20). Our names are inscribed in the records of the cities to which we belong, and in these words the Lord indicated that they were entering upon a heavenly citizenship. Later, in His farewell discourse, He spoke to them of His Father's true house which is in the heavens—that house of which the earthly temple was only the pattern and shadow—and He said, "I go to prepare a place for you" (John xiv. 2). Our place is there. Our calling is heavenly in its character and it has heaven as its end.

If these early Hebrew converts really took in these mighty facts by faith, they would without doubt have realized how greatly they had been elevated. It was truly no mean thing to have been the people of Abraham and Moses, called to a land flowing with milk and honey; but all that shrinks into comparative insignificance besides such things as being among the "many sons" who are being brought to glory, owned as "holy brethren" by the Lord Jesus, and thus called to heaven. But again, if so great an elevation for them how much greater an elevation for us, who with neither part nor lot in Israel's privileges were just sinners of the

HEBREWS

Gentiles? Only let us take time to ponder the matter and we shall find abundant cause to bend our hearts in worship of Him from whose heart of love such designs have proceeded.

Holiness and heavenliness characterize our calling, but the great thing for us is that we turn the eyes of our mind upon Jesus and earnestly consider Him. He is both Apostle and High Priest and in His greatness we may read the greatness of our calling. Verses 2 to 6 give us a glimpse of His greatness as contrasted with Moses. When, as recorded in Numbers xii., Miriam and Aaron spoke against Moses, they said, "Hath the Lord indeed spoken only by Moses? hath He not spoken also by us?" That is, they questioned his office as the prophet, or apostle, of that day. Then the Lord bore of him this remarkable testimony, "My servant Moses . . . is faithful in all Mine house." In this he was a type of Christ, who is faithful to Him that appointed Him in a supreme degree.

Yet even so we find that the relation here between type and Antitype is contrast rather than comparison. First, Moses was faithful in God's house as being part of the house himself; whereas Christ is the builder of the house. Second, the house in which Moses ministered was just Israel; he bore the burden of that nation but of that nation alone. The Lord Jesus acts on behalf of "all things." He that built all things is God, and the Lord Jesus is He by whom God built them. Third, in the small and restricted sphere of Israel Moses ministered as a faithful servant; but in the vast sphere of all things Christ ministers to the glory of God. Let us meditate on these points and we shall begin to have large thoughts of Christ.

Still we must not lose ourselves in the immensity of God's mighty universe, so we find that Christ has His own house over which He is Son, and we, the believers of today, are that house. We are His building, and He faithfully administers all that concerns us to God's glory, as Apostle and High Priest.

But, as it says here, we are His house, "IF . . ." That *if* mightily disturbs a good many people. It is intended to disturb, not the true believer, but the mere professor of the Christian religion. And here let us draw an important distinction. When in Scripture we are viewed as those born of God, or indeed viewed in any way as the subjects of God's work by His Spirit, then no *if* is introduced. How can there be?—for perfection marks all God's work. On the other hand when we are viewed from the human standpoint as those who have taken upon us the profession of Christianity, then an *if* may be introduced—indeed it must be.

Here are some who professed conversion years ago, yet today they are far from being Christian in their behaviour. What can we say as to them? Well, we aim at being charitable in our thoughts, so we give them the benefit of the doubt and accept them as believers, until conclusively proved not to be so. Still *there is a doubt:* an *if* comes in. The Hebrews, to whom our epistle was written, were many as to numbers and very varied

HEBREWS

as to their spiritual state. Some of them made the writer of the epistle feel very anxious. The mass doubtless were really converted people of whom it could be said, "But beloved we are persuaded better things of you, and things that accompany salvation" (vi. 9). Still in writing to them all indiscriminately what could be said except that all Christian privileges were theirs, *if* indeed they were *real* in their profession.

Now it is just this that the second part of verse 6 says, for it is time that tests reality. There is no more certain guarantee of reality than *continuance*. The false sooner or later let things slip, and turn away; the true hold fast to the finish. But then if any do let slip and turn away the real root of the trouble with them is, in one word, *unbelief.*

You notice of course that a parenthesis stretches from the second word of verse 7 to the end of verse 11. To get the sense we read, "Wherefore take heed, brethren, etc." It is an evil heart of *unbelief,* and not of coldness or indifference or worldliness, that we are warned against; bad as these things are for the spiritual health of believers. It was just unbelief that was the root of all the troubles of Israel in their wilderness journey, as the last verse of our chapter says. So the Israel of the days of Moses was in this a beacon of warning to the Hebrews of the Apostolic age.

In the parenthesis we have a quotation from Psalm xcv. It is introduced to our notice not as a saying of David but as a saying of the Holy Ghost, who inspired David in his utterance. In the last five verses of our chapter we have the Spirit's comment upon His earlier utterance in the Psalm, and here we have made abundantly plain what we have just stated above. Caleb and Joshua entered the land of promise because they believed; the rest did not because they did not believe. Their carcases fell in the wilderness.

A further word of explanation is necessary at this point lest we become confused in our thoughts. The history of Israel may be looked at in two ways: firstly from a national standpoint, then from a standpoint more personal and individual. It has a typical value for us whichever way we look at it.

If we take the first standpoint then we consider them as nationally a redeemed people, and that nationally they entered into the land God purposed for them, with the exception of the two and a half tribes, who became typical of earthly-minded believers, who fail to enter into that which is God's purposed blessing for them. From that point of view we do not concern ourselves with the fact that the individuals who actually entered into the land were, with two exceptions, entirely different from those that came out of Egypt. From the second standpoint we *do* concern ourselves with the actual state of the people and of individuals amongst them. Only two of those who left Egypt so believed as to actually enter Canaan. This latter point of view is the one taken in Hebrews, as also in

HEBREWS

1 Corinthians x. 1-13, where we are told that they are also in all this types or ensamples to us. They warn us very clearly of the awful end that awaits those who, though by profession and to all outward appearance the people of God, are really without that true and vital faith which is the mainspring of all godliness.

We are warned therefore against an evil heart of unbelief which departs from the living God, and bidden to exhort one another daily for sin is very deceitful. If believers are to exhort one another daily it means that daily they seek one another's company. This verse then takes for granted that, like the Apostles who, "being let go . . . went to their own company" (Acts iv. 23), we also find our society and companionships amongst the people of God. It also infers that we watch for one another's souls and care for one another's spiritual prosperity. But is this true of us all? The general spiritual health of Christians would be much better if it were. We are far more influenced by the company that we keep than many of us like to admit.

If however, any of us have professed the name of Christ without reality, then there is still in us the evil heart of unbelief, whatever we may have said with our lips; and the downward course that lies before us, except we be awakened to realities, is plainly set before us. The evil heart of unbelief is easily deceived by sin; and sin itself by reason of its deceitfulness hardens us, so that we become impervious to reproof. Then instead of holding "the beginning of our confidence stedfast unto the end," we let go and give up. But only the real, who do remain stedfast unto the end, are made partakers, or companions of Christ.

CHAPTER 4

NO WONDER THEN that chapter iv. opens with the words, "Let us therefore fear." This does not for one moment mean that we should always be filled with slavish dread, always doubting whether, enduring to the end, we shall be saved. It does mean that we should accept the warning which Israel's history affords, that we should remember the deceitfulness of sin and the weakness of our own hearts, and have a wholesome fear of in any way following in their steps.

The beginning of the second verse might more accurately be translated, "For indeed we have had glad tidings presented to us, even as they also." It is not "*the* gospel" as though both Israel of old and ourselves today had had exactly the same message presented to us. The glad tidings of deliverance from Egypt and entrance into Canaan was preached to them: the glad tidings of deliverance from sin and entrance into heavenly blessing has been preached to us. But in both cases the word preached does not profit apart from its being received in faith. The gospel is wonderful medicine for the broken heart, but it comes to us in a bottle bearing these directions

HEBREWS

—To be mixed with faith in those that hear. If those directions be not observed no cure is effected, and the rest of God is not reached.

The believer, and the believer only, enters into the rest of God. This is true whether we think of the typical rest of God in Canaan, which only Caleb and Joshua entered, or whether of the true rest of God which will be reached in a future day; and this is the simple meaning of the opening words of the third verse. The point is not that we, believers, are now entering into rest, are now in the enjoyment of peace with God—though that of course is delightfully true, and emphasized elsewhere in Scripture—but that it is believers, always and only believers, who enter into the rest of God; that rest which was purposed from the time of creation, but which has yet to be realized.

Verses 4 to 9 are occupied with an argument designed to prove that in no sense had the promise of God's rest been realized in connection with Israel's entrance into Canaan under Joshua. (The Jesus of verse 8 means Joshua, as the margin of a reference Bible shows). This argument was necessary for Hebrew readers since they might readily have taken it for granted that everything in connection with the rest had been realized in connection with their forefathers and that there was nothing more to come.

The argument might be summarized as follows:—

1. There is to be a rest, as indicated when God ceased from His works at creation.

2. Israel did not enter into the rest under Joshua, as proved by the fact that God had said, "If they shall enter into My rest" (which is a Hebrew idiom meaning, "They shall *not* enter"); and also by the fact that so long after Joshua as the time of David an offer was again made them as to entering. Such an offer would not have been made subsequently, if all had been settled under Joshua.

3. But God's promise is not going to fail of its effect; consequently a rest for the people of God—i.e., for believers—is still awaiting them.

The word used for "rest" in verse 9 means "a keeping of a sabbath." This connects the thought with what we have earlier in the chapter as to God's rest in creation, and also with what we have in verse 10. We shall only enter into the rest of God when our days of work and labour here are over for ever.

The early part of chapter iv. has established the fact that God's rest lies at the end of the believer's pathway. At the present time we are in the position of pilgrims on our way to that rest, just as formerly Israel were pilgrims on their way to the land of promise. When the rest is reached we shall cease our working, but on the way there we should "labour" or rather "be diligent" to enter in, taking warning by the fate which of old overtook so many unbelieving Israelites.

HEBREWS

The latter part of the chapter sets before us three great sources of help and guidance which are available for us on our pilgrim way. They are first, the word of God; second, the priesthood of Christ; third, the throne of grace.

The features of the Word of God are brought before us in verses 12 and 13. It is quick (i.e., *living*) and *powerful*. Like all living things it possesses amazing energy. Further it has extraordinary powers of penetration, for it can pierce its way between things most intimately connected—whether in things spiritual or things material—in a way impossible to the sharpest two-edged sword. Again, it is a discerner of the deepest thoughts and motives of men.

It is a remarkable fact that the word translated discerner is the one from which we get our word *critic*. Multitudes there are today who pose as critics of the Word of God, and their foolish criticism only betrays the fact that far from being living they are in spiritual death; that far from being powerful they are very weak, and that their supposed powers of penetration are practically non-existent. They have no real understanding of the Word which they criticise, and the phantom "authors" and "editors" etc., which they conjure up are the result, not of their powers of *penetration* but of a very undiscerning and disorderly *imagination*.

It is not man's business to criticise the Word of God, but to let the Word criticise him. Nothing tests us more than criticism. If we are proud and self-sufficient we bitterly resent it. Only if humble and walking in the fear of the Lord do we welcome the penetrating criticisms of the Word, and they are of the greatest possible help to us in pursuing our pilgrim way. Thereby we are enabled to see ourselves and scrutinize our own motives, and thus avoid a thousand snares.

The Word of God reaches us in the Holy Scriptures. Should someone ask us why we accept the Bible as the Word of God, we might well reply: Is not that word, which lives and is powerful, which penetrates and discerns the hidden and secret things, the Word of God? It is indeed. Is not the Bible marked by exactly those features? Without any question it is. Then what further need of proof have we, that the Bible is the Word of God?

Notice too how almost insensibly we pass from the Word of God in verse 12 to God Himself in verse 13. All is manifest in HIS sight. It is an all-seeing God with whom we have to do.

If the Word of God has full play in our understandings and consciences we shall become very conscious of our own insufficiency, and our weakness in the pilgrim way. How delightful then to turn to the second thing brought before us here—the priesthood of Christ.

In verse 14 we have the greatness of our High Priest emphasized, both as to His position and His Person. He has passed into (or, more accurately, *through*) the heavens. He did not stop in the first heaven nor in the second heaven when on His upward way, but into the third and highest heaven He went. Indeed, as another Scripture puts it, He "ascended up far above all heavens" (Eph. iv. 10). Still, the position of our High Priest is expressed here in this way so that Jewish readers might be reminded of Aaron going into the holiest of all. In the tabernacle the court, in which stood the altar of burnt sacrifice, was typical of the first heaven. The holy place typified the second heaven, and the holiest the third heaven in which God dwells. In entering the holiest Aaron passed through the heavens as far as the type was concerned. Our blessed Saviour and High Priest has passed through the heavens, not in type but in glorious reality. He is now in a place of infinite greatness and glory.

As to His Person our great High Priest is no less than the Son of God. This great fact settles everything in the most decisive way. There is no room for failure here. A mere man like Aaron might fail. He did as a matter of fact fail immediately, and the whole system of things which depended upon him failed likewise. Our High Priest will never fail, and all that hangs upon Him will stand for ever. We shall certainly "hold fast our profession" if we really believe this.

Then in verse 15 the graciousness of our High Priest is set before us. Having become truly Man, He passed through all human experiences and temptations, apart from sin. The rendering of our Authorized Version, "without sin." might mislead us by making us think it merely means that He went through all temptations without sinning. It means more than this. He faced all human temptations "apart from sin." He was perfectly and intrinsically holy. "In Him is no sin" (1 John iii. 5), and hence temptations proceeding from the flesh within were necessarily unknown to Him. He had no flesh within, "Every man is tempted, when he is drawn away of his own lust, and enticed" (Jas. i. 14). But this could not be said of Him.

Hence while He is said to be touched with the feeling of our *infirmities*, He is not said to be touched with the feeling of our *sins*. Infirmities are not sins but rather those weaknesses which are connected with human condition. In us they may of course lead to sin; in fact they will almost inevitably do so except we seek and obtain help from on high—the help of which verse 16 speaks.

But do not let us leave verse 15 until we have extracted therefrom the sweetness contained in two words. First, that word *touched*. A man of power and wealth may hand out much help and succour to needy folk, and yet never have time nor inclination to so enter into their sorrowful experiences as to have his heart really touched by them. We in our weakness and need may look to our High Priest in His glory and be sure that His heart is touched on our behalf. Then again that word, *feeling*. The wealthy man of many charities might go as far as being touched with the

HEBREWS

knowledge of the needs of the people he helps, but if he has no experimental understanding of their infirmities and struggles he cannot be touched with the feeling of their needs. Now the Lord Jesus has so qualified Himself by all He has passed through that He actually *feels*. He entered so truly into human life and human conditions, apart from sin, that He now knows from the human standpoint what He always knew from the divine standpoint. He possessed Himself of human feelings about human needs and human sorrows, and though now glorified on high He is still Man in heaven with all the feelings of a Man on behalf of men.

Oh, then, let us come boldly to the throne of grace! That throne is the third of the great helps which our chapter mentions. It is a "throne of grace" because graced by our great High Priest being seated there. Thence is dispensed mercy and grace for seasonable or opportune help, only we must come to the throne in order that we may get it.

What Israelite of old dared approach with any boldness the awful throne of the Almighty God? What Israelite indeed dared approach at all? When Ezekiel saw it in vision there was "the likeness as the appearance of a man above upon it" (i. 26), yet he had no boldness but rather fell upon his face. At the best his vision only pointed on to that which was to be realized in our day. Thank God it is now realized, but do we realize it? The Son of God sits on the throne, but it is the Son of God in true and tender and sympathetic Manhood. Realizing this all fear vanishes and we draw near with boldness.

The whole period of our lives down here is the time of need to us, and coming boldly all opportune mercy and grace is ours. We have but to approach in prayer and supplication. It is guaranteed to us by the character of the One to whom we come—His greatness on the one hand and His grace on the other. How rarely do we find these two things united amongst men. Here, for instance, is a very great man, with much power and ability to help others. But he cannot afford to adopt a very kindly attitude and make himself easily accessible lest he be overwhelmed by applicants. So he hedges himself about with secretaries and porters and other officials. He could do much for you if only you could approach him, but you cannot get at him. Here is another, and a kindlier, more accessible, more sympathetic person it would be impossible to imagine, but when you get at him he has no power to do anything for you. Thus it generally is amongst men; but thus it is *not* with our Lord. Both power and grace are combined in Him.

Chapter 5

THE EARLY PART of chapter v. continues this subject. The high priests of old represented men and acted for them in things relating to God. But then acting for men they had to be compassionate and sympathetic towards men. Hence they were taken from amongst men, being of the family of Aaron. Had God instituted an holy angel to act as high priest on Israel's behalf there might have been great gain Godward, as regards the accuracy and fidelity with which all priestly functions were carried out; but there would have been great loss manward, as regards such a matter as compassion on the ignorant. He who acts for men must understand mankind in an experimental way; and this is a thing pre-eminently true of Christ as we have just seen.

In Aaron's case he had, "as for the people, so also for himself, to offer for sins." In this we again find contrast and not comparison. Christ is indeed an offering priest, for it says later on, "it is of necessity that this Man have somewhat also to offer" (viii 3). But when we read on yet further in the Epistle we shall discover that Christ, "through the eternal Spirit offered Himself without spot to God" (ix. 14). There is all the difference in the world between Aaron offering FOR *himself* and Christ offering HIMSELF.

Aaron was also typical of Christ in the fact that he was called into the priestly office by God. Yet though Christ was called of God like Aaron He has not been called after the order of Aaron, but after the order of Melchizedec. He who said in Psalm ii., "Thou art My Son, today have I begotten Thee" (and this was quoted in verse 5 of chapter i.), said also in Psalm cx., "Thou art a Priest for ever after the order of Melchizedec." If at this point you refer to the psalm you will see that this was said in connection with Christ coming forth from death in resurrection, and being exalted to the right hand of God.

In verses 7 to 9 however we go back to "the days of His flesh"; that is, the days when He was upon earth before He died. Then was the great moment in the garden of Gethsemane, when He came face to face with the sorrows of death, and His cries were heard. He was heard "in that He feared," or, "for His piety." His personal perfections as Man demanded that He be heard. His cry was that He should be saved out of death—for the force of the word here is "out of" rather than "from." He was not saved from death but He was heard and saved out of it by resurrection and by Jehovah saying to Him, "Sit on My right hand, until I make Thine enemies Thy footstool."

Going into death and being saved out of it, two great things were achieved, as presented to us in verses 8 and 9. First, He learned obedience. Let us understand what this means. Far be the thought that there was ever the smallest taint of disobedience with Him. The fact is, that previous to His incarnation He had ever been in the place of supreme glory, where it was His to command. Having become Man He experienced what it was to obey. We believe we are right in saying that King George VI. was in early life a sailor. Going through that naval training, he learned the obedience which is necessary for the smooth running of the whole naval machine.

HEBREWS

When we speak of King George learning naval obedience we do not for one moment mean to infer that he started with an insubordinate and disobedient spirit, when as a young prince he became a midshipman. We mean rather to emphasize that he has acquired his naval knowledge not by the study of books but by actual experience. In just that way the Lord Jesus, though the Son of God, has learned obedience by human suffering.

The second thing achieved was on our behalf. His time of suffering and testing came to its close. He was obedient even to death—the death of the cross. Death was the supreme test and there He was perfected: that is, being ever perfect Himself, there His course of obedience came to its glorious finish and climax. But then it was exactly at that point that He effected propitiation, and thereby became the Author of eternal salvation. Not now a deliverance such as that of Israel out of Egypt, which though very wonderful was only for a time but a deliverance for eternity.

And that eternal salvation is received by those that obey Him. The value of faith was so strongly stressed in chapter iii., and the beginning of chapter iv., that we might have supposed that it would have read, "them that believe." Why does it say, "them that *obey* Him"? The obedience is of course the obedience of faith, but the point is that we should realize that the One who asks obedience from us is the One who has learned obedience Himself. In obedience the Son of God worked out eternal salvation, and that salvation is ours when we come under obedience to Him. Can we not see how divinely fitting this is? He only asks from us that obedience which He has perfectly rendered Himself.

In verse 10 we revert to the great fact established in verse 6. The verses that come between are evidently intended to impress us with the qualifications of our High Priest. Melchizedec is a mysterious personage who appears for one moment in Genesis xiv. and then vanishes. Yet he was priest of the Most High God. The One whom he typified is infinitely greater than he—the Son of God, who assumed Manhood, endured suffering, learned obedience, and by death itself became the Author of an eternal salvation to all that obey Him. To ALL that obey HIM—notice! If you obey Him and I obey Him, then we are included. Salvation is ours!

At this point the writer calls a halt to his flow of thought, and a lengthy digression ensues. Melchizedec was so important a type of Christ that there were many things to be said on the subject, and the theme was not an easy one. It required some depth of spiritual understanding if it was to be intelligently received. The thought of this fact very definitely raised the question of the spiritual state of these Hebrew believers, and of ourselves.

In the closing verses of our chapter the writer gently yet firmly upbraids his Hebrew readers because they were still but babes as to their understandings when they ought to have been like full-grown men. If we make spiritual growth our spiritual senses are exercised, we acquire spiritual

HEBREWS

habits, and we become able to assimilate the "strong meat," or, "solid food," of the truth in its wider and deeper aspects. If we do not grow, though we may have received "the word of righteousness" yet we become unskilled in it. We may even slip so far back that we need to be taught over again the simplest elements concerning foundation truth.

Thus it was with these early Hebrew believers. They doubtless were hindered by their old Jewish associations. Their tendency was to cling to the weak and beggarly elements of Judaism, and this made it very difficult for them to enter upon the simplest elements of the gospel. This may not be exactly our trouble, but we are very likely to be hindered by the elements of the world, and more particularly by the elements of that particular form of WORLDLY RELIGION in which we may have been brought up. Let us search and see if this be so; for if it is we too shall be like stunted trees in the garden of the Lord.

Let us also accept the warning of these verses to the effect that if we do not *go on*, the tendency for us is to *go back*. If we are not on the *up grade*, we shall get on the *down grade*. If we do not *advance*, we shall *decline*. We are in a scene of motion, and we shall not succeed in standing still.

Chapter 6

"LET US GO ON," is the opening exhortation of our chapter. Movement in the right direction is to mark us. We are to leave "the word of the beginning of Christ," as the marginal reading is, and go on unto "perfection." If we glance back over the last four verses of chapter v. we shall see that the point here is that we ought to grow in our understanding of the faith of Christ. We ought not to be like children staying year after year in the kindergarten, but advance until we assimilate the instruction provided for the scholars in the sixth form.

John the Baptist had brought "the word of the beginning of Christ." He laid "the foundation of repentance from dead works and of faith toward God." He put baptism in the forefront of His preaching, and spoke plainly as to eternal judgement. But things had moved on since his day. Great light shone when Jesus came forth in His ministry; and then, just as His earthly service closed, in His discourse in the upper chamber He promised the gift of the Holy Spirit. He told His disciples that He had "yet many things to say" unto them, but that they could not bear them then. He added, "Howbeit when He, the Spirit of truth, is come, He will guide you into all truth." (John xvi. 13). By the time the Epistle to the Hebrews was written ALL truth had been revealed, for it was given to Paul by his ministry to "fulfil the Word of God." (Col. i. 25). To "fulfil" in that verse means to "fill out full," or to "complete."

The whole circle of revealed truth then had been completed. Yet here were these Hebrews still inclined to dwell in their minds amongst these

HEBREWS

preliminary things, quite ignoring the fuller light which was now shining. Are we at all like them in this? In their case it is not difficult to see where the trouble lay. The special place of privilege, which belonged to the Jew nationally under the Old Covenant, had disappeared under the New. True, it only disappeared because a higher order of blessing had been introduced, so that, when converted, both Jew and Gentile are brought into privileges quite unknown before. Yet their hearts clung to the old and exclusive national position, and consequently they became dull of hearing as regards the fuller truth of Christianity. In our case we have no national position to maintain, but there is many a thing which we naturally love and cling to, which is dispossessed by the light of full and proper Christianity; and there is very real danger that we may close our eyes against that light in order to retain the things we love.

Oh, then may we heed this exhortation! May we allow it to repeat itself over and over again in our hearts—Let us go on! *Let us go on*! LET US GO ON! And then let us join the writer of the Epistle in saying, "This will we do, if God permit."

After this very encouraging word in verse 3, we drop abruptly into a very dark passage extending from verse 4 to verse 8. Though the transition is very abrupt it is not without very good reason. If Christians do not go on they invariably go back; and if it almost seems as though they *will* not go on, grave fears are aroused lest their unwillingness springs from the unreality of their profession; in which case their going back might proceed to the length of open apostasy. In the case of a Jew it would do so without fail.

It is apostasy that is contemplated in these verses, not just ordinary back-sliding—not the true believer growing cold and falling into sin; not persons, who have once professed conversion without reality, dropping their false profession and going back into the world—but that total falling away from, and repudiation of Christianity root and branch, which is APOSTASY.

No true child of God ever apostatizes, though not a few professors of the Christian religion have done so. If an Hebrew threw up his Christian profession and wished to get reinstated in the synagogue and amongst his own people, what would happen? He would find that as the price of readmission he would have to call down a curse upon Jesus as an impostor. He would have in effect to crucify to himself "the Son of God afresh, and put Him to an open shame." Now to go to such lengths as that is to bring oneself under the governmental judgment of God, just as Pharaoh did in the days of old when God hardened his heart, so that it is impossible to be renewed unto repentance.

In verses 4 and 5 it is contemplated that those liable to fall away may have shared in privileges common to believers in those times, and that in

HEBREWS

no less than five ways. We may well ask if it is possible for anyone to share in this way without being truly converted; and this question may well be specially urgent as regards the third of the five. Can it be possible to be a "partaker of the Holy Ghost" without being born again?

The answer to that question is, that it is quite possible. Only a true believer can be *indwelt* by the Holy Spirit, but all within the circle of Christian profession, whether truly converted or not, *partake* or *share* in the benefits of the presence of the Spirit. A man may be enlightened without being saved. He may taste the heavenly gift without receiving it. He may taste the good word of God without digesting it in his inward parts. He may share in "the powers of the world to come." (i.e. miraculous powers) without experiencing the real power of the world to come.

The terrible case of Judas Iscariot furnishes us with an illustration of this very thing. He walked for over three years in the company of the Son of God. What floods of light fell upon his path! What tastes he had of the heavenly gift and of the good Word of God! It could not be said of course that he was a partaker of the Holy Ghost, but he was a partaker of the benefits of the presence of Christ upon earth; and he shared, in common with the other apostles, in those miraculous powers which are here called "the powers of the world to come." He was one of the twelve to whom the Lord gave power over unclean spirits, and of whom it is said, "They cast out many devils and anointed with oil many that were sick, and healed them." (Mark vi. 13). Yet the miracle-working Judas was all the while a "son of perdition" and not a saved man at all. He fell away and it proved impossible to renew him unto repentance.

You will notice that the word here, is *"impossible"* and not *"improbable."* This one word is quite sufficient to show that there is no support in this scripture for the idea of a true believer falling away and being lost for ever. ALL those who "fall away" in the sense spoken of in this passage are for ever lost. It is not that they *may* be, but that they *must* be; and there would not be a single ray of hope for any back-slider, did it refer to such.

It refers then to the sin of apostasy—a sin to which the Jew, who embraced the Christian religion without being really converted, was peculiarly liable. By turning back to his ancient and worn out religion, thereby utterly condemning and disowning the Lord Jesus, he proved himself to be utterly bad and worthless ground. The contrast in verses 7 and 8 is not, you notice, between ground which this season is fruitful and the same ground which another season is unfruitful, but between ground which is essentially good and another piece which is essentially bad. The very form of this illustration supports the explanation just given of verses 4 to 6. Judas enjoyed "the rain that cometh oft," yet he only brought forth thorns and briars and was rejected.

In verse 9 the writer hastens to assure the Hebrews, to whom he wrote, that in saying these things he was not throwing doubt upon the reality of all them, nor even upon the most of them. The opposite to this was the fact. He stood in doubt of a minority evidently, but he was assured of the reality of the mass. He discerned in them features which gave him this assurance. He calls them "things which accompany salvation."

There are then certain things which act as a kind of hallmark upon our Christianity. The hallmark upon a silver article does not make it silver, but it gives us an official guarantee that it is silver. It assures us of its genuineness. What then are these things which assure us of the genuineness of Christians—things which so definitely accompany salvation that if they be present we know that salvation also is present? This question is answered in verse 10. And the answer is—they are many little acts which reveal genuine love for the saints.

Some of us may feel inclined to exclaim:—"How extraordinary! I should have thought that great acts of faith, great exploits of devotion to God would better have revealed reality than that." In so saying, or thinking we should be wrong. Under stress of emotion or sudden enthusiasm great acts are sometimes accomplished which are no true index to the heart. It is in these little things that we reveal our true selves far more truly. Ministering to the saints, who are the people of God, they showed their love toward God Himself.

It is one thing to minister to a saint because I happen to like him or her, and quite another to minister to a saint just as a saint; and it is this latter which is spoken about here. The former is a thing which might be done by an unconverted person; the latter is only possible to one who possesses the divine nature. Now this is just the point here. The things that accompany salvation are the things which manifest the divine nature; and things which therefore prove the reality of faith, in a way that the possession of miraculous powers or the outward privileges of Christianity never can.

Being thus assured of the salvation of the mass of those to whom he wrote, there is but one word of exhortation at this point. The writer urges them to go on doing as they had done—to continue diligently in this good way to the end, in the full assurance that their hope was not misplaced.

Hope has a very large place in connection with the faith of Christ, just as it had in the bygone dispensation. *Then*, whether patriarchs or prophets or just the people of God, they all had their eyes directed forward to the good things to come at the advent of the Messiah. *Now* the good things have been manifested in Christ—full atonement has been made, our consciences have been purged, we have received the gift of the Spirit. Yet even so we are not in the full enjoyment of the good things. For that we await the second coming of the Lord. What we actually have at the present moment we have in faith, and we enjoy by the power of the Spirit, for He is the Earnest of all we shall inherit. We are saved, in hope of all that is to come.

HEBREWS

It is very important for us to be clear as to this, and even more important it was for these converted Hebrews to be clear as to it. How often did they get reproached by their unconverted relations! How often taunted with their folly in giving up all the outward glories of the Mosaic system with its temple, its altar, its sacrifices, its priesthood—and for what? For a Master whom they could not see, for He had left them, and for a whole range of things as invisible as He! What fools they appeared to be! But were they really fools?

They were not. And if instructed in that which our chapter says they would be able to give very good reason for what they had done. They would be able to say, "It is really we and not you who are following in the footsteps of our father Abraham. Promises were made to him and you seem to have forgotten them, settling down as though contented with the shadow system of the law, which was given through Moses as a provisional thing. We have received Christ, and in Him we have the pledge of the fulfilment of every promise which ever was given, and we have fresh, and even brighter promises besides."

We need to have a hope which is resting upon a very well established basis if we are to hold it with full assurance. It is this thought which leads to verses 13-18. Abraham stands before us as a great example not only of faith but of hope also. It was when he had offered up Isaac, as recorded in Genesis xxii., that the promise of blessing was given, which culminated in "the Seed," which is Christ, according to Galatians iii. 16. That great promise had behind it not only the authority which always accompanies the bare Word of God, but also the added sanction of His solemn Oath.

How beautiful is this glimpse which we have of God, stooping to consider the feebleness and infirmities which mark even the best of His creatures! Here are Abraham and the later heirs of the promises. How easily their faith may waver! How full of uncertainties is the world in which they find themselves! Then God will condescend to their weakness and reinforce His Word by His Oath, saying, "By Myself have I sworn, saith the LORD."

His Word and His Oath. These are two immutable things—things that never change, never shift, never shake. They establish for us the immutability of His counsel. Never, *never*, NEVER, will He fail in any promise He has given, in anything which He has said that He will do.

And all this, you notice, is valid for us today. Verse 18 makes this very clear. What God was for Abraham He is for us. This is the beauty of these Old Testament unfoldings of God. What He is, He is in all times and places, and to all. The strong consolation flowing from these two immutable things is to be enjoyed by us who have embraced the Christian hope.

The Hebrews are said to have "fled for refuge to lay hold upon the hope." Why put it thus? Because it would at once carry their minds back to the regulations given concerning the cities of refuge, in Numbers xxxv.

HEBREWS

Those regulations had a typical significance which was exactly fulfilled in the case of the converted Jew. He was just like the manslayer who had fled to the nearest city of refuge.

Had Israel's national sin, in crucifying their Messiah, been reckoned as murder by God there would have been absolutely no hope. All must have fallen before the avenger of blood. The prayer of Jesus on the cross was however, "Father, forgive them, for they know not what they do." That was just as if He had said, "Father, account this sin of theirs to be manslaughter and not murder." God heard that prayer, so there was hope even for those who encompassed His death. Consequently on the Day of Pentecost Peter preached forgiveness for those who would turn in faith to the risen and exalted Jesus. That day the heavenly city of refuge was opened and there fled to it three thousand souls.

Multitudes of course did not believe, and consequently did not flee for safety, and they fell before the avenging Romans when Jerusalem was destroyed. Their unbelieving descendants in a future day have to face the great tribulation, and the judgment of God. But those who have entered the city of refuge have a hope set before them. It is connected with the moment when Jesus shall come in His glory; when He will cease to exercise His priestly functions after the pattern of Aaron and do so after the pattern of Melchizedec. Thus will be fulfilled the type as to the change of the priest (See Numbers xxxv. 25). When that takes place our hopes will be realized with Him in glory, and on earth it will be the time of jubilee, when every man will go back to his own proper inheritance.

The Christian's hope is heavenly; therefore it is said to enter into "that within the veil." *Within the veil* was the holiest of all, typical of the third heaven; that is, the immediate presence of God. *That* within the veil was the ark of the covenant, typical of Christ. Now Christ is entered into the immediate presence of God, and that on our behalf. He is entered as Forerunner and as High Priest. Our hope being centred in Him acts as an anchor of the soul, both sure and stedfast. Our hope has anchored itself already in the glorified Lord Jesus. We are already anchored to the Person and the place, to whom and to which we are going. It is as though an outgoing Atlantic liner found herself securely attached to New York by an anchor pitched in New York harbour, before ever she had got clear of the English Channel!

The fact that Christ has become our Forerunner guarantees that we who are the after-runners shall reach the place where He is. And as High Priest He ever lives to carry us through. That He should be our Forerunner is amazing grace; for in the East where these customs prevail the forerunner is a person of no consequence who clears the way for the important personage who follows after. Think of the Lord Jesus taking a place like that on our account!

HEBREWS

Chapter 7

IN THE LAST verse of chapter vi. the Lord Jesus has been presented to us in two characters. First, as the Forerunner; His arrival in heaven being the preliminary to the arrival there of the children whom God has given Him. Second, as an High Priest after Melchizedec's order; whose ministry ensures the safe arrival of the children, and the fulness of their blessing. This last verse also has completed the digression which began with verse 11 of chapter v., and has brought us back to the exact point we had reached in verse 10 of that chapter.

Consequently in the first verse of chapter vii. we resume the interrupted flow of thought, and the whole chapter is occupied with the contrast between the Priesthood of Christ and that of Aaron. We are made to see the immeasurable superiority of Christ as a Priest of Melchizedec's order; and we hear at least of some of those things, which were hard to be uttered to a people who were dull of hearing. We, being Gentiles, may not have our minds so filled with the faded glories of the Aaronic priesthood, and hence we may not find the theme so difficult.

In the first three verses of our chapter we are given a most graphic summary of all that is recorded of Melchizedec in the latter part of Genesis xiv. We learn that he is introduced there with the design of furnishing us with a type of the Son of God. His very name had a meaning, as is so often the case with Biblical names, and interpreted, it means, King of righteousness. He is presented as King of Salem, which interpreted means peace. In the coming millennial age the Lord Jesus will be manifested in just that double character.

Moreover, in the Old Testament story Melchizedec is introduced abruptly; no genealogy is given, no mention is made of his birth, his death, nor of the number of his years, no hint is given of another arising to succeed him in his priestly office. This is the more remarkable inasmuch as Genesis is exactly the book which does furnish us with just those details in regard to the other striking characters that pass across its pages. Why then were these details omitted as regards Melchizedec? Just that he might be a more accurate type of the Son of God. We believe this to be the meaning of the third verse, and not, as some have imagined, that he was some kind of supernatural personage.

Having then this condensed summary in our minds we are bidden in verse 4 to consider in detail his greatness as contrasted with Aaron or even Abraham; and that firstly, as shown in connection with *the law as to tithes*. This occupies verses 4 to 10.

Aaron and his descendants, who came out of the tribe of Levi, were supported by the tithes which they received from the rest of the children of Israel. Yet the patriarch Abraham, out of whom came Levi and Aaron and all his descendants, paid tithes to Melchizedec. Hence it is argued,

HEBREWS

Levi and Aaron, who were in this way acknowledged as superiors by the rest of Israel, themselves acknowledged Melchizedec as their superior, by Abraham their father.

And further, Abraham, who paid tithes to Melchizedec, also received blessing from him; and it is said, "without all contradiction the less is blessed of the better." So in this way also the superiority of Melchizedec to Abraham and his descendants is established. The point here, be it remembered, is not that Melchizedec was a greater man than Abraham as to his character, or that he knew more of God—as to that we have no information, one way or the other—but simply that he must be acknowledged as holding from God a higher position; and in that higher position or order he was typical of Christ.

Verses 11 to 14 are occupied with another point of the argument, based upon the fact that our Lord sprang out of Juda, and hence had no link with the priests of Aaron's order. He was an altogether *different* priest and of *a different order*. What did this show? It showed that perfection had not been reached by the Levitical order of things, and it indicated that a change had come in as regards the whole law-system of which the Levitical priesthood was a part. We shall find rather more detail as to that change when we read the next chapter.

In verses 14 to 19 the argument is enforced by another consideration. Aaron's priesthood was instituted in connection with the law. Christ's priesthood is sustained in the power of *endless life*. The law is here spoken of as, "the law of a carnal commandment," inasmuch as its commands were all aimed either at curbing and suppressing the evil tendencies of the flesh, or at bringing out of it the good that pleases God. But then, as we are told in the epistle to the Romans, the flesh is not subject to the law of God, and in it no good dwells.

Hence the commandment going before Christ has been set aside, as verse 18 informs us. Though in itself holy and just and good, it was rendered weak and unprofitable by reason of the bad and impossible nature of the flesh with which it had to deal. Verse 18 does not for one moment mean that the holy demands of God have been abated, or that they have been set aside so that now men may just act as they please. But it does mean that the whole law system has been set aside in favour of something much higher and better.

In order that this may be plainly seen we quote the passage as rendered in the New Translation by J. N. Darby, "For there is a setting aside of the commandment going before for its weakness and unprofitableness, (for the law perfected nothing,) and the introduction of a better hope by which we draw nigh to God." As in chapter vi., so here, Christianity is described as "a hope." Only it is "a better hope." When Israel entered the land of promise, they took it as a foretaste of better and larger things to come with the advent of their Messiah. We Christians have entered into good things of a spiritual sort. We have the forgiveness of sins, eternal life and the gift of the Spirit; yet they are but foretastes of the fulness of heavenly blessing which is to come. A better hope has been introduced, and by that hope—since it centres in Christ, who as High Priest has gone for us within the veil—we *draw nigh to God*, instead of being kept at a distance as was the case with the most eminent saint under the law. This thought we shall find greatly amplified when we come to chapter x.

The law, as we are reminded here, made nothing perfect. God was not perfectly made known in connection with it, nor was redemption perfectly accomplished, nor were believers perfected as regards their consciences. It came in by the way as a provisional measure, filling up the time until Christ came. Now, Christ being come, it is superseded by something which goes far beyond it, both in the standard it sets, and in what it gives and accomplishes.

In verses 20 to 22 we go a step further. Our attention is drawn to the fact that the Lord Jesus was instituted as Priest for ever *by the oath of God*. There was no such impressive and solemn word when Aaron was instituted in the priest's office. This indicates that there is a better testament, or covenant, connected with Jesus. Moreover He stands related to that covenant in a way that neither Moses nor Aaron ever were to the old covenant. He has become the Surety of it; that is, He has accepted full responsibility in regard to it, has become bail for it, so that should anything go wrong the cost of it would fall upon Him. This is of course full guarantee that nothing will go wrong with it to all eternity. All that is established in connection with the new covenant will abide.

Another contrast is brought before us in verses 23 and 24. Aaron and his descendants exercised their office one after the other and died. The Lord Jesus abides for ever and consequently His priesthood is *unchangeable*, that is, *it never has to be transmitted to another*. The happy result which flows from this is stated in verse 25. Those that avail themselves of His priestly services, coming to God by Him, are saved "to the uttermost," or, "completely," because He always lives to make intercession for them. The salvation here spoken of is that daily, momentary salvation from every adverse power, which every believer needs all the way home to glory.

This verse is often quoted to show that the Lord is able to save the worst of sinners. That is most happily true, and the verse that states it is 1 Timothy i. 15. Had that been the point here our verse would doubtless have ended, "seeing He died for them and rose again." But the word is, "seeing He ever liveth." The salvation therefore is that which flows to us by His life of unbroken priestly intercession.

Suppose a distressed Jew had applied to the high priest of his day for that compassion and help which he should be ready to give him, according to the second verse of chapter v. He finds him perhaps a most kindly and

HEBREWS

helpful man. But on going a little later, just when the crisis of his case has arrived, he learns that he has that very day died! You can easily imagine the Jew's distress. Another man who knows nothing of his case, and possibly of an entirely different disposition, becomes high priest. There was no salvation to the uttermost for him in the former high priest, and if he now gets any salvation at all he can only get it by beginning all over again with the new man. Thanks be to God, no experience at all akin to this can ever befall us. Our High Priest lives eternally.

Let us not leave verse 25 without noticing that in it believers are described as those "that come unto God by Him." It is a very prominent thought in this epistle that the Christian has boldness and liberty to come to God, whereas in the former dispensation all true access to God was forbidden. These words also indicate that the great objective in all Christ's priestly service is to bring us to God, and to maintain us there. On the one hand there is no access to God save BY HIM. On the other, all His compassionate service on our behalf, sympathizing, succouring, saving, is a means to an end. The end being this, that thereby lifted above the things that otherwise would overwhelm us, we might be maintained in the presence of God.

The last three verses of our chapter seem to clinch the whole argument and to sum up the situation, and we find that everything hinges upon *the greatness of the ONE* who is our High Priest.

What an extraordinary statement is made in verse 26! We should certainly have reversed it, and stated that seeing our High Priest was so wonderful a rather remarkable people were suited to Him. But no, the statement here is, that an High Priest of this remarkable character was suited to us! As the Holy Ghost views things, the many sons being led to glory, the Christian company, bear such a character that no less an High Priest becomes them.

The character of our High Priest is presented to us in a seven-fold way; and each item gives us a point of contrast with the priests of old. The first three items, holy, harmless, undefiled, present no difficulty. It is obvious that none of these three things characterized in an absolute way any priest of Aaron's race.

The fourth is, "separate from sinners," or, more accurately, "separated from sinners." It refers not only to the fact that He was ever wholly separate to God in His spirit and ways, even while eating and drinking with publicans and sinners, but to the fact that now in resurrection He is apart altogether from the whole scene where sinners move. "In that He died, He died unto sin once: but in that He liveth, He liveth unto God" (Rom. vi. 10). We may quote also the Lord's own words in John xvii. 19., "For their sakes I sanctify Myself, that they also might be sanctified through the truth." The root meaning of "sanctify" is *to set apart*, and the

Lord was alluding to the place He was about to take up in resurrection and in glory. In our verse, the thought of His glory comes in the fifth item which closes it, "Made higher than the heavens." Our High Priest is not merely a risen Man, but exalted above all. The heavens and all that they contain are beneath His feet. If we consider these five items alone, we can see that no high priest constituted under the law is worthy of mention beside Him.

But there is more. A sixth contrast fills verse 27. They offered up daily sacrifices, not only for the sins of the people but for their own sins as well. He offered one sacrifice, and He offered it once for all. It was for the people truly, but it was not for Himself. It was "HIMSELF," instead of being *for* Himself. He was the Sacrifice as well as the Offerer! Here we have the great truth alluded to, which we shall find expanded in all its glorious details when we come to chapters ix. and x.

Seventhly, and lastly, there comes the contrast between the persons who held priestly office under the law, and the Person who is our High Priest today. They were just men, with the usual infirmities of men. He is the Son Himself. This of course is the bed-rock fact upon which all stands. WHO HE IS, settles everything. It carries with it all the contrasts which have been dwelt upon in the chapter. Let us dwell upon it—He is the Son, who is consecrated for ever more.

The word "consecrated" is really "perfected," as the margin of a reference Bible will show. Here we get that word, *perfect* again, which we had in verse 9 of chapter v. There it was stated that His whole course of testing and obedience on earth having been brought to completion in death and resurrection, He became the Author of eternal salvation. Here we find that in the same way He became High Priest. The Son was eternally with the Father, He was Creator and Sustainer of all things. But it was not then that He assumed this office. It was when He had become Man, tasted all possible sorrows, endured all possible testings, suffered death and reached perfection in His risen glory, that He was constituted High Priest by the oath of God.

Now let us just meditate upon these things, giving them time to sink into mind and heart, and surely we shall be filled with confidence in His ability to save to the uttermost, and have our hearts filled with praise and thanksgiving to God.

Chapter 8

Chapter vii. having set before us in full detail the contrast between the temporary priesthood of Aaron and the abiding priesthood of Christ, chapter viii. opens with a summary of the whole matter. In this summary, occupying verses 1 and 2 there are four things which we shall do well to note.

HEBREWS

Firstly, the Lord Jesus is "*such* an High Priest," that is *such an One* as chapter vii. has shown Him to be. We need therefore to refresh our minds as to all those points of contrast which show forth the infinite superiority of Christ, as expounded in that chapter.

Secondly, being such He has taken His seat at the highest point of glory. The supreme Majesty has His throne in the heavens, and on the right hand of that throne He is seated—that is, in the place which signifies that all its executive functions are vested in Him. There is no weakness, no infirmity, in Him. The place He fills indicates that He wields all power. We learned that this exalted place is His when we had only read so far as verse 3 of chapter i.; but there we saw Him seated in glory as the answer to His finished work in the purging of sins. Here it is as the Priest that He is crowned with glory.

Thirdly, His priestly ministry concerns itself, not with the holy places on earth, constructed and pitched by Moses, which were the scenes of Aaron's ministry, but with that real sanctuary and tabernacle which came from the hand of God. The real sanctuary is the heaven of God's immediate presence: the true tabernacle is that mighty universe of created things, wherein the third heaven of God's presence lies. Christ's priestly service has to do with God and His presence as its centre; whilst within its circumference it embraces the whole creation of God. What a stupendous thought is this! How paltry do Aaron's glories look beside it!

Fourthly, such an High Priest as this is *ours*. "*WE have* such an High Priest"; while Israel had priests of Aaron's order. This one fact, apart from all other considerations, indicates how far in advance of Judaism is Christianity. These Hebrews, as we have seen, were inclined to slackness; some of them showed signs of going back. Let them lay hold of this, and how it would encourage them to hold fast, and keep on in the path of faith. Let us lay hold of it and we too shall feel its encouraging power.

Our thoughts turn from the High Priest Himself to His service and ministry when we read verses 3 to 6. It is helpful to notice that verse 5 is really a parenthesis; the whole verse might well be printed within brackets. The sense follows straight on from verse 4 to verse 6.

Though the Lord Jesus is not a priest of Aaron's order yet in many a way He exercises His ministry after the pattern set forth in Aaron. So it is necessary that He should have something to offer in the presence of God; and that something cannot be a gift of the kind that was customary in connection with the law, for had He been on earth He would have been no priest at all, for He did not spring out of Levi or Aaron. His priesthood is of an heavenly order. Only as risen and glorified has He formally assumed His priestly office.

What the Lord has to offer in His priestly capacity we are not told at this point; but we believe that the reference is, not to the fact that He offered up Himself, as stated in verse 27 of the previous chapter, but to what we find when we reach the last chapter of the epistle, verse 15. It is "by Him" that we offer the praise of our lips to God. He it is, who offers up to God as the great High Priest all the praises springing from those who have been constituted priests by the grace of God. What we *are* told is that His ministry is more excellent than any that was entrusted to Aaron; and that its superiority is exactly proportioned to the superiority of the promises and the covenant of which He is the Mediator.

Before considering this, however, let us make note of two things. First, that the last clause of verse 4 shows us that this epistle was penned before Jerusalem was destroyed, when the Jewish offerings ceased. "There *are* priests," it says, not, "there *used to be.*" This same fact confronts us when we come to the last chapter; and the importance of it is made manifest there.

In the second place notice that in the parenthesis (verse 5) it is made quite plain that the tabernacle and all its appointments were only a shadowy representation of heavenly things; and *not the things themselves*. This no doubt was a hard saying to a Jew, for he was very apt to think of these visible things in which he boasted as though they were the great end, beyond which nothing was needed. He should not have thought of them in this way, for from the outset they were declared to be but a representation of the things God had before Him. Moses was not to deviate one hair's breadth from the pattern shown to him in the mount. Had he deviated he would have misrepresented instead of representing the great realities which had to be shadowed forth.

This fact being digested we at once see that the Old Testament types, connected with tabernacle and offerings, are worthy of our earnest consideration. The study of them is not, as some may think, an intellectual pastime giving scope to a lively imagination, but a pursuit in which there is much instruction and profit. They must be interpreted of course in the light of the heavenly things themselves, which are revealed in the New Testament.

The ministry of Christ as Priest, the new covenant, of which He is the Mediator, and the promises on which that covenant is founded, are all brought together in verse 6.

It could hardly be said that the old covenant of law was established upon promises at all, though there were certain promises connected with it. It was established rather upon a bargain, in which Israel undertook in all things to obey, and God guaranteed certain blessings conditional upon their obedience. The bargain was hardly concluded before it was broken by Israel making the golden calf. The fact that the new covenant is established upon *promises*, that those promises are *God's*, and that they are *better* than anything proposed under the law, at once differentiates it sharply from the old. To gain some idea of these better promises you must read the latter part of our chapter, which is quoted from the passage in Jeremiah xxxi.—where the new covenant itself is promised—verses 31 to 34. God's "I will," is the characteristic feature of it. All is a question of what God is going to do, and of what consequently Israel is going to be and have.

Now of this better covenant Christ is the Mediator. We might well ask, On what ground can God thus scatter blessings upon unworthy men without infringing the claims of righteousness? The only possible answer to this is found in the mediatorial work of Christ. As Mediator He has given Himself "a ransom for all" (1 Tim. ii. 6). As Mediator too He administers the covenant which has been established in His blood.

The Lord Jesus is presented to us in this epistle in a variety of characters. We sometimes sing,

> *"How rich the character He bears,*
> *And all the form of love He wears,*
> *Exalted on the throne."*

but do we stop sufficiently to consider the richness of His character in all its variety? We have already had Him brought before us as Apostle, High Priest, Forerunner, Surety, Victim, and now as Mediator. All these offices He holds in connection with the new covenant and those who come into new covenant blessing. As Apostle He announces it. As Surety He assumes full responsibility for it. As Victim He shed the blood that ratifies it. As High Priest He sustains it. As Mediator He administers it. As Forerunner He guarantees the arrival in glory of all those blessed under it in the present dispensation.

What flaw can be discovered in this? None whatever! Where is the loophole through which evil or failure may creep? No such loophole exists! All new covenant blessing is rooted and grounded in the mighty Son of God and is as flawless and perfect as He. Is not this magnificent? Does it not fill our souls with assurance and triumph?

The first covenant of law was not faultless as verse 7 indicates. There was no fault in the law, but the covenant was faulty inasmuch as all was conditioned upon faulty man. Hence it is set aside in favour of the second, which is based upon God's purpose and God's work. As the last verse of the chapter puts it, the very fact that He speaks of a *new* covenant shows that the first has grown *old* and is ready to disappear.

Jeremiah's prophecy, which is quoted here, shows us that the new covenant is to be formally established with the house of Israel and the house of Judah; that is, with restored and reunited Israel. Under it they will enter upon the blessings of the millennial reign. By the new birth the law will be written on their hearts, so that it will be as natural to them to fulfil it as now it is natural to them to infringe it. Moreover their sins will be forgiven; they will have the knowledge of God, and be His people. But the gospel today brings us just these blessings upon an exactly similar basis.

The fact is that everyone converted today, no matter from what nation they come, is blessed upon new covenant principles, though as yet the new covenant is not formally established at all; and when it is established it will be with Israel, and not with the nations, nor even with the church. We have it, in the spirit of it, and thus we anticipate what is to come. At the same time we must carefully note that Christian blessings are by no means confined to those promised to Israel under the new covenant. On the contrary we enjoy blessings which go far beyond them. Such, for instance, are the blessings spoken of in the epistle to the Ephesians.

Chapter 9

Chapter viii. ends with the ominous words, "ready to vanish away." Thus it was that the Holy Spirit, who inspired these words, prepared the minds of the Jewish disciples for the disappearance of their venerated religious system, which came to pass within a very few years by the destruction of Jerusalem. The temple being destroyed, the priesthood slain, the sacrifices stopped, Judaism has become but the pale and bloodless shadow of its former self. And in itself, and at its best, it was only a shadow of good things to come.

Yet we must not underestimate the value of the shadows connected with the law. They had very great value *until the moment came in which the realities typified were revealed;* just as the moon is of much value until the sun rises. At the heart of this typical system lay the tabernacle and its furniture, and the first five verses of chapter ix. summarize the details connected with this. It was the sanctuary, where God placed the cloud which signifies His presence, but it was a worldly one. So also were all the ordinances of the divine service connected with it. Hence it was not the object of the writer to speak particularly of these details.

His object was rather to point out that the tabernacle was in two parts, the holy place, and then the holiest of all, and that while the priests of Aaron's line had full liberty to enter the former the latter was forbidden to them; into it they had no admittance at all. When once the divine glory had taken possession of the holiest no human foot trod there, with one exception. One man alone might enter, and he only once every year, and that under one stringent condition; he must approach, "not without blood." If we turn to Leviticus xvi. and read it, we shall get all the details of that solemn occasion.

What did it all mean? It doubtless foreshadowed the fact that the blood of Christ is the only ground of approach to God, yet what the Holy Ghost was really saying in the whole arrangement was that in the old dispensation there was no real approach to God at all. The way in was not yet made manifest. We shall find the wonderful contrast to this when we reach the nineteenth verse of chapter x. But as long as the first tavernacle had a standing before God the rule was *no admittance.*

We might say then that the law instituted *the religion of the holy place,* whereas the *holiest of all* characterizes Christianity. It was not that all Israelites had access to the holy place. We know they did not, as the sad case of Uzziah, king of Judah, recorded in 2 Chronicles xxvi., shows. But the priests, who were the representatives of all Israel, had free access there. Still, even so, the real value of the whole thing lay in its typical significance, as we have seen.

This fact is again emphasized in verses 9 and 10, where the tabernacle is "a figure for the time then present," and the gifts and sacrifices are but meats and drinks and divers washings; all of which were but ordinances of a fleshly type as opposed to anything of a spiritual nature. Out of this there flow, as a result, two things.

The first thing is, that these sacrifices could not make perfect the one who approached by their means. Here again we meet with that word *perfect;* and this time not referring to Christ but to ourselves. The Jewish sacrifices, by reason of their very nature, could not make us perfect; and this fact we shall find repeated in the first verse of chapter x. Then passing on to the fourteenth verse of that chapter we find stated, by way of contrast, the glorious fact that, "by one offering He hath perfected for ever them that are sanctified." The law not merely *did not* accomplish it, but *could not;* whereas Christ *has done* it.

But what is this perfection which has to do with ourselves? That question is answered for us here. It is a remarkable fact that the first time the word is used in this connection it is carefully defined for us by the Holy Spirit. The perfection has to do with our consciences. As we read on into chapter x. we shall see more clearly what this signifies. It means having the whole weight of sin as an accusing load completely lifted off, so that the conscience is *perfectly* cleared in the presence of God.

Now this was something quite unknown under the law. If a Jew sinned it was his duty to bring to the tabernacle the appropriate sacrifice; and having done so he was clearly entitled to enjoy the relief afforded by the words, "it shall be forgiven him" (Lev. iv. 31). That one particular sin was forgiven when once the prescribed sacrifice was offered; but that was all. If he sinned again, again he had to bring a sacrifice: and so on and on, all through life. There was no such thought as a sacrifice being offered which could settle once and for ever the whole question of sin, and so perfect the sinner's conscience.

The second thing is that the law with all its ordinances was only imposed upon Israel "until the time of reformation," that is, until the time of "setting things right." The law was after all a provisional measure. It proved beyond dispute that things needed setting right, by proving how wrong they were; but it did not put them right. When presently God blesses Israel under the new covenant the time of setting things right will have arrived. Meanwhile, as we have just seen, we have been blessed upon new covenant principles, as the result of the sacrifice of Christ; and there is no setting things right upon any other basis than that.

Verses 11 to 14 furnish us with the contrast to that which we have in verses 6 to 10. If we analyze the verses with a little care we shall see how complete and far-reaching the contrast is.

In the first place CHRIST is set before us, in contrast to the high priest of Aaron's order.

Then, the Aaronic priest just had to administer the things that existed under his hand. Christ is an High Priest of *good things to come.*

Christ has entered into the *true* holiest in the heavens, a greater and more perfect tabernacle than that made with hands in the wilderness; and He entered in *once,* instead of every year, as with the high priest of old.

Not by the blood of goats and calves, which can never really put away sins, did He enter; but by *His own blood* which obtains redemption.

The blood of the sacrificial animals did sanctify to the purifying of the flesh: the blood of Christ alone can *purify the conscience.*

The purifying of the flesh which was accomplished by the Jewish sacrifices was but temporal: the redemption obtained by Christ is *eternal.*

Notice, moreover, the majesty which characterizes the one offering of Christ. All three Persons of the Godhead stand related to it. The spotless Son of God offered Himself. It was to God that He offered Himself; and it was by the eternal Spirit He did it. No wonder that all-sin comes within its scope, and that its results abide for eternity.

The immediate effect of it, as far as we are concerned, is the "purging" or "cleansing" of our consciences. By that cleansing they are perfected and we turn from the dead works of law—dead, because done with the object of *getting* life—to serve the living God. If our consciences need cleansing from *dead* works, how much more do they need cleansing from *wicked* works!

The argument of the opening verses of chapter ix. reaches a climax in verse 14, but the Spirit of God does not immediately carry us on to the results which flow from it. Instead of that He elaborates with great wealth of detail the point He had just been making; so that when we reach chapter x. 14, we find that we are back again at the point we had started from in ix. 14. And only then do we proceed to the consideration of its results.

From this we may learn the very great importance that attaches to the

HEBREWS

truth concerning the sacrifice of Christ. It lies at the foundation of everything, and until it is thoroughly apprehended by us we are not able to appreciate what follows from it. Let us pray for the understanding heart as we consider these verses, in which the main point of the Holy Spirit is so fully developed and supported.

The main point, then, is that the blood of Christ completely purges the believer's conscience so that he is enabled to serve and worship the living God. Now this was an end utterly unattainable under the old covenant; hence it follows, as verse 15 tells us, that the Lord Jesus became the Mediator not of the old but of the new. And hence, too, His death had a twofold bearing: bringing in redemption as regards the transgressions under the old covenant, and becoming the basis whereon is fulfilled the promise connected with the new. Something had to be done for the removing of the mighty mountain of transgressions which had accumulated under the law: and equally something was needed if God was to call people with an eternal inheritance in view. Both these great ends are reached "by means of death," and that the death of Christ.

Verses 16 and 17 are a parenthesis. The word translated *testament* here, and *covenant* in chapter viii., has both those meanings. Used in relation to God it is "a disposition which He has made, on the ground of which man is to be in relationship with Him." In this short parenthesis the writer uses the word in the sense of a testament or will, which only is of force when the testator is dead. If viewed in this way, again we see the absolute necessity of the death of Christ.

There was no "death of the testator" under the old covenant, yet the necessity for death to take place was acknowledged in a typical way. If we turn to Exodus xxiv. 7 and 8., we shall find the incident referred to in verses 19 and 20., and we may note a remarkable fact. Exodus records only the sprinkling of the people with blood; Hebrews adds that the book of the law was also sprinkled.

The significance of the sprinkling of the people would seem to be that they were thereby reminded that death was the penalty of disobedience. Any breach of its demands meant the death penalty *on them*. The significance of the sprinkling of the book would indicate, on the other hand, that death was necessary as the basis of everything. Hence even the law system was not dedicated without blood; and this fact is added here by the inspired writer since it is just the point of the argument in this epistle.

Moreover at different times in connection with the sacrifices the tabernacle vessels, and indeed "almost all things," were purged with blood; and all this was intended to drive home into men's hearts the all-important lesson, that, "Without shedding of blood is no remission."

In our twentieth century we might almost call this great statement—*the most hated fact of Holy Scripture*. Nothing so moves to wrath and contempt and ridicule the soul of the "modern" theologian as this. And why?

Not because his delicate sensibilities are shocked by the idea of blood being shed, for the average modernist enjoys his slice of roast beef as much as other average people. But because he knows what this fact really signifies. It means that the death-sentence lies on mankind as creatures hopelessly lost; and that only *death* can lift this death-sentence so that remission can reach the fallen creature. The solemn witness borne to the modernist, that as a sinful creature he is under the death-sentence before God, is what his soul loathes with an intensity that amounts to hate. The prouder he is the more he hates if.

Do we not all understand this quite well? Did we not all share those feelings until grace subdued our pride and brought us into an honest frame of mind before God? The modernist, of course, deludes himself into thinking that his aversion to this truth arises from his superior aesthetic or moral sense, and we may never have victimized ourselves with that particular little piece of vain conceit. If so, we may well thank God! The moment we were brought to honesty and humility of mind we grasped the absolute necessity of *the death of Christ*.

Of that necessity verse 23 speaks. The blood of goats and calves sufficed to purify the tabernacle and its furniture, which were but patterns; the heavenly things themselves needed a better sacrifice. We might be surprised that *heavenly* things should need a sacrifice at all, did we not remember that Satan and the fallen angels have had their seat in the heavens, and have introduced the taint of sin there; and also that we, who are sinners and had our seat here, are destined as the fruit of redemption to take our seat in the heavens. As the fruit of the work of Christ not only shall there be purification wrought on earth but in the heavens also.

Consequently, in verses 24 to 26 we are introduced to the work of Christ from a most exalted view-point. He appeared once at the consummation of the ages to put away sin by the sacrifice of Himself, and now, in virtue of His blood shed, has gone into the very heaven of God's presence on our behalf. Let us mark that word, "to put away sin." How comprehensive it is! The expiation of our sins is of course included, but it is not limited to that. The judgment of sin is included, but it is not limited to that. It includes sin in all its ramifications and bearings. Sin, the root, and all the sins which are the fruit; sin as it has affected man and the earth, and sin as it has affected the heavens; sin, in its totality; all put away by His sacrifice. And His sacrifice was the sacrifice of *Himself!*

In these verses again, the work of Christ comes before us as contrasted with the service of the high priest of old, and this it is which accounts for the way things are put in the last verse of our chapter. When the Jewish high priest had entered the holy place made with hands on the yearly day of atonement, carrying the blood of the goat, the people stood outside waiting for his reappearance. Very possibly they waited with a certain amount of trepidation for they knew that to enter wrongfully into the presence of God meant death. For him they were waiting, and they hailed his appearance with a sigh of relief. Now we, Christians—and this specially applies to the converted remnant of Jews, who were addressed in this epistle—are waiting for the re-appearance of our great High Priest. We "look for" or "await" Him, and when He comes it will be "without sin" or "apart from sin." He so effectually dealt with sin at His first coming that He will have no need to touch that question at His second coming. He will appear unto the salvation of His people, and the deliverance of a groaning creation.

Thus we can see what a striking analogy exists between the actions of Aaron on the day of atonement and the great work of Christ; only with this complete contrast, that whereas Aaron's actions were typical and confined to the patterns of heavenly things, and oft repeated, Christ has to do with the heavenly realities and His work in offering for sin has been accomplished once and for ever. It is the lot of sinful men once to die, and then to face the judgment of God. In keeping with that, Christ has once been offered to bear the sins of many, and therefore those that await Him look forward not to judgment but to salvation.

You notice that here it speaks of Christ bearing the sins of *many*, not of *all*. It is true that He died *for* all, as far as the scope and intention of His work is concerned. When however the actual effect of His work is in question, then He bore the sins *of* many, that is, of those who believe. You will notice also that the words, "look for Him," have not really got the meaning so often imported into them, by which they are made to support the idea that only certain believers who are watchful are going to find salvation when the Lord comes again. The force of the whole passage the rather is, that sin has been so perfectly put away, and believers so perfectly cleared as to their consciences, and as to all liability to judgment, that they are left awaiting the coming forth of their High Priest from the heavenly sanctuary to their salvation from every adverse power.

With this thought before us, the opening words of chapter x. carry us back to the days of the law, that once more we may realize the glory of the gospel as contrasted with it. Twice already that contrast has been laid open before us; first in verses 6 to 14 of chapter ix., and then again in verses 23 to 28. In the earlier of these two passages the great point of the contrast seems to be as regards the *nature* and *character* of the law sacrifices contrasted with the sacrifice of Christ. In the later passage the contrast seems more to lie in the *absolute sufficiency* of Christ's sacrifice, which is therefore *one*, and not a repeated thing like the sacrifices of old.

CHAPTER 10

IN THE PASSAGE now before us both these contrasts reappear, but coupled with them is a third—the *supreme glory of Him who became the sacrifice*, as contrasted with both priests and offerings of old. We see Him stepping out of eternity that He might accomplish the will of God in the work that He did. The passage starts with the reminder that the law with its shadow sacrifices could NEVER make the worshippers perfect. It ends with the glorious statement that the offering of Christ *has* perfected them FOR EVER.

It is not that the law sacrifices *did not* perfect anyone as to the conscience, but that they *could not*. Their very repetition showed this. Could they have availed to cleanse the conscience, so that the offerer got complete relief as to the whole question of sin, they would have ceased to be offered; inasmuch as we never go on *doing* what is *done*. In point of fact their effect was in just the opposite direction. Instead of removing sins from the conscience as no longer to be remembered, they were formally brought to remembrance at least once every year. The blood of sacrificial animals had no efficacy to take away sins. The thing was impossible, as verse 4 says.

The statement of that verse is clear enough. Some of us, however, remembering what is said as to the forgiveness of various sins, or as to cleansing from sin, in Leviticus iv. v. and xvi. may feel that there is apparently a contradiction, and that a further word of explanation is needed. The solution of the difficulty is not far to seek, and we may reply by way of an illustration.

Here is a trader hard pressed by a creditor. He is short of cash in these hard times, though he knows well that in three months' time he will have ample funds. What does he do? He offers his creditor a three months' promissory note for £500, and his creditor well satisfied with his integrity, gladly accepts it. Now our question is this—What really has the creditor got?

That question may with equal truth be answered in two ways, apparently contradictory. Thinking of it as regards its intrinsic value, we should reply:—He has got a small piece of paper, whereon certain words are traced in ink, and in the corner of which is embossed a red government stamp, and the total value of the whole thing would be *less than a penny*. Thinking of it in its relative value—that is, of what it will be worth at its due date in view of the character of the man who drew it, we should be quite right in replying, *Five hundred pounds*.

The sacrifices of old were like that promissory note. They had value, but it lay in that to which they pointed. They were but paper; the sacrifice of Christ alone is like fine gold. In Leviticus their relative value is pointed out. In Hebrews we find that their value is only relative and not intrinsic. They can never take away sins. Hence in them God had no pleasure, and the coming of Christ was a necessity.

Hence in verses 5 to 9 we have the quotation from Psalm xl. and its application. It is quoted as the very voice of the Son of God, as He enters

HEBREWS

into the world. The Psalm mentions, "Sacrifice and offering . . . burnt offerings and sacrifices for sin;" that is, offerings of four kinds, just as there are four kinds of offerings mentioned in the early chapters of Leviticus. There was no pleasure for God in any of them, and when the Son of God came forth to do the will of God they were supplanted and taken away. In the body He took, the whole will of God was done, and by the offering of it up in sacrifice we have been set apart for God once for all.

The thing being accomplished what further need is there of the ineffectual shadows? The fine gold having appeared what use have we for the scrap of paper? That great word, "He taketh away the first, that He may establish the second," might almost be taken as the whole drift of the epistle to the Hebrews, stated in few words—put into a nutshell, as we speak.

Once more are we brought face to face with the contrast in verses 11 to 14. On the one hand, there are all the priests of Aaron's race. On the other, "this Man" in His solitary dignity as the Son of God. There, the daily ministering, and the constant offering of the ineffectual sacrifices that can never take away sins. Here, the one perfect offering, which is perfectly efficacious, and the Offerer seated at the right hand of God. There, the priests were always standing. No chair or seat of any kind was provided amongst the furniture of the tabernacle. It was not needed for their work was never done. Here, the Offerer has by His one offering perfected for ever the sanctified ones, and consequently He has taken His seat for ever at God's right hand.

The words, "for ever," occur in verses 12 and 14. In both cases they have the significance of, "as a perpetual thing," or, more briefly, "in perpetuity." Those set apart for God having been perfected as to their consciences in perpetuity, He has taken His seat at God's right hand in perpetuity. For one thing only is He waiting, and that is for His enemies to be made His footstool.

We would like to think that all our readers have entered into the tremendous significance of all this. Oh, the blessing and establishment of soul that comes when we really lay hold of it! Its surpassing importance may be seen in the way that the Spirit of God dwells upon the subject, and elaborates it in its details. Note too, how again and again it is stated that the sacrifice of Christ is one, and offered once and for ever. Six times over is this fact brought before us, in the passage beginning with ix. 12, and ending with x. 14. Search that passage and see for yourselves.

And then may the truth contained in that passage enter all our hearts in its soul-subduing, conscience-cleansing power!

It has often been pointed out that in the early part of Hebrews x. we have mention of, firstly, the will of God; secondly the work of Christ;

HEBREWS

thirdly, the witness of the Holy Ghost. The work of Christ *for* us has laid the basis for the accomplishment of the will of God *about* us, and in order that we may have the assurance of both there is the witness of the Spirit *to* us. In verse 15 of our chapter this last is brought before us.

How may we know that, as believers who have been set apart for God, we have been perfected in perpetuity? Only by relying upon an unimpeachable witness. And where is such a witness to be found? Suppose we put our feelings in the witness box, and subject them to a little cross-examination on the point. Can we arrive at anything like assurance? By no means, for they hardly tell the same story twice running. If on certain occasions they would seem to testify to our being right with God, on other occasions their witness would be in exactly the opposite direction. We must dismiss them from the witness box as utterly unreliable.

But the Holy Spirit condescends to take the place of Witness, and He is utterly reliable. It is not here His witness *in* us as in Romans viii. 16. In our passage He is viewed as testifying from without *to* us, and we are immediately referred to that which is written in Jeremiah xxxi. The words of Jeremiah were the words of the Spirit; his writings the writings of the Spirit. The witness of the Spirit to us is found in the written Word of God. The burden of His witness in favour of the believer is, "Their sins and iniquities will I remember no more."

Is there some reader of these lines who lacks assurance? Are you a prey to doubts and fears as to your salvation? What you need is to receive the witness of the Spirit in "full assurance of faith," as verse 22 puts it. Could more reliable witness be presented to you than that of God, the Holy Ghost? No! Could His witness be presented to you in a more stable or more satisfactory form than in the Scriptures of truth, which He has inspired? We venture to say, *it could not*.

Supposing God dispatched an angel to you with tidings of your forgiveness. Would that settle everything? For a short time perhaps. Angels however appear for a moment and then they are gone, and you see them no more. The memory of his visit would soon grow faint, and doubt enter your mind as to what exactly he *did* say. If you were granted a wonderful inrush of joyful feeling; would that do? It would soon pass and be succeeded by a corresponding depression, for when waves run high you cannot always ride upon their crests. Bring forward any alternative you please, and our reply will be, that though more spectacular than the Scriptures they cannot be compared with them for reliability. If you cannot or will not receive the witness of the Holy Ghost in that form, you would not receive it in any form whatsoever.

The witness of the Spirit to us is, then, that our sins are completely remitted, and being forgiven there is no more offering for sin. In verse 2

HEBREWS

the question was asked, "Would they not have ceased to be offered?" —that is, had the Jewish sacrifices been able to make the worshippers perfect. In verse 18 we learn that Christ's one sacrifice having perfected us, and the Holy Spirit bearing witness to it, there is no further offering for sin. When these words were penned Jewish sacrifices were still proceeding at Jerusalem but they were valueless as offerings for sin, and very shortly they were all swept away. The Roman armies under Titus, who destroyed Jerusalem and utterly scattered the Jews, were really God's armies (see, Matt. xxii. 7) used by Him in judgment to make their sacrifices impossible any longer. And yet a very large part of Christendom is continually bowing down before what they call, "the sacrifice of the mass." How great the sin of this! Worse really than the sin of perpetuating the Jewish sacrifices, had that been possible.

Verse 19 brings before us the great result that follows from the one perfect sacrifice of Christ. We have "boldness to enter into the holiest." No Jew, not even the high priest, had boldness to enter the holiest made with hands: we have boldness to enter the holiest not made with hands; in spirit now, and in actual presence when the Lord comes. The converted Hebrew reading this would at once say to himself—This must mean that we are constituted priests in a far higher sense than ever Aaron's family were priests of old. He would be right! Though in this epistle we are not told that we are priests in so many words, the truth enunciated plainly infers it. In the first epistle of Peter, chapter ii., the truth of Christian priesthood is plainly stated, and that epistle is also addressed to converted Hebrews.

Our boldness is based upon the blood of Jesus, since through His flesh, by means of death, He has opened up for us a new and living way into God's presence; but then we also have Himself as High Priest living in the presence of God. Verse 21 mentions this, but He is there really called, not an High Priest, but a *"Great* Priest over the house of God." Earlier in the epistle we read of Him as both Priest and Son, and then it added, "Whose house are we" (iii. 6). We are God's house, God's priestly family, and over us is this Great Priest, the Lord Jesus Christ, and we have full access to God. Verse 22 exhorts us to avail ourselves of our great privilege and draw near.

We are to draw near, "with a true heart in full assurance of faith." These two things are what we may call the necessary moral qualifications *which we ought to have.* Converted we may be, but if there be not that simplicity of faith in the work of Christ, and in the witness of the Holy Ghost as to the complete settlement of the question of our sins, which produces full assurance in our minds, we cannot enjoy the presence of God. Nor can we, except our hearts be true; that is, marked by sincerity under the influence of the truth, and without guile.

HEBREWS

The latter part of verse 22 reverts again to that which *we have* as the fruit of the grace of God—and not to that which we ought to have. We have boldness by the blood of Jesus: we have a Great Priest over the house of God: we have hearts sprinkled and bodies washed, as verse 22 says.

These two things may present a little difficulty to our minds, but doubtless to the original Hebrew readers the allusions would have been quite clear. Aaron and his sons had their bodies completely washed with pure water, and they were also spinkled with blood before they took up their priestly office and duties. Now we have the realities which were typified in this way. The truth of the death of Christ has been applied to our hearts, giving us a purged conscience, which is the opposite of an evil conscience. Also we have come under the cleansing action of the Word of God, which has renewed us in the deepest springs of our being. It was to this that the Lord Jesus alluded just before He instituted His supper in the upper chamber, when He said, "He that is washed (bathed) needeth not save to wash his feet, but is clean every whit." The word He used signifies *to bathe all over*, as the priests were bathed at their consecration. But even so they needed to wash hands and feet every time they entered the sanctuary.

We, thank God, have received that new birth which corresponds to the bathing with pure water. The "true heart" spoken of earlier in the verse would correspond pretty closely with the washing of hands and feet which was needed every time the priest entered the holy place.

But, having all, let us draw near. Let us take up and use and enjoy our great privilege of access to God. It is the great feature that should characterize us. We are people put into this nearness, having unrestricted liberty in approach to God, and that at all times; though doubtless there are occasions when we may specially enjoy the privilege, as for instance when we gather in assembly for the Lord's supper or for worship. Still it is by no means restricted to such occasions, as is plain when we remember that this epistle is silent as to the assembly and its functions; to find instruction as to that we must turn to the first epistle to the Corinthians.

The presence of God should really be the home of our hearts, the place to which in spirit we continually resort. The point here is not that we resort there with our needs and present our prayers; that came before us at the end of chapter iv. It is rather that we draw near in the enjoyment of all that God is, as revealed to us in Jesus, in communion with Him, and in the spirit of worship. We draw near not to get any benefit out of Him, but because we find attraction in Himself.

The three exhortations of verses 22—25, are very closely connected. We are to hold fast the profession of our faith, (or, our *hope*, as it really is), without wavering, since it hangs upon One who is wholly faithful. We shall most certainly do this if we enter into our privilege and draw near. We shall also find there is much practical help in the companionship of our

HEBREWS

fellow-Christians, and in the exhortation and encouragement they give. When believers begin to waver and draw back, their failure is so frequently connected with these two things. They neglect the twofold privilege of drawing near to God on the one hand, and of drawing near to their fellow-believers on the other.

It is a sad fact that today there are thousands of dear Christian folk attached to denominations in which the great truths we have been considering are very little mentioned. How could they be when things are so organized as to altogether obscure the truth in question? Services are so conducted that the individual saint is put at a distance, and he can only think of drawing near by proxy, as though he were a Jewish worshipper. Or perhaps the case is that he finds all the service conducted for him by a minister, and this of necessity tends to divert his thoughts from the supreme importance of his drawing near for himself, in the secret of his own soul.

Others of us have the inestimable privilege of gathering together according to the Scriptural form prescribed in 1 Corinthians xi-xiv. This is indeed calculated to impress us with the necessity of drawing near to God in our hearts. But let us watch lest we lose our spiritual exercises and lapse into a frame of mind which would take us listlessly to the meetings, expecting to have everything done for us by "ministering brothers." And perhaps we get quite annoyed with them because they do not perform their part as well as we think they ought to do! Then it is that, instead of holding fast, we begin to let go; the first symptom of it being very probably, that we begin to forsake the meetings and the society of our fellow-believers generally. We become very critical of both meetings and people, and consider we have very good grounds for our criticism!

If instead of holding fast we begin to let go, who can tell whereunto our drawing back will take us? Who indeed, but God Himself! He alone knows the heart. All too often this drawing back, which commenced, as far as human eye can see, with forsaking Christian company, never stops until utter apostasy is reached. This terrible sin was much before the mind of the writer of this epistle, as we saw when considering chapters iii. and vi. He greatly feared that some of the Hebrews to whom he wrote might fall into it. Hence he again refers to it here. The rest of our chapter is taken up with it. In verse 26 he speaks of sinning "wilfully." In the last verse he speaks of drawing back "unto perdition."

To "sin wilfully" is evidently to forsake the faith of Christ, with one's eyes open. No *true* believer does this, but a professed believer may do so, and it is just this fact, that we have reached perfection and finality in Christ, which makes it so serious. There is no more sacrifice for sins. This fact which seemed so unspeakably blessed in verse 18, is seen in the light of verse 26, to have a side to it which is unspeakably serious. There is beyond nothing but judgment. And that judgment will be of a very fearful character, hot with indignation.

Some of us might feel inclined to remark, that such judgment seems to be rather inconsistent with the fact that we live in a day when the glad tidings of the grace of God is being preached. So we do, but it is just that fact that increases the severity of the judgment. Verses 28 to 31 emphasize this. Grace makes known to us things of such infinite magnitude that to despise them is a sin of infinite magnitude, a sin far graver than that of despising the law of Moses with its holy demands.

In the gospel there is presented to us, first, the Son of God; second, His precious blood, as the blood of the new covenant; third, the Holy Spirit, as the Spirit of grace. Now what is it that the apostate does—especially the Jew, who having professed Christianity, abandons it, and reverts to Judaism. He treads under foot the first. The second he counts an unholy thing. The third he utterly despises. He treats with the utmost scorn and contempt the very things that bring salvation. There is nothing beyond them, nothing but judgment. He will deserve every bit of judgment he gets. All this, be it noted, is a vastly different thing from a true believer growing cold and unwatchful and consequently falling into sin.

In verse 32, we again see that, though for the sake of some these warnings were uttered, yet the writer had every confidence that the mass of those to whom he wrote were true believers. He remembered, and he called on them to remember, the earlier days when they suffered much persecution for their faith, and he appealed to them not to cast away their confidence at this late hour in their history. An abundant recompense was coming for any loss they had suffered here.

One thing only was necessary, that they should continue with endurance doing the will of God. Then without fail all that had been promised would be fulfilled to them. Their very position was that they had "fled for refuge to lay hold upon the hope set before us," (vi. 18). That hope was abundantly sure, but its fulfilment can only be at the coming of the Lord, as is indicated in verse 37.

For the third time in the New Testament that striking word from Habakkuk ii. is quoted. That "the just shall live by faith," is quoted both in Romans i. and in Galatians iii. But only here is the preceding verse quoted. Take note of the alteration in the words made by the Spirit of God. In Habakkuk we read, "IT will surely come IT will not tarry;" the "it" referring to the vision. But in our days things have become far clearer, and we have the definite knowledge of the Person to whom the indefinite vision pointed. Hence here it is, "HE that shall come will come, and will not tarry."

It is a striking fact that the word *faith* only occurs twice in the Old Testament. Once in Deuteronomy Moses uses the word negatively, complaining of the people that they were "children in whom is no faith." In Habakkuk alone does the word occur, used in a positive way. It is equally striking that the New Testament seizes upon that one positive use of the word, and quotes it no less than three times. How this emphasizes the fact that we have now left behind the system of sight for the system of faith. Judaism is supplanted by Christianity.

The point of the quotation here is, however, not that we are justified by faith, but that by faith we LIVE. Faith is, as we may say, *the motive force* for Christian living. We either go on to the glorious recompense or we draw back to perdition. No middle ground is contemplated.

Do not miss the contrast presented in the last verse of our chapter. It lies between drawing back to perdition and believing to soul-salvation. This furnishes additional proof, were it needed, that the contrast in Hebrews is not between believers who do well and believers who do ill, and who consequently (as is supposed) may perish; but between those who really do believe unto salvation, and those, who being mere professors, draw back to their eternal ruin.

Thanks be to God for that living faith which carries the soul forward with patience to the glorious recompense which awaits us!

CHAPTER 11

WE NOW ARRIVE at the passage which is pre-eminently the *faith* chapter of the Bible, and it is easy to see how thoroughly it fits into its place in the whole scheme of this Epistle. Judaism as a religious system largely appealed to sight, whereas the great realities of Christianity are unseen and only appeal to faith. The object of the Epistle being to deliver the converted Hebrews from the grave-clothes of Judaism which clung to them, and to establish them in the liberty of Christianity, the Holy Spirit naturally dwells long upon *faith*.

How fitting all this is! We do well to dwell long upon it, that the wonder of Divine inspiration may more and more appear to us. We may notice also how the great *love* chapter of the Bible is 1 Corinthians xiii., and the great *hope* passage is 1 Thessalonians iv. 13—v. 11. Now 1 Corinthians is as we may term it, the Epistle of the local assembly, and it is just in the local assembly that all the friction is created amongst believers, and the trying disagreements and disagreeables take place, and consequently *love* is so much needed. So also 1 Thessalonians is the Epistle where the saints are seen suffering at the hands of the world, and in these circumstances nothing sustains the heart more than *hope*.

The whole of our chapter is like a commentary on that little sentence from Habakkuk—"The just shall live by faith." We are shown that from the very outset of the world's history that which pleased God in His people was the outcome of faith. This may seem very obvious to us, but it doubtless was a rather revolutionary idea to the average Jew, for he had accustomed himself to consider that what pleased God was the ceremonials and sacrifices of Judaism, and the works of the law connected therewith. But here the Spirit of God goes behind the activities of these Old Testament believers to bring to light the faith that moved and inspired them. Their works were not the works of the law, but the works of faith. In this connection you might do well to refresh your memories as to the contents of Romans iv. and James ii., noticing well how Paul excludes the works of the law from our justification, and how James insists on the works of faith as evidencing the vitality of the faith we profess.

The first verse defines, not what faith *is* in the abstract, but what it *does* in practice. It is "the substantiating of things hoped for, the conviction of things not seen." The *New Translation* gives this rendering together with a footnote saying that the words "assurance," or "firm conviction," might be substituted for "substantiating." Faith then is the telescope that brings into our view the unseen verities of which God speaks; making them real to us, giving us assurance of them, and turning them into solid substance in our hearts.

Before however we are led to review how faith wrought in "the elders," we find one word is to *ourselves*. Verse 3 begins, "Through faith WE understand . . ." and the things seen in creation are brought before us. This is a very significant statement! In apostolic days it was evidently the common faith of Christians that "the worlds were framed by the Word of God." Is it the faith of all Christians today? We have just seen that faith is "the conviction of things *not* seen." We now discover that only faith can give us a proper understanding of the things that we *do* see. Nineteen centuries ago the philosophic world was full of weird theories as to the origin of creation. Equally weird theories fill philosophic minds today. All these theories, both ancient and modern, take it for granted that things that are seen *were* made of things that do appear; and the process, by which they think they were made, has received the name of *evolution*. The philosophers are very clever men, and they have provided themselves—especially in these modern days—with a really wonderful equipment for their researches. They only lack *one* thing. But that one thing is the *only* thing that counts! They lack the faith that enables anyone to understand. Through faith we understand the origin of creation. Without faith we do not understand it at all.

All the readers of this little paper have, we trust, the faith that understands creation, and so we are prepared to understand the faith which actuated the elders, the recital of which begins with verse 4.

The story seems naturally to fall into three parts. First, we have in verses 4 to 7 the three great worthies of the antediluvian world, and in them faith is seen as that which sets in right relation with God, and consequently *saves*. Second, we have the patriarchs of the postdiluvian world before the law was given. They illustrate faith as that which brings into view unseen things—the faith that *sees*. Third, beginning with Moses, the law-giver, we find the faith that gives energy in spite of all obstacles—the faith that is prepared to *suffer*. In so saying we merely allude to that which seems to be the prominent thought of the Spirit in each section, for of course no one can have faith at all without its effects being known in all three ways.

Abel's faith led to the "more excellent sacrifice" and to the knowledge that he was righteous before God; which knowledge he got by faith in God's testimony. He offered his sacrifice, not by chance nor by some happy inspiration, but by faith. Faith in what? we may ask. Doubtless in that which God had already shown as to the value of the death of a sacrifice by the coats of *skins*, about which we read in Genesis iii. 21. God testified to the value of his gift by accepting his sacrifice; and Abel knew that in accepting his sacrifice God declared him righteous. Many a professing Christian today is saying that it is impossible in this life to have the knowledge of sins forgiven; but lo! here is a man living some four thousand years before Christ, and he possessed this very thing. And may not we possess it who live nearly two thousand years after the great atoning work has been done?

Abel died; but in the case of Enoch, the next on the list, translation took place and he never saw death. And further he had the testimony, not merely of being right with God, but of pleasing God. In this connection we are reminded that without faith we cannot please God at all. Faith is the root out of which spring all those fruits that delight Him: just as in 1 Timothy vi. 10, by way of contrast, money is said to be a root out of which every kind of evil springs.

In the case of Noah we see faith which saved from judgment and condemned the world. When warned of coming judgment he took God at His word. When instructed to build the ark he yielded the obedience of faith. Thereby he was separated from the world. He received righteousness and reached God through sacrifice in the renewed earth, while the world was cut off in judgment.

The case of Abraham occupies verses 8 to 19, with the exception of one verse which is occupied with Sarah, for had she not been a woman of faith Isaac, the promised seed, had never been born. Abraham's faith was so exceptional that the Apostle Paul speaks of him as "the father of all them that believe" (Rom. iv. 11); so it is not surprising that in this chapter more is said as to him than of any other individual. What is said seems to fall under three heads. First, the faith that led him to respond to the call of God at the outset. He started forth from a city of civilization and culture without knowing where he was going. When he did know it proved to be a land of less culture than the one he had left. Yet all this mattered not. Canaan was the inheritance God had chosen for him, and he moved at the call of God. GOD was before his soul. That is faith!

Second, when in the land of promise he had no actual possession therein. He sojourned there as a stranger and pilgrim, content to dwell in tents. Finally he died in the faith of the promises without ever receiving them. His course was indeed a most remarkable one; and what accounted for it? *Faith*—the faith that endows a man with spiritual eyesight. He not only desired a better and heavenly country, but he *"looked for"* a heavenly city far more enduring than Ur of the Chaldees. Verse 13 tells us that he *saw* the promises, though they were *far off* as we count time.

Third, his faith seemed to reach a climax and express itself most fully when he "offered up his only begotten son." Isaac was a child of resurrection even as to his natural birth: he became doubly so after this event. Yet the faith was the faith of Abraham, who reasoned that the God who could bring into the world a living child from parents who were physically dead, could and would raise him from the dead. When Abraham believed in the Lord and He counted it to him as righteousness, as Genesis xv. 6 tells us, he believed in a God who could raise the dead, as the end of Romans iv. shows. The offering up of Isaac demonstrated this faith of his in the clearest fashion. It was the special work in which his faith wrought, as the latter part of James ii. declares.

After Abraham we find Isaac, Jacob and Joseph mentioned. In each case of the three only one detail in their lives is mentioned, and in two cases out of the three that detail is the closing one. Reading Genesis we should hardly recognize any faith at all in the blessing that Isaac bestowed upon his sons, and we might not see much in the way Jacob blessed his grandsons; yet the keen eye of the Spirit of God discerned it, and He notes it for our encouragement. If He had not a keen eye like this, would He discern faith in the details of our lives? We may well ask ourselves this.

The case of Joseph is more distinct. Egypt was the land of his glory, but he knew by faith that Canaan was to be the land of Messiah's glory, so he commanded that ultimately his bones were to rest not in Egypt but in Canaan.

Verse 23 speaks of the faith of Moses' parents rather than of Moses himself. The faith of Moses occupies verses 24 to 28. The first great display of it was when he refused to continue any longer in the splendid circumstances into which the providence of God had brought him. Faced with the alternative of suffering along with the people of God or enjoying the temporary pleasures of sin, he deliberately chose the former. He cast in his lot with the people of God, though he knew that, being at that moment just down-trodden slaves, it meant reproach for him. Indeed he esteemed that reproach as treasure, even greater than the treasures of Egypt, and how great those treasures were recent discoveries have reminded us. The reproach Moses endured was in character the reproach of Christ, inasmuch as it was a faint foreshadowing of the infinitely greater stoop of Christ when He came down from heaven and identified Himself with a poor and repentant people on earth, as we see for instance in Matthew iii. 13-27.

We saw that in the case of Abraham faith acted like a telescope, bringing into his view things that otherwise he had never seen. We now discover that in the case of Moses it acted like an X-ray apparatus, bringing to light things that lay beneath the surface and enabling him to see through the tinsel glory of Egypt. In this way he got down to the real root of things, and he found that "the recompense of the reward" was the only thing worth considering. It was evidently this that governed him in the whole of his remarkable career.

Having a view of the divine recompense he was able to form a correct estimate of Egypt's treasures and he ranked them far below the reproach of Christ. If Egypt's glory is not to be compared to the *reproach* of Christ, how will it look in comparison with the *glory* of Christ? Faith's penetrating sight led to faith's estimation, and this in its turn led to faith's choice and faith's refusal.

From Moses we pass on to the people of Israel in verse 29 and to Joshua—though he is not named—in verse 30, and we reach Rahab, a Gentile, one of an accursed race, in verse 31. Had it not been for this verse we might never have discerned that faith was the root of her actions and words. Reading Joshua ii. we might have supposed that she was a woman of poor morals and no principle, who was anxious to escape her doom. But the fact was that her eyes had been opened to see *God*. The Canaanites merely saw Israel. "*Your* terror is fallen upon us," said she, "all the inhabitants of the land faint because of *you*." (Josh. ii. 9). Her attitude however was this:—"I know that *the Lord* hath given you the land." This was faith; and her actions expressed the fact that she dared to side with the God of Israel. This courageous faith did not mean suffering for her since God was at once intervening in power.

Usually, however, God does not intervene at once and then suffering is entailed. So after the mention of Rahab we have a list of names in verse 32 and a further recital of the triumphs of faith and then especially of the sufferings of faith. Multitudes of saints, of whom the world was not worthy, have been through every conceivable form of persecution and suffering. They endured, not accepting deliverance which might have reached them had they recanted or compromised. Faith suffered, but it carried them through.

Verse 39 brings us back to the point from which in verse 2 we started. They obtained a good report when their "term time" was over. They emerged "the finished article," from God's school. An intimation of the recompense that awaits them in the great "prize-giving day" is furnished by the statement that although they suffered at the world's hands, the world was not worthy of them. They were infinitely its superior.

And yet they, one and all, did not receive the things promised. In due time, according to God's wise plan, another company was to be gathered and constituted, spoken of as "us" in the last verse of our chapter. Note the contrast between the "they" and the "us"—between Old Testament and New Testament saints. The saints of old days had much, but "some better thing" is provided for Christians, and we shall all reach final perfection in glory together. The perfecting in glory of Old Testament believers waits for the completion of the church and the coming of the Lord.

This verse makes it abundantly plain that God's people are found in more families than one. The saints of Old Testament times form one family; Christians form another. Saints of the coming age, when the church has been removed, will form a third. We find different companies distinguished in such passages as Revelation iv. 4; vii. 3-8; vii. 9-17; xiv. 1-5; xix. 7, 9. Much depends upon the revelation of God, in the light of which we live, and upon the purpose of God in regard to us, according to which is the calling wherewith we are called. Here however, the contrast is between that which God purposed for the saints who lived *before* Christ came, and for those whose great privilege is it to live *after*.

In Christianity the "better thing" has come to light. Indeed the word "better" is characteristic of this epistle, since, as we have seen, the great point of it is to show that proper Christianity wholly transcends Judaism. Already we have had before us, a *BETTER* Apostle, Priest, hope, covenant, promises, sacrifice, substance, country and resurrection. Run over the chapters and note these things for yourselves.

Chapter 12

THE OPENING WORDS of chapter xii. bring us face to face with the application to ourselves of all that has preceded in chapter xi. All these Old Testament heroes of faith are so many witnesses to us of its virtue and energy. They urge us on that we may run the race of faith in our day, even as they did in days before ours.

In 1 Corinthians ix. Christian service is spoken of under the figure of a race; here Christian life is the point in question. It is a figure very much to the point since a race requires energy, concentration, endurance. So here the exhortation is, "let us run with patience," and patience has the sense of *endurance*. The normal Christian life is not like a brief sprint of 100 yards, but rather like a long distance race in which endurance is the decisive factor.

HEBREWS

In this matter of endurance there were disquieting symptoms manifested amongst these Hebrew believers, as the latter part of chapter x. has shown us. Verse 36 of that chapter begins, "For ye have need of patience." Then faith is mentioned as the energizing principle of Christian life, and this is followed by the long dissertation on faith in chapter xi. Thus chapter xi. is a kind of parenthesis, and in the words we are considering in the first verse of chapter xii. we are back again on what we may call the main line of the exhortation.

We can only run the race with patience if we lay aside every weight and the sin which entangles. Sin is a very effectual hindrance. It is likened to an obstacle which entangles our feet so that we fall. In the first place however weights are mentioned, as though they were after all the greater hindrance. Many things which could by no means be classified as sins prove themselves to be weights to an earnest Christian; just as there are many things quite right, and allowable to the ordinary individual, which are wholly discarded by the athlete. He strips himself of everything which would impede his progress to the goal. And every Christian should consider himself a spiritual athlete, as 2 Timothy ii. 5 also shows.

We have heard chapter xi. spoken of as "the picture gallery of faith," and the opening words of the second verse of our chapter as setting before us "the great Master-piece which we find at the end of it." As we walk down the gallery we can well admire the portraits that we see, but the Master-piece puts all the others into the background. No other than JESUS is the Author—i.e., the beginner, originator, leader—and Finisher of faith. The others displayed certain features of faith; flashes of it were seen at different points of their career. In Him a full-orbed faith was seen, and seen all the time from start to finish. The little word "our" in the A.V. is in italics you notice, since there is no such word in the original, and here it only obscures the sense.

The One who was the perfect exemplification of faith is set before us as our goal, and as the Object commanding our faith. In this we have an immense advantage over all the worthies mentioned in chapter xi., for they lived in a day when no such Object could be known. We have noticed that faith is the eye, or the telescope, of the soul; that it is faith that *sees*. Well, here faith looks to Jesus. If He fills the vision of our souls we shall find in Him the motive energy that we need for the running of the race.

Moreover He is our Example. Every kind of obstacle confronted Him when He trod on earth the path of faith. There was not only the contradiction of sinners to be faced but also the cross, with all the shame that it entailed. The shame of the cross was a small thing to Him: He despised it. But who shall tell what was involved in the cross itself? Some of us used to sing,

The depth of all Thy suffering
No heart could e'er conceive,

HEBREWS

The cup of wrath o'erflowing
For us thou didst receive;
And oh! of God forsaken
On the accursed tree:
With grateful hearts, Lord Jesus,
We now remember Thee.

Yet though we cannot conceive all that the cross meant to Him, this we know, that He *endured* it.

In the enduring of these sufferings for sin the Lord Jesus stands absolutely alone, and it is impossible to speak of Him as an Example. In the lesser sufferings which came upon Him through men He is an Example to us, for in one way or another we suffer as following Him. He went to the extreme limit, resisting unto blood rather than turning aside from the will of God. The Hebrews had not been called to martyrdom up to the time of the writing of this epistle, nor have we been up to today; still we need to consider Him.

In this connection another thing has to be taken into account. We are so apt to consider suffering as something in the nature of a very awkward liability—as being all loss. But it is not this. It may rather be written down on the profit side of the account, since God takes it up and weaves it into His scheme of things, using it for our training. This thought fills verses 5 to 11 of our chapter.

Three words are used in this passage:—chastening, rebuking, scourging. The last does of course mean a whipping, and the second means a reproof. But the first, though it may sometimes be used for a beating, primarily means discipline in the sense of child-training; and it is worthy of note that, whereas each of the other two words is used but once in these verses, this one is used no less than eight times. This then is the predominant thought of the passage. We ARE children of God and hence we come under His training, and must not forget the exhortation addressed to us in that capacity.

The exhortation quoted comes from the third chapter of Proverbs. Turn up the passage and you will see how Solomon addresses the reader as, "my son." Here however it is assumed to be the voice of God Himself addressing us, just as again and again in the first chapter of our epistle we had the words, "He saith," introducing a quotation of Old Testament Scripture. We might say perhaps that it is the voice of the Spirit of God, for later in the Epistle we have had such expressions as, "The Holy Ghost saith," "The Holy Ghost this signifying," "The Holy Ghost is a Witness to us." The point however is this, that what looks like being but the advice of a Solomon to his son is assumed by the New Testament to be the Word of God *to us*.

We are then to take this chastening from the hand of God as being the normal thing. It is a proof to us that we are His children. Hence when we come under His chastening we are neither to despise it nor to faint under it, but to be exercised by it, as verse 11 tells us. If we are naturally light-hearted and optimistic, our tendency will be to disregard the troubles, through which God may see fit to pass us. We put a bold face on and laugh things off, and do not recognize the hand of God in them at all. In so doing we despise His chastening. If, on the other hand, we are naturally pessimistic and easily depressed, our spirits faint under quite small troubles and our faith seems to fail us. This is going to the opposite extreme, but equally with the other it means the losing of all the profit, into which our troubles were designed to lead us.

The great thing is to be *exercised* by our troubles. Chastening means trouble, for we are plainly told that "no chastening for the present seemeth to be joyous but grievous." And exercise means that we turn our troubles into a sort of spiritual gymnasium; for the Greek word used here is the one from which we have derived our English word, gymnasium. Gymnastics for the body have in them some profit, as 1 Timothy iv. 8 tells us. Gymnastics for our spirits have in them great spiritual profit in the direction of both holiness and righteousness. By them we become partakers of the very holiness of God Himself; and we are led into paths of righteousness. Righteousness itself bears fruit which is peaceable, even though the disciplinary process, through which we passed in order to reach it, was of a stormy nature.

The tendency with the Hebrews evidently was to faint under their troubles, hence in verse 12 comes the exhortation, in the light of these facts about God's chastening, to renewed energy in the race. Observe those runners at the start of a Marathon race. Their arms are firmly lifted by their sides: their step is elastic, and their knees strong. Now look at them as they approach the finish an hour or two later. Most of them have run themselves out. Their hands hang down and their knees tremble, as doggedly they stumble on.

"*Wherefore* lift up . . ." We are to renew our energies just because we know what God's discipline is designed to effect. We might have imagined that to talk to a poor feeble stumbling believer about God's chastening would be just the thing to cast him down, whereas it is just the thing, if rightly understood, to lift him up. What can be more encouraging than to discover that all God's dealings have as their object the promotion of holiness and righteousness, and also our being preserved from the sin and the weights which would impede our progress in the race?

Moreover we are to consider the welfare of others and not merely our own. Verses 13 to 17 turn our thoughts in this direction; and two classes are spoken of—the lame and the profane. By the former we understand believers who are weak in faith; and by the latter those who may have made a profession and come amongst Christians, but all the while they really prefer the world. Verses 16 and 17, in fact, contemplate just that class that

HEBREWS

already has been alluded to in this Epistle—chapters vi. and x.—who cannot be renewed to repentance, and who have nothing but judgment in prospect. Esau is the great Old Testament example of such, and Judas Iscariot is the example in the New.

We need to watch against those profane people lest they damage others beside themselves, by becoming roots of bitterness. If we read John xii. 1-8, we may see how very easily Judas might have become a root of bitterness, had not the Lord at once intervened. Those who are spoken of as lame need however very different treatment. We should aim at the healing of such and take every care that straight paths are set before them. We all need these straight paths, and we are to *make* them. There are some, alas! who seem to find a joy in making things as difficult and complicated as possible, whereas the path of righteousness and holiness is ever a very straight and simple one. And all this we are to do because we are come, not to the order of things connected with the law, but to that connected with grace.

The two systems are summed up for us in verses 18 to 24—Sinai on the one hand and Sion on the other. Now the forefathers of these Hebrews had come to Sinai, and the Hebrews themselves, before their conversion, had come to it in this sense; that it was to God, known according to the display of Himself at Sinai, that they came, when they drew near to Him, as far as they might do so in those days.

But now all was changed, and in drawing near to God in the wonderfully intimate way which the Gospel permits, they came upon another ground, and in connection with another order of things entirely. Mount Sion had become symbolic of grace just as Sinai had become symbolic of law; so that believing the Gospel, and standing in the grace of God, we may be said to have come to Sion.

It is not easy to see the connection between all the things mentioned in verses 22 to 24, but it may help us to notice that the little word "and" divides the different items the one from the other. Hence for instance, it is the innumerable company of angels which is spoken of as "the general assembly," and not the church which is mentioned immediately following.

We are regarded here as being under the new covenant, and hence as having come to all that which is clearly revealed in connection with it. Eight things are mentioned, and each is stated in a way calculated to bring home their superiority, as compared with the things which the Hebrews knew in connection with the law.

The Jew could boast in the earthly Jerusalem, which was intended to be the centre of Divine rule on the earth: but we have come to the heavenly city whence God's rule will extend over heaven as well as earth. The Jew knew that angels had served in the giving of the law: but we have come to the universal gathering of the angels in their myriads, all of them the

HEBREWS

servants of God and of His saints. Israel was God's assembly in the wilderness and in the land: but we belong to His assembly of firstborn ones whose names are written in heaven. A heavenly citizenship is ours.

So too, Moses had told Israel that, "The Lord shall judge His people" (Deut. xxxii. 36): but we have come to God as the Judge of all—a vastly greater thing. The old order dealt with just men living on the earth: we have come to the same, but as made perfect in glory. Lastly, for us it is not Moses the mediator of the law covenant, and the blood of bulls and of goats, but Jesus the Mediator of the new covenant, and His precious blood of infinite value.

To all this have we come *in faith*, and we await the hour of manifestation which is surely drawing nigh. Israel came to Sinai in a visible way and were greatly affrighted. Our coming in faith to Sion, and all connected therewith, is no less real, and in coming we are greatly comforted and established.

Yet there is a serious side to this matter, inasmuch as it adds great emphasis and solemnity to all that God says to us today. He spoke in time past to the fathers through Moses and the prophets, but now He has spoken from heaven. The fact that He has now spoken in His Son, making known to us His grace, does not lessen the solemnity of His utterance but rather increases it, as we saw when reading the second and third verses of chapter ii.

If we turn away from His heavenly voice we certainly shall not escape. At Sinai He spoke, formulating His demands upon men, and then His voice shook the earth. Now He has spoken in the riches of His mercy. But in the days between these two occasions He spoke through Haggai the prophet, announcing His determination to shake not only the earth but the heavens also. He will in fact so shake that everything that can be shaken will be shaken. Only the unshakeable things will remain. Our God —the Christian's God—is a consuming fire, and everything that is unsuited to Him will be devoured in His judgment.

Can we contemplate that day with calmness of spirit? Indeed we can. The feeblest believer is entitled to do so, for we receive, one and all, a kingdom which cannot be shaken. And just because we have an immovable kingdom we are to have grace to serve God with reverence and true piety. Let us all take it to heart that reverence becomes us in our attitude towards God, even though He has brought us into such nearness to Himself. Indeed it becomes us *because* we are brought into such nearness.

Also let us take note that we are exhorted to serve God acceptably, not in order to have the kingdom made sure to us, but because we have received it, and it never can be moved. The very certainty of it, far from making us careless, only incites us to serve.

HEBREWS

Chapter 13

The first verse of our chapter is very short but very important. The word *continue* is virtually the same as the word *remain*, which closes verse 27 of the previous chapter. Only the things which cannot be shaken are going to remain when the great day of shaking arrives; then, let brotherly love remain amongst the saints of God today. It is one of the things which will remain unshaken in eternity.

Let us recall that in the early part of the epistle believers are spoken of as the "many sons" being brought "unto glory." Christ was seen to be "the Captain of their salvation," who is "not ashamed to call them brethren." Hence most evidently Christians are brethren, and the love existing between them, the fruit of the new nature divinely implanted, is to be cultivated. In fostering it we shall not be like children building a sandcastle to be washed away by the next tide, but like those who build for eternity.

Verses 2 and 3 indicate two directions in which brotherly love is to express itself. First, in hospitality; that is, in the love of strangers. The world is usually prepared to receive those they esteem as important or influential, and thus to do honour to the distinguished guest. We are bidden to rise above merely worldly motives and to receive brethren unknown to us simply because they *are* brethren. This is true brotherly love in manifestation: a manifestation all too often but very little seen in our land. Second, it is to come out in the remembrance of brethren in adversity, particularly of those suffering imprisonment.

The word, remember, means to recollect in an active way; not merely to call to mind, but to do so with active sympathy. If one member suffer all the members suffer with it, we are told elsewhere; and what we find here is in keeping with that fact. True brotherly love would lead us so to remember all such sufferers as to sympathetically support and succour them, as far as we are able.

In verse 4 natural love is in question, and that in the world has been sadly perverted and marred. By Christians it is to be preserved intact as a sanctified thing, which originated in God. In verse 5 another "love" comes before us—the love of money. The Christian's manner of life is to be characterized as being without this altogether, since this is a love which never originated in God at all. Only when man had become a fallen creature did he lose all love for God and enthrone in his heart earthly objects, and more particularly the money which enabled him to pursue them.

The word for us is, be content with "such things as ye have," or, "your present circumstances." A very searching word it is too! The world is filled with covetousness as much as ever, perhaps more than ever. God is not in

HEBREWS

all its thoughts, which are concentrated upon material gain. Out of this spring all the strifes. Envies, jealousies, heartburnings, quarrellings are everywhere! Oh, let us so live as to present a very definite contrast to all this! May it be manifest to all that we are actuated by another love than the love of money!

"But," it may be said, "in these days of competition we must bend all our energies to the making of money, else we shall not long retain such things as we have, but shall sink into poverty." The answer to this thought is however immediately anticipated in these verses. We have the definite promise of His unfailing presence and support; consequently we may boldly count upon the Lord for all our needs, and have no fear of man.

There are two points of great interest about verses 5 and 6. The first concerns the way in which the Old Testament Scripture is quoted. It was to Joshua that the Lord said, "I will never leave thee, nor forsake thee." We might very properly say to ourselves, "But I am no Joshua. He was a very eminent man of faith, and I am a very insignificant and often a very feeble believer. Would it not be a rather forward and impertinent thing for me to calmly assume that a promise made to him is equally valid for me?" It is delightful to discover from these verses that such an application of this ancient promise is not the boldness of presumption but the boldness of faith. The fact is, of course, that what God is, He is towards His people in all time and circumstances. There is no variableness nor shadow of turning with Him. He will not be less towards His people in this dispensation than He was in a past dispensation. We may wholly count upon Him.

The Christian poetess has said,
> "*They that trust Him wholly,*
> *Find Him wholly true.*"

This of course is so, but it is well when quoting these happy words to lay the stress on the word, *find;* since it is equally a fact that He is wholly true to those who do not trust Him wholly. Their defective faith will never provoke Him to defective faithfulness. No! But their defective faith will obscure their view of His faithfulness, and possibly they may never FIND Him wholly true,—never really wake up to it, as a realized and enjoyed thing—until they discover it in glory.

The second point of interest is not so much the application of this Old Testament text but rather the reasoning which is based upon it. The skeleton outline of the reasoning runs thus, "He hath said . . . so that we may boldly say . . ." If God speaks we may accept what He says with all confidence. More than this, we may assert what He asserts with all boldness. And we may do even more than this. For if He asserts things concerning Himself in regard to His people, we may, since we are of His people, assert these things boldly *as applying to ourselves.* Indeed we may take it home with all confidence as applying to each individually; even as

HEBREWS

here we read, "The Lord is *MY* Helper, *I* will not fear." In our reading of Scripture let us form the happy habit of thus applying the words of God to ourselves.

Before leaving the first six verses let us notice the *simplicity* which is here enjoined upon believers; a simplicity all too much lost in these days of civilized artificiality. How striking a testimony would be rendered if we were marked by that brotherly love which expresses itself in hospitality and practical sympathy, by natural love preserved in undefiled honour, and by a holy contentment, the fruit of the realized presence of God, and the very opposite of the mad covetousness and discontent of the world.

The seventh verse bids us remember those who are guides or leaders, having ministered the word of God. To be a leader one needs not only to minister the word but to practise it. When this is the case faith is made evident and the "end" or "issue" of their conduct can be seen, and we can safely be exhorted to imitate their faith. Their *faith*, be it observed. It is all too easy to start imitating the speech and ways and idiosyncrasies of those we look up to. But if we imitate anything let it be the faith which underlies and inspires all else about them.

In verse 8 also our thoughts are carried back to the things with which we started in chapter i. There we discovered that the words occurring in Psalm cii., "Thou art the same, and Thy years shall not fail," were not addressed to God in a general way, but specifically to the One whom we know as our Lord Jesus Christ. This thought is amplified in the great statement that He is "the same yesterday, and today, and for ever." Of whom could such a statement be made but of One who was and is God?

Now just because the One in whom our faith centres is the same, there must be a certain kind of sameness in all the truth that also centres in Him. He can never be the Centre and Theme of doctrines which are various and strange. There is no place for that unsatisfied restlessness of the human mind that is for ever running after notions, however contradictory they may be. Now the real knowledge of Jesus establishes the heart with grace, and mere variety and novelty cease to attract. The danger immediately threatening the Hebrews was the importation of strange doctrines from their own former religion, as is indicated by the allusion to "meats."

A certain proportion of the meats consumed by the Jews reached them through their sacrifices. Leviticus vii. shows us that not only the priests, but also in some cases those who offered were privileged to eat parts of the things offered: that is, they ate of the altar. How often must unbelieving Jews have flung the taunt at their believing brethren that they now had no altar in which to claim their share! But the fact is, "We have an altar"! And of the Christian's altar the proud orthodox Jew had no right to eat, having shut himself out by his own unbelief.

HEBREWS

What is the Christian altar, and where is it to be found? "Come to us," say the Romanists, "and in our high altars, ornamented with crucifix and candles, where mass is daily said, you will find it." And so also, though with slight variations, say Greek and Anglo-Catholics. But what says the Scripture? It says, "We have an altar, . . . for . . . Jesus also, . . . suffered without the gate." Patriarchal and Jewish altars—the only altars made by hands that ever were sanctioned by God—where just types of the death of Christ. We eat of that Altar, inasmuch as every bit of spiritual blessing that we are able to appropriate comes to us from thence. We eat His flesh and drink His blood, according to our Lord's own words in John vi.; and in this there is no allusion to the Lord's supper, but rather to a spiritual appropriation of His death. Just as Baptism sets forth in figure our burial with Christ, so the Lord's supper sets forth in figure this spiritual appropriation: that is all.

In the death of Christ, then, we have our Altar; but in His death we have also the antitype of the sin offering. According to Leviticus iv., if the sin in question was of such a nature as to involve the whole congregation, then the blood of the offering had to be carried into the holy place and sprinkled before the veil, and the carcase of the animal had to be burned without the camp. Our Lord Jesus has taken up the whole question of sin in all its gravity. His blood has spoken in the fulness of its virtue in the immediate presence of God, and, true to the type, He died as the rejected One outside the gate of that very city which was the crown and glory of man's religion. We are glad to be identified with the virtue of His blood before God; are we as glad to be identified with Him in His place of rejection without the camp? Except we have come powerfully under the attraction of His love, we are not!

Verse 11 gives us the type. Verse 12 gives us the fulfilment of the type, in Jesus suffering without the gate of Jerusalem. Verse 13 gives us the exhortation based upon it, but using again the language of the type. We are not exhorted to go without the city, for here we have no continuing city as verse 14 reminds us, but to go without the camp. To the believer the world has become a wilderness.

Moreover, had the exhortation been, "Go forth . . . without the city," the words might have had a merely political significance to these early Hebrews. As a matter of fact, when a few years later Jerusalem was destroyed by the Romans, the Christians had almost to a man fled the city; but that was not the point here. The *camp* was Israel viewed religiously, Israel grouped around the Tabernacle according to the divine order. The call to these Hebrews was to go outside the religious system of Judaism, and thus to take up the reproach of Christ. Only one thing could induce them to obey this call, and that the love of Him. "Let us go forth therefore UNTO HIM."

HEBREWS

If we attentively read the Acts we become aware that the mass of believing Jews by no means broke their links with Judaism. They thought now to proceed with Christ AND Judaism. With many indeed it was a case of Judaism and Christ; for the outstanding feature with them was, "they are all zealous of *the law*," rather than zealous for Christ. When this epistle was penned the hour had struck for a decisive move. It could no longer be Christ and Judaism. It had to be Christ OR Judaism. If they wanted CHRIST, then outside the camp to HIM they must go.

A few years passed and in the fall of Jerusalem the very heart of Judaism disappeared. Temple, altars, sacrifices, priests, all were swept away. The camp strictly speaking had gone. Are we to suppose that therefore this exhortation had lost all its force? By no means, for the Jews carried on some resemblance of their religion by means of Synagogues and Rabbis, and have done so to this day. They still have a camp of a sort, though not the camp as originally instituted of God. When a Jew is converted today, this exhortation without a question calls him out of his Judaism unto the rejected Christ as effectively as ever.

And what of that sad travesty of primitive Christianity which today is called Christendom? It has almost entirely organized itself after the pattern of the Jewish camp. It boasts its priests, its worldly sanctuaries and often its sacrifices. It rests upon a worldly basis and frequently encourages alliance with the world. Has this exhortation no voice to us in connection with this? Is it likely that God would begin by calling His people out of a religious system that He had originated Himself, and then end by expecting them to remain within religious systems which He never instituted, but which were created through long ages of unfaithfulness and decay? What a reviving we should see if every Christian really heard the cry, "Unto HIM without the camp," *and obeyed it*!

Doubtless there are a thousand reasons against our obeying it. Here is one, "We should be isolating ourselves. It would be a dull and miserable business." Would it? Why then does verse 15 go on to speak of praise and thanksgiving? Those who have gone forth to Christ without the camp are filled with praise and thanksgiving! They offer it by Him, for He is their High Priest, and they are exhorted to offer it continually. The Jewish camp had the silver trumpets and the high sounding cymbals without a doubt. But what were they worth? Christendom's camp has, without a question, magnificent organs and orchestras and lovely choirs. But what about, "the fruit of lips, confessing His name"? That is another matter, and that is the thing that counts!

Here is another objection, "We should be sacrificing all our opportunities of doing good." Should we? Why then does verse 16 speak of our doing good? The fact is that unlimited opportunities for doing real GOOD lie before those who are obedient, and instead of sacrificing their opportunities, they offer real sacrifice in doing good.

HEBREWS

Again it may be said, "If you go outside the camp it will be all disorder and confusion." What then about verse 17? These Hebrews, though coming outside the camp, would have leaders or guides, raised up of God, who would watch over them for their souls good. To such it would be a pleasure to submit. This does not look like disorder but rather the reverse.

Yet once more, it may be said, "But we need the outward framework of organization that the camp supplies. Without hurdles the sheep will always be straying." But look at verses 20 and 21. Long before this, as recorded in John x., the Lord Jesus had spoken of Himself as the Shepherd who had entered the Jewish fold in order that He might call His own sheep by name and *lead them out*. Now he is presented to us as the great Shepherd of the sheep, raised again from the dead by the God of peace. In going forth unto Him they were but leaving the fold finally and for ever, in order to come altogether under His authority and His shepherd care. They were coming to Him by whom they could be made perfect in every good work to do the will of God.

All this stands as true for us today as for the Hebrew believers of the first century. If we have gone forth to Him, who is our risen Shepherd, we have come to a place where Psalm xxiii. applies, with a fulness of meaning that David himself could never have known. Instead of knowing want we shall be like sheep who lie down in green pastures, because abundantly satisfied.

On this note the Epistle ends. The writer speaks of it as "a word of exhortation," and such indeed it is. It is also "a letter . . . in few words." Though only two epistles exceed it in length yet it is indeed "in a few words" if we consider the magnitude and scope of its contents. If we have really taken in these "few words" we shall have received some knowledge of things which are so great that all eternity will not exhaust them.

JAMES

INTRODUCTION

WE INCLINE TO think that the Epistle of James is read less than any other of the Epistles. This is a pity, because it deals with matters of a very practical sort. There is in it hardly anything which could be called the unfolding of Christian doctrine, but a great deal which inculcates Christian practice. We might almost call it the Epistle of *works*, of everyday Christian behaviour. Its difficulty lies in the fact that the standpoint from which it is written differs from that of all the other Epistles. But we must not neglect it on that account.

The James who wrote it was not the brother of John. He was slain by Herod in very early years, as recorded in Acts xii. 2. The author of the Epistle was the James spoken of in Acts xv. 13, and xxi. 18. Paul calls him, "James, the Lord's brother," in Galatians i, 19, and he acknowledges him as one of the "pillars" of the Church in Jerusalem in Galatians ii. 9. He does not appear to have gone forth to Judea or Samaria or to the uttermost parts of the earth, but to have remained in Jerusalem and there attained to a position of great authority.

CHAPTER 1

THE EPISTLE IS not written to any particular assembly of believers, nor even to the whole church of God. It is addressed rather to "the twelve tribes which are scattered abroad," and it is this which accounts for its unusual character. Let us attempt to seize the view-point from which James speaks before we consider any of its details.

Although the Gospel began at Jerusalem and there won its earliest triumphs, the Christians of that city were slower than others in entering into the true character of the faith they had embraced. They clung with very great tenacity to the law of Moses and to the whole order of religion which they had received through him, as is evidenced by such passages as Acts xv, and xxi. 20—25. This is not surprising, for the Lord did not come to destroy the law and the prophets but rather to give their fulness, as He said. This they knew but what they were slow to see was that having now got the substance in Christ, the shadows of the law had lost their value. The enforcing of that fact is the main theme of the Epistle to the Hebrews, which tells us, "Now, that which decayeth and waxeth old is ready to vanish away." Shortly after those words were written the whole Jewish system,—temple, altar, sacrifices, priests,—did vanish away in the destruction of Jerusalem by the Romans.

Up to that point however, they viewed themselves as just a part of the Jewish people, only with new hopes centred in a Messiah who was risen from the dead. The same idea was common among the Jewish converts to Christ, wherever they were found and consequently their tendency was to still remain attached to their synagogues. An exception to this state of things was found where the Apostle Paul laboured and taught "all the counsel of God." In such cases the real character of Christianity was made manifest and the Jewish disciples were separated from their synagogues, as we see in Acts xix. 8 and 9. James, as we have seen, remained in Jerusalem and he wrote his Epistle from this Jerusalem standpoint, which was right as far as it went and at the time of his writing.

We might put the matter in another way by saying that the earliest years of Christianity covered a period of transition. The history of those years, revealing the transition, is given to us in the Acts, which begins with the incorporation of the church in Jerusalem, consisting exclusively of Jews, and ends with the sentence of blindness finally pronounced upon the Jews as a people and the Gospel specially sent to the Gentiles. James writes from the standpoint that was usual amongst Jewish Christians in the middle of that period. It is this which accounts for the peculiar features of his Epistle.

Although the Apostle addresses himself to the whole of his dispersed nation he does not for a moment hide his own position as a servant of the Lord Jesus Christ, who was still rejected by the majority of his people. Moreover, as we read on, we soon perceive that the believers amongst his people are really in his mind's eye and that what he has to say is mainly addressed to them. Here and there we shall find remarks specifically addressed to the unbelieving mass, as also other remarks which have the unbelievers in view, though not addressed directly to them.

Take, for instance, the opening words of verse 2. When he says, "My brethren," he was not thinking of them merely as his brethren according to the flesh, as fellow Jews, but as brethren in the faith of Christ. This is evident if we look at the next verse where their *faith* is mentioned. It was faith in Christ, and that alone, which at that moment differentiated between them and the unbelieving mass of the nation. To the casual observer all might look alike, for all were waiting on the same temple services in Jerusalem or attending the same synagogues in the many cities of their dispersion, yet this immense line of cleavage existed. The minority believed in Christ, the majority refused Him. This cleavage was manifested in the lifetime of the Lord Jesus for we read, "So there was a division among the people because of Him." (John vii. 43). It was perpetuated and enlarged at the time when James wrote, and as ever the Christian minority was suffering persecution at the hands of the majority.

They had at this time "divers" or "various" temptations. From different quarters there came upon them trials and testings which, if they had succumbed to them, would have tempted them to turn aside from the simplicity of their faith in Christ. On the other hand, if instead of succumbing they went through them with God they would be made strong by enduring, and this would be great gain in which they might well rejoice.

JAMES

Hence when the trials came instead of being depressed by them they were to count it an occasion of joy. What a word this is for us today! A word amply corroborated by the apostles Paul and Peter: see, Romans v. 3-5, and 1 Peter i. 7.

These temptations were permitted of God for the testing of their faith and they resulted in the development of endurance. But endurance in its turn became operative in them, and if allowed to have its perfect work it would carry to completion the work of God in their hearts. The language is very strong, "perfect and entire, wanting nothing." In the light of these words we may safely say that temptation or trial plays a very large part in our spiritual education. It is like a tutor in the school of God, who is well able to instruct us and to develop our minds to the point when we graduate as the finished product of the school. And yet how greatly we shrink from trial! What efforts we make to avoid it! In so doing we are like unto children who scheme with great ingenuity to play truant from school, and end up by becoming dunces. Are we not foolish? And have we not here an explanation of why so many of us make but little progress in the things of God?

Many of us would doubtless rejoin, "Yes, but these trials make such demands upon one. Again and again one is entangled in the most perplexing problems that need superhuman wisdom for their solution." That is so, and therefore it is that James next instructs as to what should be done in these perplexing situations. Lacking wisdom we are simply to ask it of God, and we may be assured of a liberal answer without a word of reproach; for we are not expected to have *in ourselves* that wisdom which is *in God*, and which comes from above. We may assuredly ask God for whatever we lack and expect a liberal answer, though whether we should always get it without a word of reproach is another matter. There were occasions when the disciples asked the Lord Jesus for things which they did not get without a gentle word of reproof: see, for instance, Luke viii. 24, 25, and xvii. 5-10. But then these were occasions when what was wanted was *faith*, and that, being believers, we certainly ought to possess.

How definite and certain is the word—"It shall be given him." Take note of it, for the more the assurance of it sinks down into our hearts the more ready we shall be to ask wisdom in faith without any "wavering" or "doubting." This simple unquestioning faith, which takes God absolutely at His word, is most necessary. If we doubt we become double-minded, unsteady in all our ways. We become like sea-waves tossed about by every wind, driven first in this direction and then in that, sometimes up and sometimes down. First our hopes run high and then we are filled with forebodings and fears. If this be our condition we may ask for wisdom but we have no ground for expecting it, or anything else, from the Lord.

We rather think that verse 7 is also intended to convey to us this thought; that he who asks of God, and yet asks with a doubting mind, is not likely, whatever he may receive, to take it *as from the Lord*. Wisdom or guidance or anything else is asked of God. Instead of there being calm reliance upon His word the mind is full of questionings and tossed about between hopes and fears. How can real wisdom and guidance be received? And if any kind of help is granted how can it be received as from God? Does not this go far to explain why so many Christians are troubled over questions concerning guidance? And when God's merciful providence is exercised towards them and things reach a happy issue, they do not see His hand in it and receive it as from Him. They attribute it to their good fortune: they say, as the world would say, "My luck was in!"

Verses 9 to 12 form a small paragraph by themselves and furnish us with an instructive example of the point of view that James takes. He contrasts "the brother of low degree" with "the rich," and not, as we might have expected, with "the brother of high degree." The rich, as James uses the term, mean the unbelieving rich, the leading men of wealth and influence and religious sanctity, who were almost to a man in deadly opposition to Christ, as is shown to us throughout the Acts of the Apostles. God had chosen the poor of this world and the rich played the part of their opressors, as is stated in chapter ii. of our epistle, verses 5 and 6. How plainly does the Apostle warn the rich oppressors of his nation of what lay ahead of them! Great they might be in the eyes of their fellows but they were like grass in the sight of God. Grass produces flowers and the fashion of them has much grace about it, but under the burning heat of the sun all is speedily withered. So these great Jewish leaders might be most comely in the eyes of their contemporaries, yet soon they would fade away.

And when the rich fade away here is this "brother," this Christian, emerging from his trials and receiving a crown of life! Exaltation reached him even during his life of toil and testing, inasmuch as God considered him worthy of being tested. Men do not test mud, except it be that kind of blue clay in which diamonds are found. Base metals are not cast into the crucible of the refiner, but gold is. God picks up this poor brother of low degree, who would have been regarded by the rich of his nation as but the mud of the streets (see, John vii. 47-49) and exalted him by proclaiming him to be an object composed of gold. Consequently He permits him to be refined by trials. If we really understand this we shall be able to say with all our hearts, "Blessed is the man that endureth temptation." The testing process itself is not joyous but grievous, as the Apostle Peter tells us, yet by means of it room is made in our hearts for the inshining of the love of God, and we become characterized as those that love the Lord. Consequently the trial issues in a crown of life when the glory appears. The tried saint may have lost his life in this world but he is crowned with life in the world to come.

Though the primary thought of this passage is the testing which God permits to come upon believers, yet we cannot rule out altogether the idea

JAMES

of temptation, since every test brings with it the temptation to succumb, by gratifying ourselves rather than glorifying God. Hence when God tests us we might be so foolish as to charge Him with tempting us. This it is which leads to the next short paragraph, verses 13 to 15.

God Himself is above all evil. It is absolutely foreign to His nature. It is as impossible for Him to be tempted with evil as it is impossible for Him to lie. Equally so it is impossible for Him to tempt anyone with evil though He may permit His people to be tempted with evil, knowing well how to overrule even that for their ultimate good. The real root of all temptation lies within ourselves, in our own lusts. We may blame the enticing thing which from without was presented to us, but the trouble really lies in the desires of the flesh within.

Let us lay hold of this fact and honestly face it. When we sin the tendency is for us to lay a great deal of the blame on our circumstances, or at all events on things without, when if only we are honest before God we have no one and nothing to blame but ourselves. How important it is that we should thus be honest before God and judge ourselves rightly in His presence, for that is the high road to recovery of soul. Moreover it will help us to judge and refuse the lusts of our hearts, and thus sin will be nipped in the bud. Lust is the mother of sin. If it works it brings forth sin, and sin carried to completion brings forth death.

Sin in this 15th verse is clearly sin in the act: for other scriptures, such, for instance as Romans vii. 7, show us that lust itself is sin in the nature. Only let sin in the nature conceive, and sin in the act is brought forth.

At this point we shall do well to think of our Lord Jesus and recall what is stated of Him in Hebrews iv. 15. He too was tempted, tempted in like manner to ourselves and not only this but tempted like us "in all things." And then comes that qualification of all importance, "yet without sin," or more accurately, "sin apart." There was no sin, no lust in Him. Things which to us had been most alluring found absolutely no response in Him, and yet He "suffered being tempted" as Hebrews ii. 18 tells us.

It is easy to understand how temptation, if we refuse it, entails suffering for us. It is because we only turn from it at the cost of refusing the natural desires of our own hearts. We may not find it so easy to understand how temptation brought suffering to Him. The explanation lies in the fact that not only was there no sin in Him but He was full of holiness. Being God He was infinitely holy, and having become Man He was anointed by the Spirit of God, and He met all temptation full of the Spirit. Hence sin was infinitely abhorrent to Him, and the mere presentation of it to Him, as a temptation from without, caused Him acute suffering. We, alas! having sin within us, and having become so accustomed to it, are very little able to feel it as He felt it.

JAMES

God, then, far from originating temptation is the Source and Giver of every gift that is good and perfect. The Apostle is very emphatic on this point; he would by no means have us err as to it. Verses 16 to 18 are another short paragraph, in which God is presented to us in a very remarkable way. Not only is He the Source of every good and perfect gift but also of all that can be spoken of as light. The light of creation came from Him. Every ray of true light for the heart or conscience or intellect comes from Him. What we really *know* we know as the result of divine revelation, and He is the "Father" or "Source" of all such light. Man's lights are very uncertain. The light of "science" so-called is very variable. It burns brightly, it dies down, it re-appears, it flares up, it goes out, finally extinguished by an oncoming generation which feels sure it knows more than the outgoing generation. With the Father of lights, and hence with all light that really comes from Him, there is no variableness neither shadow of turning. Blessed be God for that!

There is a third thing in this short paragraph however. Not only is God the Source of gifts that are good and perfect and lights that do not vary, but also of His people themselves. We too have sprung from Him as begotten of Him according to His own will. We are what we are according to His sovereign pleasure and not according to our thoughts or our wills, which by nature are fallen and debased, and also according to the "word of truth" by which we have been born of Him.

The devil is the father of lies. The world today is what he has made it, and he started it with the lie of Genesis iii. 4. In contradistinction to this the Christian is one who has been begotten by the word of truth. By-and-by God is going to have a world of truth, but meanwhile we are to be a kind of firstfruits of that new creation.

Is not this wonderful? A thoughtful reader might have deduced the fact that a Christian must be a wonderful being, inasmuch as he is begotten of God. We might have said, "If God is the Source of gifts and those gifts are good and perfect; if He is the Source of lights and those lights are without variation or turning; then if He becomes the Source of beings those beings are sure to be equally wonderful." We are not however left to deduce it. We are plainly told; and very important results flow from it as we shall see.

The nineteenth verse begins with the word, "Wherefore" which indicates that we are now to be introduced to the results flowing from the truth of the previous verse. Because we are a kind of firstfruits of God's creatures, as begotten of Him by the Word of Truth, we are to be "swift to hear, slow to speak, slow to wrath."

Every intelligent unfallen creature is marked by obedience to the voice of the Creator. Fallen man, alas! shuts his ear to God's voice and insists upon talking. He would like to legislate for himself and for everybody else, and hence come the anger and strife which fill the earth. We were always creatures, but now, born of God, we are a kind of firstfruits of His creatures. What therefore should mark all creatures should be specially characteristic of us. Hearing God's word should attract us. We should run eagerly to it as those who delight to listen to God.

We only speak aright as our thoughts are controlled by God. If we think God's thoughts we shall be able to speak things that are right. But, even if we are swift to hear God's thoughts, we shall only speak them when first we have assimilated them for ourselves and made them our own. We assimilate them but slowly and hence we should be slow to speak. A wholesome sense of how little we have as yet taken in God's mind will deliver us from that self-confidence and shallow self-assertiveness which makes men ready to speak at once on any and every matter.

Further we should be slow to wrath. The self-assertive man, who can hardly stop to listen to anything but must at once speak his own opinion is apt to get very angry when he finds that others do not accept his opinion at his own high valuation of it! On the other hand, here may be a believer of godly life who pays great heed to God's word and only speaks with consideration and prayer, and yet his opinion is equally turned aside! Well, let him be slow to wrath for if it be merely man's anger it accomplishes nothing that is right in God's sight. Divine anger will be made to serve His righteous cause, but not man's anger.

We must remember too that we are a firstfruit of God's creatures *as born of Him*. Hence not only should we be pattern creatures but we should though creatures exhibit the likeness of the One who is our Father. All evil should be laid aside and the word received with meekness. We are in the first place begotten of the Word; then with meekness we continue to receive it. These two things also appear in 1 Peter i. 23—ii. 2, where we are said to be "born again . . . by the word of God," and also exhorted as new born babes to "desire the sincere milk of the Word."

The Word is spoken of here as "engrafted" or "implanted." This supposes that it has taken root in us and grown into a part of ourselves. It is the very opposite of "going in at one ear and coming out at the other." If the Word merely flows through our minds it accomplishes for us little or nothing. If implanted in us it saves our souls. The primary thought here is the saving of our souls from the snares of the world, the flesh and the devil, a salvation which we all need moment by moment.

In verse 22 we get a third thing. Not only should we be swift to *hear* God's word, not only has it to be *implanted* in us, but we must become *doers* of it. First the *ear* for hearing. Then the *heart*, in which it is implanted. Then the *hand* governed by it, so that it comes into outward expression through us. And it is only when this third thing is reached that the Word is vitally operative in us. If our hearing does not result in doing our hearing is in vain.

JAMES

To enforce this fact the apostle James uses a very graphic illustration. When a man stands before a mirror his image is reflected therein for just so long as there he stands. But there is nothing implanted in the mirror. His face is reflected in it, but without any subjective effect in the mirror, which is absolutely unchanged, even if ten thousand things are reflected in turn upon its face. The man departs, his image vanishes, and all is forgotten. It is just like this if a man merely hears the Word without any thought of rendering obedience to it. He gazes into the Word and then goes away and forgets. If on the other hand we not only look into truth but abide in it, and hence become doers of the work which is in accordance with truth, we shall be blessed in our doing. To this matter James refers more fully in the next chapter when he discusses faith and works.

We must not fail to notice the expression he uses to describe the revelation which had reached them in Christ. The revelation which the Jew had known through Moses was a law and writing to Jews, James uses the same term. Christianity too may be spoken of as *law*—the law of Christ—though it is much more than this. In contrast with the law of Moses however it is the *perfect* law of *liberty*. The law of Moses was *imperfect* and *bondage*.

The law of Moses was of course perfect *as far as it went*. It was imperfect in the sense that *it did not go all the way*. It set forth the bare *minimum* of God's demands so that if man falls short in the smallest degree—offending in but "one point" (ii. 10)—he is wholly condemned. If we want the *maximum* of God's thoughts for man we have to turn to Christ, who fully displayed it in His matchless life and death, which went far beyond the bare demands of the law of Moses. In His earliest teachings too He plainly showed that the law of Moses was not the full and perfect thing. See Matthew v. 17 to 48.

In Christ we have the perfect law, even that of liberty. We might have imagined that if the setting forth of God's minimum produced bondage the revelation of His maximum would have meant greater bondage still. But no! The minimum reached us in what we may call the law of *demand*, and generated bondage. The maximum reached us in connection with the law of *supply* in Christ, and hence all here is liberty. The highest possible standards are set before us in Christianity but in connection with a power which subdues our hearts and gives us a nature which loves to do that which the revelation enjoins upon us. If a law were imposed upon a dog that it should eat hay it would prove to be to the poor animal a law of bondage. Impose the same law upon a horse and it is a law of liberty.

It is clear then, from verse 25, that we are to be doers of the work and not merely hearers of the word. Even our doings however need to be tested, for a man may seem to be religious, zealous in all his works, and yet his religion be proved vain by the fact that he does not bridle his tongue. He has not learned to be "slow to speak" as verse 19 enjoined. In giving rein to his tongue he is giving rein to self.

Now pure and undefiled religion, which will stand in the presence of God, is of a sort which shuts self out. He who visits the fatherless and the widows in their affliction will not find much to minister to the importance or the convenience of self. He will have to be continually ministering instead of finding that which will minister to himself, if he moves amongst these afflicted and poor folk. The world might minister to self in him. Yes, but he keeps himself separate from the world so that he may not be spotted by its defilements.

"Unspotted from the world" is a strong way of putting it. The world is like a very miry place in which all too many love to disport themselves. (see 2 Peter ii. 22). The true Christian does not wallow in the mire. Quite true! But if he practices pure religion he goes further. He walks so apart from the miry place that not even splashes of the mud reach him.

Alas! for the feebleness of our religion. If it consisted in outward observances, in rites, in ceremonies, in sacraments in services, Christendom might yet make a fair show of it. Whereas it really consists in *the outflow of divine love* which expresses itself in compassion towards and service to those who have no ability to recompense again, and a *holy separateness* from the defiling world-system that surrounds us.

CHAPTER 2

THESE EARLY JEWISH Christians were far too much controlled by the ordinary thoughts of the world, and as a consequence of being spotted by the world, they despised the poor. They should have been controlled by the faith of the Lord Jesus, and not by the standards and customs of the world. Though he was the Lord of Glory yet He ever stooped to the poor and the fatherless. Poverty and need may be incompatible with human glory, but they are quite compatible with Divine glory.

As a consequence when some rich Jew pompously entered their "assembly" or "synagogue"—this latter is the right word—attired in all his finery, he was met with servile attention, as much by the Christians as by the non-Christians apparently. When a poor man entered he was unceremoniously put in an obscure place. Quite natural of course according to the way of the world; but quite foreign this to the faith of Christ. They might constitute themselves judges of men in this way, but they only thereby proved themselves to be "judges of evil thoughts" or "judges having evil reasonings."

In verses 5 to 7 James recalls to his brethren what the situation really was. The rich Jews were in the main the proud opposers of Christ and His people, blasphemers of His worthy name. God's choice had in the main

JAMES

fallen on the poor; and with this agree the words of the Apostle to the Gentiles, in 1 Corinthians i. 26—31. These chosen poor ones—true Christians—were rich in faith and heirs of the coming kingdom. When servile attention was paid to the proud blasphemers and persecutors, because they were rich, and contempt was meted out to the followers of Christ because they were poor it only proved the blindness and folly of those who so acted. They viewed both rich and poor with the world's superficial gaze, and not with the penetrating eye if faith.

Notice that the Kingdom is said to be "promised to them that love Him." Most of those to whom James wrote would have stoutly contended that the kingdom was promised to the Jew nationally, and that in an exclusive way. This was now seen to be a mistake. It is promised to lovers of God, and that whether Jew or Gentile, as we find in Paul's writings.

Notice also the expression, "that worthy name by the which ye are called." The rich Jew blasphemed it but God pronounces it a *worthy* Name. By it they were called—this seems to indicate that, when James wrote, the name *Christian* had travelled from Antioch where first it was coined (Acts xi. 26) to Jerusalem. The poor were the objects of persecution not so much because they were poor, as because they were identified with Christ, and He was the object of the world's hatred.

This having respect of persons is not only contrary to the faith of Christ, but even to the law itself which bids us love our neighbours as ourselves. This is called in verse 8 the "royal" or "kingly" law. It sums up in one word that which must be observed by every king who would reign righteously and govern according to God. To have respect of persons is to break that law and stand convicted as a transgressor.

If we stand before God on the ground of law keeping and are convicted in one point of law-breaking, what is the effect?

Nothing could be more sweeping than the statement made in verse 10, and at first sight some of us might be inclined to question the rightness of it. We have to remember however that the law is treated as a whole, one and indivisible. An errand boy, carrying a basket of bottles, may slip and break one bottle in his fall, and his employer cannot with any justice accuse him of breaking all of them, for every bottle is separate and distinct from each of the others. If however the lad were carrying the basket suspended from his shoulder by a chain, and in falling he also broke one link of the chain, his master could rightly tell him that he had broken the chain. If in addition he indulged in rough horseplay with other boys, and hurling a stone misdirected it through a large shop window, it is rightly spoken of as a broken window.

It is thus with the law. The chain may have many links yet it is one chain. The window may comprise many square feet of glass yet it is one pane. The law has many commandments yet it is one law. One commandment may be

JAMES

carefully observed as verse 11 says, indeed many commandments may be kept, yet if one commandment is broken the law is transgressed.

If that be so then must we all plead guilty, and we might begin to enquire if then after all we are to stand before God and be judged by Him on the basis of the law of Moses? To this question James replies in verse 12. We stand before God and shall be judged on the basis of the "law of liberty"—an expression which means the revelation of God's will which has reached us in Christ, as we saw when considering verse 25 of the previous chapter. We shall have to answer as being in the much fuller light which Christianity brings. Being in the light of the supreme manifestation of God's mercy in Christ we are responsible to show mercy ourselves. This thought brings us back to the matter with which the paragraph started. Their treatment of "the poor man in vile raiment" had not been according to the mercy displayed in the Gospel. They set themselves up as "judges of evil thoughts," but, lo! they would find themselves under judgment.

A serious position indeed! Are we in a similar position? We shall have to answer to God as in the light of Gospel mercy and as under the law of liberty, even as they.

Notice that the last phrase of verse 13 is not, "Mercy rejoiceth against *justice*," but, "against *judgment*." Divine mercy goes hand in hand with righteousness, and thereby it triumphs against the judgment that otherwise had been our due.

The change of subject that we find in verse 14 may strike us as rather abrupt but it really flows quite naturally from the profound insight which James had by the Spirit into the foolish workings of the human heart. He began the chapter by saying, "My brethren have not . . . faith." They might wish to rebut his assertion by saying, "Oh, yes! we have. We have the faith of the Lord Jesus as much as you." Is there any certain test which will enable us to check these contrary assertions and discover where the truth lies?

There certainly is. It lies in the fact that true faith is a living thing which manifests its life in works. Thereby it may be distinguished from that dead kind of faith which consists only in the acceptance of facts, without the heart being brought under the power of them. We may profess that we accept the teaching of Christ, but unless that which we believe controls our actions we cannot be said to really have the faith of Christ. Hence the latter part of this second chapter is of immense importance.

It must be carefully noted that the works, upon which James so strenuously insists in these verses are *the works of faith*. Having noted this we shall do well to turn at once to Romans iii. and iv., and also to Galatians iii., where the Apostle Paul so convincingly demonstrates that our justification is by faith and is not of works. These works however which Paul so completely eliminates are *the works of the law*.

JAMES

A great many people have supposed that there is a clash and a contradiction between the two Apostles on this matter, but it is not so. The distinction we have just pointed out largely helps to remove the difficulty that is felt. Both speak of works, but there is an immense difference between the works of the law and the works of faith.

The works of the law, of which Paul speaks, are works done in obedience to the demand of the law of Moses, by which, it is hoped, a righteousness may be wrought that will pass in the presence of God. "This do, and thou shalt live," said the law, and the works are done in the hope of thereby obtaining the life—life upon earth—that is proffered. No one of us ever did obtain this abiding earthly life by law-keeping, since as James has just told us we became wholly guilty directly we had transgressed in one point. Hence we all lie by nature under the death sentence, and the works of the law are dead works, though done in the effort to obtain life.

The works of faith, of which James speaks are those which spring out of a living faith as its direct expression and result. They are as much a proof of faith's vitality as flowers and fruit prove the vitality and also the nature of a tree. If no such works are forthcoming then our faith is proclaimed as dead, being alone.

Is there any contradiction between these two sets of statements? By no means. They are indeed entirely complementary the one to the other, and our view of the matter is not complete without both. Works done *for* justification are rigorously excluded. Works flowing *from* the faith that justifies are strenuously insisted on, and that not only by James but by Paul also; for in writing to Titus he says, "These things I will that thou affirm constantly, that they which have believed in God might be careful to maintain good works." (iii. 8). The works that are to be maintained are those done by "*they which have believed*"; that is, they are the works of faith.

The above considerations do not entirely remove the difficulty for there remain certain verbal contradictions, such as, "We conclude that a man is justified by faith without the deeds of the law" (Rom. iii. 28), and in our passage, "Ye see then how that by works a man is justified, and not by faith only." Again we read, "If Abraham were justified by works, he hath whereof to glory; but not before God" (Rom. iv. 2), and in our passage, "Was not Abraham our father justified by works, when he had offered Isaac his son upon the altar?" Some puzzled reader may wish to ask us if we can extricate ourselves from the contradictory conclusions that in the distant past Abraham both *was* and *was not* justified by works; and further that in the present a man is justified *by faith without works*, and also *by works and not by faith alone*?

We should reply that there is really no difficulty from which to extricate ourselves. We have but to remark that in James the whole point is that

JAMES

which is valid *before man*, as verse 18 of our chapter shows. A man has the right to demand that we display our faith in our works, thus justifying ourselves and our faith before him. In Romans the whole point is that which is valid *before God*. The very words, "before God," occur in Romans iv. 2, as we have seen. Our faith is quite apparent to *His* all-seeing eye. *He* does not have to wait for the display of the works that are the fruit of faith, in order to be assured that the faith really exists.

In the world of men however works are a necessity, for in no other way can we be assured that faith exists of a living sort. The illustrations of verses 14 to 16 are quite conclusive. We may profess faith in God's care for His people in temporal things, but except our faith in that care leads us to a readiness to be the channel through which it may flow, our faith is of no profit to the needy brother or sister; nor indeed to ourselves. Our faith as to that particular point is dead and consequently inoperative, as verse 17 tells us, and we must not be surprised if it is challenged by others.

A man may come up to you and say, "Well, you say that you believe but you produce no visible evidence of your faith, kindly therefore produce your faith itself for my inspection." What could you do? Obviously, nothing! You might go on reiterating, "I have faith. I have faith." But of what use would that be? Your confusion would be increased if he should further say, "At all events I have been doing such-and-such a thing, and such-and-such, which clearly evidence that I personally do believe, though I am not in the habit of talking about my faith."

So far the Apostle has urged these very practical considerations upon us in connection with matters of every day life in the world, but they stand equally true in connection with matters of doctrine, matters connected with the whole faith of the Gospel. In verse 19 the very fundamental point of faith in the existence of the one true God is raised. "Oh, yes," we each exclaim, "I believe in Him!" That is good; but such faith if real is bound to affect us. We shall at least tremble, for even demons, who know right well that He exists and hate Him, go as far as that. The multitudes, who in a languid way accept the idea of His existence and yet are utterly unmoved by it, have a faith which is dead.

"What!" someone may remark, "Is such a thing as *trembling* counted as a work?" It certainly is. And this leads us to remark that James speaks simply of works, and not of *good* works. The point is not that every true believer must do a number of kindly and charitable actions—though it is of course good and right for him so to do—but that his works are bound to be such as shall display his faith in action if men are to see that his faith is real. This is an important point: let us all make sure that we seize it.

As an illustration, let us suppose that you go to visit a sick friend. You enquire for his health when he at once assures you that he is perfectly certain to get well. As he does not seem particularly cheerful about it, you ask what has given him this assurance—upon what his faith rests? In reply he tells you he has some wonderful medicine, as to which he has read hundreds of flattering testimonials; and he points you to a large bottle of medicine standing on the mantelpiece. You notice that the bottle is quite full, so you ask him how long he has been taking the stuff, when he surprises you by saying that he has not taken any! Would you not say, "My friend, you cannot *really* believe that this medicine will cure you without fail, otherwise you would have begun to take it?"

You would be even more surprised however if in response to this he calmly remarked, "Oh, but my faith in it is very real, as may be seen by the fact that I have just sent £5 to help our local charities." "What has that to do with it?" you would exclaim. "Your gift seems to show that you have a kindly heart, and that you believe in local charities, but it proves nothing as to your belief in the medicine. Start taking the medicine: that will demonstrate that you believe in it!"

Here is a rich man who, when requested, will draw out his cheque-book and sign away large sums for charitable services. There is a poor woman who is astonishingly kind and helpful to her equally humble neighbours. What do their works show? Their faith in Christ? Not with any certainty. True it *may* be that their kindly spirit is the result of their having been converted, but on the other hand it *may* only spring from a desire for notoriety or for the approbation of their fellows. But suppose they both begin to display great interest in the Word of God, together with a hearty obedience to its directions, and a real affection for all the people of God. Now we can safely draw the deduction that they really do believe in Christ, for that is the only root from which springs such fruit as this.

Two cases are cited in verses 21 to 25—Abraham and Rahab. Contrasts they are in almost every respect. The one, the father of the Jews, an honoured servant of God. The other, a Gentile, a poor woman of dishonourable calling. Yet they both illustrate this matter. Both had faith, and both had works—the works exactly appropriate to the particular faith they possessed, and which consequently showed it to others.

Abraham's case is particularly instructive since Paul also cites him in Romans iv. to establish his side of this great question; referring to that which happened under cover of the quiet and starry night, when God made His great promise and Abraham accepted it in simple faith. James refers to the same chapter (Gen. xv.) in our 23rd verse; but he cites it as being fulfilled years after when he "offered Isaac his son upon the altar," as recorded in Genesis xxii. The offering of Isaac was the work by which Abraham showed forth the faith that had long been in his heart.

Many a critic is inclined to object to the offering of Isaac and to denounce it as unworthy of being called a "good work." That is because they are entirely blind to the point we have just been endeavouring to make. When Abraham believed God on that starry night, he believed that He was going to raise up a living child from dead parents. How could he have so

JAMES

believed except he had believed that God was able to raise the dead to life? And what did his offering of Isaac show? It showed that he really did believe in God, just in that way. He offered him "accounting that God was able to raise him up, even from the dead" (Heb. xi. 19). His work showed forth his faith in the most precise and exact way.

With Rahab it was just the same. She received the spies from Joshua and sent them out another way. Again our critic is far from pleased. He denounces her action. It was unpatriotic! It was treason! She told lies! Well, poor thing! she was but a depraved member of an accursed race, groping her way towards the light. Her actions can easily be criticised, yet they had this supreme merit—they clearly demonstrated that she had lost faith in the filthy gods of her native land and had begun to believe in the might and mercy of the God of Israel. Now this was exactly the point, for the faith she professed to the spies was, "I know that the Lord hath given you the land . . . for the LORD your God, He is God in heaven above, and in earth beneath" (Joshua ii. 9-11). Did she believe this? She did, for her works showed it. She risked her own neck to identify herself with the people who had JEHOVAH as their God.

Is not all this very wholesome and important truth? It is indeed. It is reported that Luther was betrayed into speaking of James with contempt, and referring to his Epistle as "the Epistle of straw." If so, the great Reformer was mistaken, and did not grasp the real force of these passages. If we have grasped their force we shall certainly confess it to be more like "an Epistle of iron." There is a sledge-hammer directness about James hardly equalled by any other New Testament writer.

The sum of the matter we have been considering is this—that, "as the body without the spirit is dead, so faith without works is dead also." We may talk of our faith in Christ, or of our faith in this, that and the other detail of Christian truth; but unless our faith expresses itself in appropriate works it is DEAD! That is a sledge-hammer hit! Let us allow it to exert its full effect in our consciences.

CHAPTER 3

WITH CHAPTER III. a fresh series of exhortations commences. James turns from the subject of the works of faith to exhort his brethren against the very common failing of wishing to be a master of others when one has in no sense learned to be master of oneself. The word translated "masters" really signifies "teachers," and if we glance at Romans ii. 17-21 we shall see that the Jew especially fancied himself in this direction, and when converted the same tendency would doubtless remain in him. He would still be very inclined to pose as a teacher, and correspondingly have a disinclination to be taught and to receive with meekness the engrafted word.

JAMES

Other Scriptures make it abundantly clear that God is pleased to raise up teachers in the church, amongst other gifts, and all such gifts are to be received with thankfulness. The verses before us do not in the least militate against that, but they do warn us against the desire so natural to the flesh to be continually instructing and legislating for other people. The fact that those who teach will receive greater judgment, as compared with those who are taught, may well make us pause.

James is here only enforcing that which the Lord Jesus Himself taught in Matthew xxiii. 14, when addressing scribes and Pharisees, who were the self-constituted religious teachers of that day. It is evidently a fact, in the light of these words, that there are differing degrees of severity in the Divine judgment, and that those who have more light and intelligence will have more expected of them and be judged by higher standards. It is also evident that we shall be judged according to the place that we take, whether we have been called into it by God or not. In the light of that let none of us rush into the position of being a master or teacher. On the other hand if God has really called any man to be a teacher, or to take up any other service, woe betide him if he shirks the responsibility and ties up his pound in a napkin.

The plain truth is that "in many things we offend all," i.e., we all often offend. Moreover our most frequent offences are those connected with our speech, and to offend against God in our words is especially serious if we be teachers, since it is by words that we teach. This is illustrated by the case of Moses. He was a teacher divinely raised up and equipped, and hence his words were to be the words of God. When he offended in word he had to meet severer judgment than would have been meted out to an ordinary Israelite sinning just as he did.

How terribly common are sins of speech! Indeed we all do *often* offend, and in respect of our words *very often*. So much so, that if a man does not offend in word he may be spoken of as a perfect man—the finished article, so to speak. Further, he will be a man able to control himself in all things. As we think of ourselves or as we look at others we may well ask where this completely controlled and perfect man is to be found? Where indeed? We do not know him. But it should teach us to be slow in taking the place of a master, for it is eminently right that he who aspires to be master of others should first be master of himself.

The Apostle is going to speak to us very plainly about our tongues, and he uses two very expressive figures of speech: first the bridle or bit used for the direction of the horse; second the rudder which is used for the steering of a ship.

The bit is a very small article when the large bulk of a horse is considered, yet by this simple contrivance a man gains complete control and, when once the animal is broken in and docile, it suffices to turn about its whole body.

JAMES

Ships are large and driven by fierce winds, or, in our days, by the fierce force of steam or motor driven propellers, yet are they turned about by means of a very small rudder as compared with the bulk of the ship.

Even so the tongue is a little member. Yet it is an instrument of very great things either for good or evil. If men's tongues are used for the proclamation of the Glad Tidings, why then their very feet upon the mountains are beautiful! Alas, as the tongue is ordinarily used among men it is rightly declared by James to be "a fire, a world of iniquity." Small as it is, it boasts great things. It may be like a little spark of fire, but how many a ruinous conflagration has been started by a little spark!

The Apostle had first alluded to the danger of the tongue in chapter i. 26. In chapter ii. he contrasts the works of faith with the mere use of the tongue in saying that one has faith. In the chapter before us he uses the very strongest language as to it in verses 6 and 8. Yet who, that knows the fearful havoc that the tongue has caused, will say that his language is too strong? What mischief has been caused amongst Christian people by the rash and foolish and wicked use of the tongue. When we read, "so is the tongue among our members, that it defileth the whole body," the context indicates that James was referring to the human body, yet it would be equally true if we read it as referring to the church which is the body of Christ and of which we are all members. More defilement has been brought into the church of God by it than by anything else.

Then again there is not only the direct mischief of the tongue, but think of the indirect mischief! The whole course of nature may be set on fire by it. Every instinct and faculty of man may be roused. The deepest and basest passions stirred into action. And when the tongue is thus used we may be quite sure that the tongue itself was originally set on fire of hell. It has been enslaved by the devil to be used for his ends. It was he who struck the spark which by means of the tongue has fired the whole train of evil.

Another feature that marks the tongue is brought before us in verses 7 and 8, and that is its unruly character. Man can tame all kinds of creatures but he cannot tame his own tongue. The reason for this is fairly evident. Speech is the great avenue by which the heart of man expresses itself, and hence the only way to really tame the tongue is to tame the heart. But this is a thing impossible to man. The grace and power of God are needed for it. In itself the tongue only gives expression to the deadly poison which lurks in the human heart.

In verse 9 and onwards a still further feature is mentioned. There is a strange inconsistency about the tongue when it is a question of the people of God. Unconverted people do not bless God, even the Father. They do not really know God at all, and much less do they know Him as Father. Christians know Him and bless Him in this way, and yet there are times when utterances of a very contrary sort come out of their lips. Sometimes they even go so far as cursing men who are made in the likeness of God; so that out of the same mouth goes forth both blessing and cursing. No wonder that James so emphatically says, "My brethren, these things ought not so to be."

Nature teaches us this. Fountains of sweet fresh water can be found, and also fountains of water that is salt or bitter. But never a fountain that produces both out of the same opening. Fruit trees of various kinds may be found each producing its proper fruit. But never a tree violating the fundamental laws of nature by bearing fruit not of its own kind. Why then do we behold this strange phenomenon in Christian people?

The answer of course is twofold. First, they to begin with were sinful creatures, possessing an evil nature, just as the rest. Second, they have now been born again, and consequently they now possess a new nature, without the old nature having been eradicated from them. Consequently within them there are, if we may so speak, two fountains: the one capable only of producing evil, the other capable only of producing good. Hence this strange mixture which the Apostle so strongly condemns.

Someone may feel inclined to remark that, if the case of a believer is thus, he hardly ought to be so strongly condemned if his tongue acts as an opening from whence may flow the bitter waters of the old nature. Ah, but any who think this are forgetting that the flesh, our old nature, has been judged and condemned at the cross. "Sin in the flesh," as Romans viii. 3 puts it, has been condemned, and the believer, knowing this, is responsible to treat it as a judged and condemned thing, which consequently is not allowed to act. The believer therefore IS to be reprimanded if his tongue acts as an outlet for the evil of the flesh.

The Apostle James does not unfold to us the truth concerning the cross of Christ. This ministry was committed not to him but to the Apostle Paul. He does however say things that are in full agreement with what the Epistle to the Romans unfolds. The wise man is to display his wisdom in meekness which shall control both his works and manner of life. If the contrary is manifested—bitter envying and strife, out of which spring all the evils connected with the tongue—such an one is in the position of boasting and lying against the truth.

What is this truth, against which we all far too often are found lying? Every outbreaking of the flesh, whether by the tongue, or whether in some other way, is a practical denial of the fact that sin in the flesh was condemned in the cross of Christ. Which is truth?—the cross of Christ, or my bitter strife and fiery tongue? They cannot possibly *both* be truth. The cross of Christ is TRUTH, and my evil is a *lie against the truth*.

It is also a lie against the truth that we are born of God, and that He now recognizes us as identified with that new nature which is ours as born

JAMES

of Him and not with the old nature which we derived from Adam by natural descent.

In verse 15 the two wisdoms are plainly distinguished. If we wish to find the two natures plainly distinguished we must thoughtfully read Romans vii. The two natures lie at the root respectively of the two wisdoms. The wisdom which is of God brings into display the characteristics of the new nature, and like the nature which it displays it is from above. The other wisdom brings into display the characteristics of the old nature, and like the nature which it displays it is from the earth; it is sensual or natural, it is even devilish, for alas! poor human nature has fallen under the power of the devil, and has taken on characteristics which belong to him.

Its character is summed up in verse 16. At the root of it lies envy or emulation. This was the original sin of the devil. By aspiring to exalt himself, as envying that which was above him, he fell. When this is found there is bound to be strife, and strife in its turn results in confusion and every kind of evil work. Many of these evil things, perhaps all of them, would be counted as wisdom by fallen men. It looks wise enough to the average man to scheme and fight for oneself—to be always out for "number one" as it is called.

How great the contrast in the wisdom from above, as detailed in verse 17! Its features may not be of the kind which make for a great success in this world, but they are delightful to God, and to the renewed heart; and he who manifests them may count upon having God upon his side. Notice that purity comes first upon the list, before peace even. If we reflect we shall at once realize that this must be so, since all is of God. He never compromises with evil, and hence there can be no peace except in purity. Again and again this was the burden of the prophets. See for instance, Isaiah xlviii. 22; lvii. 21; Jeremiah vi. 14; viii. 11; Ezekiel xiii. 10, 16.

Peace and gentleness, yieldingness and mercy should indeed mark us but always as the handmaidens of purity and never as compromising with evil.

There is however another side to the question even in this matter. Though the wisdom from above is first of all pure, and only then is peaceable and gentle, it always proceeds upon the lines of making peace. It is never marked by the pugnacious spirit. The last verse of our chapter makes this very plain. Those who are making peace are faithfully sowing that which will make for a harvest of the fruit of righteousness. Peace and righteousness are not disconnected, and much less antagonistic, in Christianity. Rather they go hand in hand.

Ancient prophecy declared that, "The work of righteousness shall be peace; and the effect of righteousness, quietness and assurance for ever" (Isa. xxxii. 17). This will be fulfilled in the day of Christ's kingdom, yet the Gospel today brings us peace on exactly the same principle. Romans iii.

JAMES

speaks of righteousness manifested, and established in the death of Christ. Romans iv. speaks of righteousness imputed, or reckoned, to the believer. Romans v. consequently opens with, "Therefore being justified by faith we have peace with God through our Lord Jesus Christ."

This being so, peace-making is on the part of the Christian simply practical righteousness which will produce the fruit of righteousness in due season. Purity must be first always, but even purity must be pursued in a spirit not of pugnacity but of peace-making.

Chapter 4

THE LAST NOTE struck, as we closed chapter iii. was that of *peace*. The first note of chapter iv. is the exact opposite, that of *war*. What lay behind the peace was the purity that is the first mark of the wisdom that is from above. So now we discover that what lies behind the wars and fightings, which are so common among the professed people of God, is the impure lust of the human heart, the lust connected with that wisdom which is earthly, sensual, devilish.

You will notice that the marginal reading for "lusts," in verses 1 and 3, is "pleasures." That is because the word used means the pleasure that comes from the gratifying of our desires, or lusts, rather than the desires themselves. If our desires run riot and we find a sinful pleasure in their gratification, we at once have the root of endless contentions and warfare.

Verses 2 and 3 tell us the way this evil works. First, there is the desire for what we have not. Now this desire may carry a man to the point of killing in order to achieve his end, but at any rate it fills him with envy if he cannot accomplish his desire. And after all there is a very simple way in which we may receive what we desire, if indeed we are Christians. We may struggle and strive and move heaven and earth, and yet receive nothing. Yet the Saviour Himself has told us to ask and we shall receive. We have not, because we ask not.

Does someone say in a rather aggrieved tone, "But I have asked, time and again, yet I have never received." The explanation may be that you have asked "amiss" or "evilly"; your object in asking being simply the gratification of your own desires. Had you received it, you would have just spent it upon your own pleasures. Hence God has withheld from you your desire.

How plainly this teaches us that God looks at the heart. He scrutinizes the motive that lies behind the asking. This is very searching, and it explains a lot of unanswered prayer. We may ask for thoroughly right things and be denied, because we ask from thoroughly wrong motives.

You may be serving the Lord. Perhaps you have started to preach the Gospel, and then you certainly desire that your words may be marked by grace and power. Is not that right? It is eminently right, yet beware lest you ask for this just because you have an over-mastering desire to be a successful preacher. Your prayer will sound quite beautiful to us all, but God will know the thought that lies behind it.

Here I am, writing this article. I have asked the Lord to guide so that it may bring light and help to many. Yet I ask myself very seriously, Why did I ask this? Was it that I had a genuine care for the spiritual prosperity of others, or was it just that I might enhance my reputation as a writer of magazine articles of a religious sort? Again I say, this is very searching.

Verse 4 brings in another consideration. We cannot very well be set on our own pleasures without becoming entangled with the world. The world is, so to speak, the arena wherein pleasures disport themselves, and where every lust that finds a place in man's heart may be gratified. Now for the believer alliance with the world is adultery in its spiritual form.

The apostle James is exceedingly definite on this point. The world is in a state of open rebellion against God. It was ever thus since man fell, but its terrible enmity only came fully to light when Christ was manifested. Then it was that the world both saw and hated Him and His Father. Then it was that the breach was irrevocably fixed.

We are speaking, of course, of the world-system. If it be a question of the people in the world, then we read, "God so loved the world." The world-system is the point here, and it is in a state of deadly hostility to God; so much so that friendship with the one entails enmity as regards the other. The language is very strong. Literally it would read, "Whoever therefore is minded to be the friend of the world is constituted enemy of God." It does not say that God is his enemy, but the breach is so complete on the world's side that friendship with it is only possible on the basis of enmity against God. Let us never forget that!

And let us also never forget that we, as believers, are brought into such close and intimate relations with God that if we play Him false and enter into guilty alliance with the world the only sin amongst mankind with which it can be compared is the very terrible one of adultery.

Verse 5 is difficult, even as to its translation. The New Translation renders it thus, "Think ye that the Scripture speaks in vain? Does the Spirit which has taken His abode in us desire enviously?" The force then would seem to be—Has not the Scripture warned you of these things, and does it not always mean what it says? Can you for one moment imagine that the Holy Spirit of God has anything to do with these unholy desires? If we read it as in our Authorized Version we should understand it to mean that all along the Scripture had testified that man's own spirit is the source of his envious lusts. The truth to which it leads us is the same, whichever way we read it.

JAMES

The chapter opened with the lusts of the flesh. It passed on to warn against alliance with the world. Now in verse 7 the devil is mentioned, and we are told that if resisted he will flee. But how thankful we should be for the verse which precedes this mention of the devil, containing the assurance that "He giveth more grace." The flesh, the world, the devil may exert against us power which is *much*. God gives us grace which is *more*. And if the power against us becomes more and *abounds*, then grace *super-abounds*. The great thing is to be in that state which is truly receptive of the grace of God.

What is that state? It is that condition of humility which leads to submission to God and consequent nearness to Him. This comes out very clearly in these verses. God gives grace to the humble while He resists the proud. The wise king of olden time had noted the fact that "Pride goeth before destruction, and an haughty spirit before a fall" (Prov. xvi. 18); though he does not tell us why it is so. Here we get the explanation. The proud get no grace from God but rather resistance. No wonder they go down. And with none is the fall so manifest as with proud believers, since God deals promptly with His children in the way of government. The worldling He often leaves untouched until the final crash comes, as eternity is reached.

If we are marked by humility we shall have no difficulty in submitting to God, and as we submit to God we shall be enabled to resist the devil. All too often things work the other way round with us. We start by submitting to the devil, which leads to our developing the pride that marks him, and consequently resisting God; and as a result of that God resists us and a fall becomes inevitable, with its consequent humiliation. If only we were humble we should escape much humiliation.

The order then is clear. First, humility. Then, submission to God, which entails resistance as regards the devil. Third, drawing near to God. No one of course can draw near to God except as happily submitting to Him. Drawing near to Him He will draw near to us. This is the way of His government. If we sow the seed of a diligent seeking of His face, we shall reap a harvest of light and blessing from a realized sense of His nearness to us.

Let us always keep clear the distinction between God's grace and His government. In His grace He took the initiative and drew near to us, when we cared nothing for Him. From that all has flowed. But saved by grace we are brought under the holy government of God, and here we reap as we sow. If we seek Him He will be found of us, and the more we draw near to Him the larger will be our enjoyment of His nearness and all its benefits.

Immediately we think of drawing near to God the question of our moral fitness is raised. How can we draw near except as cleansed and purified.

JAMES

Hence, what we find in the latter part of verse 8 and in verses 9 and 10. James speaks very strongly as to the state of those to whom he wrote, accusing them of sin and double-mindedness and a good deal of indifference to their real condition, so that they were filled with laughter and jollification in spite of their sorry state. What they needed was to purify themselves not only externally—the "hands"—but internally—the "hearts," and also to repent, humbling themselves before God.

Are we sometimes conscious that our hearts are far from God? Do we sometimes feel as though it were impossible for us to draw near to Him? These verses then will explain matters for us and show us the way. The only road into the Divine presence that is available for us is that of purification, within as well as without, of repentance and of freshly humbling ourselves before God. Then it is that He will lift us up, and we shall be in the full enjoyment of the light of His countenance.

In verses 11 and 12 the Apostle again reverts to the matter of the tongue. No sin amongst Christians is more common than that of speaking evil against their brethren. Now those to whom James wrote were very familiar with the law and greatly reverenced its commandments, so he reminds them how distinctly the law had spoken on this very point. Knowing what the law had said, to speak evil of and judge their brother would be tantamount to speaking evil of and judging the law which forbad it. Instead of obeying the law they would be setting up to legislate for themselves. These early Jerusalem Christians were "all zealous of the law" (Acts xxi. 20). But that only made the matter more serious for them. We are not under the law but under grace, still it will do us all good to remember the word which the Lord spake unto Moses saying, "Thou shalt not go up and down as a tale-bearer among thy people" (Lev. xix. 16).

Another sad feature of those days was a lack of piety, and as to this James utters words of rebuke in the paragraph extending from verse 13 to the end of the chapter. The Jew true to his nature was out for gain and moved from city to city buying and selling. If unconverted he thought of nothing but the demands of his business and laid his plans accordingly. The converted Jew however had claims which were higher than the claims of business. He had a Lord in heaven to whom he was responsible, and every movement must be planned and made subject to His will.

True piety brings God and His will into everything. It is wholesome to recognize our own littleness and the brevity of our days. In a boastful spirit we may begin legislating for our own future, but it is evil work. We have no power to legislate, since we cannot even command what shall be on the morrow. But why should we wish to legislate when we are the Lord's, and He has a will about us? Shall we not recognize His guidance and be satisfied with that?

Not only should we recognize His guidance but we should be glad to acknowledge it in all our ways and by word of mouth also. We "ought to

JAMES

SAY, If the Lord will, we shall live, and do this, or that." And notice please that "we OUGHT to say." It is not something which we *may* say, and find that God approves of it. It is something we *must* say if we wish to give Him His proper place in our lives.

Knowing this let us be careful to do it, for a very striking statement closes our chapter. Sin is not only the doing of that which is wrong: it is also the not doing of that which we know to be right. Hence to know is a great responsibility.

Shall we therefore shrink from knowledge? But that would only make matters worse, inasmuch as it would entail closing our eyes against the light; and those who do that will have no ground of complaint against God, should He do for them what long ago He did for others, and shut them up in hopeless darkness. No, let us welcome the light, and let us look upon the responsibility to put into practice the good that we know, as being also a very great privilege.

Chapter 5

IN THE CLOSING verses of chapter iv. James was addressing those of his own people belonging to the prosperous commercial class, who professed to receive Jesus as their Lord. In the opening of the fifth chapter his thoughts turn to the rich Jews, and these, as we have before mentioned, were almost to a man found amongst the unbelieving majority. In the first six verses he has some severe and even scorching things to say about them, and to them.

The accusation he brings against them is threefold. First he charges them with fraud, and that of the most despicable character. They took advantage of the humblest people who were least able to defend themselves. Second, they were utterly self-indulgent, thinking of little but their own luxuries. Third, they persecuted and even killed their brethren who had embraced the faith of Christ, who are spoken of here as "the just."

As a consequence, self-enrichment was their pursuit and they were successful in it. They "heaped treasure together." Meanwhile the labourers who could not defend themselves cried out in their poverty, and the Christians, who very possibly might have defended themselves, followed in the footsteps of their Master and did not resist them. The rich men succeeded famously and seemed to have matters all their own way.

Appearances however are deceitful. In reality they were but like brute beasts being fattened for killing. "Ye have nourished your hearts, as in a day of slaughter," is how James puts it. If Psalm lxxiii. be read we discover that this is no new thing. Asaph had been greatly troubled observing the prosperity of the wicked, coupled with the chastenings and sorrows of the people of God; and he found no satisfactory solution of the problem until he went into the sanctuary of God.

JAMES

In the light of the sanctuary everything became clear to him. He saw that the course to both the godless rich and the plagued and downtrodden saints could only be rightly estimated as the end of each came into view. A few moments before he had been near to falling himself because he had been consumed with envy at the prosperity of the wicked: now he exclaims, "How are they brought into desolation, as in a moment!" Asaph himself was one of the godly, plagued all the day long and "chastened every morning." Yet in the sanctuary he lifts his eyes to God with joy and confesses, "Thou shalt guide me with Thy counsel, and afterward receive me to glory." The end of the one was, *brought into desolation*. The end of the other, *received to glory*. The contrast is complete!

And that contrast is very manifest in our chapter. The amassed wealth of the rich was corrupted and cankered. Utter misery was coming upon them. As for the tried saints they had but to wait with patience for the coming of the Lord; then their glad harvest of blessing would be reaped, as verses 7 and 8 make manifest.

These inspired threatenings of judgment found an almost immediate fulfilment in the destruction of Jerusalem under Titus. History informs us that most Christians took warning and left the city before it was invested by the Roman armies, while the unbelieving mass were entrapped and such miseries came upon them as all their weepings and howlings could not avert. Yet while *a* fulfilment it was not *the* fulfilment of these words. "Ye have heaped treasure together," it says, "for *the last days*." That means, not merely the last few years of that sad chapter of Jerusalem's history, but the days just preceding the coming of the Lord.

You will notice how James corroborates his fellow-apostles, Paul, Peter and John. All four of them present the coming of the Lord as imminent, as the immediate hope of the believer. They say to us such things as, "The night is far spent, the day is at hand." "The end of all things is at hand." "Little children, it is the last time." "The coming of the Lord draweth nigh." And yet nearly nineteen centuries have passed since these words were written. Were they mistaken? By no means. Yet it is not easy to get their exact view-point, and so understand their words.

An illustration may help. A drama is being enacted on the stage, and the curtain rises for the last act. It is the first public performance, and someone who has already witnessed it privately whispers to a friend, "Now for the finish! It is the last act." Yet nothing seems to happen. The minutes pass, and the players appear to be absolutely motionless. Yet there is something transpiring. Very slow, stealthly movements are going on. Something is slowly creeping on to the stage. It needs good opera glasses and a very observant pair of eyes behind them to notice it! The crowd becomes openly impatient, and the man who said, "Now for the finish," looks a fool. Yet he was perfectly right.

JAMES

In the days of the Apostles the earth was set for the last act in the great drama of God's dealings. Yet because God is full of longsuffering, "not willing that any should perish, but that all should come to repentance," (2. Pet. iii. 9.) He has slowed down the working of iniquity. It is a very long time coming to a head—as we count time. It was perfectly true when the Apostles wrote that the next decisive movement in the drama was to be God's public intervention, in the coming of the Lord; though for His coming we are still waiting today. We shall not wait for it in vain!

His coming is our hope, and these words of exhortation ought to come to us with tenfold force today. Are we tested, our hearts oppressed with the burden of unrighted wrongs? "Be ye also patient," is the word for us. Do we feel unsettled, everything around and within seemingly insecure and shaking? The message comes to us, "Stablish your hearts." Does it seem as if we are everlastingly sowing without effect? Do we plough and wait, and plough and wait, until we are tempted to think that we are but ploughing sands? "Be patient," is the word for us, "unto the coming of the Lord." Then we shall enjoy our grand "Harvest-home."

We must remember however that the Lord's coming will not only mean the judgment of the ungodly and the uplifting of the saints, but it will entail the righting of all that has been wrong in the relations of believers one with another. Verse 9 bears on this. What is more common than grudges or complainings of believers one against another, and what more disastrous in its effects upon the spiritual health of the whole body of saints? Are we inferring that there are no causes of complaint, nothing that might lead to the cherishing of a grudge? There are probably more causes than we have any notion of, but let them not be turned into grudges. He who will sit in judgment, and assess everything—even as between believers—in perfect righteousness, is standing with His hand upon the handle of the door ready to enter the court; and he who is readiest to entertain and nurse a grudge will probably be himself the first to be condemned.

In all this we should be encouraged by the example of the prophets who have gone before, and particularly by the case of Job. We see them suffering affliction, enduring patiently and, in many cases, dying as the result of their testimony. Job's case was special. Satan was not permitted to take his life and so remove him from our observation. He was to live so that we might see "the end of the Lord" in his case. And what a wonderful end it was! We can see the pity and tender mercy of God shining through all his disasters as we view them in the light shed by the finish of his story.

Job's case was just a sample. What God wrought out for him He is working out for all of us, for He has no favourites. We cannot see to the finish of our own cases, but in the light of Job's case God invites us to trust Him, and if we do we shall not grudge against our fellows any more than Job bore a grudge against his three friends when God had reached His end with him. Why, Job then was found fervently praying for his friends instead of grumbling at them! Let us trust God and accept His dealings, assured that His end according to His tender mercy will be reached for us at the coming of Jesus, and we shall see it then.

How important it is then that the coming of the Lord should really be our HOPE. If faith be vigorous it will be kept shining brightly before our hearts, and then we shall endure with patience, we shall be lifted above grudges and complaints, and we shall be marked too by that moderation of language to which verse 12 exhorts us. He who lives in an atmosphere of truth has no need to fortify his words with strong oaths. The habitual use of them soon has the contrary effect to that intended. Even men of the world soon doubt the veracity of the man who cannot be content with a plain yes or no. The last words of the verse, "lest ye fall into condemnation" seem to infer this.

While we wait for the coming of the Lord our lives are made up of many and varying experiences. Going through a hostile world there are frequent afflictions. Then again there are times of peculiar happiness. Yet again, seasons of sickness come, and sometimes they come upon us as the direct result of committing sin. From verse 13 to the end these matters are taken up.

The resource of the afflicted saint is prayer. We do not always realize this. So often we merely betake ourselves to kindly friends, who will listen to the recital of our troubles, or to wealthy and influential friends, who perchance may be able to help us in our troubles, and prayer falls into the background, whereas it should be our first thought. It is affliction which adds intensity to our prayers. You attend a meeting which may be described as "our usual prayer-meeting," and it is, we trust, a profitable occasion. But even so how different it is when a number meet together to pray about a matter which burdens their hearts to the point of positive affliction. In meetings of that sort the heavens seem to bow down to touch the earth.

But here, on the other hand, are believers who are merry indeed, their hearts are full of gladness. It is spiritual gladness, at least to begin with. The danger is however that it will soon degenerate into mere carnal jollification. If spiritual gladness is to be maintained it must have an outlet of a spiritual sort. That spiritual outlet is the singing of psalms, by which we understand any poetical or metrical composition of a spiritual sort which can be set to music. The happy heart sings, and the happy Christian is to be no exception in this.

Just think of the range of song that is within our compass! Earth's great singers have their portfolios of familiar songs, their *repertoire* they call it. We read that Solomon's songs were one thousand and five, but how many are ours? In his days the heights and depths of love divine were not made known as they are in ours. We have the breadth and length and depth and height of divine revelation and the knowledge of the knowledge-surpassing love of Christ as the subject matter for Christian song. There are moments, thank God, when very really we break forth with,

> *Sing, without ceasing sing,*
> *The Saviour's present grace.*

only let us be careful that our singing is of such a character as may further lift us up, and not let us down.

As to sickness the Apostle's instructions are equally plain. It is viewed as being God's chastening hand upon the saint, very possibly in the form of direct retribution for his sins. In this the church would be interested, and the elders of the church should be called in. They, *at their discretion*, pray over him, anointing him with oil in the Lord's name and he is healed, his sins being governmentally forgiven. It is evident from such a scripture as 1 John v. 16 that the elders were to exercise their spiritual discernment as to whether it was, or was not, the will of God that healing should be granted. If they discerned it to be His will then they could pray the prayer full of faith and confidence, which would be without fail answered in his recovery.

Is this all valid for today? We believe so. Why then is it so little practised? For at least two reasons. First, it is not an easy matter to find the elders of THE church though the elders of certain religious bodies may be found easily enough. The church of God has been ruined as to its outward manifestation and unity, and we have to pay the penalty of it. Second, assuming the elders of the church are found and that they come in response to the call, the discernment and faith on their part, which are called for if they are to offer such a prayer of faith as is contemplated, are but very rarely found.

The faith, be it observed, is to be on the part of those who pray, that is of the elders. Nothing is said as to the faith of the one who is sick, though we may infer that he has some faith in the matter, sufficient at least to send for the elders in accordance with this scripture. We may infer too from the words that immediately follow in verse 16 that he would confess his sins, if indeed he have committed them. We point this out because this passage has been pressed into service on behalf of practices not warranted by this or any other scripture.

The confession of which verse 16 speaks is however not exactly confession to elders. It is rather "one to another." This verse has nothing official about it as verses 14 and 15 have. There is no reason why any of us should not practice prayer for healing after this sort.

The case supposed is that of two believers, and one has offended against the other, though neither apparently are entirely free from blame, and

JAMES

consequently both are suffering in their health. The main offender comes with heart-felt confession of the wrong he committed. The other is thereby moved to confess anything which may have been wrong on his side, and then melted before God they begin to pray for each other. If they have really forsaken their wrong-doing and are going in the way of righteousness they may expect to be heard of God and healed.

In connection with this Elijah is brought before us. Verse 17 is particularly interesting inasmuch as the Old Testament makes no mention of the fact that he prayed that it might not rain, though we are given very full details of how he prayed for rain at the end of the three and a half years in 1 Kings xviii. He is introduced to us very abruptly in the opening verse of 1 Kings xvii as telling Ahab that it would not rain, so this verse in James gives us a peep into scenes before his public appearance—scenes of private and personal dealings with God. Though of like passions to ourselves he was righteous, and burning with the fervency of a passion for the glory of God. Hence he was heard, and he knew that he was heard with an assurance that enabled him to confidently tell Ahab what God was going to do. Would that we resembled him, if only in a small degree!

We may learn in all this what are the conditions of effectual prayer· Confession of sin, not only to God but to one another; practical righteousness in all our ways; fervency of spirit and petition. Fervent prayer is not that which is uttered in loud stentorian tones, but that which springs from a warm and glowing heart.

The closing verses revert to the thought of our praying for one another for healing and restoration. Verse 19 alludes to the conversion or bringing back of an erring brother, and from this we pass almost insensibly to the conversion of a sinner in verse 20. He who is used of God in this blessed work is an instrument in saving souls from death and the covering of many sins. Do we realise what an honour this is? Some people are for ever on the tack of uncovering sin, whether of their fellow-believers or of the world. The covering of sins *in a righteous way* is what God loves. Let us go in for it with all our hearts.

1 PETER

INTRODUCTION

WE BEGIN BY noticing certain features which characterize the whole epistle:—

1. It is definitely called in its heading a *general* or catholic epistle, inasmuch as it is not written to any particular church, nor to an individual, as most of the others.

2. It definitely addresses the *"strangers scattered"* in the provinces of Asia Minor, yet *"elect"*—*i.e.*, Peter writes to converted people of his own nation scattered throughout the regions to the north of Palestine. Peter was the apostle to the circumcision (see Gal. ii. 7, 8), yet it was Paul who traversed these lands and evangelized the Jews while carrying the Gospel to the Gentiles; so Peter exercised his ministry towards them by pen and ink.

3. It is a definitely *pastoral* epistle. Peter manifests throughout it his shepherd care for the spiritual well-being of those to whom he wrote. He gives instruction in Christian truth, but even before he concludes his instruction and turns to exhortation, he pauses to deal with the practical state of their souls, as witness verses 13-17 in the midst of chapter i. In all this Peter was true to his commission to "feed" or "shepherd" the sheep and lambs of Christ (John xxi. 15-17).

4. These things being so, there are a very large number of allusions to Old Testament Scripture, with which his original readers were so well acquainted. This is especially marked in chapters i. and ii., wherein he unfolds the place and condition and hopes which now were theirs as Christians. He *quotes* plentifully from the Old Testament; but beyond this, almost every sentence contains an *allusion* to the ancient Scriptures, and it is the catching of these allusions that so greatly helps in the understanding of the Epistle.

CHAPTER 1

COMMENCING THEN OUR reading of the Epistle, we find the opening address in verses 1 and 2. To whom does he write? To "strangers scattered" or "sojourners of the dispersion," to people who were a standing witness to the fact that the Jew had forfeited his ancient privileges, to folk who had lost all the earthly foothold they ever had, though it was a big foothold as originally granted. Yet the sojourners he addressed were not by any means all the scattered Jews of those provinces, but such of them only as were "elect," or chosen of God.

1 PETER

Three things are mentioned as to God's choice of them, connected respectively with the Father, the Spirit and Jesus Christ. Note the prepositions used:—

"According to," indicating *character*.

"Through," indicating the *means* employed.

"Unto," indicating the *end* in view.

God's choice of them—and of us, for both Jew and Gentile come into the same Christian blessings on the same ground, as Paul's epistles show—was characterized by His foreknowledge as Father. What a comfort this is! How far removed it is from the blind fate which is supposed by some to preside over human destiny. God's election is never capricious and the idea of a sinner earnestly desiring salvation, and yet prevented by an adverse decree, is a nightmare of human reason and not Scripture. God chooses, knowing the end from the beginning, and therefore His choice is always right and justifies itself in its results.

His choice is made effectual "through sanctification of the Spirit." The root idea of "sanctification" is "setting apart for God" and the Holy Spirit is He who, by His inward life-giving work, sets apart the one who is the subject of it.

The end in view is that the one so set apart should be marked by the obedience of Christ—that is, obey even as He obeyed—and also come under the efficacy of His blood to this end. The words "of Jesus Christ" refer to both the obedience and the sprinkling of blood, but why, we may ask, is this order observed; why not the reversed order, for do we not need the cleansing of His blood before we can obey at all? The answer is, because of the reference there is to Old Testament Scripture.

They belonged racially to the people who were God's elect nation, chosen in Abraham, and sanctified, that is, set apart, as Exodus xiii. 2 testifies. Now read Exodus xxiv. 3-8, and you will observe there the order, *first* the obedience promised which the law demanded, *then* the sprinkling of the blood of the sacrifice in ratification. Peter, addressing believers who were very familiar with this, carefully observes this order, only showing that we Christians have these things on a far higher plane in a vital and spiritual way, and the blood of Jesus Christ instead of being like that of the sacrifices of Exodus xxiv. 8, which had a *penal* force (that is, it indicated that death was the penalty attached to disobedience to the law's righteous demands) is wholly *purifying*, and the righteous basis of all our standing and relations with God. Sanctified by the Spirit and sprinkled by the blood of Christ we are committed to a life of obedience after the very pattern of Christ. With so exalted a course set before us we certainly need the multiplication of both grace and peace!

Verse 3 opens the apostle's message in striking a note of praise to God, now revealed as the God and Father of the Lord Jesus Christ, since He

1 PETER

has begotten us again to a living hope by the resurrection of Jesus Christ. As belonging to the commonwealth of Israel they had formerly had national hopes which centred in a Messiah upon earth, but the light of those hopes was quenched in their hearts when He died rejected, crucified between two thieves. The story of the two going to Emmaus, as told in Luke xxiv., is a telling illustration of this; but, when those two had their eyes opened and beheld Him risen, a new hope dawned in their hearts which nothing on earth could quench. It was a living hope because centred in a Saviour living beyond the power of death. How aptly the very words of verse 3 would have sprung from their lips as they entered the upper room in Jerusalem to tell the news to the rest after their return journey of three-score furlongs! They were like men who had been born again into a new world of hope and expectation, in the great mercy of God.

Israel's hopes, when brought out of Egypt, centred in the land that was to be given to them as their inheritance. The Christian's hope also has an inheritance connected with it, as verse 4 shows, but what a contrast is here! Palestine as an inheritance proved a sad disappointment. The land itself was all that a land should be, still it was capable of being corrupted, and consequently it was speedily defiled by those who inherited it, since they were left to their own responsibility. Thus, bit by bit it was forfeited and it faded away. Our inheritance is reserved in the heavens and consequently it is beyond the possibility of corruption, undefiled and unfading; and we, for whom it is reserved, are being kept by the power of God for it. There shall, therefore, be no slip betwixt the cup of the inheritance and our lips!

The power of God keeps us and not our fidelity, yet God's power works through faith. Faith is our side of the matter. God is sovereign in exercising His power, and we are responsible as to the exercise of faith. Many are puzzled as to how to put these two things, God's sovereignty and man's responsibility together, and regard them as quite incompatible and irreconcilable. Yet here, in this fifth verse, they are found going hand in hand, preserving the believer to the salvation that awaits him in the last time. The salvation mentioned here is future. It is the final deliverance that awaits the believer at the coming of the Lord. That final deliverance is a certainty before us; yet we cannot await it with self-confidence, for nothing short of the power of God is needed to keep us, nor can we await it with carelessness, for God's power is effective through faith, on our side. How then do we await it? Why, with exultation, yet tempered with the heaviness of many trials, as verse 6 declares. The coming glory shone brightly before the faith of these early Christians and filled them with great rejoicing, so that they were like ships with sails set and filled with heaven's breezes. On the other hand they had plenty of ballast in the shape of heavy trials. These trials are permitted in love, for they only come *"if need be."* In one way or another we all do need them. If we try to rejoice in the world and its pleasures we need trials to dislodge us from the world by stirring up the comfortable nest we would fain build below. If we are exulting in the coming glory we need them as sobering and steadying ballast, lest our exulting should overbalance us.

The heavy trials, however, are "*now, for a season,*" even as the "pleasures of sin," which charm the poor worldling are "for a season" (Heb. xi. 25). Soon the worldling will say good-bye to his pleasures, and the Christian to his trials.

Moreover, the very trials themselves are profitable as working in us—in our character and lives—the qualities that glorify God. Hence verse 7 declares that faith (which is much more precious than gold) being tested by the fire of persecution, will come out to the praise and honour and glory of God when Christ appears. Many a bold confessor, suffering fiery trial—even to death perhaps—may have been tempted to think that, their light being extinguished, all was *lost*. The apostle tells them that, on the contrary, all would be *found* in that day. Christ being revealed in His glory, everything to His praise and honour will come into the light and be displayed.

Then Christ will appear, or be unveiled, as the word is. At the present time He is unseen. These dispersed exiles had never seen Jesus in the days of His flesh for they had been driven far outside the land of Promise, nor were they then looking on Him. Yet they loved Him, and He was the Object of their faith and this caused them to exult with a joy beyond words and full of glory.

We, like them, have never yet seen the Lord, but is faith as active with us? Faith, remember, is the telescope of the soul, bringing into the field of our spiritual vision what is unseen to mortal eyes. Then we see Jesus as a living, bright Reality, and our joy is filled with the glory of what He is and the hope of what He is going to be, which is beyond all human language. Believing we *rejoice*, and believing we *receive* the salvation of our souls, for *soul*-salvation is the end, or result, of faith in the risen Saviour.

Love, faith, joy and hope are all found in verse 8, though the last is inferred and not explicitly named. How excellent must be the spiritual state marked by these things! Yet all produced not by being occupied with one's spiritual state, but by Christ Himself being the loved Object of faith's vision.

Those to whom Peter wrote were quite familiar with the idea of a salvation which consisted of temporal deliverance, such as the deliverance of their fathers from Egypt, and they had expected a supreme salvation of that kind at the advent of their Messiah, as promised through the prophets; but by faith in the risen Christ (verse 3) a salvation of a spiritual sort affecting their souls had reached them, though they were externally still under the iron heel of Rome. Of this salvation the prophets had also spoken, for the theme of their testimony was twofold—first, the sufferings of the Christ, and second, the glories that were to follow. As the immediate result of His first advent to suffer there is a soul-salvation for those who believe. As the direct result of His second advent to reign in glory the bodies of the saints will be saved from the power of death and public and universal salvation will be established for those who enter His kingdom.

Three very important things should be noted in verses 10 to 12.

(1). The reality of *inspiration*, and its remarkable character. The prophets ministered, but the source of their prophecies, whether oral or written, was the Spirit. The Spirit *in* them testified *through* them, and He was so really the source of their utterances that they had to search diligently their own words and inquire as to their real force, only to discover that their full meaning was beyond the apprehension of the age in which they lived, and that they were really writing for the instruction of saints in a coming age—even for us.

(2). Though in the bygone age Christ had not been manifested, yet the Spirit in the prophets and speaking through them, could be spoken of as "the Spirit of Christ." Christ was accordingly the Speaker by His Spirit even in Old Testament days. We shall see the bearing of this when we consider verses 18-20 of chapter iii.

(3). The strong difference drawn between the age before and the age after Christ. The soul-deliverance, which is the common possession of believers today, was for even the prophets of the bygone age a subject of enquiry; it is spoken of as "the grace that should come unto you," *i.e.*, it was not come in the previous age. Further, the things now reported to us by the apostles and others who have preached the Gospel by the Holy Ghost sent down from heaven are the things which were only prophesied before. Then *predicted* by the Spirit; now *reported* by the Spirit. Then the Spirit was in the prophets for the purpose of inspiration, but now the Spirit is sent down from heaven. The present age is marked by the sufferings of Christ having been accomplished and consequently by grace having come, soul-salvation being realized, things that angels desire to look into being reported, and the Holy Ghost having been sent down from heaven.

Having unfolded these great and blessed facts, the apostle turns aside to exhortation in verses 13 to 17. The great advance which marks Christianity as compared with Judaism entails a corresponding advance in the character of Christian life and behaviour. We are now children and call upon God as our Father, but we are to be obedient. On the one hand, we are to be braced up mentally, marked by sobriety and confident hope; on the other hand, we are to avoid the old desires which mastered us when we were in ignorance of God, and to be holy in all our conduct as God Himself is holy. What God has revealed Himself to be sets the standard for all our conduct. Moreover, the One whom we call Father is the impartial Judge of the work of each, hence, reverential fear becomes us. He is Judge, but He is our Father, and we are before Him, therefore, in filial fear.

These exhortations, which spring out of the truth unfolded in verses 1 to 12 (notice the word "wherefore," commencing verse 13), are reinforced by the further details of truth expounded from verse 18 onwards to verse 10 of chapter ii., as witness the word "Forasmuch" with which verse 18 starts.

They knew, and so do we, that we are redeemed with the precious blood of Christ. Their fathers had been redeemed with silver and gold—a typical redemption carried out under Jewish law. Sometimes actual money was given as in Exodus xxx. 11-16; Numbers iii. 44-51. Sometimes it was by sacrifice, as in Exodus xiii. 13-15; still, even then, silver and gold were involved, since they were needed to purchase the animal used for sacrifice. Silver and gold are the least corruptible of metals, yet they *are* corruptible. The price of our redemption was incorruptible and precious.

The Jewish manner of life had degenerated into a matter of mere tradition received from their fathers. This was quite manifest in Isaiah's day (Isa. xxix. 13), and the Lord Jesus charged it home upon them, quoting Isaiah's words, in Mark vii. 6-13. Even the right things they did, they did not because they were enjoined of God, but because ordered by tradition. Thus their manner of life had become corrupt and most offensive to God. Our Gentile manner of life was pure darkness and lawlessness, and equally corrupt. Whether, however, it were we or they, we have been redeemed out of our old manner of life by the precious blood of the One who was typified as the unblemished and spotless lamb of Exodus xii. 3-6; only He was ordained not a mere matter of four days before sacrifice, but from before the foundation of the world. Our redemption, therefore, was according to the eternal counsels of God.

The Lamb of God was ordained in eternity, but manifested in time. He appeared "in these last times"—the "end of the world," or the "consummation of the ages" of Hebrews ix. 26—and that not only as the *Redeemer* but as the *Revealer*. God was perfectly revealed in Him so that it is *by Him* that we believe in God. We do not believe in God by the wonders of creation, nor by the law as given through Moses, nor by visions of angels, but by Christ, once dead but now risen and in glory. Our faith and hope repose in God who is known to us as He who raised Christ up from the dead and gave Him glory. How wonderfully this fits in with Paul's testimony in Romans iv. 23-25, and x. 9.

From this it is clear that if we desire to win the faith of men for God we must present Christ to them—Christ once dead; Christ as risen; Christ

1 PETER

now in glory. Every other theme is useless. We may possibly find subsidiary matter elsewhere. Useful illustrations may abound in the fields of creation and providence. They may be furnished sometimes by the facts, or even the speculations of science—though as to the latter, the greatest caution must be exercised as they are mostly *wrong*, as witnessed by the ease with which the oncoming generations of speculators dispose of the hypotheses (or, *guesses*) of their predecessors. Still, the fact remains that if men really believe in God it is by Christ that they believe in Him. Let us therefore preach CHRIST, whether by life or lips or pen.

Redemption is, of course, a work accomplished *for* us. We need also a work wrought *in* us. Of this the apostle proceeds to write.

The truth of the Gospel had brought their souls into subjection and obedience in the energy of the Spirit. This had wrought a mighty work of purification. The purifications of the law had consisted in "divers washings" of water (Heb. ix. 10), purely external. This was a soul-purification, a moral renovation with love as the outcome, for love is as native to the new nature as hatred is to the old.

If verse 22 presents the work wrought *in* them and us as it might be observed and described by man, verse 23 lets us into the real secret of it all, from a point of view impossible to man and only to be known because revealed by God. We are born again.

The necessity of this new birth for Israel was alluded to, though in veiled terms, in Ezekiel xxxvi. 25-27. The Lord Jesus yet more strongly enforced its necessity when speaking to Nicodemus in John iii. Nicodemus should have known the passage in Ezekiel, hence the Lord's words, "Art thou a master of Israel, and knowest not these things?" The teaching of the Lord is based upon Ezekiel's words, though He greatly expands and clarifies them. Even so, the Lord did not drop all figurative language and still spoke of "water." In the main, however, He stressed the Spirit's sovereign action in new birth. "That which is born of the Spirit is spirit."

Peter's epistle was written in the full light of Christianity. It was not now the Lord Jesus on earth speaking to a Nicodemus, but the same Jesus, risen and glorified after the accomplishment of redemption, speaking through His inspired apostle to Christians. Hence, figures are dropped and the matter stands out with full clearness. Here the energy of the Spirit is only alluded to in verse 22 and the main stress is laid on what we are born *of* and *by*.

The life of Adam's race, to which we belong, whether Jews or Gentiles, is utterly corrupted; its nature wholly evil. We must be not only redeemed, but purified. The Spirit of God works to this end and we obey the truth. The real inwardness of the matter, however, is that the Spirit uses the Word of God in such a way that we are born again of incorruptible seed. Consequently, we possess a new nature, springing from a divine source and beyond the taint of corruption. Here, then, is a purification of a most profound and fundamental sort brought about through the Spirit of God by the agency of the Word of God—the "water" of John iii. and Ezekiel xxxvi. It is not difficult to see how apt a figure "water" was.

You will find it helpful to glance at 1 John iii. 9, which carries the matter a step further. The expression "born *of God*" emphasizes the divine source whence we spring. The seed of God remains in us and is incorruptible, as Peter has told us. This is the essential character of our new nature, as will be plainly manifested when the last trace of the old nature is eliminated from us at the coming of the Lord.

Returning to our passage we note that the Word of God by which we are born again is living and it abides for ever, and in this it is directly in contrast with ourselves as the children of Adam. All flesh is as grass which grows up and speedily withers. All man's glory is as the flower of grass, which falls away and disappears even more rapidly than grass itself. Man's glory speedily fades, and man himself passes away into death. The Word of the Lord lives and abides for ever, and by it we are born again.

How wonderful this is! That which is born partakes of the nature and character of that which gives its birth. "That which is born of the Spirit is spirit." It is equally true that that which is born of incorruptible seed is incorruptible, and that which is born by the living and abiding Word of God is living and abiding. And that enduring Word of the Lord has reached us in the gospel message that we have believed. We shall not be surprised therefore when in the next chapter we find ourselves spoken of as "living stones" and as connected with a "house" which is incorruptible and abiding.

Chapter 2

THE LATTER VERSES of chapter i. have shown us that the new birth which has taken place with each believer has a purifying effect, therefore the first verse of chapter ii. takes it for granted that we lay aside those ugly features which are the nature of the flesh in us. Of the things specified, malice, envy and evil speakings specially concern our relations with our fellows, and they are particularly mentioned because Peter is now going to bring before us truth which shows us the believer in intimate relation with all his fellow-believers as a stone in a spiritual house, and as one of the priestly family. In such connections, nothing will proceed rightly unless these evils are laid aside.

It is not enough, however, to lay aside evil, we must go in for that which is good. We must not merely put on good as an outward dress or adornment, but imbibe it as spiritual food. There is "the sincere milk of the Word" suitable for the new-born babe, and we are to earnestly desire it. If we feed upon the Word we grow up. But even then we still need the

1 PETER

Word, for it is meat for those of full age as well as milk for babes, as Hebrews v. 12-14, tells us.

This furnishes us with a very clear answer to the oft-repeated question—Why do some Christians make such good spiritual progress and some hardly any at all? Because some feed heartily and regularly upon pure, spiritual diet. They feast their souls upon the Word, whether as milk or meat. Others feed upon it but little and are half-starved spiritually. Others again, choke up their minds and hearts with light and foolish reading. Some go in for sentimental love stories, slightly flavoured with the gospel perhaps; such, naturally, do not progress spiritually any more than a child would progress physically whose diet consisted only of sweetmeats.

Others take up reading of a more intellectual sort but with a strain of infidelity in it; and progress no better than would the child brought up on solid food with small quantities of poison in it.

Food for our minds and hearts we must have. Let us see to it that it is the Word on which we feed, seeing it is by the Word we have been born again, if indeed, we have tasted the goodness of God—for all this supposes that we are truly converted people, that we have really come to the Lord.

And who and what is the Lord to whom we have come? He is the "Living Stone." This is a remarkable title of our Lord. It sets Him forth as the One in whom is life, who became Man, and who, by death and resurrection, has become the Head and Foundation of this new structure which God is building composed of men who live through Him and in Him. He is the "chief corner stone, elect, precious" (verse 6), "the head of the corner" (verse 7). The men who, as "living stones," have been built into this "house" of a living sort, became such by coming to Christ, the Living Stone.

Evidently, the Apostle Peter never forgot his first interview with the Lord Jesus, as recorded in John i., and in these verses we have a definite allusion to it. John i. introduces the Lord Jesus to us as the Word, in whom was life, become flesh that as Man He might die as the Lamb of God, and then in resurrection baptize with the Holy Ghost (verses 1, 4, 14, 29, 33). Then Andrew brings his brother Simon to Jesus, as the Christ. The Lord Jesus, knowing that which was before Him, and conscious of all that He Himself was—whatever Simon might know or not know Him to be—instantly assumed possession of him and changed his name to Peter, which means "a stone." It was as though the Lord said to him, "Coming to Me in faith you have become—even though your faith is partial as yet and incomplete—of the same nature as Myself."

Neither did Peter forget the subsequent interview recorded in Matthew xvi. On this occasion Peter had confessed the Lord Jesus as the Son of the Living God, which was virtually to confess Him as the Living Stone. The

1 PETER

Lord Jesus in reply reminded Simon that his real name now was Peter—"a stone"—while He Himself was the Rock; and that Peter as a stone was not to be left in isolation, but to be with the others builded into the church or assembly which Christ called His own—"*My Church.*"

When the Lord Jesus spoke thus to Peter all was future, for He said, "I *will* build." Now Peter writes to others who also had come to Christ and thereby become living stones, and he can speak of all as a present and existing thing, though not an absolutely completed thing. He says in verse 5, "Ye are built up"—or, "Ye are being built up a spiritual house." A spiritual house they were, yet it was not a completed thing for other living stones were continually being added.

Now a house exists for its occupant, and we are thus builded together as a dwelling-place for GOD; not a material house of the sort they had been accustomed to as Jews, but a *spiritual* house. Moreover, where God dwells there He is to be praised and so, by His work and ordering, we fill a further capacity as "an holy priesthood, to offer up spiritual sacrifices, acceptable to God by Jesus Christ." These spiritual sacrifices are "of praise to God continually, that is, the fruit of our lips giving thanks to His name" (Heb. xiii. 15).

Every true believer is a living stone in the house, and a priest as belonging to this holy priesthood.

Had we approached one of the sons of Aaron and asked him how he became a priest, he would doubtless have told us that it was, firstly, by his birth; and that, secondly, being born of the priestly family, he was put into the priest's office by the washing of water, the sprinkling with blood, and the anointing with oil, as ordered in Exodus xxix. We, too, are priests by birth. Being born of God, we are priests of God. We, too, have had the washing of water by the Word (i. 22, 23). We have been redeemed by blood, the precious blood of Christ (i. 19), and we have received the Spirit, who was typified of the oil; though that particular feature is not brought before us in the passage we are considering. We have come to Christ (ii. 4), and thus we are priests, just as Aaron's sons were priests as having come to Aaron, and being thus associated with him in the priest's office.

Every believer today is then a priest. But we must remember that it is one thing to be a priest, another to really enter into and exercise our priestly functions. The first exercise of our priesthood is Godward, in the offering up of the sacrifice of praise. This is "acceptable to God by Jesus Christ," for He is the Great High Priest, as the Epistle to the Hebrews makes so manifest. All that we offer we offer by Him; and this of course accounts for its acceptability to God, since He is the chosen One and precious in God's sight, as the sixth verse shows.

1 PETER

It must never be forgotten, however, that He is not elect and precious, nor is He the acceptable One, in man's esteem. The very reverse, He is disallowed and rejected. The fact is that man has become a disobedient creature as verse 7 reminds us. Instead of falling in with God's plans, he wishes to push ahead with plans of his own. Instead of being content with God's building and with being called to have a part in it as a living stone, man wishes to create a building on his own account—a building which shall conform to his own fallen ideas and result in his own glory. When the Lord Jesus appeared, men attempted to work Him into their building and failed. Had He consented to fall in with man's ideas it would have been otherwise. They would have been delighted if so great an One as He had been a supporter of, or even a developer of, Roman government, or Greek philosophy, or Jewish religion. Coming as He did, on God's behalf, He exposed their folly and fitted in with none of their notions. He was, as it were, a stone of such peculiar formation that there was not a single niche in the imposing temple of man's fame where He fitted in. Hence He became "the stone which the builders disallowed," and "a stone of stumbling and a rock of offence" to the proud men who rejected Him, whilst being elevated of God into the headstone of the corner in the divine building.

Consequently, we who are priests of God in association with Him are no more of man's building, of man's world-system, than He is, though we have another priestly function which has direct reference to the world through which we pass. We are "a chosen race, a kingly priesthood, a holy nation, a people for a possession"—as verse 9 has been rendered. We are those whom God has chosen out and separated to Himself. In the coming age the kingly character of our priesthood will be more manifest than it is at present, but now we are commissioned to show forth the praises, the virtue or excellences, of God in this disobedient world. This is our priestly function manward.

In the coming age the saints are going to judge the world, as 1 Corinthians vi. 2 tells us. As kingly priests we shall then be commissioned to dispense His judgment. We are kingly priests today, but commissioned to dispense His excellent righteousness expressed in grace, to set forth His character as light and love. This, of course, we do even more by what we *are* than by what we *say*. It is the character and spirit and attitude of the royal priest that counts for so much.

Do some feel inclined to declare this an impossible task? Nay, not impossible! Difficult perhaps, because not natural to us as men in the flesh, though natural enough to the born-again, redeemed, Spirit-indwelt priesthood to which we belong. *Possible*, indeed, because we ourselves have been the subjects of the grace that we are now to "show forth" to others. We have been called "out of darkness into His marvellous light."

1 PETER

Can you not imagine one of the converted Jews to whom Peter wrote, crying out at this point—"*Darkness!* But, Peter, you forget, we were never benighted heathen as were others"? And we, who were brought up in conditions controlled by an enlightened and christianized civilization, might say the same. "I know it," the Apostle would have replied, "but your Judaism was darkness, for all that." God was not fully revealed, it was not "in the light" (1 John i. 7), if Judaism be considered in its original purity. When it was corrupted into a mass of traditions and observances by the Pharisees it was darkness indeed.

All was darkness for us whether we were called out of Judaism or heathenism, or a nominal and corrupted Christianity, and now we are in a light which is marvellous; we are the people of God, having obtained mercy.

Marvellous light! Is this how we feel about it? The world plunges on, deeper and ever deeper into its darkness and unbelief. Its learned scientists and philosophers fill the air with triumphant shoutings as to their investigations and their discoveries. Yet really they are as men who clutch at elusive shadows while their science is an enshrouding mist. Their discoveries enable them to do lots of clever and curious things in the world, but not a ray of light shines in them as to things beyond the grave. And here are we, put in the light of God fully revealed in Christ, in the light of His grace, His purposes, His glory. Are we studying these things, so as to become even more and more enlightened, and consequently, luminous ourselves?

On a cloudless night at the season of full moon we get the benefit of our satellite shining in the light of the sun. How marvellous must be the sunlight that can make a dark body shine so brightly! Well, the world is still in the dark, for its back is turned towards God. We are in the light of His truth and grace,—the light of the knowledge of Himself. How marvellous that light is may be discerned in the fact that it can make dark and unattractive people, like to ourselves, show forth His excellences and reflect Himself.

Oh! to be more fully in the unclouded brightness of God's MARVELLOUS LIGHT.

At verse 11 of chapter ii. the apostle Peter turns the "marvellous light" of God upon the daily lives of the holy and royal priests to whom he writes, addressing them as "strangers and pilgrims."

They were, of course, strangers in the lands of their dispersion, as the first verse of the Epistle told us, but this is not what is alluded to here. *Every* Christian is a stranger and pilgrim, and we need not be surprised at this, since by the very fact that we are brought into such near and honoured relationship with God there must be a corresponding severance from the world. The world is entirely antagonistic to God and we cannot

1 PETER

hold with both at the same time. It must be one or the other. For us it is relationship and communion with God, and hence strangership and pilgrimage in the world. The world itself began with Cain, who was "a fugitive and a vagabond" (Gen. iv. 12). We may summarize the matter thus:—

A fugitive is a man who has fled from home.
A vagabond is a man who has no home.
A stranger is a man who is absent from home.
A pilgrim is a man who is on his way to home.

The actual presence of God is the true home of our souls and we are disconnected from the world-system so as to be strangers in it, though left in it for a time to show forth the excellencies of God. Still, we do not wander aimlessly for we are pilgrims also; and this means that we have an objective before us—a fixed point of destiny to which we wend our way.

The world is consumed with fleshly "lusts" or "desires," and consequently, given over to the gratification of those desires. The Christian has other desires of a spiritual sort which proceed not from the flesh at all, and the only way to foster these is to abstain from the desires of the flesh. This is a very personal matter.

Verse 12 deals with our lives in relation to others. The Gentiles were naturally very critical of these Jewish sojourners in their midst and disposed to speak against them. When any of them became Christians the Gentiles were more likely than ever to denounce them, as witness the way in which a Christian today gets denounced if he gives the world the smallest occasion for it. Therefore, their whole manner of life was to be right and honest. The Jew, with his notoriously strong instincts in the matter of profit-making may have particularly needed this exhortation, but who of us does not need it at all? If we maintain righteousness, ultimately our very antagonists will glorify God. They may do so in a way that will ensure their own blessing. They will certainly do so when God visits them in judgment.

Verses 13 to 17, inclusive, work this exhortation out for us, in its details. These dispersed Christian Jews might very possibly be inclined to resent many of the Gentile authorities who were over them, whether kings or governors, and also the many ordinances and laws and regulations that had been instituted, so many of them very different to what had been given of God through Moses, to which they and their forefathers had been accustomed. Still, they were to submit. Government, they had to recognize, was a divine institution. Hence they and we are to be subject for the Lord's sake. The Christian is of course, free for he stands in the liberty of Christ. Still, he must not use his freedom as "a cloke of malice"—in any way to vent his spleen upon others—but he must regard it as liberty to serve God, and the service of God demands the subjection to rulers which is here laid down.

1 PETER

The matter is tersely summed up in verse 17, and we find what becomes "the servants of God." As to all men—honour. As to the brotherhood, *i.e.*, all believers—love. As to God—fear. As to the king, the representative of all human authority—honour. Carrying out this we do the will of God and silence foolish adversaries.

Having thus exhorted all Christians to submission, the apostle specially addresses servants in verse 18. The word used means not exactly "slaves" but "household servants." These, too, are to be subject to authority and specially to the masters whom they serve. These masters may be often men of the world and ill-tempered. The servant may consequently often have to suffer wrongfully. There is no credit to the Christian if, suffering for wrong doing, he takes it patiently. Such is the divine way of thinking, though nowadays people—even Christians—are very intolerant of a small rebuke for their faults. What does please God is to take patiently suffering which is endured for doing well and acting with "conscience toward God." Nothing is harder to us naturally than this. How indignant we feel when our well-doing only serves to bring trouble upon us!

What will help us in this? Two things. Firstly, the example of Christ. Secondly, His atoning sacrifice and its results.

Verses 21 to 23 give us the first. No one ever did well like the Lord Jesus. No one was so misjudged, reviled and persecuted as He. Moreover, He did no sin, no guile was ever in His mouth. There was nothing in Him or His life to justify the smallest slur being cast upon Him. Yet no one suffered as He, and no one ever took the suffering with such meekness and perfection. He fulfilled the word of Isaiah liii., "He was oppressed and He was afflicted, yet He opened not His mouth; He is brought as a lamb to the slaughter, and as a sheep before her shearers is dumb, so He openeth not His mouth." In all this He was an example for us, for we are called to His path, and to follow His steps. The consideration of Christ in all the glory of His perfection cannot fail to have its effect on us, conforming our thoughts and ways to His. If called upon to suffer we, too, shall commit ourselves to Him that judges righteously, instead of attempting to avenge ourselves.

Yet even so, we are not as He was, for we have sins and He had none. We needed, therefore, the atoning sacrifice of which verse 24 speaks. He who did no sin "bare our sins in His own body on the tree." This is something altogether beyond us. We cannot follow in His steps here.

Every part of this wonderful verse deserves our most careful attention. *His own self* became the Sin-bearer, and no other. He *bare our sins*. Isaiah liii. had said He should bear our griefs and carry our sorrows, but it also predicted that He should be "wounded for our transgressions" and "bruised for our iniquities," and be striken for "the transgression of My people," and His soul be made "an offering for sin." These sins were *ours*,

1 PETER

for the verse definitely speaks of the work of Christ, not in its Godward aspect as propitiating Him, but in its believer-ward aspect as bearing his sins—*his* sins, and not the sins of everybody.

Moreover, He bore our sins *in His own body*. He was definitely our Substitute. We had sinned in our bodies, and having become a true Man, apart from sin, He bore our sins in His holy body as a sacrifice for sin. This He accomplished *on the tree*, for it was exclusively in His death that atonement was effected. He did not bear our sins during His life, but in His death, and we are healed by His stripes as Isaiah liii. had also declared.

But then He bore our sins and delivered us from the stripes that our sins deserved, not in order that we should go on in our sins, but rather that we should henceforward be dead to the old life of worldly corruption and the sins which it entailed, and now live unto practical righteousness. Our sins have been atoned for and dismissed as to their judicial sentence, in order that we should be delivered from the practice of them and from their power.

This verse may be helpfully compared with the truth set forth in Romans vi. There *sin* is in question—sin as a tyrant and a master—here *sins*. There we are to reckon ourselves dead to sin and alive to God. Here we are to be dead to sins and live unto righteousness. In both cases the cross of Christ is that from which all flows, but Romans vi. is the believer taking up the reckoning of faith in his experience. Here it is the practical result which follows. The consistent believer becomes as a dead man to all the sins that formerly pleased him, and he lives now for the will of God which is practical righteousness. And this because of the fact that the One who died for him as the Lamb of sacrifice now lives as the Shepherd and Bishop of his soul. We were indeed "as sheep going astray"—a last reference to Isaiah liii.—but now we have a living Shepherd to lead us in the paths of righteousness for His Name's sake.

Chapter 3

The opening verses of chapter iii. continue the exhortation to submission. The apostle commenced this exhortation at verse 13 of chapter ii. In verse 18 he applied it to those who *socially* are in the subject place. Now he applies it to those who hold the subject place in that great *natural relationship* which is the foundation of all human relationships.

The Christian wife is to be in subjection to her husband. If he is a Christian he *obeys* the word and she *obeys* him. A most excellent and delightful arrangement made according to the wisdom of God! Subjection, be it remembered, does not mean inferiority. In business partnerships two men may be equal partners and yet one is recognized as the senior with whom the final decision rests. So in the marriage bond the man has been creatorially fitted for the senior, directing place in the partnership, the woman for the subject place, though she is an heir together with her husband of the grace of life, and a sharer together with him in his exercises and prayers. If the husband loves and honours his wife as a fellow-heir and partner, and she honours and obeys him, an ideal marriage is the result.

But, as the first verse indicates, some believing women may have husbands who, not being converted, do not obey the word. In this case, the converted wife is still to act towards him as the word directs. She, at any rate, is to be a Christian woman and let her Christianity shine in her pure manner of life (v. 2), her avoidance of worldly artifices for self-adornment and self-display (v. 3), her meek and peaceful spirit, which is so great a thing in God's estimation (v. 4), and her subjection to him, coupled with the doing of good and a spirit of calm confidence in God (vv. 5, 6). By such "conversation" or "manner of life" many a husband has been won "without the word."

The "church," dominated by the principles of the twentieth-century world, may cut the word "obey" out of its marriage service, but see what you Christian wives are going to miss if you cut it out of your hearts and minds! Should your husband be unconverted you may miss the joy of winning him. Should he be a Christian, how much of the grace of life and of prayer may be forfeited.

Verse 8 brings us to the final word of the apostle in connection with the matter of subjection. The gracious, gentle, humble spirit is to characterize the whole Christian company. We are never to indulge in evil or recrimination on the principle of tit for tat, but always to be in the spirit of blessing since blessing we receive from God, and this because we are left to pursue our pilgrim way under His holy government.

The principles of God's government of His people do not change. When David wrote Psalm xxxiv., it was the age of law and God's people were in the place of servants. Today is the age of grace and we are before God as His sons, as Galatians iii. 23—iv. 7, shows. Yet the apostle Peter can quote David's words from Psalm xxxiv. as applying equally to us. We reap what we sow in the government of God; and the way to "see good" is to "do good," as verses 10 to 13 of our chapter show. Many a disagreeable event in our lives is clearly the result of our own disagreeableness. If we sowed more good we should reap more good.

At this point let us notice the remarkable way in which the apostle has set before us in its main outlines the truth set forth typically and in historical fashion in the books of Moses.

Genesis is the book of ELECTION. It shows us how God chose Abel and Seth and not Cain, Shem and not Ham. Abram and not Nahor, Isaac and not Ishmael, Jacob and not Esau, Joseph and not Reuben, Ephraim

1 PETER

and not Manasseh. Peter brings before us first of all God's electing mercy (i. 2).

Exodus is the book of REDEMPTION. Israel was redeemed out of Egypt, and brought to God. Peter proceeds to tell us how we have been redeemed with the precious blood of Christ and brought to God with our faith and hope in Him (i. 18-21).

Leviticus is the book of the PRIESTHOOD. It contains directions as to sacrifices for priestly guidance, and as to customs and cleanness for priestly fitness. Thirdly, Peter sets before us the Christian priesthood, its constitution and its privileges (i. 22—ii. 10).

Numbers is the book of the WILDERNESS. It specially reveals the wilderness journey of Israel with all its vicissitudes and lessons. Fourthly, Peter instructs us as to our pilgrimage and the conduct that befits us in it (ii. 11—iii. 7).

Deuteronomy is the book of the GOVERNMENT OF GOD. In it Israel were warned of the consequence of their disobedience, the reward of obedience. And we have just got to the part of the epistle in chapter iii. where Peter warns us that though we are as Christians set in the grace of God we still come under His government and have to make our reckoning with it.

Verse 14 introduces another consideration. We may of course suffer for our own folly in the government of God. We may, on the other hand, be receiving blessing in the government of God, and yet be called upon to suffer for righteousness' sake. If so, God guarantees our happiness in it and under it. We are not to be afraid of men but, sanctifying the Lord God (or "Lord Christ" as it probably is) in our hearts, to testify meekly to the truth while maintaining a good conscience by holy living.

Notice in passing how verse 15 makes manifest the true force of the word "sanctify." It is not primarily "to make holy," for the Lord cannot be more holy than He is. He can, however, in our hearts be *set apart* in His own proper place of glory and supremacy and authority. To sanctify is to set apart.

Now no one ever suffered as Christ. He is our supreme Example. Yet His sufferings as verse 18 presents them, were in a class by themselves and altogether beyond us, for He suffered for sins as a Substitute—the Just for the unjust ones. The actual word substitution does not occur in our English version, but that which the word represents is very clearly in this verse. Note the object of His substitutionary sufferings—"that He might bring us to God," making us thoroughly at home in His presence, having a fitness to be there. Are we all in our own hearts and consciences happily at home with God?

The Lord Jesus suffered for sins even to death and He rose again by or "in" the Spirit, the day of His flesh being over. In the Spirit also He had

1 PETER

preached before the flood to those who now are spirits in prison. These people who now are spirits in prison once walked the earth as men and women in Noah's day and through Noah's lips Christ in Spirit (or, the Spirit of Christ) spoke. They were disobedient, hence their present imprisonment in *hades*, the unseen world. The Spirit of Christ spoke in the Old Testament prophets, as we noticed when reading chapter i. verse 11. He also spoke in Noah.

If any of our readers have doubts as to whether this is the correct explanation of the passage, let them turn to Ephesians ii. and read verses 13 to 18. Having done so they will find that the "He" of verse 16 (which "He" refers also to verse 17) is undoubtedly the Lord Jesus. In verse 17, "you which were far off" were Gentile: "them that were nigh" were Jews. The passage states then, that having endured the cross the Lord Jesus "*came and preached peace*" *to the Gentiles*. When? How? Never, in a personal way. Only by the lips of the apostles and others who were filled with His Spirit did He do so. Exactly the same figure of speech is used in this passage as in the one we are considering in Peter.

As a result of this ante-diluvian testimony of the Spirit of Christ only eight souls were saved through the waters of the flood; a tiny handful that, the merest remnant of the former age. Now baptism, which is but a figure, has just that force. The flood cut off that little remnant of the antediluvian age that through the waters of death they might be disassociated from the old world and enter the new. The converted Jews to whom Peter wrote were exactly in that position. They, too, were but a small remnant, and in their baptism they were dissociated from the mass of their nation that was under wrath and judgment, that they might come under the authority of their risen and glorified Messiah. Baptism is in figure dissociation by means of death and in that sense it saves. The Jews as a nation were like a foundering ship, and to be baptized was to formally cut one's last link with them which meant salvation from their national doom. Hence Peter's words in Acts ii. 40. "*Save* yourself from this untoward generation." What followed? "Then they that gladly received his word were *baptized*."

Baptism accomplishes nothing vital and eternal, for it is "a figure." It is, however, not a mere ceremonial washing as were Jewish "baptisms." It is rather the "answer" or "demand of a good conscience toward God," as we see with the eunuch and with Lydia (see Acts viii. 36; xvi. 15). A good conscience gladly accepts it, and even demands it, accounting it as faithfulness to the Lord to be in figure cut off from the old life, even as He was actually cut off in death; and thus identified with Him.

All, however, is only effectual "by the resurrection of Jesus Christ." For if there were not really and actually a new world of life and blessing opened for us by His resurrection who would cut their links with the old? It was by the resurrection that these Christians had been begotten again to a living hope, as chapter i. verse 3 told us. They would cheerfully go down into the waters of baptism, and so bid a formal goodbye to the old Jewish footing with its impending judgment (See 1 Thess. ii. 14-16), in view of the vast range of grace and glory with its living hopes, that stood revealed to them and secured for them in the resurrection of the Lord Jesus.

Not only is Christ risen, however, but He is gone into heaven and is already at the right hand of God, which signifies that He is the appointed Administrator of all God's will. A man of large business interests who has someone of great ability acting for him and carrying out his wishes, will often speak of him as "my right-hand man." The Lord Jesus is indeed the "Man of Thy right hand" of whom the Psalmist spoke (lxxx. 17), and we have been baptized to Him and come under His authority. To Him all angels and authorities and powers are subject.

How great an encouragement for us! All these verses (15-22) have sprung, remember, out of the thought that we may have to suffer for righteousness' sake. It was just when the converted Jew formally severed his links with Judaism by being baptized that he did suffer. But then being baptized to the Lord Jesus he came under the authority of the One who sat in the place of supreme authority and administration and since all powers were subject to Him, no power could touch them without His permission.

Similarly, when we, who are converted Gentiles, cut our links with the world, we have to taste suffering, but we, too, are under the mighty authority of Christ and need have no fear.

CHAPTER 4

THOSE OF YOU who have carefully followed our Scripture Portion thus far, have possibly noticed that the thought of suffering, both for Christ Himself and for His followers, has been very prominent from chapter ii. verse 11, where we started the practical and hortatory part of the epistle.

That suffering must be expected by the Christian is very clear. His life is to be one of well doing, but he may suffer for doing well (ii. 20). It is to be a life of righteousness, but he may suffer for righteousness' sake (iii 14). The first verse of chapter iv. reverts to this matter, and instructs us that we are to be armed for the conflict with the mind to suffer. It was the mind that animated Christ. He suffered for us in the flesh, and that even unto death (iii. 18). There is, of course, a difference. He suffered for us in atonement, and this we can never do. He "suffered being tempted" (Heb. ii. 18), because being perfectly holy, the very thought of sin was abhorrent to Him. We suffer in refusing temptation and in ceasing from sin, because, alas! sin is alluring to the flesh within us. If we gratify the flesh we do not suffer, but we sin. If we refuse temptation and have done with sin, the flesh suffers instead of being gratified. But it is just that suffering that is incumbent upon us.

1 PETER

In our unconverted days we lived in the gratification of our natural desires without any reference to the will of God. Now we are on exactly opposite lines, as verse 2 indicates. We do well to remember that God divides up our lives into two parts; "the time past of our life," and "the rest of our time in the flesh," the hour of conversion marking the boundary between them. In the earlier part we wrought the will of the nations who never were put under the law of God. Now we are to carry out the will of God, which has been made known to us not merely in the law but in Christ.

By the very fact however that we do not act as the world does we are open to the world's dislike and criticism. There are always many to be found who think and speak evil of what they cannot understand. This need not disturb the believer for there is One who is ready to judge the living and the dead and the accusers will stand before Him.

Now the ground of all judgment will be the testimony as regards God and His truth which may have been rendered to those who are subject to judgment; in other words, the responsibility of each will be measured by the divine testimony they have heard. "The gospel" of verse 6 is not the Christian gospel in particular. It is just "glad tidings" such as has at different times been preached to people of bygone ages, now.dead. In particular it refers to the glad tidings of salvation by the ark through the flood, for "the dead" refers to the same people as the Apostle had alluded to in chapter iii. verses 19 and 20. All through the bygone ages there was also glad tidings of a coming Deliverer and always then, as now, the glad tidings separates those who hear it into two classes; those who refuse or neglect it and have to stand their judgment as men in the flesh, and those who receive it and consequently live in the spirit as regards God. Those who thus pass from death to life by the hearing of Christ's word of glad tidings do not come into judgment, as another Scripture assures us.

Now we Christians have to remember that we have come to the end of all things. Obviously Peter did not mean that when he wrote—somewhere about A.D. 60, —*the end of this dispensation* was reached, but rather that *the end dispensation* was reached, that it is "the last time." The judge is quite ready as verse 5 has told us. He stands "before the door" (Jas. v. 9), ready to enter the court and take His seat so that the judgment may begin. All things then were quite ready for judgment at the very start of this epoch in which we are living, and it is only the longsuffering of God which holds the judgment back as Peter's second epistle tells us. How sober and watchful unto prayer should we therefore be.

More than this, we should be marked by fervent love amongst ourselves, and the utilization of every gift and ability to the glory of God, from whom all such things proceed. The world is a cold and critical place, the Christian circle should be a place of warm love. When love amongst

1 PETER

Christians exists in fervour it expresses itself passively in covering a multitude of sins and actively in giving and hospitality. There are alas many sins even with true believers. The antagonistic world delights to advertize the sins of believers, proclaiming them upon the housetops. Love in the Christian circle feels them as though they were its own and covers them. When a Christian busies himself in advertizing the sins of some other Christian, he thereby advertizes his own carnal condition. Many of us would be rather careful not to advertize the sin of some other believer who happens to meet with us in our public gatherings. Are we as careful in regard to believers who do *not* meet with us?

Whatever we may have received from God we are to hold it in trust for the benefit of all saints. The grace of God is very manifold and various. This one may speak, that one may serve. He who speaks is to speak as God's mouthpiece. He who serves as in strength that God supplies; and thus those who benefit by the speaking or serving will trace all up to God and glorify Him and not the one who happens to be the vessel or channel of supply. Speaking "as the oracles of God" does not mean, "according to the Word of God," though of course we always should so speak. It means, speaking as a mouthpiece of His word. If a speaker comes to us telling us what *he thinks*, what are *his impressions and conceptions*, we end by thinking him a very wonderful man, and doing him homage as a kind of spiritual hero! If he, on the other hand, just gives us what really is the word of God, we are subdued and we glorify God instead of glorifying him.

If fervent love prevails we shall not only give one another our due but give God His due also. Things will be right within the Christian circle even if the world without is very antagonistic.

In verse 12 the Apostle returns to the matter of suffering for the Christian, and he speaks of it with increased plainness and with prophetic foresight. There lay before these early Christians a "fiery trial," it was indeed already upon them. It very soon became as we know literally a trial by fire. They were not to account it "some strange thing." We are taught by this remark that suffering from the world is the *normal* thing for the Christian. We may hardly realize this, living, as we do, in a land of christianized culture and toleration. We may easily come to regard a life of ease and pleasantry in the world as the normal thing for us and persecution as a very abnormal thing. Then should persecution come upon us we would feel aggrieved and scandalized.

It is this wrong view of things and the "softness" which shrinks from "hardness" (2 Tim. ii. 3) which largely accounts for the great weakness of today. Only a small minority of Christians are prepared to stand up for anything, or stand out against anything in the world. A weak spirit of compliance and compromise is in the air. Suffering is avoided but power and joy are lost.

1 PETER

How does Peter present this matter of suffering? In verse 13 he holds out to us the *honour* of partaking in Christ's sufferings—i.e., we enter into sufferings that have the same character as those which He endured as the great witness to God in a rebellious world. This is, according to his account a matter of *rejoicing*,—and here he only preaches what he himself practised as recorded in Acts v. 41. We are to rejoice now, while the suffering proceeds, and thus shall we be manifestly conquerors in the presence of our foes. The day of Christ's glory hastens on however and then we shall be glad "with exceeding joy." We shall "rejoice with exultation," the suffering being over and the day of reward having arrived. Christ's supreme sufferings are to be crowned with His supreme glory. It will be our honour and joy to share in both. Which shall we see to be the greater honour in that day? Let us call shame on our faint and cowardly hearts!

But we shall get not only persecution in the world, but *reproach*, and often this is the harder to bear. Well, supposing reproach rolls in upon us, are we to be specially commiserated? Not at all. We are declared to be happy or blessed if the reproach be "for" the name, or "in" the name of Christ; which means that the world sees in us His representatives. The Lord Jesus was once in this world as the Great Representative of Jehovah, and He consequently had to say "The reproaches of them that reproached Thee are fallen upon Me" (Psa. lxix. 9). That was assuredly no disgrace to Him, and to be reproached in the name of Christ is an honour to us. Men may blaspheme Him and reproach us, but we glorify Him and the Spirit who indwells us rests upon us as the Spirit of glory and of God. Many a Christian who has been through reproach of this sort looks back afterwards to the occasion as a time of the greatest spiritual exaltation and blessing.

We are to be most careful not to suffer for evil doing of any sort but only as Christians. Then we have no need to be ashamed for we can glorify God "on this behalf," or "in this name." Here we have the Spirit of God accepting and sanctioning the name *Christian* as applied to believers. It was first used as a descriptive nickname at Antioch (Acts xi. 26). It had come into general use later (See, Acts xxvi. 28) and now is formally accepted by the Spirit of God. We may accept it therefore, and as Christians we glorify God even as Christ Himself did.

One further thought as to suffering is expressed by the Apostle in verse 17. Though it comes upon Christians from the world it is overruled of God to serve the ends of His government—the government of which he had spoken to us in chapter iii. Now God's governmental dealings especially apply to His own. He is of course the Judge of all, and beneath His judgment all will ultimately come. But He keeps specially short accounts with those acknowledged as in relationship with Him, those who are of His household. When failure supervenes and sin invades the holy precincts of

1 PETER

His house He begins to make the weight of His judgment felt in the way of His governmental dealings.

That this is God's way was manifest in Old Testament times. Read chapter viii and ix. of Ezekiel and see. Judgment was to be set in Jerusalem and the instruction was "Begin at My sanctuary." So it had begun to be in the church of God. These early Christians had to accept these fires of persecution as permitted by God for the purifying of His house. We all know there is nothing like persecution for weeding the false out of the midst of the true.

But if judgment thus starts at God's house, if God does not spare these, what about those that are not in relationship with Him at all? What shall their end be? If the righteous is saved with difficulty where shall the ungodly and sinner appear? These are tremendous questions which only admit of answers of most terrible import.

The righteous may come through with difficulty, as many an Old Testament Scripture illustrates, but he IS SAVED, nevertheless. He may have even to suffer to the extreme point of death according to God's will, as verse 19 indicates. If so he has but to go on doing well and thus commit his soul into the hands of God "as unto a faithful Creator." We know God not merely as Creator but as Saviour and Father. Still we do not lose the benefit of knowing Him as Creator, and as faithful to His own handiwork.

How happy for us to know God in all these varied ways.

Chapter 5

WHEN CHRISTIANS ARE passing through times of persecution and suffering, so much depends upon there being a right and happy condition amongst themselves. The Apostle Peter, therefore, supplements his warnings as to the persecution with some words of admonition addressed respectively to the elder and the younger amongst the disciples. Between such friction may easily develop, as we know right well.

The tendency to develop friction has always existed but never more so than now, inasmuch as the rapidity with which world changes have occurred has never been as pronounced as in the last few decades. The consequence of this is that great changes in thought and habits and outlook have supervened within the limits of a single generation; and hence children look upon their parents as behind the times and their grandparents as thoroughly antique, and the older people look upon the younger as revolutionary in their ideas. If verses 1—7 of our chapter be observed and obeyed, all friction would cease and harmony reign inside the Church of God whatever conditions prevail without.

Peter addresses himself first to the elders as being the more responsible. These were men recognized as holding the office of an elder, and not merely Christian men advanced in years. He claims a right to exhort them as being an elder and more than an elder—a witness of Christ's sufferings. To those sufferings he could render testimony since he had seen them, having been with Him in the days of His flesh. Once he thought that he could easily share in those sufferings, even to prison and death, and we all know the painful breakdown in which his self-confidence involved him. If, however, he then failed, the Lord in His grace indicated to him that he should partake in some measure before his course was finished (see, John xxi. 18, 19). Here he simply speaks of himself as a partaker of the coming glories as the fruit of grace.

His one exhortation to the elders is, "Feed," or "Shepherd the flock of God." The Holy Ghost thus gives exactly the same injunction to the elders by the lips of Paul in Acts xx. 28, and by the pen of Peter here. The elders should extend towards their younger brethren all the care which a shepherd takes of his sheep. Nothing but the outflow of divine love in their hearts will produce the watchful oversight which such care demands, and it is well for the younger believers to see in the care of their older brethren an expression of the love of Christ the Chief Shepherd, which He will richly reward at His appearing.

It is most important that the "elder" should exert his spiritual authority in the right way and spirit, hence the three things stipulated in verses 2 and 3. He is to take up his service *willingly, readily*, and as himself a *model* to the flock. The Holy Ghost who inspired these words foresaw what a tendency there would be to take up such work, either from *compulsion*, or for *love of gain*, or for *desire for power and influence*. How much these words were needed is borne witness to by church history, which tells us how the simple "elders" or "bishops" of apostolic days were gradually magnified into "princes of the church," who lorded it over God's people as though they were their own possessions. It is, indeed, remarkable with verse 3 before us, that anyone professing to be a Christian "bishop" should call himself, or suffer himself to be called, "lord."

Those of us who rank amongst the younger believers, have to pay special attention to verse 5. The elder may indeed be willing and ready in the exercise of oversight, and also may himself carry out what he enjoins on others, so as to be an example himself; all will be in vain if the younger are not prepared to listen to him and be subject. We beg every young Christian to remember that though there may be much advance in certain branches of human discovery and knowledge, so that the older generation may in these things easily fall behind the times, there is no such advance in the revealed truth of God. Consequently, spiritual maturity is still only to be gained as the fruit of years well spent in the school of God—and by that we mean, the study of His Word, supplemented by Christian life, experience and service. The younger Christian may indeed have superior zeal, energy, endurance, and possibly superior mental equipment, even so he

1 PETER

will more effectually serve his Master if he is subject to the mature and wise guidance of the "elder," who may be in most other respects decidedly his inferior.

All this will be easy if the humble spirit prevails. *All* are to be clothed with humility in their dealings with each other. The person of humble mind is not uppish, and hence does not readily come into collision with others. Better still, he does not come into collision with God; for God sets Himself against the proud, whilst He gives grace to the humble. The mighty hand of God is upon His people in the way of training, and often in very painful dealings, as was the case in the persecutions of these early Christians, yet under it we are to bow and in due time we shall be exalted. Meanwhile, we are to cast all the cares, which this painful state of things might produce, upon Him in the full assurance that He cares for us.

Although as believers we are privileged to take all our trials, even our persecutions, as connected with "the mighty hand of God," yet we are not to overlook the fact that the devil has a hand in them. The case of Job in the Old Testament illustrates this, and the fact is recognised here. In the persecution of saints the devil moves about as a roaring lion, aiming thereby at breaking down our faith. If faith be a mere matter of mental enlightenment, mere head-conviction and not heart-trust, it fails and he devours us. We are therefore to be sober and watchful. We must recognize that the devil is our adversary, and that he is to be resisted in the energy of a live faith which cleaves to the faith made known to us in Christ, remembering also, that if we taste suffering we are only sharing what is the common lot of our brethren in the world.

The "But" that opens verse 10 lifts us in the most glorious way out of the murky atmosphere of the world with its persecutions and trials and the power of Satan. We are suddenly transported in thought into the presence of "the God of all grace." Are we conscious of needing grace in an infinite variety of ways? Well, He is the God of *all* grace. The powers of the world and the devil may be against us, but He has called us unto His eternal glory by Christ Jesus, and nothing shall frustrate His purpose. He will permit us to suffer for a little while, but even that He will overrule. He will, as it were, take up the suffering and use it as material which He weaves into the pattern and design of His own choice as regards our characters and lives; and thus make it contributory to the perfecting, the establishing, the strengthening, the settlement of our souls.

As to His purpose for us, He has called us to His eternal glory. As to His disciplinary ways with us, He overrules even the activities of the adversary against us, for our spiritual perfecting and establishment. Grace, *all* grace, shines out in both His purposes and His ways. Who would not ascribe glory and dominion to the ages of ages to such an One as this?

The last three verses give us Peter's closing words. It is interesting to find Silvanus (or, Silas) and Mark mentioned, both of them brethren who had intimate relations with the Apostle Paul, since the latter part of verse 12 is evidently an allusion to the Apostle Paul's labours.

These scattered Jewish Christians had been evangelised, be it remembered, by Paul and his companions. If they stood in grace it was the fruit of his labours, and the grace in which they stood had been opened out to them through his ministry. Now Peter is led to write to them, in fulfilment of his commission as Apostle to the Jews, testifying as to the grace of God, and thus confirming that the grace in which they stood was the "true grace of God." When we remember how once at Antioch, Peter and Paul came into pretty sharp collision over questions concerning law and grace, and how Paul had to exclaim, "I do not frustrate the grace of God" (Gal. ii. 21), for Peter was committing himself to a line of action which threatened to do this very thing, we can rejoice in noting how thoroughly now they are in accord. We find a similar happy spirit of accord at the close of the second epistle (iii. 15, 16).

Let us never forget that we stand in grace—*the true grace of God*. All our relations with God are on the basis of grace. He began with us in grace at our conversion to Himself. He continues with us on the footing of grace through all the vicissitudes of our Christian life and service. With grace He will end—only, there is no end—for we shall enter His eternal glory as called to it and brought into it by the "God of all grace," as verse 10 has told us.

We are not so likely to overlook the start and the finish as we are the course between. It is *now*, amidst the failures and difficulties of our pilgrimage that we need an abiding sense of the grace that carries us through, the grace in which we stand. Soon, as we sometimes sing,

> "Grace all the work shall crown,
> Through everlasting days;
> It lays in heaven the topmost stone,
> And well deserves the praise."

2 PETER

CHAPTER 1

IN HIS SECOND EPISTLE the apostle Peter addressed himself to the same believers—Christian Jews scattered throughout Asia Minor—as in his first. This fact is not directly stated in the opening verses, but the first verse of chapter iii. makes it quite apparent. In the salutation with which the Epistle opens he simply describes them as those who had received a like precious faith to himself "through the righteousness of God and our Saviour Jesus Christ."

They had believed the gospel just as he had believed it, and such faith wherever found in the heart is indeed precious. Still the reference here is to the faith of Christianity which is precious beyond all words. The Jews religion could not be called a *faith*. It began with *sight* at Sinai. It consisted in a law of demand coupled with a *visible* system—"ordinances of divine service and a worldly sanctuary" (Heb. ix. 1)—which was a shadow of good things to come. They had turned from this, which looked like the substance but was only the shadow, to embrace the precious faith of Christ which looks to unbelievers like a shadow, but which is really the substance.

This precious faith has only come to us by the advent of the Lord Jesus as Saviour, and He came as the demonstration of the righteousness of *our* God. The word "our" should be inserted as the margin of a reference Bible will show, and it is worthy of being noted. Writing as a converted Jew to converted Jews "our God" would signify "Israel's God" who had displayed His righteousness in His faithfulness to His ancient promises and intervened on their behalf, and on ours, by the sending of the Saviour, as the result of which so precious a faith is ours.

Now the Lord Jesus who came as our Saviour, according to verse 1, also is the Revealer by whom we have the true knowledge of God, as verse 2 indicates and all grace and peace is enjoyed by us in proportion as we really know God Himself and the Lord Jesus. Indeed it is through the knowledge of our Saviour God that all things relating to life and godliness are ours.

It will help to the understanding of this passage if you begin by noting that:—

1. Verse 3 and the first part of verse 4 speak of things which are given by the power of God to each and every believer.

2. The latter part of verse 4 gives us the object God had in view in what He has given.

3. Verses 5 to 7 indicate the way in which we are responsible to work out into practical effect that which we have received, so that God's object is reached. We are to be marked by expansion and growth. That which "divine power" (verse 3) has given, our "diligence" (verse 5) is to expand.

2 PETER

What has divine power given to us? All things relating to life and godliness. We have not merely received life but with it all these things necessary that the new life may be manifested in practical Christian living and godly behaviour. The Apostle does not stop to specify the things given save to remind us that we have promises of an exceedingly great and precious kind. He really uses in fact the superlative word "greatest," for nothing could surpass the hopes of the Christian which centre in the coming of the Lord. Still a few moments' reflection might serve to remind us of *some* of the gifts that divine power has conferred upon us: —the Holy Spirit indwelling us, the Word of God written for us, the throne of Grace opened to us, to name but three. We have received however, not *some* but ALL things that have to do with life and godliness. Hence we are sent forth thoroughly furnished. Nothing is lacking upon God's part.

All these things have reached us through the knowledge of God as the One who has called us "to" or "by glory and virtue" (See margin). We are of course called *to* glory (See 1 Pet. v. 10). Here the point is that both glory and virtue characterize our call. We are called to live in the energy of that glory which is our destiny and end, and of that virtue or courage which will carry us through to the end.

These things, one and all, are ours that by them we might be "partakers of the divine nature." Every true believer is "born of God" and in that sense partakes of the divine nature (See 1 John iii. 9); consequently he does righteousness and walks in love (See 1 John ii. 29, iii. 10). The meaning of our passage however is not that by the things given to us we might be born again, for Peter was writing to those who were already "born again" (1 Pet. i. 23). It is rather that by these things we might be led into a practical and experimental partaking of the divine nature. In one word, *love* is the divine nature and hence verses 5 to 7 depict the growth of the believer as culminating in love. "Charity" or *love*, the divine nature, is the ultimate thing. The believer whose heart is full of the love of God is truly partaker of the divine nature, in the sense of this passage.

All the corruption that is in the world is the fruit of lust. The word "lust" covers all the desires which spring from man's fallen nature. The law of Moses came in and imposed its restraint upon man's fallen desires, but instead of the law really restraining lust the lusts of men broke through the restraints of law and continued to spread their corruption around. All the corruptions of the world originate in man's fallen nature. We, believers, are brought to partake in the divine nature, whence springs holiness, and hence we are lifted out of and escape the corruption. In the strength of what is divine we are lifted out of what is natural to us as sinners, and there is no other way of escape than this.

Now note the words with which verse 5 begins. "*And beside this.*" That is to say, beside all that is freely conferred upon us by "His divine power"

2 PETER

there is needed something on our side. And that something is *"all diligence."*

The work, even in our hearts and lives as believers, is all God's work, yet we must not because of that drop into a kind of fatalism as though there were nothing for us to do. We must rather remember that it pleases God to use human means in connection with much of His working, and that He has ordained that the way to spiritual prosperity for each individual believer should be by means of that believer's own spiritual diligence. This is not surprising for it is quite in accord with what we see in natural things. In the book of Proverbs we have divine wisdom applied to natural things and there we read, "Seest thou a man diligent in his business? he shall stand before kings; he shall not stand before mean men." (xxii 29).

Hence with all diligence we are to add to our faith virtue and all the other things enumerated in verses 5 to 7. Another version renders it, "In your faith have also virtue, in virtue knowledge" &c. If the former translation gives the idea of building, as though one were adding brick to brick, the latter gives the idea of growth. The bud upon the apple tree in the spring has within it in germ the luscious apple that hangs in autumn time in the same spot. Yet in the production of the apple many things have played their part, the sunshine and the rain, and the life energies of the tree which have enabled it to suck up from the soil the required moisture and other matter. Without the life energy of the tree all else would have been in vain as far as the production of an apple was concerned.

Now we are to be marked by diligent energy after this fashion. The beautiful traits of Christian character which lie in germ in every Christian are then expanded in us and in our faith is found virtue or courage. If there be not virtue which enables us to stand out clear and distinct from the world our faith becomes itself a very sickly thing.

In virtue we are to have knowledge. Virtue imparts great strength to one's character, but except strength is used according to knowledge, and that knowledge the highest and best of all—the knowledge of God and His will—it may become a dangerous thing.

In knowledge we must have temperance, or moderation. If ruled by knowledge only we may very easily become creatures of extremes. The believer of great intellectual clearness may easily so act as to imperil the welfare of his less discerning brethren, as Romans xiv. and 1 Corinthians viii. show us. Hence the need of temperance.

In temperance we are to have patience, or endurance. We are bound to be tried and tested. The believer of endurance wins through.

In patience, godliness, or piety. We learn to live in the consciousness of the presence of God. We see God in our circumstances and act as beneath His eye.

2 PETER

In godliness, brotherly kindness; for we are now able to adjust ourselves fittingly in regard to our fellow-believers. We view them too in relation to Christ and as begotten of God, and not according to our whims and fancies, our own partialities, our likes or dislikes.

In brotherly kindness we are to have charity, or love; that is divine love, the love that goes on loving the naturally unlovely, since now the fountain of love is within and hence love has not to be excited by the presentation without of what may appeal to one personally. The believer who by diligent spiritual growth loves after this fashion is a partaker of the divine nature in a very practical manner, and is fruitful as verse 8 plainly declares.

These things, you notice, are to be *in* us and abound. They are not like garments to be put *on* us for then they might be put *off* on occasions. Like fruit they are the product and expansion of the divine life within, and if they abound in us they prove us to be neither "barren"—or "idle"— "nor unfruitful in the knowledge of our Lord Jesus Christ."

Idleness is the opposite to diligence. Which are we, idle or diligent? Some Christians are very diligent in money-making and even diligent in pleasure-seeking, but idle in the things of God. Is it any wonder they spiritually languish? Others while paying the necessary heed to their business or work are diligent in the things of God. No one need be surprised that they spiritually flourish.

Verses 8 and 9 of our chapter present to us a strong contrast. The diligent believer who grows spiritually, and in whom consequently the fruit of the Spirit is found abundantly, is neither idle nor unfruitful in the knowledge of the Lord Jesus. On the other hand, it is alas! possible for a believer to be, temporarily at least, both idle and unfruitful and to be consequently in the sad plight that verse 9 portrays. Such are blind and short-sighted, and their spiritual memory is decayed.

The backslider of verse 9 is evidently a true believer. It does not say that he *never was* purged from his old sins; much less does it say that having been once saved he is *now no longer purged* from his sins; but that he has forgotten the purging of his former sins. *Purged* he was, but he has forgotten it. We must distinguish, therefore, between the backsliding of this verse and the backsliding referred to in Hebrews vi., and in the parable of the sower (See, Luke viii. 13).

In Hebrews, the backslider is an apostate who falls away from the Christian faith into such a repudiation of it as involves the crucifying *to himself* of the Son of God afresh, and his case is altogether hopeless.

In the parable of the sower, the backslider is one who receives the word in the mind and emotions, without it ever penetrating to the conscience. Such profess conversion, but without reality, and presently fall away. Their case, though difficult, is not hopeless, for they may subsequently be really and truly converted to God.

2 PETER

Here, however, it is the true believer, and, if any were disposed to question whether these things could ever be true of such, we can point to a sad episode in Peter's own history where he illustrated what he states in this verse. Had we seen Peter's *blindness* as to his own weakness on the night of the betrayal, had we seen him *short-sightedly* running into the most perilous position as he warmed himself by the fire amid the enemies of the Lord, and then when entrapped by the maidservant, breaking out into a painful exhibition of his former sins of cursing and swearing, we should have seen how, for the moment at least, he had *forgotten how he had been purged.*

And we certainly are no better nor stronger than Peter. How often have we each sadly illustrated verse 9?

Our preservation from it lies, of course, in that diligence to which Peter exhorts us. The way not to go back is to go on. Having these things abounding *in* us (verse 8) and *doing* them (verse 10) we shall be preserved from falling, and thus it will be manifest that we are indeed the called and chosen of God.

How did the other disciples regard Peter after his disastrous backsliding? Probably they feared for a moment that he might prove himself to be a second Judas. Evidently they questioned if, indeed, he were really one of themselves. Hence the special message, "Tell His disciples *and Peter*" (Mark xvi. 7). They were not at all sure of his "calling and election."

To the earnest simple-hearted Thessalonian Christians, the Apostle Paul wrote, "Knowing, brethren beloved, your election of God." How did he so confidently *know*? Read the first chapter of the 1st Epistle and see what amazing progress they had made in the short time since their conversion. It was impossible, therefore, to doubt their election. They had made it sure.

The vitality and fruitfulness which mark the diligent believer not only give demonstration of his calling and election in the present, but also are full of promise for the future. Ahead of us lies "the everlasting kingdom of our Lord and Saviour Jesus Christ," and though every Christian will enter that kingdom, it is the fruitful Christian who will have an abundant entrance, as verse 11 makes plain.

The "everlasting kingdom" is not heaven. No one gains heaven as the result of diligence or fruitfulness; nor do some gain an abundant and others a meagre entrance there. There is no entrance into heaven save through the work of Christ—a work perfect and available alike for all who believe— so that all who enter at all enter in the same way and on the same footing without distinction.

The everlasting kingdom will be established when Jesus comes again, and in connection with it rewards will be given as the parable of Luke xix. 12-27 teaches us, There will consequently be great differences as to the places that believers will occupy in the kingdom, and our entrance into it

2 PETER

may be abundant or the reverse. All will depend upon our diligence and faithfulness. The remembrance of this will certainly stir us to zeal and devotedness.

Knowing this, and knowing also how very easily and quickly we forget even the things that we are well acquainted with, the Apostle Peter, as a diligent shepherd of souls, reminded them of these things again and again. They knew these things; indeed they were established in the truth that had come to light in Christ—the *present* truth—yet what they needed was to be "put in remembrance." How much more do we need these reminders, the object being as Peter said, "*to stir you up.*"

Take note of this! We may listen to addresses or read articles which contain no truth that is new to us. Let us not therefore despise them. The main function of a teacher may be to instruct in the truth of Christianity, truth which however old in itself, is largely new to those whom he instructs. The main function of a pastor or shepherd is to get at the hearts and consciences of believers, applying to them the things in which they have been instructed, stirring them up and keeping them in an exercised and watchful condition. Do not most of us need the latter ministry more than the former? To practise more consistently what we do know is probably for us a more urgent necessity than to enlarge the area of our knowledge.

Now Peter looked on to the hour of his death. The Lord Jesus had hinted at his death and the manner of it, as recorded in John xxi. 18, 19. By this time he knew that it was to take place shortly. Is it not striking that Peter should *need* to be told that he is going to die? What a testimony to the fact that not death but the coming of the Lord is really the hope of the Christian.

But see what use Peter made of this knowledge, and how he practised the diligence which in this chapter he has pressed upon others. Verse 15 more literally translated runs:—"But I will use diligence, that after my departure ye should have also, at any time [in your power] to call to mind these things"—and then he goes on to enforce the reality and certainty of the coming kingdom of which he began to speak in verse 11, without stopping to indicate just what he purposed to do. It is very evident, however that what he purposed and accomplished under the guidance and inspiration of the Holy Spirit, was the writing of the Epistle that we are now reading. By means of it we can now at any time call to mind these things, though Peter's voice is long since silent.

Observe that there is here no mention of the rising up of a further race of apostles or inspired men, no apostolic succession. What is indicated as taking the place of the apostles is *Scripture*—particularly the apostolic writings, in other words, *The New Testament.* No teacher can possibly speak with the inspired authority of Scripture. If we neglect our Bibles, we shall listen to the best of men in vain.

2 PETER

We have just had our minds stirred up by the fact that diligence is to have its reward when the day of the everlasting kingdom of our Lord is come. Peter, however, was writing to people who had from the days of their fathers cherished the hope of Messiah's kingdom, and who had lived to see Him rejected and crucified. Were they tempted then to wonder if after all the prophecies of His glorious and actual kingdom embracing both earth and heaven were to be interpreted as but figures of speech—glowing and poetic descriptions of what was after all but a spiritual and invisible estate in heaven? It may well have been so, for we are naturally creatures of extremes. People who once thought everything of Messiah's promised advent in public glory and nothing of His advent in humiliation, are likely, when convinced of His coming to suffer, to think everything of that and nothing of His kingdom and glory.

The power and coming of our Lord Jesus Christ so long foretold in prophetic testimony, is, however, no "cunningly devised fable," and Peter is able to bear such a witness to its substantial reality as is conclusive. In verses 16 to 18 he says to us, in effect, "The prophetic testimony is true and the kingdom foretold is a substantial reality to be displayed in its season, *for we have seen it already in sample form.* He alluded, of course, to the transfiguration scene recorded in three out of the four gospels, and witnessed by himself, James and John.

Not many years ago a few men began to talk of a new kind of silky fabric produced not from the cocoons of a caterpillar, but from *wood*—of all things in the world! Folk were incredulous, it sounded like a fable. Proof was soon forthcoming though, of a quite conclusive sort. The stuff was produced in sample; not tons of it but ounces only. The substantial reality of artificial silk was as fully proved then by those ounces as it is now by the countless thousands of stockings displayed in shop windows all over the world.

The glorious kingdom of our Lord Jesus has long ago been seen in sample form by chosen witnesses. Indeed, the manifestation of it appeared not only to their eyes, but to their ears also. They were *"eyewitnesses* of His majesty," and also "this voice which came from heaven we *heard"*—the voice which came from the "excellent glory" saying, "This is my beloved Son, in whom I am well pleased."

Some may, however, wish to enquire in what way the transfiguration scene was a sample of the "power and coming" of the Lord, and thus confirmatory of His glorious kingdom? It was so, inasmuch as He was the central and glorified Object of all. Saints enjoying a heavenly portion were represented in Moses and Elijah. Saints upon earth were represented by Peter, James and John. The heavenly saints associated with Him, and entering intelligently into His thoughts in conversation. The earthly saints blessed by His presence, though dazzled by His glory. It was a sight of "the Son of man coming in His kingdom" (Matt. xvi 28); a sight of "the kingdom of God come with power" (Mark ix. 1); a sight of "the kingdom of God" (Luke ix. 27).

The glorious and everlasting kingdom of the Lord Jesus is then a blessed and substantial reality. It is certainly coming. We shall enter into it as called of God to its "heavenly" side (2 Tim. iv. 18). The question that remains to be settled is—in what way shall we enter it? Will your entrance and mine be an abundant entrance? Shall we enter like a trim and well-appointed ship entering port in full sail? Shall we enter rather as a battered and tattered wreck? The answer to that is going to be given by us each in the spiritual diligence or spiritual sloth and carelessness that marks us day by day.

The transfiguration of the Lord Jesus was not only a special and particular confirmation of the reality of His coming kingdom, but it also in a general way was a confirmation of the whole prophetic testimony of the Old Testament. This is what the opening words of verse 19 state, "and we have the prophetic word made surer" (N.Tr.). This is not difficult to understand if we search the Old Testament and observe how all its glowing predictions centre in the Messiah's Kingdom on earth, so that to establish the reality of His glorious coming Kingdom, was to establish the whole prophetic witness of the Old Testament.

These early Jewish Christians were perhaps somewhat inclined to ignore Old Testament prophecy, as though it were superseded by the developments as to the sufferings of Christ, so unexpected by them. The Apostle Peter here assures them of its value and importance for it is as a "light [or, lamp] that shineth in a dark place." The word in the original translated "dark" is one which means "squalid" or "filthy." This world with all its clever inventions and elegant splendour is only a squalid place in God's estimation, as also in the estimation of every Christian who is taught of Him. The only real light shed in the squalor is that which comes from the lamp of prophecy. Men indulge in vain imaginings as to the "millennium" which they will evolve from the present filth. Such imaginings are just a Will-o'-the-wisp. The lamp of prophecy brings us into the light of God's purpose and God's coming work of both judgment and salvation, and it enables us to see the squalor of the world that is, as well as the glory of the world to come.

We are to take heed to the light of the prophetic lamp "until the day dawn, and the day star arise in your hearts." "The day" is of course *Christ's day*—the day of His glory—then the lamp will be no longer needed. Before the day dawns however the day star arises, and before it actually arises, it is to arise in our hearts.

The "day" or "morning" star is an allusion to Christ coming for His own, who wait for Him, before He appears publicly to the world as "the Sun of

2 PETER

righteousness." As the day star He is distinctively the Christian's hope, and when the day star arises in a believer's heart, that believer is in the joyful expectation of the coming of his heavenly Saviour. We are to take heed then to the word of prophecy until the day of Christ's glory dawns, and until we are led thereby into the full enjoyment of our proper Christian hope, for New Testament prophecy has brought into view that which was never mentioned in the Old Testament. To put the matter into other words, the end of prophecy is twofold:—First, to shed its beams in the darkness until the day of Christ's glory actually arrives. Second, to conduct the believer's heart meanwhile into the full realization and enjoyment of his proper hope.

As a matter of fact many Christians fight shy of prophecy altogether because, they say, it has become a mere battleground of rival schools of interpretation amongst true Christians, and too often a kind of hunting ground to the leaders of false religious systems, wherein they pursue their heretical notions. There is all too much truth in this, but the remedy is not to ignore prophecy but rather to take heed to it well, paying all attention to the first rule for its proper use as given in verse 20.

"No prophecy of the Scripture is of any private interpretation" or, more literally, "of its own interpretation." This does not mean as the Romanists pretend that no private person has any right to concern themselves as to what Scripture means, but only to trustfully accept what the Romish "church," as represented by Pope or council, declares its meaning to be. It is rather a warning against treating each individual prophetic utterance as though it were by itself, a kind of self-contained saying to be interpreted apart from the mass of prophetic teaching. All prophecy is connected and inter-related and to be understood only in connection with the whole. It was never uttered by the will of man but by inspiration of the Spirit of God. He used different men in different ages, but His one mind pervades it all. Each individual prophetic utterance will only therefore be properly understood and interpreted as it is seen in relation to the whole, of which it forms a part.

If an artist in furniture designed an exceptionally fine wardrobe and entrusted the work in twelve sections to twelve different joiners, anybody who endeavoured to "interpret" any one of the resulted pieces of joinery *by itself* would surely reach some strange conclusions. No reliable or satisfactory interpretation would be found until it was seen as related to the whole design. Thus it is with every prophecy of the Scripture, and here is found the reason of the many opinions and even heresies which we have to deplore.

Notice how inspiration is spoken of in verse 21. "Holy men of God" spake and wrote "moved by" or "borne along by" the Holy Ghost. They put their pens to paper under His power, hence He is the real Author of what they thus wrote.

2 PETER

Chapter 2

YET EVERYTHING OF GOD, and therefore good, is counterfeited by Satanic power, consequently chapter ii. begins with a warning. When in old time the Holy Ghost was moving holy men to give us utterances from God the great adversary moved and brought in among the people false prophets. We have many examples of this in the Scripture. In the days of Ahab things had reached such a pass that Elijah could say, "I, even I only remain a prophet of the Lord; but Baal's prophets are four hundred and fifty men" (1 Kings xviii, 22), and even after the destruction of the prophets of Baal there were about four hundred prophets luring Ahab to his death against one prophet, Micaiah, the son of Imlah, who told him the truth; and all these prophets spoke not in the name of Baal but said, "Go up to Ramoth-gilead, and prosper; for the LORD shall deliver it unto the king's hand" (1 Kings xxii. 12).

Now once again God was giving prophetic testimony by inspired utterances through the apostle and others, and the adversary was preparing to repeat his tactics. Peter therefore warned these early Christians that they must be on their guard against false teachers who would bring in privily "damnable" or "destructive" heresies. Satan is never more dangerous than when he works privily or by stealth; when instead of delivering a frontal attack, boldly denying truth, he creeps in on the flank, making merchandise of the people of God with feigned words, as verse 3 puts it. Indeed the very word translated "privily shall bring in" means literally "shall lead in sideways."

The flank attack invariably succeeds in much larger measure than the frontal attack. Illustrations of this are common. Many years ago, a bold direct attack on the Deity of Christ was launched, and a Unitarian body was formed. It remains to this day a comparatively insignificant movement. Of more recent years unitarian doctrine has been brought sideways into professedly orthodox denominations and the plague has spread like wildfire.

Be on your guard then against these false teachers. They will have a wholly pleasing exterior and their words will be "feigned" or "well-turned"—cleverly adapted to throw the simple believer off his guard. They will tell you how they believe in "the divinity of Christ"—but then of course they hold every man to be more or less divine. They accept the truth of "the atonement"—as long as you permit them to print it, "at-one-ment." They can juggle marvellously with the word "eternal" and show you that it merely means "age-long" when it stands in connection with punishment. And so on.

They go even to the length of "denying the Lord that bought them." He *bought* them for by His death He bought the whole of the world for the

2 PETER

sake of the treasure hid therein (see, Matt. xiii. 44). It does not say that He *redeemed* them, for redemption applies only to the true believer. Revealing thus their true character they bring upon themselves swift destruction—which means, not that destruction will reach them in a very short time, but that when it comes it will fall upon them swiftly for their guilt admits of no question, and no lengthy judgment process will be necessary to establish it. Their judgment will not slumber. Yet alas! many will follow them, as we see; and the effect of their heresies is not merely the ruin of themselves and of their dupes but the bringing of the way of God into disrepute so that it is blasphemed. This is ever Satan's way. In his blind hatred he may desire to ruin souls, but he even more ardently desires to discredit God and His truth.

God, however, is more than equal to dealing with the situation thus created. He is perfectly able to disentangle all the confusion, as verses 4 to 10 tell us. Read those seven verses, and notice that not one full stop comes until the last word of verse 10 is completed. They are one tremendous sentence. "If God spared not the angels . . . and spared not the old world . . . and . . . condemned with an overthrow [the cities] . . . and delivered just Lot . . . the Lord knoweth how to deliver the godly . . . and to reserve the unjust . . . to be punished." A most consoling fact this for the believer, however fearful it may be for the ungodly.

The "god" created mentally by "modern theology" who being too weak or too indifferent, spares everybody and everything, that thereby he may show himself to be "love", is no more the God of the New Testament than he is of the Old. The God of the New Testament is the God of the Old as this Scripture emphasizes. When of old the angels sinned He did not spare them, but holds them in chains reserved for judgment. When the antediluvian world had filled up the cup of its iniquity God did not spare them though He saved a little remnant of eight souls in the ark. Later He overthrew Sodom and Gomorrha yet He delivered righteous Lot. So it shall be again. He will deliver the godly and reserve the unjust to judgment, and this specially when they are marked by licentiousness and the despising of authority.

However much destructive heresies are brought in, and consequently people are deceived and the way of truth blasphemed, the Lord will know how to disentangle His people and judge the ungodly. We usually find it impossible even to discern, and much less can we disentangle. Who of us, reading only the story of Lot as unfolded in Genesis could discern with any certainty what was his true state before God? He shared Abraham's path for a while, but did he at all share in Abraham's faith? His subsequent history did not look like it, so who of us could tell? Our Scripture however sets all questions at rest. He is pronounced to have been a righteous man, though sadly enmeshed by the world and living a life of continual vexation in consequence. God knew him and delivered him by angelic hands.

2 PETER

What a voice this has for us. How pitiful for us if we get so entangled that, though true believers, it would not be possible for our fellows to decide that we were such except God Himself made a pronouncement on the point. It is intended on the contrary that we stand out from the world clear and distinct as epistles of Christ, "known and read of all men" (2 Cor. iii. 2, 3). This will be profitable for us in the day that is coming. It will deliver us too at the present time from much of that vexation of soul, that mental torment, that Lot suffered. The worldly believer is well nigh the most miserable of all men.

The two evils mentioned in verse 10 seems always to accompany "damnable heresies" as their natural result. The flesh finds an attraction in the heresies, because it loves to gratify itself and to do its own will and to despise and speak against all that would hold it in check. The truth puts the sentence of condemnation on the flesh; the heresy on the contrary fosters it.

These twin evils—*self-gratification* and that of the lowest character, and *insubordination* under the plea of obtaining a larger liberty—are very prominent in the latter part of this second chapter. The contrast between verses 11 and 12 is very striking. These false teachers are but men. Angels who are greater than man in their power and might would never impeach those in dignity or authority, however much they might deserve censure, in the reckless way these men do. But as a matter of fact these teachers, who speak of dignities in a way that would suggest that they themselves were greater than the angels, are really just like—not angels—but "natural brute beasts made to be taken and destroyed." The poor animal *without reason*—for that is what the word "brute" means—may heedlessly destroy what it is not capable of understanding, like the proverbial bull in a china shop. These men are like that, they violently attack and destroy, as far as words can do it, what they do not understand.

Many teachers there are of "modernist" persuasion who exactly exemplify this. How trenchantly they attack the old foundations of the faith. What is the authority of a Paul, a Peter, a John or even indeed of Jesus Himself before their slashing words and pens? As a matter of fact however the simplest person, who being born again has become a child of God, is conscious that they have not the least comprehension of that which they attack. The most costly china is to a bull just what the truth of the Scriptures is to them.

Are some of us, who are old-fashioned believers in Christ, to tremble and be intimidated by these assaults? There is really no need for it. It may look as if nothing can stand before them in their mad career, but it is only so because God is very patient and has plenty of time in which to settle accounts. We remember a nursery picture and rhyme book which amused us in childhood's days. There was the story of the bad dog who ran amuck

2 PETER

and bit a large slice out of a man's leg. The last words of the rhyme however were:

> *The man recovered from the bite*
> *The dog it was who died*!

We are irresistibly reminded of this by the closing words of verse 12. The faith of God survives in unbroken health; the false teachers "perish in their own corruption," and receive the due reward of their unrighteousness.

How terrible is the indictment laid against them in verses 13 and 14! The adultery laid to their door may not be *literal* in all cases, but in its *spiritual* significance it certainly applies to all false teachers, for they all either teach or sanction *unholy alliance with the world*. Hence not only do they sport themselves in their own deceits—the foolish ideas engendered in their own minds—but they beguile unstable and unestablished souls. They destroy themselves, but they also bring themselves under the curse of destroying others.

In verse 15 their secret motives are unmasked. They have followed the way of Balaam. There is then nothing original about their performances. They follow in a well beaten track first trodden by Balaam of infamous memory, who sold his prophetic gifts for money. He was not the first person to prophesy for hire, for this has always been a custom in idolatrous religions, but he appears to have been the first to offer to prophesy *in the name of the Lord* for hire. With Balaam the supreme question was "Will it pay?" If a paying proposition he would prophesy to order—as far as he could. This was terrible madness involving terrible moral degradation. In verse 12, notice, the false prophets are *on a level* with the "natural brute beasts"; in verse 15 Balaam is *below* them. A dumb ass was able to rebuke him.

What then is the secret motive behind the many and various onslaughts of the modern false teachers? It is the same old story. The real drive behind them is in this—IT PAYS.

Generally it pays *financially*. When years ago the late "Pastor" Russell conducted a great campaign in London, hiring the most expensive halls and advertising on lavish scale, he was reported by a daily paper to have said, that he really did not know what to do with the money that poured in upon him.

It always pays if *fame and notoriety* is the desired thing. The sensational newspaper always patronizes the man retailing a false novelty. Thoroughgoing modernism is alas! a high road to preferment in ecclesiastical circles.

And when preferred and in high office, what have they to give? Just, *nothing*. They are "wells without water" and so no spiritual thirst can ever be slaked by them. They are as "clouds carried by a tempest" which deposit little or nothing to refresh the weary earth.

Do they accomplish anything? Yes, alas! they do. They speak "great swelling [or, high-flown] words of vanity" to the ensnaring of many souls. Oh! with what deadly accuracy are the inspired words of Scripture aimed. Certain secular papers have recently been making merry over the amusing medley of scientific jargon used at the recent meetings of the British Association. "Great high-flown words" were in plenty of evidence; and "words of vanity" they were also, wherever they touched upon "the things of God" known by no man "but the Spirit of God" (1 Cor. ii. 11). By these vain words they capture some "who have just fled those who walk in error" (N.Tr.), promising them liberty.

Liberty! That word has a very familiar sound. Has not someone said to you in effect.—"Why be enslaved by blind adherence to a Bible which you imagine to be inspired? Why not adopt the enlightened modern view? Treat it as an ordinary book, classical and interesting of course, but of no supernatural authority. Thus you will emancipate your mind from its trammels and begin to move with full *liberty* in the vast fields of modern speculation." Oh, how enticing the proposition! How fatally it works amongst well-meaning folk of unsettled minds, just fled from those walking in error and from the gross pollutions of the world, yet though thus reformed not born again. It opens up before them a way, quite high-class and scientific, right back into the old corruption from which they had just emerged.

The poor victims of these false teachers, who are thus freshly and finally entangled in the world's pollution so that their latter end is worse than their beginning, are not truly converted souls, but merely people who through a certain knowledge gained of the Lord are outwardly reformed in their ways. They are consequently likened to the dog and the sow, both unclean animals. Such is dog nature that it has the unpleasant habit of returning to its own vomit. Such is sow nature that however well washed it loves the mire and plunges into it at the first opportunity. The person who may be intellectually enlightened and consequently reformed in outward actions, yet without that fundamental change of nature produced by the new birth, falls an easy victim. The false teacher promises him liberty and by his great high-sounding words of vanity cuts the slight mental leash that held him in restraint, and there he is back again in the old ways of sin, whether vomit—uncleanness generated from within, or mire,—uncleanness from without.

They had a "knowledge of the Lord and Saviour," they knew "the way of righteousness," they "escaped from them who live in error," yet back they went to their own eternal loss. Sad, sad for them, but what pen can portray the judgment that will overtake the false teachers who have encompassed their ruin? In due season it will not slumber, as verse 3 states.

2 PETER

Chapter 3

CHAPTER II, THEN, is a very dark one. It introduces by way of parenthesis a very necessary warning. With the third chapter the apostle Peter returns to his main theme, the immense importance of *true* prophecy. The true believer, being born again, has a *pure* mind. Yet though pure it needs to be stirred up to constant mindfulness of what God has said whether by the holy prophets of Old Testament days or by the apostles and prophets of the Lord Jesus in New Testament Scripture. The chapter plainly shows us what is the effect of bringing prophetic truth to bear upon the pure mind of the believer; he is thereby separated in heart and life from the world that must come not only spiritually but also materially under judgment and so disappear (see, verses 10-14).

This, be it noted, is exactly the opposite of what is found in chapter ii. There it is the iniquitous teaching of the false prophet with the inevitable effect of *entangling* its votaries in the world and its corruptions. Here it is the light of truth given through the prophet raised up of God, which has the effect of *separating* those who receive it from the world and its corruptions.

This distinction stands true everywhere and always. So much so, indeed, that we may be able to judge of the truth and soundness of any teaching set before us by asking ourselves this simple question,—if I receive this teaching as truth will it have the effect in my mind of separating me from the world or of confirming me in it? There are other tests, of course, which we must not ignore, but this one alone is quite conclusive.

It would seem that immediately the apostle Peter returned to the subject of true prophecy he was conscious of the fierce antagonism to it on the part of adversaries. Hence first of all he issues a warning and that especially as to the opposition to be expected in the last days from scoffers, walking after their own lusts. Wishing to give free rein to their carnal desires they deride that which most would put a check upon them.

There have always been scoffers of this sort. Verse 4 however predicts that in the last days they will base their scoffing upon the steady continuity of all things from time immemorial, which, they will assert, makes any sudden catastrophe, in days to come, such as the coming of the Lord, an unthinkable thing. Verse 5 follows this up by stating that to fortify their denial they will also deny that such a catastrophic intervention as the flood could ever have taken place in times past. They "willingly [*i.e., wilfully*] are ignorant" of it. The thing is hid from them because they will to have it so.

This prediction of verses 3 to 6 is really most cheering for us. Here is a prophecy of the Scripture the fulfilment of which is being dinned into our ears almost every day. During the last century there has been a greatly revived expectation of the coming of the Lord amongst true Christians, and during at least the last half century the idea of His coming has been resisted with increasing scorn, for it cuts right across the evolutionary theories which are all the rage. To a mind obsessed with evolution the flood of the past, as recorded in Genesis, and the personal coming of Christ in the future are equally unbelievable. They remain wilfully ignorant of the one and they scoffingly deny the other. For over nineteen centuries scoffers have scoffed. Only during the last half century have they scoffed *on these grounds*. But the scoffers are to scoff on these grounds *in the last days*. Therefore the conclusion is definite and unmistakeable: *we are in the last days*. This is indeed most cheering. We may well praise God! This day is this Scripture fulfilled in our ears (see, Luke iv. 21).

How did the flood take place? The answer is, "by the Word of God." By "the same Word" the existing heavens and earth are reserved unto fire in the coming day of judgment. The Word of God overthrew the flimsy unbelief of men in the past and it will do so again. The eye of faith sees written upon the finest construction of men's hands, the ominous words, "RESERVED UNTO FIRE."

The mocking question of the scoffer springs of course out of the fact that many centuries have elapsed since the Lord left this earth with the promise that He would come again quickly. We have therefore to recognise the fact, stated in verse 8, that God's ideas of time are very different to ours. A thousand years are as one day to Him, as indeed Psalm xc. 4 had told us; one day is also as a thousand years, as is illustrated in verse 10 of our chapter. We must not therefore count Him slack if much time has elapsed to our way of thinking.

The reason for the long waiting time is not slackness but long-suffering. The second advent will mean the striking of a tremendous blow in judgment. This though necessary is no joy to God. He does not desire that any should perish but that all should come to repentance. The alternative is very clearly stated in these words. It is *repent* or *perish*.

Yet the judgment blow *will* be struck when the time arrives. The Lord *will* come when men do not expect Him, as a thief in the night, and thus usher in His day. That "day" will comprise a thousand years as other Scriptures show. It will commence with His coming and not close until the passing away of the earth and its surrounding heavens, dissolved by fire. This will not take place until the end of His thousand years' reign is reached, as stated in Revelation xx. 7-11. That same destruction of the heavens and the earth will usher in the "day of God" of which Revelation xxi. 1-8 speaks,—the eternal state. The "day of the Lord" and the "day of God" are like two circles touching each other and just overlapping at the point where the heavens and earth are destroyed, so that their destruction may be said to be in both of them.

2 PETER

The day of the Lord is the period especially characterized by the exaltation of Christ, as Lord and Administrator of the will of God, when righteousness will reign. It lasts for 1000 years. The day of God is the succeeding eternal state in which God shall dwell with men in a new heaven and new earth and there righteousness shall dwell without a solitary foe to challenge its peace.

These things are plainly declared in the prophetic Word and we know them. But to what end are they made known to us? The answer to this question is found in verse 11 and in verses 14 to 18. All is designed to have a present effect upon our characters and lives.

We know that the dissolution of the earth and all its works is decreed by the Word of God. Then we shall be marked by "holy conversation"—*i.e.*, a separate manner of life—and godliness. We shall be as those who expect and hasten the coming day. The Christian who spends all his energies in making the best of *this* world may affirm that he knows these things, but he hardly *believes* them in the true sense of the term. Lot struck his roots deeply into the soil of Sodom but it was because he did not know its doom was decreed. What would he have done had he known it? In very deed the light of true prophecy has a separating and sanctifying effect.

We know too that we shall enter into the blessedness of the eternal state in the new heavens and the new earth. Then we shall be *diligent*—here Peter returns to the word he had used in chapter i. 5—to walk now in peace, spotless and unblameable. The eternal state will be a scene of peace because no spot nor blame shall be there. Well, we shall aim at the characteristics of the new heavens and new earth before they actually arrive.

Further, we shall account that the present longsuffering of our Lord is salvation, consequently we shall not chafe under the waiting time it imposes upon us. We shall know that every day of waiting and perhaps suffering which is entailed for us means the salvation of multitudes. And not only this—for the "accounting" will not stop with a mere mental recognition of the fact but express itself in action—we shall bend our energies to the setting before men of that which is ordained for their salvation, until the Lord comes. The gospel of God is "the power of God unto salvation to every one that believeth" (Rom. i. 16).

As Peter opened his first epistle (i. 12) it appears as if he referred to Paul's labours amongst these dispersed Jews. Now at the close of the second Epistle he specifically names him and not only "all his epistles" in a general way but also some special writing or epistle which he had addressed to them, according to the wisdom given him from on high. So evidently Paul wrote to the Hebrews. It *may* of course have been a writing not intended for preservation as part of the Scriptures, and hence not extant today. It is much more likely to be that wonderful Epistle to the

Hebrews that we possess for our soul's rejoicing. In that Epistle he does indeed "speak of these things." See particularly chapter xii. 25 to 29. He speaks of them in his other epistles too.

Notice how Peter writes of Paul, the man who had to withstand and rebuke him once at Antioch (See Gal. ii. 11). Not a trace of bitterness is there, nor a trace of that Judaizing spirit which Paul had to withstand. Martyrdom was approaching for both of them, and it is, *"our beloved brother Paul."* Delightful—is it not? The freest flowing forth of Christian affection and the fullest acknowledgement of the grace and gift bestowed upon another than himself. We can see the warm and loving heart that beat in Peter without the taint of egotism, which marred it when he was young, and thought he loved more than all the other apostles.

Yet he had to say that in Paul's epistles there were things "hard to be understood." In so saying he wrote doubtless as the apostle to the circumcision identifying himself with the believers of his own nation. All the truth concerning the church, its place in the purposes of God, its privileges, its composition of an election gathered from Gentiles as well as Jews, all that which Paul speaks of, in short, as "the mystery of Christ" (Eph. iii. 4) was bound to be "hard" to a Jew. It cut across every fibre of their national feeling which had been fostered for centuries. The truth was simple enough from an intellectual point of view but the eyes of their *hearts* needed opening to see it. This was recognized by Paul in Ephesians i. 18, where the word "understanding" should be "hearts". Except we too have the eyes of our hearts opened we have to sadly confess when we read God's Word it is hard to be understood.

Scripture too may be wrested or distorted to the destruction of those who so treat it. Those who do so are "unlearned and unstable." "Unlearned," or "untaught," means of course untaught, not in the wisdom of the world, but in the things of God. Here Peter may have been especially referring to a Gentile danger, the sort of thing that Paul himself warns Gentiles against in Romans xi. 13 to 29. If Gentiles misunderstand and misuse God's truth so as to become "wise in their own conceits" they are very near destruction. Still even if Peter did especially refer to this his words are capable of a much wider application. Let us all beware of twisting the Word of God!

Now, we have been forewarned. Thus we are forearmed against the error of the wicked, lest we should fall. The error of the wicked was fully exposed in chapter ii. It is not enough however to be warned against evil; we must be in the positive enjoyment of truth. The way not to go back is to go on. Like a man on a bicycle, the Christian must go on if he would avoid falling off. Hence we must "grow in grace and in the knowledge of our Lord and Saviour Jesus Christ."

This word just summarizes the main teaching of the Epistle. Spiritual growth was the great theme of chapter i. and to it the apostle returns in his

2 PETER

closing words. All true growth is in grace, *the grace of God*. Then as we expand in grace we grow in graciousness of spirit. All true growth too is in the knowledge of the Lord Jesus, in whom the grace of God has reached us.

Who shall set a limit to our expansion in grace and in the knowledge of the Lord? Both are alike illimitable. Planted here, we are like trees that have struck their roots down into a subsoil of fertile richness that is without a bottom!

"To Him be glory both now and for ever, Amen."

1 JOHN

INTRODUCTION

THE MOST CURSORY reading of the first Epistle of John is enough to show us that it bears a very strong likeness to the Gospel of John. The same themes are prominent in both. In the Gospel they are set forth, mainly but not exclusively, in the Lord's own words, and as illustrated in His life. In the Epistle they are still enforced, but the main point now is that they are to be demonstrated in the lives of the children of God. The Gospel shows us things that are *true in Him*. But the Epistle speaks of "a new commandment . . . which thing is true in Him *and in you*" (ii. 8). This brief sentence furnishes us with a key to the whole epistle.

This epistle was amongst the last to be written. There were already "antichrists" about, as the second chapter states. These men laid claim to superior knowledge. They claimed that their teachings were a moving forward, an improvement on what had gone before. But under pretence of moving *forward* they moved clean *away* from the foundation which had been laid in Christ, and from the life which from the beginning had been manifested in Him, when He came amongst us in flesh. Hence the first thing needful was to make very plain that there had been a real, true, objective manifestation of the eternal life in Christ.

CHAPTER 1

WE MUST NOT confound "from the beginning" with the words, "In the beginning," with which the Gospel opens. There, the eternal existence and deity of the Word is stated, and we travel back to the beginning, and even beyond the beginning, of all things that can be said to have had a beginning. Here, we are concerned with the fact that all Christian truth begins with the revelation which reached us in Christ incarnate. *That* was the beginning of the true manifestation of God and of life eternal. *That* was the basis of all apostolic teaching. The antichrists pushed their seductive teachings which merely originated from their own foolish minds. The apostles declared that which was from the beginning, and not something which had been introduced since.

In verses 1 and 2 the Lord Jesus is not mentioned personally, for the point is rather that which was presented to us in Him. He was "the Word of life." In John i., He is "the Word," and being such He creates, so that creation may express something at least of God. Also He becomes flesh and dwells amongst us that He may express God fully to us. Here the thought is similar, but more limited. Life is the point: He was "that eternal life which was with the Father" and in Him it has been manifested unto us. We are to have the life in having Him; but the first thing is to see the full character of the life as it came out in Him.

The life was eternal life, but it also was "with the Father." This statement, we are told, gives the *character* of the life; so that it is not merely a statement of the fact that it *was* with the Father, but rather that it was *such a life as that*. It was with the Father inasmuch as He, who is the Fountain Head of that life, was with the Father, and in Him it has been manifested unto us. He became flesh that it might be manifested.

By the fact of His becoming flesh He placed Himself within the reach of three out of the five senses or faculties with which man is endowed. He could be heard, seen and felt. Hearing comes first, for in our fallen condition it is to that faculty that God specially addresses Himself. "Faith cometh by hearing, and hearing by the word of God" (Rom. x. 17). And so in the first place the apostles *heard* the Word of life, and thus were able to apprehend Him.

But then they also *saw* Him with their eyes, and even "looked upon," or "*contemplated*" Him. There had been in earlier days fleeting manifestations of this great Person as "the Angel of the Lord," only then it was impossible to contemplate Him for He was seen but for a moment. Now, come in flesh, all was different. The apostles spent years with Him, and could scrutinize Him with attention. They gazed at Him long and earnestly, even though they did not properly understand all that they observed until they had received the gift of the Holy Ghost.

Also they came into physical contact with Him. Their hands actually *handled* Him. This guaranteed that He was no mere Spirit manifestation. He was amongst them in a real human body of flesh and blood. After His resurrection He sojourned among them in His risen body of flesh and bones, and we may remember how He specifically enjoined them to handle Him and see He was not a Spirit after His resurrection.

All this establishes then beyond a doubt that there had been this real manifestation of eternal life before them. John i. shows that in Him the Father was *declared* (ver. 18); Colossians i., that God was perfectly *represented* in Him as His Image (ver. 15); Hebrews i., that as the Son He is the Word, and that He is the *expression* and outshining of God's Being and glory (vers. 2, 3). Here we find that He furnished the only true, objective *manifestation* of eternal life. It is remarkable that, just as we have four Gospels setting forth His life from differing aspects so we have these four passages which set forth from differing aspects all that which came into revelation in Him.

The reason why John laboured this point in his opening verses was that the anti-christian teachers belittled it, or even denied it altogether. They were called "Gnostics," because they claimed to be "the knowing ones." They preferred their own subjective impressions and philosophic speculations to the objective facts established in Christ. Now everything for the apostles and for us begins with well established facts. The faith once delivered to the saints is rooted and established on facts. We cannot be too clear and emphatic as to this. That which is (as we shall see) subjectively

1 JOHN

produced in the saints is strictly in keeping with that which has been objectively manifested in Him.

The manifestation was made in the first place to the apostles. They were the "we." But then, "that which we have seen and heard declare we unto you." The "you" were the saints generally. The manifestation made before the apostles brought them into "fellowship ... with the Father, and with His Son Jesus Christ." They have made known to us that which was manifested, that we might be brought into the same wonderful fellowship. The Father and the Son are made known to us. The eternal life connected with the Father and the Son has been manifested to us through them. The things of the Father and the Son have been revealed. Nothing could be more wonderful than this: nothing more absorbing, if once by the Holy Spirit we begin to lay hold of it. Nothing more calculated to fill our hearts with abiding gladness. No wonder the Apostle adds, "These things write we unto you, that your joy may be full."

Verse 4 makes it quite clear that the communication of these things to us by the apostles is through the Scriptures. "These things *write* we ..." The apostles heard, saw and handled. We must *read*. Thank God for the Holy Writings which bring the knowledge of these things to us for our joy.

In verse 5 John begins his message. Where does he start? With this great fact that "God is light" and not, as we might have expected, with the fact that God is love. All the emphasis would no doubt have been on His love had the manifestation been made in regions of unsullied purity and light. As however the manifestation has been made in this world, so filthy with sin and full of darkness, the first emphasis must be laid on light.

As to light—who can define it? Men have formulated theories to account for the light of creation, but they cannot really explain it. Who then shall explain the uncreated Light? We know that light is necessary if life is to exist in any but its lowest forms. We know that it is healthful, that it illuminates and exposes all things, and that if it enters darkness flees. In God there is no darkness at all, for darkness stands for that which is removed from the action of light, that which is hidden and sinful.

Not only is God Himself light but, as verse 7 tells us, He is "in the light." Once the Lord had said, "that He would dwell in the thick darkness" (2 Chron. vi. 1); and the fact that Solomon built Him an house did not alter it, for His presence was still found in the Holy of Holies, where all was dark. This was altered by the coming of the Lord Jesus, for God stepped into the light in Him. The God who *is* light is now *in the light*.

This fact is used as a test in verse 6. We have in this verse the first of many tests which are propounded. The presence of many false teachers with their varied and boastful claims made these tests necessary; and we shall notice that none of them are based upon elaborate or far-fetched considerations. They are all of the simplest sort and based upon the fundamental nature of things. Here, for instance, the fact that God is light, and that He is in the light, tests any claim that is made of being in fellowship with Him. Such an one cannot possibly be walking in darkness, for as we read elsewhere, "What communion hath light with darkness?" There is no communion (or fellowship) at all between the two. They are diametrically opposed.

The point here is not whether we always walk *according to* the light that we have received. We are all found offenders as to this at some time or other, as we know to our sorrow. To "walk *in* darkness" is to walk in ignorance of the light that has shone in Christ. A reference to Isaiah L. 10, 11, at this point may be helpful. The one who "walks in darkness and has no light" is to "trust in the name of the Lord, and stay upon his God." However, even in Isaiah's day there were those who preferred to "kindle a fire" and walk in the light of the fire and the sparks that they kindled. It was just like this in John's day, and still is so in our own. There are all too many false teachers who prefer the sparks of their own kindling to the light of God's revelation. Consequently they and their followers are in darkness in spite of all their pretensions, and they have no fellowship with Him.

The true believer walks in the light of God fully revealed. The light has searched him of course. It could not be otherwise. But he walks happily in the light because he has learned in that light that "the blood of Jesus Christ His Son cleanseth us from all sin." Every spot of defilement exposed by the light is removed by the Blood.

The word is "cleanseth"—the present tense. From this some have deduced that the blood is to be continually applied. But the present tense is also used to denote the nature or character of anything; just as we say, "Cork floats." "Fire burns." "Soap washes." Such are their respective natures. Those properties belong to them. So it is the nature of the blood of Christ to cleanse from all sin. That blessed property is inherent in it. The idea that the Blood has to be continually or repeatedly applied contravenes the teaching of Hebrews ix. 23—x. 14. We are "ONCE PURGED" by the "one offering," so as to have "no more conscience of sins."

Not only were men found who professed to have fellowship with God while yet walking in darkness, but there also were found some who went so far as to say, "We have no sin." No test is propounded in regard to this wicked pretension. None was needed since they must of necessity soon be found out. They were deceiving themselves, and John tells them so plainly. They would hardly deceive anyone else; and if for a moment they did, the deception would soon be dispelled by sin being manifested in them all too plainly. If any indulge in such high and unfounded claims they do

1 JOHN

not show that *sin is not in them*. They only make it very manifest that *the truth is not in them*.

It is very difficult to imagine true believers deceiving themselves in this way, save for a very brief time. The only true and honest attitude for us is that of confessing our sins, and doing so at once. It is true of course that the only honest thing for the unbeliever, when conviction reaches him, is to confess his sins; then forgiveness, full and eternal will be his. The believer is in question here however. It is, "If *we* confess . . ." The sin of a believer does not compromise or upset the eternal forgiveness which reached him, when as a sinner he turned to God in repentance. It does nevertheless compromise his communion with God, of which we have just been reading. That communion will be suspended until he confesses the sin that has broken in upon it.

When we confess, God is faithful and just to all that Christ is, and has done, and the sin is forgiven so that fellowship may be restored. This is what we may call *paternal* forgiveness, to distinguish it from the *eternal* forgiveness which reached us as sinners.

Not only does He forgive, but He also cleanses from all unrighteousness. The honest confession of sin by the saint not only ensures forgiveness but it also has a cleansing effect. Confession of sin means the judgment in our own hearts and minds of what we confess. And that means cleansing from its influence and deliverance from its power.

A third pretension comes before us in verse 10. Some may be so far deluded as to say that they "have not sinned." A test is propounded in regard to this; namely, the Word of God. To make such a preposterous statement is to place ourselves in opposition to the Word of God and to make Him a liar. He plainly states that we have sinned, which ends the matter. We cannot contradict His Word, and yet have His Word abiding in us.

As surely as we are in the light, shall we know that we have sinned and that sin is still in us. Yet we shall also know the value of the blood of Christ and its cleansing power, as also the restoration that reaches us upon honest confession. Thus communion in the light with the Father and His Son is established for us, and also maintained. We are enabled to know and rejoice in the life which has been manifested, and in all that from the beginning has been set forth in the blessed Son of God.

Our joy being full in such things as these, we shall not feel inclined to run after the men who would entice us with their professed improvements and enlargements of "that which was from the beginning." The sparks they display before us may be quite pretty, but they are only of their own kindling, and they die out into darkness.

1 JOHN

Chapter 2

THE CLOSING VERSES of chapter i. have shown us that we cannot say that we have no sin, nor that we have not sinned. The opening words of chapter ii. act as a counter-balance, lest we should rush to the conclusion that we can excuse ourselves for sinning by assuming that we can hardly help it, that it is practically inevitable. It is nothing of the kind. John wrote these things that we might not sin. Other scriptures speak of special provision made to keep us from falling: the point here is that, if we enter into the holy fellowship of which verse 3 of chapter i. speaks, we shall be preserved. The enjoyment of that fellowship excludes sin; just as sin excludes from the enjoyment of that fellowship, until it is confessed.

There is ample provision made for us that we may not sin, even though sin is still in us. We ought not to sin. There is no excuse for us if we do sin; but there is, thank God! "an Advocate with the Father" for us in that case. The word translated, Advocate, here is the same as is translated, Comforter, in John xiv.—a word meaning literally, "One called alongside to help." The risen One, Jesus Christ the righteous, has been called *alongside the Father* in glory for the help of His saints, if and when they sin. The Holy Spirit has been called *along to our side* here below for our help.

It is "the Father," you notice. That is because the Advocate appears for those who are already the children of God. The first words of the chapter are, "My children" (N. Trans.)—the word used is not the one meaning "babes," but one for "children" in a more general way. In this loving way the aged Apostle embraced as his own all the true children of God. We have been introduced into this blessed relationship by the Saviour, as John i. 12 tells us. Being in the relationship, we need the services of the Advocate when we sin.

The righteousness of our Advocate is stressed. We might have expected that His kindness and mercy would be: yet we find elsewhere that emphasis is laid on righteousness when sin is in question, and so it is here. The One who takes up our case in the Father's presence when we sin, will see to it that righteousness shall prevail. The *Father's glory* shall not be tarnished by our sin, on the one hand. And, on the other hand, He will deal with *us* righteously, so that we may come to a proper and righteous judgment of our sin, be brought to confession, and be forgiven and cleansed.

He who is our Advocate on high is also "the propitiation for our sins." This fact brings us back to the rock foundation upon which all rests. By His propitiatory sacrifice every claim of God against us has been met, and He takes up His advocacy with the Father upon that righteous basis. His propitiation has settled for us *as sinners* the eternal questions which our sins have raised. His advocacy now settles the paternal questions which are raised, when *as children of God* we sin.

Propitiation is what we may call the Godward side of the death of Christ. It is concerned with the most fundamental matter of all; the meeting of the Divine claims against sin. The meeting of the sinner's need must be secondary to that. Hence when we have the Gospel unfolded by Paul in the epistle to the Romans, we find that the first mention of the death of Christ is "a propitiation through faith in His blood" (iii. 25). We do not get substitution clearly stated until reaching chapter iv. 25, we read of Him as "delivered for our offences."

Being the Godward aspect of His death the widest possible circle is in view—"the whole world." When the substitutionary side is stated believers only are in view: it is "our offences," or, "the sins of many." But though only believers stand in the realized benefits of the death of Christ, God needs to be propitiated in regard to every sin that ever has been committed by men, in regard to the whole great outrage which sin has wrought. He has been thus propitiated in the death of Christ, and because of this He can freely offer forgiveness to men without compromising in the smallest degree one feature of His nature and character.

Propitiation is a word which often rouses to much wrath and scornfulness many opponents of the Gospel. They assume that it means what it does among the heathen—the pacifying by much blood-shedding of some angry, antagonistic and blood-thirsty power. But in the Scriptures the word is lifted on to an altogether higher plane. It still carries the general sense of appeasing or rendering favourable by sacrifice, but there is no ground for regarding God as antagonistic or blood-thirsty. He is infinitely holy. He is righteous in all His ways. He is of eternal majesty. His very nature, all His attributes must receive their due, and be magnified in the exaction of the appropriate penalty: yet He is not against man but for him, for what righteousness has demanded love has supplied. As we read presently in our epistle, "He loved us, and sent His Son to be the propitiation for our sins" (iv. 10). God Himself provided the propitiation. His own Son, who was God, became it. Propitiation, rightly understood, is not a degrading idea but uplifting and ennobling. The only thing degrading is the idea of the matter falsely entertained by those who oppose. They attempt to foist their degraded idea into the Gospel, but the Word of God refutes their idea.

We now pass to the consideration of another claim that was being made falsely on occasions—"I know Him." It is indeed possible for the believer to say with great gladness that he knows God, inasmuch as "fellowship with the Father and with His Son Jesus Christ" is granted to us, and there can be no fellowship without knowledge. Still, again a test is needed lest such a claim be mere pretension. The test is that of obedience to the commandments which He has given to us. The knowledge *of* Him is inseparably connected with obedience *to* Him.

1 JOHN

In keeping His commandments we know that we have come to know Him. Apart from this obedience there cannot be this knowledge, and the claim, if made, would only reveal that the truth is not in the claimant. Compare verse 4 with verse 8 of chapter i. The truth is not in the one who claims *to have no sin*, any more than it is in the one who claims *to have the knowledge of God*, and yet is not obedient to His commandments.

Let us clearly grasp the fact that there are commandments in Christianity, though they are not of a legal order: and by that we mean, not given to us in order that we may thereby either establish or maintain our footing before God. Every definite expression of God's will has the force of a command, and we shall find this epistle has a great deal to say to us about His commandments, and they "are not grievous" (v. 3). The law of Christ is a law of liberty, inasmuch as we are brought into His life and nature.

From keeping His commandments we pass, in verse 5, to keeping His word. This is a further thing. His word covers all that He has revealed to us of His mind and will, including of course His commandments, but going beyond them. A man might give his sons many definite instructions—his commandments. But beyond these his sons have gleaned an intimate knowledge of his mind from the daily communications and intercourse of years, and with filial devotion they carefully observe his word even when they have no definite instructions. So it should be with the children of God. And, when it is so, the love of God is "perfected" in such, for it has produced in them its proper effect and answer.

Moreover, by such obedience we know "that we are in Him." Our being "in Him" involves our participation in His life and nature. There is of course a very intimate connection between knowing "that we know Him," (ver. 3) and knowing "that we are in Him," (ver. 5). The second introduces us to a deeper thing. Angels know Him, and obey His commands. We are to know Him, as those who are in Him, and hence the slightest intimation of His thought or desire should be understood by us, and incite us to glad obedience.

Being in Him, we are to "abide in Him;" which means, as we understand it, abide in the consciousness and power of being in Him. Now it is easy for any of us to say, "I abide in Him," but if so we must produce that which proves the claim to be real. Such an one "ought himself also so to walk, even as He walked." If we are in His life, and also in the power and enjoyment of it, that life is bound to express itself in our ways and activities just as it did in Him. The grace and power of our walk, compared with His, will be poor and feeble; yet it will be walk of the same order. The difference will not be in kind but only in degree.

What extraordinary elevation then is to characterize our walk! How far beyond the standard that was accepted in Old Testament times! When John wrote these words a good many may have felt inclined to protest that he was setting too high a standard and introducing what was entirely new.

1 JOHN

Hence in verse 7 he assures them that what he was saying was not new—in the way that the teachings of the antichrists were new—but rather an old commandment. At the same time it was in another sense a new commandment. There is no contradiction here, though there is a paradox. It was an old commandment, for it had been from the beginning set forth in Christ, as being God's holy will and pleasure for man: and so there was nothing about it which resembled the new notions of the Gnostics. Still it was a new commandment, for now it was to be set forth in those that were Christ's, and hence came as a new thing for them. The thing, said John, "is true in Him and in you." The life which was manifested in Christ, and which at the first was exclusively in Him, is now to be found in believers, who are in Him. As they abide in Him the life will express itself in them in the same way, and bring forth similar fruits.

And so we read, "the true light now shineth." There is the closest possible connection between life and light. If the true life was manifested in Christ, the true light equally shone in Him. If we have part in that true life, the true light will also shine in us. "The darkness is passing," is what the Apostle wrote, and not, "is past." We must wait for the world to come to say it is past: yet clearly it is passing away, for the true light has begun to shine in Christ and in those that are His. When God acts in judgment and the false life and light of this world are put out, then the darkness will be past indeed. At present we can rejoice in the assurance that it is passing, and that the true light is shining. The more we walk as He walked, the more effectively the light will shine through us.

But further, if the light is now going to shine in and through us, we ourselves must be in the light. Do we claim to be in the light? Well, there is a simple test by which it may be known if that claim is a genuine one. If any one says he is in the light and yet he hates his brother his claim is false, and he is in darkness; that is, he does not really know God—he is not in the light of God revealed in Christ. No one can be in the light of God who is not in the life of God, which is love. Hence a little later in the epistle we read, "He that loveth not his brother abideth in death" (iii. 14). So now we discover that life, light and love all go together; and in the very nature of things they act as tests, the one upon the other. The one who loves his brother manifests *the life*, according to chapter iii. Here the point is that he abides in *the light*.

John adds the remark, "there is none occasion of stumbling in him." This is in contrast to what follows in verse 11, where the one who hates his brother is described as being in darkness, walking in darkness, and not knowing where he is going. We have no light in ourselves, just as the moon only has light when it is in the light of the sun. So the one who hates his brother, being in darkness, is all dark himself, and consequently becomes an occasion of stumbling to others. He stumbles himself and acts as a stumbling-block. Such were the antichrists and their followers. The one who loves, as the fruit of having the divine life, walks in the light, and neither stumbles nor is a stumbling-block.

The loving of one's brother is of course the loving of each and all who equally with ourselves are begotten of God. It is the love of the divine nature, extended to each who has entered the divine family,—loving children of God as children of God, apart from all human likes or dislikes.

A fresh paragraph begins with verse 12. In verse 4 of chapter i. John indicated the *themes* as to which he wrote. Now we have the *basis* on which he wrote. All those whom he addressed stood in the wonderful grace of sins forgiven, and all were in the children's place. The word translated "little children" is the one for children rather than babes. It includes all the children of God without distinction. The forgiveness which is ours has reached us solely for His Name's sake. The virtue, the merit is wholly His. As forgiven, and brought into divinely formed relationship, we are addressed.

On the other hand, there *are* distinctions in the family of God, and they are brought before us in verse 13. There are "fathers," "young men," and "little children," or "babes." In this way John indicated the differing stages of spiritual growth. We all must of necessity begin as babes in the divine life. Normally we should develop into young men, and finally become fathers. Each of the three classes is characterized by certain things.

Verse 13, then, states *the characteristic features* of those to whom he writes, not the themes concerning which he writes, nor the basis on which he writes. The fathers are characterized by the knowledge of Him that is from the beginning; that is, they were matured in the knowledge of Christ, that "Word of life," in whom the eternal life had been manifested. They really knew the One in whom had been revealed all that is to be known of God. All other knowledge shrinks into insignificance compared with this knowledge. The fathers had it.

The young men were characterized by having overcome the wicked one. Later verses in the chapter show more exactly the force of this. They had overcome the subtle snares of the devil through antichristian teachings, by having been built up in the Word of God. In our earlier years as believers, before we have had time to be well grounded in the teachings of the Word, we are much more likely to be led away by subtle teachings contrary to the Word, and thus overcome by the wicked one.

This is the danger to which the babes are exposed, as we shall see. Yet they have a beautiful feature characterizing them—they know the Father. The human babe soon manifests the instinct which enables it to recognize its parents; and so it is with the children of God. They have His nature, so they know Him. There are many things for them still to learn about the Father, yet they know the Father. As the children of God let us be exercised that we do not remain babes. There we must begin, but let us aim

1 JOHN

at that acquaintance with the Word of God which will develop our spiritual growth, and lead us to become young men and even fathers in due season.

Having given, in verse 13, the features which characterize respectively the fathers, young men and little children, the Apostle begins, in verse 14, his special message to each of the three. He commences again with the fathers.

His message to them is marked by the utmost brevity; moreover it is expressed in exactly the same words as those used in the previous verse, when he described their characteristic feature. This is remarkable, and we may well inquire what is the reason for it. The reason we believe to be that when we come to the knowledge of "Him that is from the beginning" we reach the knowledge of God in a fulness which is infinite and eternal, beyond which there is nothing. He who is "Son," and "the Word," the "Word of life," manifested amongst us, is the One that is from the beginning. In Him God is known to us, and there is nothing beyond this knowledge of such infinite profundity.

Now the fathers knew Him in this deep and wonderful way. The God who is love had become the home of their souls and dwelling in love they dwelt in God and God in them. They had but to go on deepening in this blessed knowledge. Nothing needed to be said to them beyond this.

The young men had not as yet grown up to this, but they were on the way to it. They were characterized by having overcome the wicked one, as verse 13 told us. We now learn how this overcoming had been brought to pass. They had been made strong by the Word of God abiding in them.

We all enter upon the Christian life as little children, but if healthy growth marks us we advance to be young men. Now the *knowledge* of the Word of God must come first. We cannot abide in that of which we are ignorant. Here then we are brought face to face with the reason why so many true believers of many years standing have remained little children—just stunted babes. They have never become really acquainted with the Word of God. The great adversary of the work of God knows the need of this right well, and it is easy to see the skill of his deeply laid designs in the light of this fact.

Romanism takes the Scriptures out of the hands of its votaries on the ground that, being God's Word, it is far above the layman and only fit to be in the hands of the doctors of the church, who alone can interpret it. Modernism is prevalent in the Protestant world. In its full-blown form it denies the Word of God entirely: the Bible is to them only a collection of doubtful legends interspersed with obsolete religious reflections. In its diluted form—which often seduces real Christians, and therefore is the more mischievous as regards ourselves—it weakens the authority of the

1 JOHN

Word, and therefore dooms its followers to perpetual spiritual babyhood. And where these evils are absent, so frequently people are content to take their knowledge of the Word from the texts upon which their minister may happen to preach. They do not read, and mark and learn and inwardly digest the Word for themselves. Hence their growth also is stunted.

But the Word is not merely to be known, *it is to abide in us*. It is to dwell in our thoughts and in our affections; in this way it will control us, governing the whole of our lives. If that point is reached by any of us, then it can be said that we are strong, for our lives will be founded upon the impregnable rock of Holy Scripture. Even so however, strength is not everything, for we have yet to be conducted to that knowledge of Him that is from the beginning, which characterizes the fathers.

The young men are faced by a danger which, if it prevails, will hinder them advancing still further into this blessed knowledge. That danger is the world, and the love of it: not merely of the world as an abstract conception, but of the concrete, material things that are in the world. We *use* a great many of these things, and occasionally at least we *enjoy* them, but we are not to *love* them. That which we love dominates us, and we are not to be dominated by the world but by the Father. The love of the world and the love of the Father are mutually exclusive. We cannot be possessed by both. It must be one or the other. Which possesses us?

If the love of the Father possesses us, we shall see the world in its true light. We shall possess a spiritual faculty which acts after the fashion of the much prized X-rays. We shall get down beneath the surface of things to the skeleton framework on which all is built. That skeleton is revealed to us in verse 16 as, "The lust of the flesh, and the lust of the eyes, and the pride of life;" all of which spring not from the Father but are wholly of the world.

The lust of the flesh is the desire of *having*—the desire to possess oneself of those things that minister to the flesh. The lust of the eyes is the desire of *seeing*, whether with the eyes of the head or with those of the mind, all the things that minister to one's pleasures. It would cover man's restless intellectual cravings as well as his continual hunt for spectacular pleasures. The pride of life is the desire of *being*—the yearning to be somebody, or something that ministers to pride of heart. This is the most deep-seated evil of the three, and often the least-suspected.

Here then we have exposed for us the framework on which the world system is built; every item of it totally opposed to the Father, and to that world which is to come, when the present world order is displaced. "The world passeth away," we are told, and so does the lust of it. We are not surprised to hear it. What a mercy that it does, for what greater calamity could there be than that the world and its lusts should be perpetuated for ever! The world will disappear; the Father and His world will abide. We

1 JOHN

shall indeed be foolish if we are filled with love for that which vanishes away instead of love for Him who abides.

How striking the contrast in verse 17! We might have expected the end of the verse to have been, "but the Father abides." That however is so obvious as hardly to need stating. "He that doeth the will of God abideth for ever;" that is the wonderful fact. It is the world that passes away. When believers die we remark that So-and-so has "passed away." The world gets on very well without them and seems perfectly stable. The Apostle John views things from the Divine side, and helps us to do the same. Then we see the world about to pass away, and the doer of the will of God, though he be withdrawn from earthly scenes, is the one who abides for ever. He serves the will of God. The will of God is fixed and abiding. The servant of that will is abiding too.

From verse 18, onwards to verse 27, the "little children," or "babes," are addressed. Without any preface the Apostle plunges into a warning against the anti-christian teachers which were beginning to abound. "Antichrist" is a sinister personage, whose appearance in the last days is predicted. He is not yet come, yet many lesser men, who bear his evil character in greater or smaller degree, have long been on the scene. This shows us that we are in the last time; that is, the epoch immediately preceding the time when evil will come to a head and meet with summary judgment.

Now the antichrists, who had appeared when John wrote, had once taken their place amongst the believers, as verse 19 shows. By this time however they had severed their connection and gone out from their midst By this act they made it manifest that they never really belonged to the family of God—they were not "of us." The true believer is characterized by holding fast the faith. They had forsaken it and gone out from the Christian company, thereby revealing that they had no vital connection with the children of God. The real child of God has an Unction from the Holy One, and this was just what the antichrists had never possessed.

The "Unction" of verse 20 is the same as the "Anointing" of verse 27, and the reference in each case is to the Holy Spirit. Indwelling the children of God, He becomes the Source whence proceeds their spiritual understanding. Now the simplest babe in the Divine family has received the Anointing, and so may be said to "know all things." The word for *know* is the one meaning *inward, conscious knowledge*. If it be a question of acquired knowledge, there are ten thousand details of which at present the babe is ignorant; but the Anointing gives him that inward capacity which brings all things within his reach. He knows all things potentially, though not yet in detail.

Hence even the babe may be said to "know the truth," and he possesses the ability to differentiate between it and what is a lie. He may at the

1 JOHN

moment only know the Gospel in its simplest elements; yet in the Gospel he has truth undiluted—foundation truth out of which all subsequent truth springs—and every lie of the devil can be detected if it be placed by way of contrast against the bright background of the Gospel.

Every lie of the devil is in some way aimed at the truth concerning the Christ of God. He is no mean marksman, and even when he appears to be directing his shots at the outer rings of the target he is calculating on a rebound action which will ultimately land them fairly on to the bullseye. In the Apostle's day he aimed at the centre openly. The antichrists boldly denied that Jesus was the Christ: they denied the Father and the Son. In our day some of them are still doing this. Many more however hardly do this; they introduce teachings of a more subtle kind, not so harmful on the surface but ultimately leading to just the same denials, whereby the centre of the target is hit.

The Antichrist, when he appears, will be the full and perfect denial of the Father and the Son. He will "magnify himself above every god, and shall speak marvellous things against the God of gods." (Dan. xi. 36), and this prediction is amplified in 2 Thessalonians ii. 4. The "many antichrists" who have preceded him all run on similar lines. Their denials relate more particularly to the Son who has been manifested on earth, and they may profess that they have nothing to say as to the Father or against Him. Such a profession is unavailing. To deny the Son is to deny the Father. To confess the Son is to have the Father also. Though distinct in person They are one in the Godhead, and he who has the Anointing (the Holy Spirit), who also is one with Them in the Godhead, knows this right well, and is not likely to be deceived on the point.

The whole drift of the *Old* Testament is that Jesus is the Christ, as is shown by Acts xvii. 2, 3. The truth as to the Father and the Son is disclosed in the *New* Testament. It is not that just then the relationship of the Father and the Son began to be; but that this eternally existing relationship in the Godhead was then for the first time fully disclosed. The fellowship into which we are brought is with the Father and the Son, as we were told in the opening of the epistle; and therefore the denial of this truth must be destructive of our fellowship.

It is worthy of note that error most frequently takes the form of denying truth. Denials are dangerous: they should be issued with care, based upon wide knowledge. Usually more knowledge is needed to deny than to assert. For instance, I may assert that a certain thing is in the Bible, and I need know but one verse in the Book, where it is stated, in order to prove what I say. If I deny that it is in the Bible, I shall need to know the Bible from beginning to end, before I am sure I cannot be successfully contradicted.

From the beginning then Jesus had been manifested as the Christ, and as Son He had revealed the Father. To this knowledge even the babes had come and it was to abide in them, as also it is to abide in us. Jesus is the Christ, that is, the Anointed One: we have received the Anointing so that the truth may abide in us, and then as a consequence, we shall abide in the Son and in the Father.

The Apostle Paul instructs us that we are "in Christ" as the fruit of God's gracious work. The Apostle John instructs us as to the revelation of the Father and the Son, and as to the communion established in connection with that relationship, into which each child of God—even the youngest babe—is brought, so that we may continue "in the Son and in the Father." The Son comes first, since we can only continue in the Father as we continue in Him. To "continue" is to abide in the conscious knowledge and enjoyment of the Son and the Father, possible for us inasmuch as we are born of God and have received the Anointing.

This continuing in the Son and in the Father is eternal life. There was the promise of eternal life even "before the world began," as stated in Titus i. 2. The Lord Jesus spoke of eternal life as, "that they might know Thee the only true God and Jesus Christ, whom Thou hast sent" (John xvii. 3). Verse 25 of our chapter carries this a step further. He who abides in the Son and in the Father is abiding in the life which is eternal. The Eternal Life had been manifested and had been seen; but that had been the privilege of the Apostles only. Now we may possess that life and be in it; and this is for all of us, for these things were written to the babes in the family of God.

All this the Apostle had been saying in order to fortify the babes against the seducing teachers. In verse 27 he reverts again to the Anointing, for it was by the Spirit given to them that all these things were made available for them. What a comfort it is to know that the Anointing abides in us. There is no variation or failure there. Again the Anointing not only abides but teaches of all things. Instruction may reach us from without, but it is by the Holy Spirit that we have the capacity to take it in. We do not need that any man should teach us. This remark is not intended to discredit teachers whom the Lord may have raised up and gifted to do His work, otherwise we might use it to discredit the very epistle we are reading. It is intended to make us realize that even gifted teachers are not absolutely indispensable, but the Anointing is.

The Anointing Himself is truth. This is repeated in slightly different words in chapter v. 6. Christ is the truth as an Object before us. The Spirit is truth, bringing it into our hearts by divine teaching. To these babes John could say, "even as it hath taught you," for the Anointing was already theirs.

Thank God, the Anointing is ours also. Hence for us also the word is, "Ye shall abide in Him." We may be but babes; our knowledge may be small; but may nothing divert us from this life and communion in which we are set. It all centres in Him. Let us abide in Him.

The paragraph especially addressed to the babes, or "little children," which begins at verse 18, ends at verse 27. We have the words "little children" in verse 28, but the word there is not the one meaning "babes," but the word for "children" in a more general sense, the same word as is used in verses 1 and 12, and also in the next chapter, verses 7, 10 and 18.

With verse 28, then, the Apostle resumes his address to the whole family of God, to all those who are His children, irrespective of their spiritual growth or state. He had just assured the babes that the Anointing was theirs, and that consequently they might "abide in Him." Now he turns to the whole family of God and exhorts them to "abide in Him." What is good for the babes is good for all, and this abiding is the way of all spiritual fruitfulness and growth. When we are diverted from Him and our hearts' affections and interests abide in the things of the world, then we are feeble and unfruitful. The Apostle looked on to the manifestation of Christ, when all of us will stand revealed in our true character; and he desired that we all may have confidence in that day and not be ashamed.

He will be manifested, and we too shall be manifested at His coming; and there is evidently the possibility of the believer being put to shame in that solemn hour. It is very likely that in these words the Apostle indicated his own sense of responsibility toward them, and he wished them to do him credit—if we may so put it—in that day. But they also surely indicate that we each may be put to shame on our own account. Let us each so really abide in Him that we may be fruitful now and have confidence then; and so neither we may be put to shame nor those who have laboured over us, whether as evangelists or shepherds.

Chapter 3

Verse 28 of Chapter ii stands as a short paragraph by itself, and the second chapter would more fittingly have ended with it. Verse 29 begins another paragraph which extends to verse 3 of chapter iii. At this point someone might well have desired to enquire—But who are the children of God, and how exactly may they be distinguished from those who are not?

The answer given here is that those who are born of God are the children of God, and that they may be distinguished by the doing of righteousness. The doing is something habitual and characteristic. It is not that they do righteousness off and on, now and again; but that they practise it as the habit of their lives. They are far from being perfect in it— only One was that. Still, as born of God they necessarily have His nature. He is righteous: we know that right well. Then of necessity those born of Him are characterized by righteousness: it could not be otherwise.

1 JOHN

Therefore when we see anyone really practising righteousness we are safe in assuming that such an one is a true child of God.

The practice of righteousness is a very big matter, going far beyond the paying of one-hundred pence in the pound. We have to begin with God and render to Him that which is His due, and then consider rendering to all others that which is their due. No unconverted man can be said to practise righteousness for such have never begun at the beginning. They do not practise what is right in regard to God.

We know God. He is righteous. Here is someone who practises righteousness. We are safe in regarding that one as born of God. He belongs to the Divine family. But then what amazing love this is! And it is bestowed upon us by the Father Himself!

The word that John uses here is "children" rather than "sons." It is a more intimate term. Angelic beings are spoken of in Scripture as "sons of God," and all things are of Him as creatures of His hand; but to be His children we must be "born of Him." This is something more profound as well as more intimate, and we may well marvel at the manner of the Father's love which has bestowed upon us such grace as this. Into this new relation we have been brought by God's own act, wrought within us by the power of the Holy Ghost. It might have pleased Him, while saving us, to have brought us into a relation with Himself far inferior to this. But no; such has been the manner of His love.

But further, just as this act of His in begetting us has *connected* us with Him in this new relationship, so also it has *disconnected* us from the world, and that in a most fundamental way. When Christ was here the world knew and understood neither Him nor His Father. That was because in origin and character He was totally opposite to them. He said to them, "Ye are from beneath; I am from above: ye are of this world; I am not of this world." And again, when they claimed that God was their Father He said, "If God were your Father ye would love Me" (John viii. 23, 42). The trouble with them was that they had not the nature which would enable them to know or understand Christ. Now we, thank God, have the nature which knows Him and loves Him; but for that very reason we also are not known and understood by the world. It must be so in the very nature of things.

The children's place is ours NOW. The love of the Father, which is proper to the relationship, is ours NOW. Yet there is that for which we wait. What we shall be has not yet appeared; but it is going to appear when He appears. When He is manifested in His glory, we shall not only be with Him but like Him, for we are going to see Him as He is. The world will see Him in that day, arrayed in His majesty and His might. They will see Him in His official glories. We shall see Him in His more intimate personal glories. The kings of this world are seen by the populace

1 JOHN

in official trappings on state occasions: but by members of the royal families they are seen in private *as they are*.

Now we must be like Him to see Him as He is. Only as bearing the image of the Heavenly One can we tread the heavenly courts and gaze upon Him in this intimate way. We are actually going to be LIKE HIM. The children of God today are nothing much to look at. They are often a very poor and despised people. In the autumn we may see a number of dull, uninteresting caterpillars crawling upon the nettles. What they are going to be does not yet appear. Wait till next summer, when they will emerge as gorgeous butterflies! Even so we shall emerge in His likeness in the day of His manifestation. We shall be seen then in the estate which is proper to the children of God.

Such then is our hope in Christ. As we contemplate it we must surely be conscious of its elevating and purifying power. If this is our high and holy destiny we cannot possibly be content to accept the defilements of this world, whether they are within or without us. We must purify ourselves with such a hope in view. We might rest content with the defilement if these things were mere notions or theories to us, but not if they are a real hope. Burning as a hope within our hearts, we must purify ourselves, and this process will continue as long as we are here, for the standard of purity is "even as He is pure." We may make an application of Mark ix. 3, which speaks of His raiment as "exceeding white as snow; so as no fuller on earth can white them." No fuller on earth can white us to that standard: we shall only reach it when like Him in glory.

Passing from verse 3 to verse 4 of our chapter, we are conscious of a very abrupt change. We have just been told how we may discern the true children of God by their practice of righteousness. We are now to see the complete contrast that exists between the children of God and the children of the devil. There are two distinct seeds in the earth from a moral and spiritual standpoint, diametrically opposed the one to the other. They cannot be confused or mixed, though an individual may be transferred from one to the other by an act of God, by being begotten of Him.

But first of all the true nature of sin must be exposed. One of the few blemishes of our excellent Authorized Version occurs in verse 4, where the word for lawlessness is translated as "transgression of the law." "Every one that practises sin practises also lawlessness; and sin is lawlessness." (New Trans.). If sin really had been the transgression of the law, then there would have been no sin committed in the world between Adam and Moses, as Romans v. 13, 14 says. But sin is something deeper than that, for lawlessness is the denial and repudiation of all law, and not merely the breaking of it when given. If the planets that encircle our sun were suddenly to repudiate all law, the solar system would be destroyed. Lawlessness amongst the intelligent creatures of God's hand is equally deadly, and destructive of His moral order and government.

1 JOHN

Sin therefore is utterly abhorrent to God, and cannot be permitted to continue for ever. Hence Christ has been manifested—One in whom sin was entirely absent—that He might remove it. Verse 5 only goes as far as this, that He was manifested to remove our sins, the sins of the children of God. Our sins are only a part of the whole, but they are the part in question here, for the point is that the children of God have been brought out of the lawlessness that once marked them and into obedience.

The One in whom is no sin has been manifested, and as a result He has taken away our sins, so that we may abide in Him and sin not. Verse 6 presents the contrast from an abstract point of view and must be read in connection with verse 4, so that "sinneth" has the special force of "practiseth lawlessness." The children of God are characterized by this: they abide in Him who has been manifested to take away our lawlessnesses, consequently as under His control they do not practise lawlessness. On the contrary, the one who does practise lawlessness has not seen nor known this blessed One.

The righteousness of verse 7 is in contrast with the lawlessness of verse 6. We are not to be deceived upon this point for the tree is known by its fruit. We may reason of course from the tree to its fruit, and say that he that is righteous doeth righteousness. Here however we reason from the fruit back to the tree, for John declares that he who practises righteousness is righteous, according to the righteousness of the One by whom he has been begotten. This is apparent if we connect the verse with verse 29 of chapter ii.

On the other hand, he who practises lawlessness is not of God at all. He is of the devil since he is displaying the exact character of the source from whence he springs. From the beginning the devil sins. He was committed to lawlessness from the outset; and the Son of God has been manifested that He might destroy his works. What the devil has done, leading men into lawlessness, the Son of God came to undo.

Verse 9 emphasizes what has just been said in verses 6 and 7, putting it in a still more emphatic way. No one that has been begotten of God practises lawlessness, and this for a very fundamental reason. The Divine seed remains in him, and hence as begotten of God he cannot sin. Here are dogmatic statements of great strength. No qualifying statements are allowed to enter and modify their positive force. Consequently they have presented a great deal of difficulty to a great many minds.

Two things help to clear up these difficulties. The first is a simple understanding of the force of abstract statements. When we speak abstractly we purposely eliminate in our minds and utterances all qualifying considerations, in order that we may more clearly set forth the essential nature of the thing of which we speak. To take the simplest of illustrations: we say, cork floats, alcohol intoxicates, fire burns. Thereby we state the essential character or nature of these things, without committing ourselves to the consideration of what may look like contradictions in practice. The old lady in yonder cottage, for instance, might say that on this cold and windy day she only wished that her fire *did* burn. We all know that this unfortunate abnormality, occurring at certain times, does not alter the truth of the abstract statement—fire burns.

The second thing is that we read this passage in the light of verse 4, which acts as a preface to it. There is no mention of sin from verse 12 of chapter ii. down to verse 4 of chapter iii. But between verse 4 and verse 9 we have the word in different forms about ten times; and at the outset the exact meaning attaching to the word is given to us. The word is defined for us; hence the mistranslation of the definition is particularly unfortunate. The point all through is the practice of righteousness, which expresses itself in obedience, in contrast with the practice of lawlessness, which expresses itself in disobedience.

In verse 9 the one begotten of God is viewed in his abstract character. If viewed apart from his abstract character he is found with sin in him and with sins that have on occasion to be confessed and forgiven, according to earlier statements in this very epistle (i. 8.—ii. 1). Viewed abstractly he does not practise lawlessness, indeed he *cannot* be lawless just because he is begotten of God.

What a wonderful—perfectly wonderful—statement this is! Such is our nature as begotten of God. At present the fact is often obscured by reason of the flesh still being in us, and our giving place to it. But when we are with Him and like Him, seeing Him as He is, the flesh will have been eliminated for ever. There will be no qualification then. The fact will be *absolute*, and not only abstract. When we are glorified with Christ it will not only be that we do not sin but that absolutely we cannot sin. We can no more sin than He.

If any desire further help on this matter they may get it by contrasting our passage with verses 7 and 8 of Romans viii. There the flesh is viewed in its abstract nature, and it is the precise opposite of what we have here. It is essentially lawless, and completely opposed to God and His nature.

In verse 10 another feature that characterizes the true children of God is brought forward. They not only practise righteousness but they also are marked by love. Other scriptures show us that love must characterize our dealings with the world. Here we are told that we display it towards our brethren; that is, all others who with ourselves are begotten of God. So those who have their origin of God and those who have their origin of the devil are sharply differentiated by those two things. The one have righteousness and love: the other have neither.

Love and righteousness are closely connected yet distinct. Love is entirely a matter of nature. "God is love," we read, while we do not read that God is righteousness. Love is what *He is* in Himself. Righteousness expresses *His relation* to all outside Himself. We are begotten of Him: therefore we display His nature on the one hand, and act as He acts on the other.

In the child of God love must necessarily flow out to all others who are His children. It is the love of the Divine family. The instruction that we should love one another was not something new, rather it had been given from the beginning. From the outset love had been enjoined. See how fully the Lord enforced it in John xiii. 34, 35.

In just the same way the hatred which marks the world—those who find their origin in the devil and his lie—is a very ancient thing. It also goes back to the beginning, the outset of the devil's activities amongst men. No sooner was there a man begotten in sin, and in that way morally the seed of the devil, than the feature was seen in him. Cain was that man, and the hatred that belongs to the seed of the devil came out in full force. He slew his brother. There was no love there but hatred. And why? Because there was no righteousness but lawlessness.

So the illustration is complete. Cain the seed of the devil, was a lawless man who as a result hated and slew his brother. As begotten of God we have *love* as our proper nature, and are left here to practise also *righteousness*. Loving our brother and practising righteousness, we make it plainly manifest that we are children of God.

May that fact be more and more plainly manifest in all of us.

Each created thing reproduces itself "after his kind." This fact is intimated ten times over in Genesis i. In our chapter we find that the same law holds good in spiritual things. Those who are "begotten of God" are characterized by love and righteousness. Those who are "children of the devil" are characterized by hatred and lawlessness, just because they are after his kind. The two seeds are clearly manifest in this: and they are wholly opposed the one to the other.

There is nothing surprising therefore if the believer is confronted by the hatred of this world. The "world" here is not the world-system—that cannot hate—but the people who are dominated by the world-system. The child of God does not hate them. How could he, when it is his very nature to love? The world hates him, for the same reason as he who does evil hates the light, for the same reason as Cain hated Abel. It must be confessed as a sad fact that very often we do marvel when we are hated, but it is very foolish of us. It is rather that which we should expect in the very nature of things.

The Christian does not hate, he loves. But in verse 14 it does not say by way of contrast that we love the world. If it did we should be in danger of a collision with verse 15 of the previous chapter. It is true that we should

1 JOHN

be characterized by love towards men generally, as shown in Romans xiii. 8—10, but what is said here is that we love the brethren; that is, all others who have been begotten of God. Love is the very life of the family of God.

How do we pass from death unto life? One answer to that question is given to us by John v. 24. It is by hearing Christ's word and believing on Him that sent Him. In the passage before us the answer evidently is, by being begotten of God—the context makes this clear. Putting the two scriptures together, we get, what we may call, our side of the matter on the one hand, and God's side of the matter on the other. To decide precisely how the two sides, the Divine and the human, combine is of course beyond us. The exact mode in which the Divine and the human are united must ever be beyond us, whether in Christ Himself, or in Holy Scripture, or anywhere else.

But the fact remains that we have passed from death unto life, and the proof of it is that we love the brethren, for love is practically the very life of the family even as it is of the Father Himself. Here the Apostle John corroborates the sweeping statements made about love by the Apostle Paul in the opening verses of 1 Corinthians xiii. He tells us that if any of us do not love our brother we abide in death, no matter what we may seem to be. Paul tells us that, no matter what we may seem to have, if we have not love we are nothing—we simply do not count at all in God's reckoning.

Verse 15 puts the case even more strongly. The fact is that in this matter we cannot be neutral. If we do not love our brother we hate him; and he who hates is potentially a murderer. Cain was an actual murderer, but in Matthew v. 21, 22 the Lord Jesus lays the emphasis not on the act but on the anger and hatred which prompted the act, and so does our scripture here. He who is possessed with a spirit of hatred is possessed with the spirit of murder, and no such person can be possessed of eternal life. As we have seen, eternal life is ours as continuing or abiding "in the Son and in the Father" (ii. 24, 25). Abiding in Him, eternal life abides in us, and the essential nature of that life is love.

But though love is the simple breathing forth of the life that we possess, we none of us have it as though we were each a little self-sufficient fountain of it. The subjective display of love in us can never be disconnected from the objective display of it in God. Hence we ever need to look outside ourselves if we would really perceive love, as love really is in itself. "Hereby we have known love, because He has laid down His life for us" (New Trans.). This was the supreme display of the real thing.

We have to ponder very deeply upon all the virtue and excellence and glory that is compressed into the "HE," and then contemplate the sin and wretchedness and misery that characterized the "us," if we desire in any adequate way to perceive the love. It is very important that we should do so, for only then can we possibly face the obligation which as a consequence is laid upon us. He manifested the love by laying down His life for us. As the fruit thereof we live in His life which is a life of love. A beautiful circuit is completed. He loved. He laid down His life for us. We live of His life. We love.

Now for the obligation. "We ought to lay down our lives for the brethren." Love with us ought to go as far as that. Priscilla and Aquila went as far as that for Paul, since they "laid down their own necks" for his life. Would they have done so for some very lowly and utterly undistinguished saint, we wonder? Very likely they would, for they are placed at the very head of the long list of Christian worthies who are saluted in Romans xvi. At any rate that is the length to which love of a divine sort goes.

If love goes to that length, it obviously will go to any point that falls short of it. There are many ways in which the child of God may lay down his or her life for the brethren which do not involve dying, or even facing actual death. The household of Stephanus, for instance—of whom we read in 1 Corinthians xvi. 15—"addicted themselves to the ministry of the saints," or "devoted themselves to the saints for service." If they did not lay **down**, they at least laid **out** their lives for the brethren. They were serving Christ in His members, and displaying the love in very practical fashion.

The love of God was dwelling in them, and it is to dwell in us, as verse 17 shows. If it does it must necessarily find an outlet towards others who are children of God. God has no needs for us to meet. The cattle upon a thousand hills are His, if He needed them. It is the children of God who are afflicted and who have need in this world. The practical way of showing love to God is to care for His children, as we see them have need. If we have this world's substance, and yet we refuse compassion to our brother in need in order to eat our morsel alone, it is very certain that the love of God is not abiding in us.

At this point we may remark that one word which is very characteristic of this epistle has already been translated by four different words in English:—abide, continue, dwell, remain. The four words used are no doubt quite suitable and appropriate in their place, but it is as well that we should know this fact, for it helps us to preserve in our minds the continuity of the Apostle's thought. Dealing, as he does, with what is fundamental and essential in the Divine life and nature, he necessarily has to speak of things that **abide**.

Verse 18 is not addressed to the babes, but to all the children of God irrespective of their spiritual growth. We all have to remember that love is not mere sentiment, not a matter of endearing words uttered by the tongue. It is a matter of action and of reality. The love that we have perceived, according to verse 16, did not exist in mere words but came out in an act of supreme virtue. The love of God dwelt in Him and He laid down His life for us. If the love of God dwells in us, we shall express our love towards our brother in action and work, rather than in word alone.

If we love thus **IN truth** it will be manifest that we are **OF the truth.** We are, so to speak, begotten of the truth, and hence truth expresses itself in our actions; and not only will other people be assured that we are of the truth, but we shall gain assurance for our own hearts as before God. A man may buy what is stated to be an apple tree of a certain variety, and to assure him he is handed a certificate signed by the horticulturist who raised the tree. That is good, but a mistake is possible. When in due season he picks from that tree apples of just that variety, he has as perfect an assurance as it is possible to have. When the love and the truth of God bear their fruit in the life and in deed, our hearts may well be assured.

"Alas! I am none too positive. This desirable fruit has often been lacking in me." That is what many of us would have to say. That is just what the Apostle anticipates in the next verse. Considering these things, our hearts condemn us. How solemn then is the fact that "God is greater than our heart, and knoweth all things." Solemn, and yet very blessed. For see how this great fact worked in the heart of Simon Peter, as recorded in John xxi. 17.

Peter who had so confidently boasted of his love to the Lord, had signally failed to show it in deed. He had instead thrice denied Him with oaths and curses. The Lord now thrice questions him on the point, letting down a probe into his conscience. Instead of having assurance, Peter's heart condemned him, though he knew that at bottom he did love the Lord. If Peter had some sense of his failure the Lord who knew all things saw the depth of it as Peter did not. And yet by that very fact He also knew that, in spite of the failure, genuine love was there. So Peter said, "Lord, Thou knowest all things; Thou knowest that I love Thee." He was glad to cast himself upon the fact that "God is greater than our hearts, and knoweth all things." So may we be, when in a like situation.

On the other hand there are times—God be thanked—when our heart does not condemn us; times when the life and love and truth of God in our souls has been in vigour, expressing themselves in practice. Then it is that we have confidence and boldness before God. We have liberty in His presence. We can make request of Him with the assurance of being answered, and receiving in due season that which we have desired.

The word "whatsoever" in verse 22 presents us with a blank cheque, leaving us to fill it in. But the "we," who are presented with it, are limited by what follows as well as by what precedes. They are those whose heart does not condemn them, who keep His commandment, and do the things that are pleasing in His sight. Such individuals can be entrusted with the blank cheque. They are Christians who love in action and not merely in word, they are marked by that obedience which is so pleasing to God. He who is characterized by love and obedience will have his thoughts and desires brought into harmony with God's, so that he will ask according to His will, and consequently receive the things that he desires.

We keep His commandments; but there is one commandment which stands out in a very special way, and which divides into two heads—faith and love. We are to believe on the Name of Jesus Christ, God's Son, and then love one another as He commanded His disciples; notably in John xiii. 34, 35, for instance. We recognize here the two things that are so often mentioned together in the epistles. Paul had not been to Colosse, but he gave thanks to God on their behalf having "heard of your faith in Christ Jesus, and of the love which ye have to all the saints" (Colossians i. 4). These two familiar things are proof of true conversion, evidence of a genuine work of God.

What perhaps is not so familiar to us is both of them being treated as a commandment. It is worthy of careful note that of all the apostles John is the one to write a great deal to Christians about the **commandments** given to us. He wrote when the other apostles had gone, and when the tendency to turn grace into license was becoming pronounced; hence this particular emphasis, we believe. They are not commandments of a legal sort, to be carried out in order that we may establish our righteousness in the presence of God, but they are commandments nevertheless. What John declares to us in this epistle is in order that we may be introduced into fellowship, or communion, with God. If we enter into the communion, we soon discover the commandments, and there is nothing incompatible between them. They are wholly in agreement, for only in obedience to the commandments is the communion enjoyed and maintained.

This is emphasized in verse 24, where we find that it is the saint walking in obedience that abides in Him. At the end of the previous chapter the children—all the family of God—were exhorted to abide in Him, for it is the way of proper Christian life and fruitfulness. Here we find that the abiding is contingent upon obedience. The two things go together, acting and reacting upon each other. He who abides obeys, but equally true it is, that he who obeys abides.

But obedience leads to His abiding in us, as well as our abiding in Him. If we abide in Him we necessarily draw from Him all the fresh springs of our spiritual life, and as our practical life is thus drawn from His, it is His life which comes into display in us, and He is seen to be abiding in us. Here, we believe John sets forth in **principle** what Paul states as his own **experience** in Galatians ii. 20. It was as he "lived by the faith of the Son of God" that he could say, "Christ liveth in me."

1 JOHN

By the Spirit, who has been given to us, we know that Christ abides in us. The Spirit is the energy of the new life that we have in Christ, and other scriptures show us that He is "the Spirit of Christ." Other people may know that Christ abides in us by observing something at least of His character being displayed by us. We know it by His Spirit having been given to us.

The Holy Spirit has been alluded to in chapter ii., as the Unction or Anointing, thus giving even to the little children a capacity which enables them to know the truth; but now we are thinking of Him as the Spirit by whom Christ abides in us so that we may manifest Him here. He was also dwelling here in order that He might give utterance to the Word of God. This He did at the beginning through the apostles and prophets whom He inspired. He is the power by whom the Word of God is **given,** as well as the power by whom it is **received.**

This fact furnished the "antichrists" with a point of attack. These earliest "antichrists" were known as **gnostics,** a word which signified, the **knowing ones.** They too would speak by power that was obviously of a spirit. They claimed that they knew, and set up their ideas in opposition to that which had been revealed through the apostles. It was because of this that the Apostle digresses a little from his main theme in the opening verses of chapter iv.

The digression was important in that day, and it is no less important in ours, as we shall see.

CHAPTER 4

AMONGST THE WILES of the devil imitation takes a foremost place. In the Old Testament, for instance, we find that when God wrought powerfully through Moses in the presence of Pharaoh, the Egyptian magicians imitated what was done as far as they could, in order to nullify the impressions made on the mind of the king. Again we find that when the sanctuary had been established in Jerusalem with its ordinances of divine service, Jeroboam easily diverted the ten tribes from it by the simple device of establishing an imitation religion connected with Bethel and Dan. The early verses of chapter iv. indicate that very soon after the faith had been delivered to the saints through the chosen apostles, Satan commenced his deceptive imitations.

The Apostle John, the last of the apostolic band, lived long enough to see that, "many false prophets are gone out into the world." The Apostles whether by word of mouth or in writing, had communicated the inspired Word of God, manifestly moved and borne along by the Holy Spirit. Before long other men rose up. They too spoke as those borne along by the power of a spirit, and consequently their utterances also were inspired.

1 JOHN

But what they said was very different from what the apostles had taught, though they claimed that their teachings were just an improvement and amplification of their words. It all sounded rather attractive, and hence was seductive. But was it true? How could the matter be tested?

We have before remarked upon the way in which all pretension is tested in this epistle, and it is evident that the more we are faced by imitations the more necessary tests become. The question now is a supremely important one. How may we distinguish between "the Spirit of God" and the "spirit of Antichrist;" between "the spirit of truth and the spirit of error"? The spirits have to be tried: but what is the criterion by which we may try them?

In the first place, Christ Himself and the truth concerning Him is the test. Does the spirit confess Jesus Christ, come in flesh? If so, He is of God: if not so, he is not of God. This is a very simple test, and if we meditate thereon a little we shall see that it is a very profound one.

We cannot rightly speak of ourselves as having "**come** in flesh." Long ago the Lord had said, "My Spirit shall not always strive with man, for that he also is flesh" (Gen. vi. 3). We **are** flesh. And even apart from this consideration we should not speak of ourselves as coming in flesh, for we had **no** previous existence, and we had **no** option as to how we came. To be of the human race we **must** be found here in bodies of flesh and blood. Now it was otherwise with Jesus Christ. He had previous existence, and He might have come in other modes. Indeed we believe He did appear in other modes in Old Testament days; as "The Angel of the Lord," for instance.

The truth is that Jesus Christ—that Person, the eternal Son of God—came in flesh, so that He was a true Man amongst us. The antichristian teachers did not confess this. They were not sound as regards His Deity, as verse 22 of chapter ii. showed us. They were not sound as to His Manhood, as this verse shows. History informs us that one of the first heresies to afflict the early church is that which John is meeting here. It is known as Docetism: the teaching being that, as matter was evil, Christ could not have had a true human body of flesh and blood; it must only have **appeared** to be such, being in reality a phantasy. Another form of error as to Christ's humanity also troubled the early church, when men arose who recognized that the seat of sin is found in the spiritual part of man rather than in his material body. These denied the spiritual part of His humanity, while emphasizing the reality of His flesh; but they rose up a century or two later and there is no reference to them here.

Jesus Christ came in flesh of a perfectly holy kind, and hence there was in Him that wonderful manifestation of eternal life, of which the first verse of the epistle speaks. To deny His coming in flesh would mean the denial not only of the possibility of this clear manifestation amongst us, but also of there being in Him the Divine fulness to be manifested. But the

1 JOHN

matter is put here even more strongly. We need not wait for a flat denial; for even non-confession of the truth betrays the spirit of antichrist.

In verse 4 we have the contrast between the saints (the word here is again that for the whole family of God, and not the babes merely) and these false prophets. The one "of God," the other "of the world." In chapter ii. we saw how the Father and the world are wholly in contrast: here we find that there are two families springing respectively from these two sources; and they are as much in contrast as the sources whence they spring. Moreover there is in each an indwelling power, though the mode of indwelling is doubtless different. There is "He that is in you," and "he that is in the world." The children of God have the Anointing of the Spirit of God. As for the world it "lies in the wicked one," (v. 19. New Trans.)—the wicked one is consequently in it.

What an immense encouragement it is to know that the Spirit of God is greater than all the power of the adversary. Herein lies the secret of the marvel that the faith of Christ has survived. We have the best authority for the statement that, "the children of this world are in their generation wiser than the children of light." We are not a wise folk judged by ordinary standards; and that, alas, does not exhaust the story: there has been much unfaithfulness. The greatest and heaviest blows against the faith have been given by those who have professed it. Yet the faith has survived all the blows against it struck **by** unfaithful believers, as well as all the blows aimed by the wicked one **at** faithful believers, by reason of the indwelling Holy Spirit. The point here however is that by Him we overcome the seductive teachings of the antichrists. In chapter ii. we saw that we overcome them by the Word of God abiding in us. But then of course it only does abide in us as we are governed by the Spirit of God. The Spirit and the Word go together.

The first five words of verse 5, "They are of the world," stand in sharp contrast not only with what goes before, "**Ye** are of God," but with what follows in the next verse, "**We** are of God." The "We" here evidently means the Apostles and Prophets of the New Testament, through whom the Word of God has reached us; since the contrast lies in the utterances of the one and of the other. Those who are of the world speak of the world; that is, the world characterizes both their own origin and their utterances. Those who are of God speak as of God.

This fact presents us with another criterion by which we may test teachings that reach us. The false teachings are "of the world," for they proceed from worldly principles and bear a worldly stamp. As a result worldly folk enjoy them, understand them and receive them. They are flattered and confirmed in their worldliness, instead of being disturbed and dislodged from it.

The apostolic teaching was of another order altogether. They spoke of and from God, and the power and authority of their utterances was at once recognized by those who were of God and knew God, whilst those not of God did not hear them.

Here we have a third criterion. Do those who come to us as teachers of truth accept the authority of the Apostles, or do they not? If they do not "hear" them, we may safely assume they are not of God.

This test, you observe, is the same as that stated by the Lord as applying to Himself, in John x. "My sheep hear My voice," whereas those who were not His sheep did not believe. When the Lord was on earth those who were of God were marked by hearing **Him** with the hearing of faith. When the Apostles were here those who were of God were marked by hearing **them** with the hearing of faith. And now that they are gone, we have the Apostolic writings, the inspired Scriptures; and those who are of God are marked by hearing **them** with the hearing of faith. The mode of communication may be different, but what is communicated is in each case of equal authority. An earthly king may speak in person, or he may speak through the lips of his duly accredited ministers, or they may commit the message to writing: there is difference as to the mode, but none as to the authority of the message.

It is well to be quite clear on this point for there are not wanting today those who discredit the Apostles and their inspired writings under the specious cry of "Back to Christ!" They begin by claiming that only His direct utterances must be quoted as having full authority; but they do not long stop there. There is no secure foothold in such a position, for every recorded utterance of His has been reported to us through apostolic or prophetic writings. Hence they soon reach the position of only "hearing" so much of His reported teaching as they wish. They end therefore, by believing in their own powers of discrimination and selection, that is to say, **in themselves.** How exceedingly dull and commonplace is all this high-sounding modern infidelity when subjected to a little analysis.

We may indeed be thankful that God over-ruled the uprising of these early heresies to the giving us of these simple tests, which are still as valid as in the day they were first propounded. Hereby indeed we may know the spirit of truth and the spirit of error. If we are wise, when confronted with doubtful teachings, we will at once apply these tests instead of leaning to our own understanding.

With verse 7 we come back again to the main line of the Apostle's thought. It is necessary now and again to digress in order to guard against evil; but we are mainly concerned with that which is good and of God. Now love is of God, and as children of God our first business is to love one another. Thereby we display the Divine nature, and make it evident that we are born of God and know Him. He who is born of God loves after this divine sort. He who loves after this divine sort is for a certainty born of God. Both statements are true; the only difference being that in the

1 JOHN

former we reason from the source to the outflow, and in the latter back from the outflow to the source.

On the contrary, he who does not love after this divine sort does not know God; for the simple reason that God is love. At the outset of the epistle we heard that God is light. That fact lies at the very basis of all that has come to light in Christ. In our chapter we get twice over the companion fact that God is love. On the surface there may seem to be a clash between the two. Sin was introduced by the devil in order that there might be a clash between light and love in God. The whole of Scripture may be regarded as the working out of the answer of God to the challenge—the story of the wonderful way in which both light and love move harmoniously to the establishment of His glory and our blessing.

God is love. This is indeed a dogmatic statement; and if men seek confirmation of this dogma, in the sinful and disordered world that surrounds them, they will fail to find it. We must look in the right direction. There has been a perfect manifestation of God's love, but only in one direction, as verses 9 and 10 so plainly state. The sending of the Son, and all that was therein involved, completely manifested it. The Son was sent into the world, where we lay under the weight of our sins spiritually dead. He came with the object that we might live through Him, and to this end He made propitiation for our sins. Life was the objective, but if we were to live propitiation was a necessity.

Life and propitiation—two immense things! When just converted the second mainly engages our thoughts. We have been convicted of our sins and know how we needed forgiveness; and how great has been the relief of discovering the propitiation wrought by the Son, who was sent into the world as the gift of God's love. Then presently we begin to realize that propitiation has opened the door to life for us, and that God's purpose is that we should live through His Sent One.

Here the great fact is stated in a general way: we live **through** Him, for He has brought it to pass. In the next chapter we find that the life we have is **in** Him: it is because we are in Him that we have it. In Galatians ii. 20, we find that in a practical way our life is **by** Him, for He is the object of it. In 1 Thessalonians v. 10, we learn that our life is to be **with** Him for ever. We may well be filled with praise and thanksgiving that He came into the world that we might live through Him; especially when we consider what His coming involved both to Him and to the God who sent Him. It was love indeed!

This marvellous love imposes upon us an obligation. The word which indicates obligation is, "ought." It is not that we **may**, or even that we **do**, but that we **ought** to love one another as having received such great love. Let us not shirk the thought of obligation. It is not legal obligation; something which must be, if we are to establish our standing before God.

1 JOHN

It is an obligation based upon grace, and upon the nature which is ours as born of God. As children of God it is our nature to love, but that does not alter the fact that we ought to do it.

We ought to love one another because, as verse 12 says, the love of God is thereby perfected as regards us. The love has flowed forth upon us, and its end is completely, or perfectly, reached when it flows out through each saint to all the rest. Then indeed God dwells or abides in us—for He is love—and He can be seen as reflected in His children. This verse should be compared with John i. 18. Both verses begin in the same way. In the Gospel, God is declared in the Son. In the Epistle, He is to be seen as dwelling in His children. That is clearly inferred in this verse.

If God dwells in us He will certainly be seen in us, but our knowledge of His dwelling is by the Spirit which He has given us. Compare verse 13 with the last verse of the previous chapter. There it was His abiding in us. Here it is our abiding in Him and He in us. But in both cases our knowing these great realities is said to be by the Spirit having been given to us. Being born of Him, we have His nature which is love; but in addition to this He has given us of His Spirit; and by this anointing we know that we abide in Him and He in us.

Moreover the Spirit is the power for testimony, and hence that which is the characteristic testimony of the children of God comes before us in verse 14. The "we" of this verse may again be, primarily at least, the Apostles. They had seen Him as the Saviour of the world in a way that the rest of us have not. But in a secondary sense we can all say it. We know that the Father sent the Son with no smaller design in view than that. It has often been pointed out how the Gospel of John leads our thoughts away from everything that was limited to the Jew to the larger designs connected with the world.

In John i., for instance, He is announced not as the Deliverer of Israel, but as the One who "taketh away the sin of **the world.**" In John iv. the Samaritans hear Him for themselves and discover Him to be "the Christ, the Saviour of **the world.**" Now, what they discovered we all have discovered; and having made the discovery, it has become the theme of our testimony.

How wonderful is the sequence of all that we have been considering. God is love. His love was manifested in the sending of the Son. We live through Him. The Spirit is given to us. We dwell in God. God dwells in us. We love one another. God, who is invisible, is reflected by us before men. We testify to men that the Father has sent the Son as the Saviour of the world. All hinges upon love—Divine love—made known to us and now operative in us.

And the more love is operative in us, the more effective will be our testimony to the Saviour of the world.

1 JOHN

When John wrote his epistle it was a matter of common knowledge that a man—Jesus of Nazareth—had appeared in the world and died on the cross. There was no particular need to testify as to that. The testimony that had to be rendered concerned the truth as to **who** He really was and **what** He came to do. Hence we declare that He was the Son, sent of the Father, with the salvation of the world in view. All those who receive the Christian witness believe on Jesus as the Son of God, and confess Him as such. Now, whoeoever does so confess Him, "God dwelleth in him, and he in God."

We have before remarked how this word—variously translated as, abide, dwell, remain, continue—characterizes the epistle. In chapter ii., from verse 6 onwards, we have four references to our abiding in Him. There is a fifth reference to this in verse 6 of chapter iii., and a sixth in the last verse of that chapter. But in this sixth reference the corresponding fact of His abiding in us is introduced: and we know that He does abide in us by the Spirit who is given to us.

In chapter iv. this second thought of His abiding in us comes into prominence—verses 12, 13, 15, 16. It is not disconnected from our abiding in Him, but evidently it is the truth now emphasized. But the order observed is clear and instructive. We must first be established as to our abiding in Him, and then, as flowing out of that, He abides in us. In these four verses His abiding in us is connected with (1) our loving one another; (2) the gift to us of His Spirit; (3) the confession of Jesus as Son of God; (4) our abiding in love, God Himself being love. He abides in us in order that His character, His love, His truth, may be manifested through us.

We may observe in passing how all this runs parallel with the teaching of the Apostle Paul. We read the opening chapters of the Epistle to the Ephesians, and find, "in Christ" to be that which characterizes everything. We are in Him. Turning to the Epistle to the Colossians, "Christ in you," is the theme. We are in Christ in order that Christ may be in us. There is this difference however: with Paul it is more a question of our standing and our state; with John it is more a question of life and nature.

Another thing worthy of note in our epistle is that when we read of "abiding in Him," the "Him" refers sometimes to Christ and sometimes to God. For instance, in ii. 6, ii. 28, iii. 6, the reference pretty clearly is to Christ. In iii. 24, iv. 13, 15, 16, it is to God. In ii. 24, it is abiding "in the Son and in the Father." In ii. 27, it would be difficult to say which is in view. The whole treatment of this matter here is surely intended to teach us how truly the Son is one with the Father, so that we cannot be in the Son without being in the Father, and we can only be in the Father by being in the Son. For that reason the Son comes first in ii. 24.

But in our verse it is God who is in question. We abide in Him, and He is to abide in us. In the Epistle to the Colossians we are seen as the body of **Christ,** and **He** is to be manifested in us. Here we are the children of **God,** forming His family, deriving from Him our life and nature, hence **He who**

1 JOHN

is Father is to abide in us, and be displayed. God is love, and he who dwells in love is dwelling in God, and the God who is love will be seen as abiding in him.

A wonderful thing this—to be abiding in love! Any kind of vessel, flung into the ocean, and remaining in the ocean, is full of ocean: so the child of God, immersed in the love of God, is filled with it. Depend upon it, this is the thing that is needed if our testimony as to the Father sending the Son is to be effectual. That we testify by word of mouth is necessary and good; but when in addition to this God, in the fulness of His love, is seen as abiding in His children, then the testimony is bound to have effect. A Christian full of the love of God wields a power, which though unconscious is most effective.

In verse 17, "our love" is literally "love with us" as the margin shows. Love has been perfected with us: that is to say, the love of God as regards ourselves has been carried to its full end and climax. And it has been perfected "herein," or "in this," referring no doubt to what has just been stated. He who dwells in God because dwelling in love, and in whom consequently God dwells, must of necessity have boldness in the day of judgment. Indeed he will have boldness as to the day of judgment before it arrives—at the present moment.

It is a most wonderful thing that the love of God should shine upon us at all: but that we should be brought to dwell in it, so that God, who is love, should dwell in us, carries us to the very climax of the story. It means this, that "as He is so are we in this world." This short statement composed of nine monosyllables is very profound in its meaning. It is perfectly true if we read it in connection with our standing and acceptance before God. But that is an application of it, and not the interpretation of it in its context. When the Son became incarnate, there was found **the perfect Man,** who dwelt in God and in whom God dwelt, whether in His sojourn here, or in His present glory above. And now again we have to say, "Which thing is true in Him and in you" (ii. 8). Here are the children of God, and **they** dwell in God and God in them. They are as He is, and they are that now.

Very marvellous, this climax of love! If we apprehend it, though only in a very small degree, we shall certainly have boldness in the day of judgment. Though that day means the terror of the Lord to those that know not God, it can have no terror for the heart of the one who at the present moment and in this world is dwelling in God, and God dwelling in Him.

This is what verse 18 tells us. There is in truth "no fear in love." This perfect love on God's side—for all proceeds from Him—must of necessity cast out fear with all its torment. It is contemplated however, that there may be found some who entertain fears, whether in regard to the day of judgment or anything else. Such are not made perfect in love. On God's side love has been perfected in regard to us: on our side we may not be made perfect in regard to it. We may quite believe that God loves us, and yet not be so consciously abiding in love that fear finds no place in our hearts.

The love of God, known and enjoyed by us, not only casts all fear out of our hearts but also produces love by way of a response to itself. We have no capacity for love of a divine sort apart from the inflow of the love of God. In this matter we are only like tiny cisterns. He is the ever-flowing Fountain. Brought into connection with the Fountain it is possible for love to flow forth from us.

We are warned by John, in verse 20, that we must be practical in this matter. A man may say, "I love God," a general sort of way. He may even say it in a highly elaborated style: he may address God as though in the spirit of worship, expressing beautiful thoughts and using endearing words. Still, it must all be tested; for God is unseen, and to some active minds beautiful thoughts and words come easily and cheaply. What will test the genuineness of such a profession as this?

Why, there is the brother who can be seen! If I myself am born of God, every other who is also born of God is a brother to me. The God whom I cannot see is presented to me in the one who is begotten of Him, this brother whom I can see. That being so, the test propounded by John's question is quite irresistible—"He that loveth not his brother whom he hath seen, how can he love God whom he hath not seen?" The same test is stated in a positive and dogmatic way in the first verse of the next chapter, "Every one that loveth Him that begat loveth him also that is begotten of Him."

This is the third time in this comparatively short epistle that this matter of the believer's attitude towards his brother has come up. In chapter ii., verses 9—11 were occupied with it; in chapter iii., verses 10—23. So it is evidently a matter of very great importance. We deduce this not only from the amount of space that is given to it, but from the fact that again in verse 21 of our chapter it is spoken of as a commandment. That we should love one another as brethren is not only the **message** "that ye heard from the beginning," (iii. 11), but "His [God's] **commandment**, . . . as He [His Son Jesus Christ] gave us **commandment**," (iii. 23). It is the commandment of the Lord Jesus ratified and endorsed by God. A commandment therefore of the utmost solemnity.

The sad history of the church shows how much it has been needed. Far more dishonour to the Name of God, and disaster to the saints, has been brought about by dissension, and even hatred, within the Christian circle than by all the opposition, and even persecution, from the world without. Had love been in active exercise with us, we should not have escaped difficulties but we should have met them in a different spirit, and instead

1 JOHN

of being defeated by them we should have prevailed. Are we not told elsewhere that "Love never faileth"?

CHAPTER 5

WHEN WE CONTEMPLATE the responsibilities which are ours in connection with our brethren, we are always apt, if the flesh prevails with us, to fall back upon Cain's question, asking, "Am I my brother's keeper?" Not exactly his **keeper** perhaps, but we certainly are to be his **helper** in the spirit of love. We are also apt to fall back upon a question similar to the one asked by the lawyer in Luke x. Wishing to justify himself, he asked, "And who is my **neighbour**?" We may ask, "And who is my **brother**?" The answer to this question is given to us in very direct fashion in the opening words of chapter v. "Whosoever believeth that Jesus is the Christ is born of God." So then we have to recognize as our brother every one that believes in Jesus as the Christ, whoever he may be. There can be no picking and choosing.

Many of these believers, who are born of God, may not appeal to us in the slightest degree upon a natural basis. By upbringing and habits we may have very little in common; moreover we may not see eye to eye in many matters connected with the things of God. Now these are just the ones to put us to the test. Are we at liberty to disclaim all interest in them, and pass by on the other side? We are not. If I love the brother who is nice and agreeable to me I am only doing what anybody might do. "If ye love them which love you, what reward have ye? do not even the publicans the same?" (Matt. v. 46). If I love my brother because he is begotten of God, even though he be not nice and agreeable to me, I am displaying the love which is the nature of God Himself. And nothing is greater than that.

Verse 2 seems to sum the matter up in telling us that we know that we love the children of God when we love God and walk in obedience. The **love** of God **moves** us to love His children, and the **commandment** of God **enjoins** us to love His children. Then for a certainty when we **do** love God and keep His commandments, we **do** love His children. Moreover love and obedience go together, as we have previously seen in this epistle, so that it is impossible to love Him without being obedient to Him.

Perhaps we have seen before now a child full of apparent love for the mother—"Oh, mother I do love you!" followed by many hugs and kisses. And yet within five minutes mother has given the child directions which slightly cross its wishes, and what an outburst of anger and disobedience has ensued! The onlookers know how to appraise the "love" that was so loudly protested a few minutes before. It is worth exactly —nothing. Well, let us remember that "this is the love of God, that we keep His commandments."

The child may have found its mother's demand to be grievous in some small degree, as keeping it from its play. If we stray into ways of disobedience we have not even that excuse, for, "His commandments are not grievous." What He enjoins is in exact keeping with love, which is the Divine nature. And we possess that nature, if indeed we are begotten of God.

It would indeed be grievous if we were commanded that which is totally opposed to our natures—just as it would be for a dog to eat hay, or a horse to eat meat. The law of Moses brought "heavy burdens and grievous to be borne," but that was because it was given to men in the flesh. We have received commandments, but we have also received a new nature which delights in the things commanded; and this makes all the difference. John's word here is corroborated by Paul when he says, "God . . . worketh in you both to **will** and to **do** of His good pleasure" (Phil. ii. 13). James also corroborates in speaking of "the perfect law of **liberty**" (Jas. i. 25).

We gladly recognize every true believer as our brother, inasmuch as he is begotten of God. Now, in verse 4 we discover that another feature marks him—he overcomes the world. Moreover, this victory over the world is connected with our faith. "Faith" here, we believe, is not merely that spiritual faculty in us which sees and receives the truth, but also the truth which we receive—the Christian faith. The very essence of that faith is that Jesus is the Son of God, as verse 5 shows us.

Now, see the point at which we have arrived. We have had before us the Christian circle, the family of God, composed of those who have been begotten of Him. God is love, and hence those begotten of Him share His nature, and dwell in His love. Abiding in Him, He abides in them, and they love one another and thus keep His commandments. But also they overcome the world, instead of being overcome by the world. Though they pass through the world, the family of God are **separated** from the world and **superior** to it.

The secret of the overcoming is twofold. First, the Divine work wrought **in** the saints. Second, the faith of Jesus as the Son of God, presented as an Object **to** us, and to be received **by** us in faith.

In verse 14 of chapter ii., we found that overcoming "the wicked one" was possible for those born of God. In verse 9 of chapter iii., that the one born of God "doth not commit sin." Now we have it that the one born of God overcomes the world. So the fact really is that this Divine begetting ensures victory over the devil, the flesh and the world.

But another element enters into the question. Not what is done in us, but what is set before us in the Gospel. Jesus is the Son of God. He was not merely the greatest of the prophets, to bring in an order of things on this earth to which the prophets had looked forward. He was the Son in the bosom of the Father, and He made known **heavenly things lying far outside and above this world.** Let faith once lay hold of **that,** and the world loses its attraction, and can be laid aside as a very little thing. He who is born of

1 JOHN

God, and lives in the faith of Jesus as the Son of God, cannot be captured by the world. He overcomes it.

Of course in all this we are still viewing things abstractly. We are looking at things according to their fundamental nature, and for the moment eliminating from our minds other considerations connected with our present state down here, which would introduce qualifying clauses. It is of great value to view things in this abstract way, for thereby we are instructed in the true nature of things, and see things as God sees them. Moreover we are seeing things as they will be displayed in the day to come when God has finished His work with us, for He "will perform it until the day of Jesus Christ" (Phil. i. 6).

If it be a question of our realized state today, how far are we from what we have been considering! How little do we dwell in love, and consequently dwell in God, and God in us! Let us be honest and acknowledge it; while at the same time we maintain the standard, and judge ourselves by it. This will contribute to our spiritual health and fruitfulness.

The faith that Jesus is the Son of God lies at the very heart of everything Jesus Christ—that historic Personage—has been in this world. No one can successfully deny that fact. But who is He?—that is the question. Our faith—the Christian faith—is that He is the Son of God.

That being settled, another question arises. How, and in what manner, did He come? The answer to this lies in verse 6: He came "by water and blood."

This is another of those brief statements which occur so frequently in John's writings; very simple as to form, though rather obscure as to meaning, and yet yielding to devout meditation a rich harvest of instruction. The reference clearly is to that which happened when one of the Roman soldiers with a spear pierced the side of the dead Christ, as recorded in John xix. 34. No other of the Evangelists records this event, and John lays very special emphasis on it in recording it, saying, "He that saw it bare record, and his record is true: and he knoweth that he saith true, that ye might believe." John wrote his Gospel that we might "believe that Jesus is the Christ, the Son of God" (xx. 31). So evidently this episode of the blood and the water bears witness to the fact that He is both Christ and the Son; and these two points are before us in our passage.

In the first place, the water and the blood witness to His true Manhood. The Son of God has come amongst us in flesh and blood; a real and true Man, and not a phantom, an apparition. This fact was never more clearly established than when, His side being pierced, forthwith there came out blood and water.

Water and blood each have their own significance. The water signifies **cleansing,** and the blood, **expiation.** We may further say therefore that the coming of Jesus Christ was characterized by cleansing and expiation.

1 JOHN

These two things were absolute necessities if men were to be blessed: they must be cleansed from the filth in which they lay, and their sins must be expiated, if they were to be brought to God. The one settles the **moral** question, the other the **judicial;** and both are equally necessary. Neither a moral renovation without a judicial clearance, nor a judicial clearance without a moral renovation, would have met our case.

Here then is another witness to the fact that Jesus is the Son of God. He was indeed a true Man, but no mere man could come in the power of cleansing and expiation. For that He must indeed be the Son, who was the Word of Life.

In the Gospel it is "blood and water," in the Epistle it is "water and blood." The Gospel gives us, what we may call, the historic order: first our need of forgiveness, second our need of cleansing. But in the Epistle the great point is that which is wrought in us, inasmuch as we are born of God; and the holy and blessed characteristics of our new life, a life so essentially holy ("he cannot sin, because he is born of God") that a wonderful cleansing has thereby reached us. Very appropriately therefore does water come first; and it is linked in our thoughts with the death of Christ, for we must never separate in our minds the work wrought in us and the work accomplished for us.

But though the water is mentioned first, it is specially emphasized in verse 6 that His coming was not by water **only,** but by "water and blood." His coming into the world was not only for moral cleansing but also for atonement. This is a peculiarly important word for us today, for one of the pet ideas of modern religious unbelief is that we can discard all idea of atonement while holding that Christ came as a reformer to set a wonderful example to us all, and to cleanse men's morals by the force of it. They hold that He did come by water only. His death, as the supreme example of heroic self-sacrifice, is to exorcise the spirit of selfishness from all our breasts. His death, as an atonement by blood for human guilt, they will not have at any price.

Those who deny the blood, while admitting the water, will have ultimately to reckon with the Spirit of God, whose witness they deny. The Spirit who bears the witness is truth, therefore His witness is truth; and they will be exposed as liars in the day that is coming, if not before. In the Gospel, where the historic fact is related, the Evangelist is content to take the place of bearing witness himself, as we have seen. By the time he wrote the Epistle however men had arisen who were challenging all that was true, so John steps back, as it were, from himself the human channel of witness, to the Spirit who is the Divine and all-important witness-bearer, and points out that He who is truth has spoken. His witness establishes **who** it is that came, and **what** His coming really signified.

The larger part of verse 7 and the opening of verse 8 have to be omitted, as having no real authority in the ancient manuscripts. The Revised, and other later versions show this. It simply is, "For there are three that bear record, the Spirit, and the water, and the blood: and these three agree in one." The Spirit of God is the living active Witness. The water and the blood are silent witnesses, but all three converge on one point. The point on which they converge is found in verses 11 and 12. Verses 9 and 10 are parenthetical.

We are to realize that the witness, whether rendered by the Spirit or the water and the blood, is the witness of GOD; and it demands that it be treated as such. We certainly do receive the witness of men: we are bound to do so practically every day of our lives. We do so in spite of the fact that it is frequently marred by inaccuracy, even when there is no wish to deceive. The witness of God is far greater in its theme and in its character. **The Son** is the theme, and **absolute truth** its character. When the Son was on earth He bore witness **to God.** Now the Spirit is here, and the witness of God is borne **to the Son.** Very remarkable, is it not?

Moreover, he who believes on the Son of God now has the witness in himself, inasmuch as the Spirit who is the Witness has been given to indwell us. We begin, of course, by believing the witness to the Son of God that is borne **to** us, and then "by the Spirit which He hath given us" we have the witness **in** ourselves. No unbeliever can have this witness within, for, believing not the witness which God gave of His Son, he has in effect "made Him [God] a liar." A very terrible thing to do.

The witness of God is concerning His Son: but in particular it is that God has given to us believers eternal life, and that this life is in His Son. The Spirit of God is the living and abiding witness of this. He is spoken of elsewhere by the Apostle Paul as "the Spirit of life in Christ Jesus." To this also the water and the blood bear witness, only in a more negative way. When we see the life of the Son of God poured forth in death on behalf of those whose lives were forfeit, we know it means that there was no life in them. The Apostle Paul again corroborates this in saying, that if He "died for all, then were all dead." That is it: all were dead, and hence the Son of God yielded up His life in death. The water and the blood testify that there is no life in men—the first Adam and his race—but only in the One who yielded up His life and took it again in resurrection.

The witness then is that eternal life is ours. It has been given to us of God; and it is "in His Son." He who has the Son has the life, and he who has not the Son of God has not the life. The issue is perfectly clear. No one could "have" the Son who denied the Son, as these antichristian teachers did. In chapter ii. 22, 23, we saw that no one could "have" the Father who denied the Son. Here we see that they cannot "have" the Son, and consequently cannot have life.

Verse 13 indicates the significance of the word "have" used in this way. The better attested reading here is as the R.V., "These things have I written unto you, that ye may know that ye have eternal life, even unto you that believe on the name of the Son of God." We might have expected John to say, "These things have I written unto you that have the Son;" instead of which he inserted what is involved in having the Son—believing "on the name of the Son of God." It is the believer on the Son of God who has the Son, and has eternal life; and John was led to write these things that we who believe might know it.

No doubt, when John wrote these things he had in view the help and assurance of simple believers who might be overawed and shaken by the pretentious claims of the antichrists. They came with their advanced philosophies and their new light; and the simple believer who pinned his faith to "that which was from the beginning," would be treated by them as quite outside the high intellectual "life" that they enjoyed. After all however it was just the believer on the name of the Son of God, who had the Son, and the life; and the life he had was the eternal life—the only life that counts.

And there the verse stands, with all its happy applications for trembling believers today. The Apostle John has given us the characteristic marks of the life in what he has written; and we may know that the life is ours, not only because of what God has said, but also because the marks of the life come out into display. Happy feelings, which some people think so much about, are **not** the great characteristic of the life: love and righteousness **are**.

Verse 14 seems to present us with an abrupt and complete change of thought. The Apostle picks up a thread, which he pursued for a few verses in chapter iii., dropping it at verse 22. If we compare the two passages we shall find that the change is not so complete as it appears. There the point was that if we love in deed and in truth our hearts will have assurance before God, and hence have boldness in prayer. Here the sequence of thought seems similar. As the fruit of what John has written to us we have happy knowledge—conscious knowledge—that we have eternal life. Hence we have confidence (or, boldness) in Him, to the effect that "if we ask anything according to His will, He heareth us." And if He hear us, our petitions are certain to be granted.

As having the life, His will becomes our will. How simply and happily then can we ask according to His will. This is the normal thing for the believer, resulting in answered prayer. Alas, that so often our actual experience should be the thing that is abnormal—because we walk according to the flesh—rather than normal.

Verse 16 assumes that we are not selfish in our prayers but concerned about others. We pray in an intercessory way for our brethren. The boldness that we have before God extends to this, and is not confined to merely personal matters. But it also makes it plain that, though we have boldness, there are certain things which we may not and cannot request. The government of God in regard to His children is a very real thing and

1 JOHN

cannot be waived at our request. The death spoken of here is the death of the body, such as we see, for instance, in the case of Ananias and Sapphira.

We may ask life—and doubtless anything short of that also—for any whose sin is not unto death; and all unrighteousness is sin, so that we have a very large field that may be covered. But if the sin is unto death our lips are sealed. It is possible that in writing this the Apostle had some definite sin in his mind, connected with the antichristian deceptions which were abroad, but he does not specify; so we are left to take heed of the broad principle. We know that hypocrisy and false pretence was the sin unto death in the case of Ananias, and gross disorder and irreverence at the Lord's Supper was the sin unto death among the Corinthians.

In verses 16 and 17 we have things looked at practically as they exist amongst the saints, for the one who may sin a sin unto death is a "brother." In verse 18 we come back to the abstract view of things. The one begotten of God does not sin, if we consider him according to his essential nature. This we have seen earlier in the epistle. Moreover, that being so, such are enabled to keep themselves so that the wicked one does not touch them. This last remark rather supports the thought that the sin unto death, which John has in view, is something connected with the wiles of the devil through antichristian teaching. Viewed abstractly, the one born of God is proof against the wicked one. Viewed practically, since the flesh is still in believers though they have been born of God, the brother may be seduced by the wicked one and bring himself under the discipline of God, even unto death.

We have now reached the closing words of the Epistle and things are summed up for us in a very remarkable way. Abiding in that which was from the beginning, there are certain things that we know. We know the true nature of those who are born of God, according to verse 18. But then we know that we—who are of the true family of God—are of God; and thereby wholly differentiated from the world, which lies in "wickedness," or, "the wicked one." There was no such clear differentiation before the time of Christ. Then the line was rather drawn between Israel as a nation owned of God, and the Gentiles not owned of God, though doubtless faith could always discern that not all Israel were the true Israel of God.

Now the line is drawn altogether apart from national considerations. It is simply a question of who are born of God and who are not, no matter what nation they may have belonged to. The family of God are wholly and fundamentally separated from the world.

Further we know what has brought all this to pass. The Son of God is come. That Person has arrived on the scene, and the life has been manifested in Him. Here we are brought back to the point at which the Epistle started, only with an added fact brought to light. At the outset our thoughts had to be concentrated on what was brought to light by His coming. But what has been subsequently unfolded in the Epistle has

1 JOHN

brought us to this, that as the fruit of His coming we have been given an understanding, so that we may know and appreciate and respond to the One who has been revealed. It is easy to see that if the understanding be lacking the most perfect revelation before us would be in vain.

Thank God, the understanding is ours. We have been begotten of God, and He has given us of His Spirit, as the Epistle has shown us, and we could never have been possessed of that Anointing if the Son of God had not come. Now we know "Him that is true," for the Father has been made known in the Son. Yet the next words tell us that we are "in Him that is true, even in His Son Jesus Christ." So, "Him that is true," is an expression that covers both the Son and the Father, and we pass almost insensibly from the One to the Other. Another witness to the fact that the Son and the Father are one in Essence, though distinct in Person.

Then, having thus brought us to "His Son Jesus Christ," John says very pointedly, "This [or, He] is the true God, and eternal life." No stronger affirmation of His Deity could we have. Also He is the eternal life, and, as we have seen, the Source of it for us.

What a marvellous summary of the Epistle is this brief verse! The life has been manifested, and Him that is true made known in the coming of the Son of God. As the fruit of His coming we have received an understanding, so that we may be able to appreciate and receive all that has come to light. But then not only is "Him that is true" revealed, and we rendered capable of knowing Him, but we are in Him, by being in the One who has revealed Him. Apart from this we might have been merely wondering onlookers, without vital connection with God. But, thank God, that vital connection exists. And the One, in whom we are, is the true God and eternal life.

How apposite then the closing words, "Children [the word meaning all the family of God] keep yourselves from idols." An idol is anything which usurps in our hearts that supreme place which belongs to God alone. If we live in the reality and power of verse 20, we shall certainly say like Ephraim, "What have I to do any more with idols?" (Hosea xiv. 8).

Once let the Son of God, and all that He has done and brought, fill our hearts, and the idols, that charmed us once, will charm us no more.

2 JOHN

BEFORE WE COME to the details of this short Epistle we may point out several features of a more general nature.

The Author's name is not mentioned. This feature characterizes also the first and third Epistles, yet in each case there can be no doubt that John is the writer. The style is identical, agreeing also with the Gospel that bears his name. It is quite remarkable that not once does John mention his own name in his writings, save in the Revelation. Yet there is something very fitting in this. His Gospel and Epistles deal with such a transcendent theme—God revealed in One, who was no less than "the Son of the Father"—that the human writer is not noticed in the glory of that light.

This second Epistle, as also the third, comes in as a kind of appendix or postscript to the first Epistle. It was evidently in the first place a communication of a private nature to a certain Christian lady and her family, but has been brought by God into permanency in the pages of Scripture, because it supplies very needful instruction not found elsewhere. It is the only Epistle addressed to a woman, and the instruction gains force from that fact.

In verses 1 and 2 the greatest possible emphasis is laid upon **truth.** The Epistle itself gives directions as to the action necessary for the defence of the truth; and the first thing we find is that all Christian relationships and affections are founded upon truth, and are to be governed by it. The love that is proper to Christians is **"in the truth;"** since it springs forth as the fruit of our having been begotten of God, as the first Epistle has shown us. Being begotten of God we are "in Him that is true," and love according to truth springs up within our hearts. Therefore the love, that John bore toward the elect lady and her children, found a place also in the hearts of all those who had been brought to a knowledge of the truth, as begotten of God.

But that love not only found its origin in the knowledge of the truth, it also found expression **" for the truth's sake."** The truth is of surpassing importance—since the world is filled with error and delusion—and we should be ready to suffer for the sake of it. Many have suffered, even to a martyr's death. Here, however, it is not a question of **suffering** for the sake of the truth, but **loving** for the sake of the truth. That bears in two directions: the love must be sincere and without the partiality which is so natural to the flesh; and also it must be intolerant of evil, since truth and error can never agree together. It is the **second** of these two considerations which is stated in this Epistle. The third Epistle deals with the **first.**

The two statements as to the truth, which verse 2 contains, are very pregnant with meaning. The truth (1) "dwelleth in us." and (2) "shall be with us for ever." We connect the two thoughts with two sayings: that of the first Epistle, "the Spirit is truth," and the saying of our Lord in the Gospel, "I am the truth."

2 JOHN

The truth "dwelleth in us," inasmuch as the Spirit indwells us, and He is truth. He is not mentioned in this short Epistle, but He is implied in these words. He is truth **subjectively,** within us; for He does not speak "of" or "from" Himself, but He glorifies Christ who is the truth, and taking of His things He ministers them to us. Hence every Spirit-indwelt believer has truth **dwelling in him**—an immense privilege and preservative in a world of error.

This fact leads us to the conclusion that the detection and refusal of evil doctrine is not for the believer primarily a matter of intellect or brain-power. It is primarily a matter of what we may call spiritual instinct. Mere intellect again and again leads even true believers astray. All the errors, that have afflicted the church during her nineteen centuries of history, have been in the first place launched by men of intellectual prowess. And on the other hand, very unlettered believers, when false teaching has been pressed upon them, have been heard to say, "Well, I can't help feeling it is all wrong, though I don't understand their ideas and cannot criticize them." This fact justifies the Apostle in writing the instructions of this Epistle to even a lady and her children.

It is also a fact, thank God, that the truth "shall be **with us for ever,**" inasmuch as Christ is the truth **objectively,** and we are never to be separated from Him. Truth as well as grace fully arrived on the scene when the Lord Jesus came. In Him all that God is stands fully disclosed. In Him light and truth shine about everything, and the darkness, the error, the unrealities disappear. As we turn our eyes upon Jesus we contemplate the One in whom truth is personified. The truth is "with us," to be considered and adoringly admired, and by which, as a standard, everything may be tested.

This is of deep importance to us at the present time, while Satan the deceiver is still at large. Yet we shall **ever** need the truth personified before our eyes, and He is to be with us for ever. Let us not forget for present emergencies that He as the truth is the test for everything that may be presented to us in the way of doctrine, and that the Spirit who indwells us, forming our instincts, is truth likewise.

Since Christ is the truth objectively before our eyes all the error of which Satan is the originator is aimed, whether directly or indirectly, at Him. Not without reason therefore is His glory so fully unfolded in verse 3. Jesus is stated to be not only Lord and Christ but also "the Son of the Father." This is the only place where this exact expression occurs, though He is frequently called the Son of God. The Father of our Lord Jesus Christ has many families both in heaven and earth, as we are told in Ephesians iii. 14, 15, yet He is the only One who has the supreme place of **the** Son of the Father—the supreme Object of His love. That is **who He is:** a little later in the Epistle we shall see **what He became.**

2 JOHN

The Apostle had much joy because he had found some of the children of the elect lady walking in truth. They were not merely confessing the truth and holding it, but they were walking in it—that is, their ways and activities were governed by it. The Father Himself has commanded this: His truth has reached us in order that we may be controlled by it. Nothing less than this is pleasing to Him. And now, turning to the elect lady herself, the Apostle beseeches her to proceed on just those lines; having in view the instruction he is about to give her as to those who propagate not truth but error.

First of all however, in verse 5, he enforces the great commandment that we love one another—the commandment with which we are already very familiar, as having read the first Epistle. He repeats here that this is not a new commandment, something only now issued. It is the commandment which we have had from the beginning, from the very first moment that the true light began to shine in Christ. The love of God was manifested in Christ, and it demanded and produced love in those who were the recipients of it.

But then love manifests itself practically in obedience to the will of God. There may be love on the lips without obedience in the life; but love in the heart must produce obedience in the life. And in particular the commandment of love is that we should walk, and continue to walk, in all that which from the outset has been made known to us in Christ. The danger now threatening was that under various specious pretexts some should be moved away to follow and obey ideas which were foreign to that which had been from the beginning.

In verse 7 John speaks very plainly. Many had "entered" or "gone out" into the world who were nothing but deceivers. He does not say you notice, "gone out into the church," but "into the world." He alludes apparently to the same kind of people as those that he warned us against in chapter ii. of his first Epistle. Those, he said, "went out from us," giving up all pretence of being connected with the church. They turned their backs, it appears, upon the church of God, and they went forth into the world as missionaries of greater "light" than any which the church had possessed. Influenced by the powers of darkness they became heralds of notions which were a skilful blend of heathen philosophies and Christian terms. They still talked about Christ, but their "Christ" was not the Christ of God.

All through the nineteen centuries notions of this deadly kind have been advanced, but the earliest form of them was that which is alluded to here—the denial of Jesus Christ come in flesh. This particular point is mentioned also in the opening of chapter iv. of the first Epistle. When considering that passage we saw that the denial covers both His Deity and His Manhood; for the fact that He came "in flesh" shows that He was indeed a Man, and the fact that He existed so as to "come" in that way shows

2 JOHN

that He was more than Man, even God. The non-confession of the truth as to Christ stamped these propagandists as deceivers and antichrists.

Verse 8 contains a salutary word for all who labour in the word and doctrine. If saints to whom they minister are turned aside from the truth they cannot expect a full reward in the coming day. Their reward is bound up with the faithfulness and prosperity of the saints. In this note of warning sounded by John there is something which reminds us of the notable words uttered by Paul, as recorded in Acts xx. 31.

Verse 8, however, is parenthetical, and verse 9 picks up the thread from verse 7. These anti-christian deceivers were not abiding in the doctrine of Christ. They were transgressing or going forward, as they thought, to newer and better things. We have this kind of thing quite full-blown today in what is known as "Modernism." The Modernist believes that religion or theology is a human science, and that like all sciences it must not stand still but advance with the times and with the increase of all human knowledge. Hence he goes forward with much confidence to what he conceives to be greater light. No doctrine is sacred to the out-and-out Modernist. There is hardly one doctrine of the Scripture which he leaves intact.

And there are forms of modernism which would hardly be classified as "Modernist" in the religious world. They are not the less mischievous on that account. They may as yet only "transgress" or "go forward" in certain particulars. But it is the whole idea of "going forward" that is wrong. If there may be development as to **some** details of the faith, why not as to **all**?

There should indeed be growth in our apprehension of the truth. That is another thing entirely, and it is quite clearly stated and enforced in chapter ii. of the first Epistle. The babe should become the young man, and the young man in due time become the father. That as increasing apprehension of that which has been made known from the beginning. The faith of Christ is divine. It has come from God, and consequently cannot be improved upon or developed. Let us lay hold upon that fact very firmly.

It is possible of course to hold that the truth has come from God, and yet not to abide in the doctrine of Christ, because simple faith becomes swamped in intellectualism and reasoning. This danger specially threatens those who think more of **talking of** truth than **walking in** truth. It may in effect lead to just the same departure from the doctrine of Christ.

Now such departure means that the transgressor has not God. He has neither the Father nor the Son, for it is impossible to have One without the Other. He who abides in the doctrine—that is, in the truth—has Both.

In order that there may be obedience to the commandment, "That, as ye have heard from the beginning, ye should walk in it," (ver. 6), there must be a clear-cut refusal of all that denies or does not confess the truth

2 JOHN

as to Christ; and verse 10 makes this very plain. The refusal of evil and error is not inconsistent with love of a Divine sort, it is rather an expression of it. Even amongst men if the parent has genuine love for the child, that love will be as much expressed in the refusal of all that would imperil it as in feeding it with all that is good.

So even this lady and her children were to have nothing to do with the man who came to the house not bringing the true doctrine of Christ. They were not to give him entrance into the house, not even to bid him God speed. They were to meet him with the completest possible refusal. It is very striking that action such as this should be incumbent upon a lady and her children. Such as these would ordinarily be esteemed as having less responsibility in such matters than any other saints. The inference then is obvious: it is a responsibility then which rests upon **all of us as individuals,** and which we cannot shelve with impunity.

We are not asked to judge as to his spiritual state, we have only to judge as to the doctrine he brings. The point is not as to whether or not he is well instructed as to details, dispensational, prophetic, and the like. It is just this: does he, or does he not, bring the doctrine of Christ. A Christian woman or her children are assumed to be capable of discerning this, and acting rightly.

Notice too that the man who comes is a **propagandist,** a travelling preacher. He comes to your door as the herald of something better than that which you have known. The case contemplated is not that of a believer of weak understanding, who gets entangled in what is false as to Christ. All too often in these days, when a multiplicity of errors are propagated, true saints get confused and waver and fall under the influence of what is false. Such should be treated differently, as indicated in Galatians vi. 1, Jude 22, 23, and elsewhere.

When the man who preaches a false Christ comes to your door the refusal of him and his doctrine cannot be too complete. Even to bid him God speed is to partake of his evil. We are not to lend ourselves to the smallest or slightest association with such a thing.

This should teach us how exceedingly precious and valuable a thing is the doctrine of Christ! It is the corner stone of our most holy faith, and if that be shaken all will collapse in ruin. It must be guarded at all cost.

Verse 12 also indicates this. There were many other things that the Apostle had to say to the elect lady and her children—things, no doubt, of spiritual importance. He looked forward a little and saw a time not far distant when he would be able to convey these things by word of mouth—a much more joyful method. This matter about which he wrote however brooked no delay. Paper and ink might be a poorer medium, but it was an urgent matter to put them on their guard in defence of the truth.

2 JOHN

Lastly notice that though John does not mention his name he speaks of himself as "the elder." The Epistle furnishes us with an example of the kind of service which was rendered by the elders, or presbyters, of Biblical days. They exercised an oversight of a spiritual sort. They gave guidance, in the way of practical directions, to those who were less instructed in the ways of the Lord. They shepherded the flock of God.

The Apostle John by this brief yet inspired letter was shepherding the souls of the elect lady and her children, and guarding them from the threatened ravages of some of Satan's wolves.

3 JOHN

IN CERTAIN FEATURES the third Epistle of John is very like his second, yet in its main theme it is the converse, and at the same time the complement, of the second, as we shall see.

Like the second it is an epistle of a private nature, yet containing in its brief verses instruction of such an important kind that the Spirit of God has seen it needful to give it a permanent niche in the inspired Word. We cannot say with any certainty whether Gaius, to whom it was written, is to be identified with one of the others bearing that name, of whom we read. The Gaius of Acts xix. 29, was a man of Macedonia. The Gaius of Acts xx. 4, was "of Derbe," a city in Asia Minor. The Gaius of 1 Corinthians i. 14, was a Corinthian, and he was almost certainly the Gaius of Romans xvi. 23, who was host to the Apostle Paul. This Gaius may very well have lived on to old age, and still exercised his hospitality when John wrote. If so, he presents us with a very delightful picture of one who did not grow weary in well-doing.

Be that as it may, the Gaius of our Epistle is presented to us as a saint characterized by spiritual prosperity. John bears witness, in the second verse, to the fact that his soul prospered to such an extent that he could only desire that his bodily health might equal the health of his soul. There are seasons when we express our wishes and desires the one for the other. How often are we able truthfully to indulge in a wish like that? Not often, we fear! With the most of us the health of the body exceeds the health of the soul. We meet one another and enquire, How are you? Taking it for granted that the enquiry refers to the body, we say cheerfully (as a rule) Quite well, thank you. If the enquiry were, How is it with your soul?— what should we say?

The assurance that John had as to the spiritual prosperity of Gaius was not gained by personal contact, for he was at a distance and communicating by letter. It was gained through testimony borne by others. Certain brethren had arrived in John's locality and they spoke of him; and what they had to say bore witness to the fact that the truth was dwelling in him and that it found expression in his life, for he walked in truth. That which is **in** us comes **out** in our activities.

The Lord Himself laid down as a principle that, "out of the abundance of the heart the mouth speaketh" (Matt. xii. 34). Here we find another principle of life which is a companion to it—**that which dwells in us characterizes our walk.** If Satan's lie dwells in us we are bound to walk in falsity and crookedness in regard to God. When truth is in us by the Spirit of God (as we saw when considering verse 2 of the second Epistle) we shall walk in the truth, even though we walk in the midst of this crooked world. The walk of a Christian is to be light in the midst of darkness, and truth in the midst of error.

3 JOHN

In the second Epistle John tells us that he rejoiced **greatly** in finding the children of the elect lady walking in truth. Here he goes even a step further, in saying that **no greater** joy was his than this. Gaius appears to come under the term, "my children." If this means that he was a convert of John, it would mean that he was not one of the others named Gaius, who are mentioned in Scripture. However John probably uses the term in a pastoral way here, as he evidently does in his first Epistle (ii. 1; iii. 7; etc.). He had a fatherly interest in all the saints who came within the sphere of his ministry. Peter warns the elders not to act as "**lords** over God's heritage." By his example John shows us that the true attitude for an elder is that of a **father** filled with love and solicitude for his children. It would have been well if all who have exercised rule amongst the saints had followed his steps.

In verses 5, 6 and 7 we discover what it was that moved the Apostle to write in this strain. The brethren who had come and testified of the truth that was in Gaius, were evidently these humble labourers in the Lord's service, to whom he had shown hospitality and whom he had helped forward on their journey. The love he had shown them and the service which he had rendered to them, just because they served the Lord and went forth in His Name, was a clear proof of the truth that was in him: and the more so because they were strangers to him.

The end of verse 5 might lead us to suppose that there were two classes in question: (1) the brethren, and (2) strangers. The better attested reading however appears to be, "the brethren, and that strangers." It was right to serve the brethren who were well known to him; but to serve brethren who were complete strangers just because they served the common Master, was indeed to act "faithfully." The truth is that the saints are one, and that the Name of the Lord Jesus binds all who serve in that Name together, and that love is the cementing power in the Christian circle. To this truth Gaius was faithful. It was in him, and he walked in it.

Not only did these brethren go forth for the sake of the Name, but they took also the place of dependence upon their Master. They did not take anything of the Gentiles, or nations; though they moved among the nations and preached the Word in their hearing. They made it very plain that they were not seeking any gain of a material sort for themselves, but seeking to give to their hearers that which would be gain of a spiritual sort. In this they were followers of the Apostle Paul, who himself was a follower of the Lord, who said, "It is more blessed to give than to receive" (Acts xx. 33—35).

These were the people whom Gaius had received into his house, showing them loving hospitality, although on arrival, they were strangers to him. Not only did he entertain them but he set them forward on their journey "after a godly sort," or "worthily of God." That being so, he must have treated them with no mean kindness! Had he set them forward in a way that was worthy of a prince, it would have been something great; but he did it in a way that was worthy of God! He evidently viewed them in the true light. However insignificant in themselves, they were servants of Christ, identified with the Name that is above every name. As being such, Gaius received them. He saw them, not in the light of his own personal likes or dislikes, but in the light of what they were as the little servants of an illustrious Master; and so Gaius walked in the truth and proved that the truth was in him.

The example of Gaius is placed permanently before us in the Scriptures not merely that we may admire it, but that we may follow it. Moreover, it is not merely something which we **may** do; something which is within our rights, and permissible, and which no Diotrephes can rightly object to our doing. It is something which we **must** do if we would be walking in the truth. Note that in verse 8 the word "ought" is used. It is not, "We therefore may receive such," but, "We therefore OUGHT to receive such." Now "ought" is a word which expresses obligation and not what is optional. It is "such" that we ought to receive; that is, those who truly come in His Name. If we do not receive SUCH, we are not walking in the truth.

On the other hand by receiving such we become "fellow-helpers to the truth." This is a very encouraging statement, especially to those of us who may not be possessed of any shining gift. There is the ever-present danger for the man of one talent that he should hide it in the earth and do nothing. Now though we may not have the gift that would qualify us to be preachers of the truth, or even to be active propagators of the truth in other and lesser ways, we may take our share and become helpers with the truth by identifying ourselves with those who do more actively labour, and helping them by caring for their needs.

It is frequently the case that our true convictions and attitude are most effectually seen **in quite small details.** In the days of long ago Rahab showed that she really did believe in the God of Israel and cast in her lot with Him by receiving the spies in peace. At the judgment of the living nations, which is yet to come, according to Matthew xxv., those who are the sheep and blessed of God, reveal the state of their hearts by receiving the messengers of the Son of Man, whom He owns as His brethren. And these today, who go forth with the truth, are to be received, if we too are of the truth and fellow-workers with it.

This is the converse of the instruction contained in the second Epistle. There, he who does not bring the truth is to be refused access to the believer's house, and there is to be not the least identification with him. Here the brother, even though a stranger, who is diligently carrying the truth for the sake of the Name, is to be received, and we are glad to be identified with him because of the truth he brings. In either case the truth is the test, and all merely personal considerations are ruled out of the question.

In verses 9 and 10 we find an exposure of the sad state of things in a certain church, which made it needful for the Apostle to write in this way. Nothing is said as to the locality of "the church" in question. It was elsewhere probably than where Gaius lived. Diotrephes was a prominent man in it, and very possibly Demetrius, mentioned in verse 12, was in it too. Diotrephes would by no means receive these brethren. He took a very strong line against them, forbidding others to receive them and even casting out of the church. Also he would receive no directions from the Apostle, seeking to overthrow the apostolic authority by malicious talk.

It would seem to have been a case of the local elder or bishop lording it over God's heritage, the assembly, just as is forbidden in Peter's Epistle; and he who would do a thing of that kind must of necessity take up an insubordinate position as regards apostolic authority. The one who would fly in the face of what Peter had written years before, would not now be likely to bow to what is written by John.

Why did Diotrephes act in this way? The excuse very probably was that these travelling brethren were unauthorized men, and that he was standing for what was orderly and official. But the underlying motive of his attitude and action is unmasked in the words, "who loveth to have the preeminence." The work of these men was in some way a challenge to the place that Diotrephes held, and loved to hold. Hence he could not tolerate them.

Again and again the Spirit of God has worked outside of officialism, and we do well to note it. It was so with the prophets that God raised up in the midst of Israel. It was so in supreme measure in the case of our Lord Himself. He was regarded as an unofficial upstart by the religious leaders of His day, and His authority was strongly challenged (see Matt. xxi. 23). Paul too, entered upon his career in an unofficial way, as Galatians i. 15-23 bears witness. The fact is that the Lord raises up servants according to His sovereign pleasure, and asks neither permission nor counsel of any man. Every distinct awakening or revival in these later days has been marked by this same feature. Officialism has not helped, even if it has not opposed.

It is worthy of remark that, whether in this epistle or the previous one, the only test proposed in regard to professed servants of the Lord is that of the truth. Did they bring it or did they not? If the Apostles had undertaken to authorize and send forth preachers of the Word, or if they had appointed a committee to do it, the presence or absence of the authorization would have been the test. We live in a day in which human authorization of that kind abounds, and the results of it are obvious. Men abound who have the authorization right enough, but they do **not** bring

3 JOHN

the truth. They use the authorization to accredit the **error** they propagate, which is a fearful evil.

It is quite a common idea that **the man should accredit the message**—So-and-so is duly ordained, so what he says must be right. Or it may take this form: So-and-so is such a good man, so earnest, so gifted, so spiritual, therefore he cannot be wrong. The whole principle however, is a false one. The true principle is just the reverse. **The message accredits the man.** The Lord's words in Luke ix. 49, 50, virtually enunciate this principle; and it is clearly stamped on both 2 John and 3 John. The man is not the test of the truth: the truth is the test of the man. How important then that we should be so established in the truth that we can use it as a test.

The action of Diotrephes did not lack anything as regards vigour. He did not receive these stranger brethren, and hindered others doing so. He would not have them in the assembly. And further he would not receive the Apostle, as regards his authority at least, and spoke against him with malice. Very possibly he regarded his vigour as a proof of his being faithful to what was orderly and dignified. The root from which it sprang, however was the old Pharisaic one of the love of place and pre-eminence. It was Gaius who was faithful and not he (see verse 5).

The casting of these brethren out of the church may not have been full excommunication, as it was his personal doing and not assembly action; but evidently he would allow them no place or liberty in the assembly. In the same way "receiveth us not" hardly means that he did not receive John to break bread, for John was at a distance. It does mean that he would not receive his authority as an Apostle, and did his best by malicious talk to undermine his authority in the minds of others.

Now all this was but "evil," as verse 11 indicates; and we are not to follow it. We solemnly believe that this "prating against" the servants of the Lord "with malicious words" is a very sore evil today. To blacken a man's character because you cannot refute his arguments is a well-known controversial trick, but it is doubly despicable when indulged in amongst those who have to contend as to the truth. Let us eschew it as an evil, and follow what is good. In the latter part of verse 11 we have another instance of how John reasons in the abstract, as to good and evil, but we do well to allow its full force in our consciences. How do we stand as to it? Are we of God, or have we not seen Him?

Demetrius is brought before us as an example we may well follow. All knew that he was a follower of the good, and John himself could bear witness to that effect. But above all this the truth itself bore witness to him. The truth presents us with an unerring standard of what is good, and if the course of Demetrius were examined in the light of the truth, the truth itself gave a good report in his favour. We shall all of us be ultimately examined in the light of the truth when we stand before the judgment seat of Christ What is our report going to be? Good or bad?

3 JOHN

Our little Epistle closes in very similar fashion to the second. As with the elect lady, so with Gaius, the face to face conversation was far better than the letter. But as it was an urgent thing, brooking no delay, to fortify the one against the subtle approaches of evil, so it was urgent to confirm the other in his reception and support of those who were good and true, even when others refused them.

In the closing sentences the Apostle speaks of the brethren who were with him and those with Gaius as "the friends." This carries our minds back to chapter xv. of his Gospel, where we find the Lord saying, "Ye are My friends, if ye do whatsoever I command you;" and again, "I have called you friends; for all things that I have heard of My Father I have made known unto you." The obedient saint is the one to be brought into this wonderful **intimacy,** and therefore to be acknowledged as a **friend** of Christ.

In contrast with the wilful and disobedient Diotrephes there were those who were indeed the friends of Christ, and such were acknowledged as friends by the Apostle and all those who walked in truth.

We each may well ask ourselves in closing this question—If the Apostle John were amongst us today, would he acknowledge me as a FRIEND?

JUDE

THE EPISTLE OF JUDE bears a very strong resemblance to 2 Peter ii. 1—iii. 14, which lies upon the surface and must be apparent to every reader. Both refer to very evil men, who come in amongst the saints, and both unmask their true character. Both quote Old Testament examples by way of illustration and warning; and amongst the examples both mention the angels that sinned, and Sodom and Gomorrah. Both remind us that even holy angels would not assume authority as these men do. Both quote the case of Balaam. Both use a succession of very vigorous and graphic similes to impress us with their terrible evil and sin. And both turn to account what they have to say about the evil, by using it to urge the saints on to that which is good.

Yet with all these resemblances there is an underlying difference which we must endeavour to seize. In Peter the men in question are distinctly **false teachers,** who themselves are going to destruction, and who influence for evil and drag with them to destruction unstable souls who, by making a profession of Christianity, have left behind them in an outward way the corruptions of the heathen world. In Jude the evil men are not spoken of as teachers in the same definite way, but the position of antagonism they take is even more pronounced. They are marked by regular **apostasy,** and in keeping with this the angels who await judgment are spoken of not merely as sinning, but as not keeping their first estate; that is, in other words, apostatizing. Jude therefore seems to contemplate a state of things just a degree worse than that which Peter contemplates.

The Apostle Paul also warns us as to the character of the last days in 2 Timothy iii. 1—iv. 5; giving instructions to the servant of God in view of that which he predicts. The words used differ very slightly. Paul, and Peter also, speak of "the last days." Jude speaks of "the last time." John also in his first Epistle speaks of "the last time;" only there it is more accurately, "the last hour," and a somewhat different sense is attached to the word, for they were in the last hour when he wrote. No fresh "hour" was going to intervene between the time of his writing and the coming of the Lord, which will take place when the Antichrist has appeared. Already many lesser antichrists had appeared as forerunners of the great one to come. Each of the other inspired writers, Paul, Peter and Jude, looks on to the coming of the Lord as the final sweeping away of the evil.

Jude addresses himself to the "called" ones; that is, to those who are genuinely the called people of God, and that without distinction. He does not write to the saints composing any particular assembly nor to Jewish believers as distinct from Gentile ones: all saints are before him. He views them in a twofold way: first in relation to God the Father, and then in relation to Jesus Christ. The word "beloved" seems to be better attested than "sanctified." They, and we, are "beloved in God the Father, and preserved in Jesus Christ."

How very beautiful is this note!—the first that is struck in this Epistle. The saints universally are addressed, as called out from the world. All are

JUDE

beloved in God the Father, as begotten of Him; and as under the mighty hand of Jesus Christ all are **preserved.** The true saints of God are the objects of Divine love, and in spite of all the evil which may invade the Christian circle they will be preserved to the end. Moreover, mercy and peace and love are to be multiplied to such, though evils multiply around them. What encouragement there is in all this! How assuring and how fortifying! In the strength of it we can proceed to consider the evils that are exposed and predicted.

Jude had purposed to write a treatise concerning "the common salvation," but found himself turned aside from that design to write this short Epistle exhorting rather to the defence of the faith. This is a remarkable confession and quite unique. The "common salvation," that is, the salvation in which we all participate, is indeed an inexhaustible theme, and it may well be that on another occasion Jude fulfilled his original purpose, though not in an inspired way. As a matter of fact an inspired exposition of that salvation was already available in Paul's Epistle to the Romans, and in the inspired Word God does not repeat Himself. There was, however, still a niche in Scripture which required to be filled, so Jude's original thought was set aside and he was honoured of God in being pressed into the service of filling it.

It was now needful that those called of God should be exhorted to **contend** for the faith. It was given only to the Apostles to authoritatively **expound** the faith, and commit it to the inspired Writings. It was given to few, comparatively speaking, to be pastors and teachers and give **instruction** in the faith. How likely then that the mass of believers should jump to the conclusion that **the defence of the faith and contention for it** was also the business of but a few. Hence the need for this word of exhortation. Is it not extraordinary and reprehensible that with this exhortation before us there should today be so many who consider that contending for the faith is no concern of theirs, and would like to relegate it to a few who have high scholastic qualifications or some kind of official status?

The faith is unspeakably precious. It embodies all we know of God in Christ. If it goes, everything goes, as far as we are concerned. Hence it must be held in its integrity at all costs, and not only held passively but contended for actively. The faith has been "once delivered unto the saints." There are three things in that statement which need to be carefully noted.

First, the faith has been **delivered,** not discovered. It is not something which has been worked out by men and added to bit by bit, as the "sciences" have been, but something handed over by God through His Holy Spirit. The sciences have been built up by observation and experiment and reasoning. The faith has been revealed of God that our faith may receive it.

JUDE

Second, the faith has been **once** delivered; that is, once for all. The delivery of it took some little time. It "began to be spoken by the Lord, and was confirmed unto us by them that heard Him." However, by the time that Jude wrote, the delivery of it was finished: the circle of revealed truth had been completed in the Apostolic writings. The men of science are always awaiting fresh discoveries: they have very little that is certain, and settled beyond all question. We have a faith delivered once for all. God has spoken. His Word has been committed to writing, and we await no further revelation. It cannot be amended, though it may be rejected. We receive it, desiring help of God that we may increasingly understand it.

Third, it has been delivered **to the saints.** It was not delivered to the Apostles and prophets, but delivered **through** them **to** the saints. The saints consequently are its custodians, and not merely prominent or gifted men amongst the saints. This is a fact of deep importance. The faith addresses itself to the faith of every one of us. Each of us is to receive it and understand it, and each of us is to be set for its maintenance and to contend for it as may be necessary. In the light of this one can see how disastrous has been the idea that it was right to have in the church a special class of men officially appointed, whether as priests or ministers, to whom all such things belong. It has been a master-stroke of the adversary, for where that idea has prevailed the great mass of saints have been put out of action in the conflict of faith, and kept in a state of spiritual infancy.

Every true believer then should contend for the faith, and contend **earnestly** as having a vital interest in it. Details of how we should contend are not stated by Jude in this short Epistle. Elsewhere we find that we must avoid all carnal weapons, and that our spirit should be that of the meek and lowly Jesus whom we serve (see 2 Cor. x. 4; 2 Tim. ii. 24, 25). Jude does give us instruction as to how we should fortify ourselves in the faith which must be preliminary to contending for it. But that comes toward the end of the Epistle.

With verse 4 there begins his exposure of the state of things that was developing, which made his message so urgent. Men of a very depraved type had crept in unawares—ungodly, turning the grace of God into utter license, and denying the great Master whom they professed to serve. In reading John's first Epistle we saw how there were antichrists who "went out," whilst the men of whom Jude speaks "crept in." The former were apparently men of a high class type, intelligent and philosophic, who took their departure when their notions were refused. The latter were anything but high class, men of a dissolute type, who used the grace of God as a cloke to cover up their sin.

We sometimes hear people today objecting to the doctrines of grace on the ground that they may be abused. The answer to that is that they have been abused, and the abuse was in full swing before the first century had reached its end; and that the Scriptures tell us of the way they were

JUDE

abused, but that, instead of recommending us to drop the doctrines of grace, they urge us to contend for them!

In verses 5—7, we have three cases cited, which show how the irrevocable judgment of God lies upon the kind of evil that these ungodly men were committing. In the case of Israel it was plain and thorough **unbelief,** and the unbelievers were destroyed in spite of the fact that at the outset they participated in many privileges. In the case of the angels, their sin was in one word, **apostasy.** They totally abandoned their original place and state. That is apostasy: and for any creature to do that, whether angel or man, is to be hopelessly doomed. Sodom and her sister cities gave themselves up to utter **license,** breaking through boundaries that God had set, and their judgment is eternal. Three awful warnings!

Now the men that Jude was denouncing were marked by similar things. They defiled themselves by fleshly sins, and at the same time were characterized by an arrogant refusal of authority. This leads up to the remarkable verse about the contention between Michael the archangel and the devil. What Jude cites is quite unrecorded in the Old Testament. The devil, though now fallen, was once a high dignity in the angelic realm, and until he is finally dispossessed by God his dignity is to be respected. Even so high an angelic dignity as Michael respected it. He did not take it upon himself to rebuke him, but left the Lord to do it.

In passing let us learn from this not to do ourselves what even Michael shrank from doing. How often we may hear people speak of Satan in a very light and mocking way, and we may have done it ourselves. Let us not do it again. Satan is a spirit being, who once held a leading place, if not the leading place, in the angelic hierarchy. Though fallen, he still wields immense power, which we cannot afford to despise. Yet, under the sheltering power of our Lord we need not fear him.

Verse 10 contains a very trenchant indictment. Men who are ignorant as well as arrogant usually fall to abusing what they do not understand. These men not only did this but they also corrupted themselves in things of nature which they did understand. The New Translation is rather striking here, "But what even, as the irrational animals, they understand by mere nature, in these things they corrupt themselves." Things spiritual they rail at: in things natural they corrupt themselves. Truly a terrible indictment!

Now the course of these men, and more particularly perhaps of the evil that characterized them, and which would be perpetuated in their successors, is graphically sketched in verse 11. Again three cases are cited from the Old Testament, which exactly set the position before us. In this matter there is nothing new under the sun. Again and again evil takes the same forms, runs the same course, and comes to the same end. Jude does not mince his words. These men and their successors have nothing but woe before them.

JUDE

The beginning of their course is a going in the way of Cain. This is a way of **self-will in the things of God.** Cain was the first to take that way, and his name is left upon it. He would approach God, and this in itself was good: but he would do it in his own way, and not in God's way. Now, by His action in clothing our first parents with coats of skins, God had indicated that death was His way, and Abel's faith had seized this. Cain had no faith, only his own thoughts. Why should not God be satisfied with the way that seemed right to Cain? He would take his own way in self-will.

These men trod the way of Cain, and it is still immensely popular. Multitudes there are who prefer their own thoughts to God's Word. Why should not God be pleased with their efforts and their approach? As long as they recognize Him, may they not draw near and worship Him as they please? At any rate that is what they intend to do. Alas, still they go in the way of Cain; and there is a woe at the end of it.

To "run greedily after the error of Balaam for reward" is the next step. This is sheer **self-seeking in the things of God.** Religion of a sort is indulged in, and it becomes a profitable business. Balaam was a spiritist medium, who adopted so much as was profitable to him of the true knowledge of God. That was the error that Balaam practised. The error that he taught, and by which he ensnared many of Israel and brought them under the judgment of God, was that of sinful alliance with the idolatrous world. And in all that he practised and taught the one thing before him was money-making—the love of reward.

Our Epistle speaks of "the way of Cain" and "the error of Balaam;" it is in 2 Peter that we read of "the way of Balaam." But in both Epistles the thought connected with him is the same, for in Peter we find him described as loving "the wages of unrighteousness." His course there is described as "madness." Alas! his madness has had many followers from the day in which Jude wrote to our own. The evil men that Jude was exposing "ran greedily" after his error, and we believe those two words are still applicable to very many. It is a striking fact that Balaam and his evil teaching appear in the Lord's address to the church at Pergamos (Revelation ii.), inasmuch as that church sets forth prophetically the epoch when the church accepted the patronage of the world, and the corruptions of the Roman system began.

In that system we see religion as a money-making power carried to its highest pitch. Years ago in Spain we saw a paper in which it was pointed out that all the supposed benefits which Rome offered from birth to death cost money; that in fact there was nothing without it. Moreover after death it was still money, money, for there was purgatory to be shortened. The title of the paper, translated into English, was **"The religion of money."** The history of Rome through the ages furnishes us also with many and terrible examples of men who have turned the grace of God into lasciviousness, just as Jude says. Many other forms of error have

JUDE

a strong strain of money-making in them, though not perhaps to the same extent.

Finally there is the gainsaying of Korah, the details of which are given to us in Numbers xvi. Korah's sin was **self-assertion in the things of God,** and it brought upon him swift destruction. Cain lived many a year after he took his self-willed way. Balaam lived for sufficient time to do much havoc in Israel by his error, and for a time at least his self-seeking seemed to be profitable. But the self-assertion of Korah was met by rapid and drastic judgment.

This is the third and final stage in the progress of the evil that fills Christendom today. We believe that we speak soberly when we say that terrible examples of it abound on every hand. Never were men more confident of themselves and of their powers in matters of religion. Korah asserted himself as against Moses and Aaron: today men who call themselves Christians are quite prepared to assert themselves against Christ. "Jesus Christ" say they, "thought this and said that. But we know better now as belonging to this enlightened age." A very sinister sign! Judgment cannot now be long delayed.

Let us, who love the Lord Jesus Christ, see to it that in everything we are subject to **His will,** that we seek **His glory** and not our own, and that instead of asserting ourselves we assert **His rights.** Thus we shall be pleasing to Him.

If verse 11 sketches for us the development and end of the evil leading to apostasy, we come back in verses 12 and 13 to the men who embodied the evil in Jude's day, and there is a further exposure of their character in a series of graphic figures, the meaning of which we must attempt to seize.

They were "spots" in the love-feasts of these early Christians. It appears that the word translated thus has the meaning of a jagged rock especially one with the sea washing over it. So these evil men who had crept in unawares, and who now were boldly taking their place in the social life of the believers, were a terrible menace, just as is the sunken rock which endangers the ships. To feed themselves was their passion, not to feed the flock. Jude warns us of their true nature so that we may avoid them.

Then, changing the figure, they are like clouds borne along on the winds, yet without water. In the land where Jude wrote the clouds were welcome as giving promise of rain. So these men had the appearance of bringing refreshment to God's weary heritage; but they had nothing to give, being themselves impelled by Satan's power, of which the wind is a figure.

Then again they are like trees "whose fruit withereth," or, "autumnal trees." Now it is in the autumn that we expect to find fruit on the trees; but they are without fruit. These men are marked by promise without performance, for they are twice dead—first by nature and then as coming

JUDE

under the judgment of God. In speaking of them as rooted up, Jude no doubt views them prophetically as having come under judgment.

They are also like waves of the sea raging and foaming, for they were uncontrolled save by the power of Satan; and it was their own shame that they displayed. The word, we are told is in the plural "shames"; and means the things which were a shame to them, and not that they felt any shame in them. Probably they did not, but gloried in them.

Fifthly, they were like wandering stars or meteors, in that their light was soon to be quenched in the blackness of darkness for ever. This again speaks of judgment, and brings us back to the point we reached at the end of verses 11 and 12. We all know the speed with which the meteor sweeps across the heavens and burns out into darkness. Thus it would be with them. They had no steady light to give.

We find then that the last words of each of the three verses (11, 12, 13) indicate judgment; and now in verses 14 and 15 Jude tells us plainly how the judgment will fall upon these apostates. It will be by direct intervention of the Lord, appearing in His glory, which had been predicted even from the days of Enoch.

All the information that Scripture affords as to this remarkable man is found in very few words, yet those words are full of significance. Genesis v. tells us of the exalted character of his life, walking with God for no less than three hundred years. It tells us also of his glorious finish, translated into God's presence. Hebrews xi. tells us of his faith, the power of both his life and his translation. In Jude we discover that he was a prophet, and, as far as we know, the earliest of all the prophets.

The first prophet spoke of the closing scenes as regards man's day, when the Lord will come with myriads of His holy ones for the execution of judgment. His words make it very evident that when He does come man's iniquity will have reached its climax, and be so open and flagrant that judgment by conviction and execution is inevitable. The repetition of the word **ungodly** in verse 15 is very striking. It will be a case of ungodly men doing and saying the most ungodly things in very ungodly fashion. At His coming the Lord will convict them, bringing home their guilt to them so that they have to acknowledge it: then He will execute judgment upon them.

From the very earliest times then it has been a revealed truth that the Lord Himself will appear to deal with man's unblushing evil; though not until New Testament times did it appear that the Lord Jesus is the Jehovah who is to come. He will not come because the Gospel has prepared the world to receive Him, as so many still think. He will come to cleanse the earth by judgment, attended by His saints. Other scriptures inform us who these saints are, and how they reach the heavens in order to come forth with Him. The Gospel will have accomplished its appointed work in

JUDE

gathering saints out of the world for heaven. Then judgment will take its course.

We have further description, and exposure of these men who crept in unawares, in verses 16 to 19. It is really very remarkable how the Spirit of God labours to make their character clear to us so that we may be able to identify them. They are said to be murmurers and complainers; that is, unsatisfied persons with grievances; the reason of it all lying not in those against whom they have the grievance, but in their own lusts. Their lusts so dominate them that nothing would satisfy them. They talk great things —about themselves no doubt—and they love grandiose language, while at the same time they fawn upon and flatter influential people in order to get something out of them for their own benefit. What a contemptible picture all this presents to us!

Jude also bids us remember the things that had been said by the Apostles of the Lord before he wrote this Epistle. It is in 2 Peter iii. 3 that we read about mockers coming in the last time walking after their own lusts, but evidently the other Apostles had testified to the same effect. The men that Jude had in view were of that stamp: they were sensual or natural men, not having the Spirit. To have the Spirit is the infallible mark of really belonging to Christ. Jude describes them also as "they who separate themselves." It is very much open to question whether the word "themselves" is really in the original, and the R.V. puts it simply "who make separations." The Holy Spirit is the power of unity. These men without the Spirit were the fomenters of disunity. With this word Jude's description of them comes to an end.

A darker picture of ungodliness it would be impossible to conceive. The description begins with the turning of the grace of God into lasciviousness, and the denying of the only Master and Lord. It ends with the making of divisions, as being utterly destitute of the Spirit of God. Yet they had crept in among the saints unawares. Still God would find them out, and as apostates they will perish.

Now Jude does not only enlighten us as to the evil; he uses it as an incentive to the diligent pursuit of what is good, as far as we are concerned. In verse 20 he again appeals to the true saints of God, and he indicates what is to mark them in the presence of all these difficulties. His instructions fall naturally under four heads.

First, we are to build ourselves up on our most holy faith. Note the wording carefully. It does not say that we are to build up the faith. We have already seen in the Epistle that the faith is committed to us as a perfect and completed thing. It needs no building up: we can add nothing to it. It is we who need the building up. We may have received the faith, and taken our stand upon it in faith. That is the right and true beginning, but we must not stop at that point; we need to be built up on it so that it becomes our very life. We can never be too fully instructed in it or too solidly established on it. Jude speaks of it as "most holy." We have not got today a most holy place as Israel had of old: we have instead a most holy faith. It is not to be trespassed upon or tampered with. None shall do so with impunity. Only fools rush in where angels fear to tread.

Let us recall at this point that the main burden of the Epistle is that we should earnestly contend for the faith. Our being built up on it is undoubtedly a prerequisite for this. Some folk, who love a fight for its own sake, would rush into conflict on behalf of a cause which they understand but imperfectly, if at all. But this is not to be the way of the called ones who are beloved in God the Father and preserved in Jesus Christ. The faith must be the **basis** on which we are built up before it becomes the **banner** for which we fight. And the more we are really built up on it, the more we shall be morally and spiritually equipped to enter into the conflict.

In the second place there must be this "praying in the Holy Ghost." Not, "**to** the Holy Ghost," as though we were to conceive of Him as an Object of faith, outside ourselves. It is "**in**" Him that we are to pray. Now prayer is the expression of dependence upon God, who **is** outside ourselves. We are very dependent, and we are to know it, and confess it practically in prayer. In this we shall be the very opposite of the ungodly men whom Jude has described to us. They feel themselves to be entirely sufficient unto themselves, and because of it they despise dominion and are not afraid to speak evil of dignities.

Our prayers however are to be in the Spirit; that is, we are to pray as those who are controlled by the indwelling Spirit, and who consequently ask for the things that are according to His mind. Prayer, which springs from the Holy Spirit acting in the hearts of the saints, is sure to be both fervent and effectual.

In the third place we are to keep ourselves in the love of God. In the consciousness and warmth and power of it we are to dwell. We are persuaded of course with Paul that nothing "shall be able to separate us from the love of God, which is in Christ Jesus our Lord" (Rom. viii. 39). His love has a firm hold on us, and He will never let us go. But we are also to have a firm hold upon it in the quiet recesses of our hearts. We are to be bathed in it, just like a bucket or other vessel which has been flung into the ocean. Then it is in the ocean, and the ocean is in it. So if we keep ourselves in the love of God, the love of God will be in us, imparting its beautiful character to our lives.

Again let us remind ourselves that this is said to saints who are exhorted to contend earnestly for the faith. In the warmth of contention nothing is easier than to get irritated, and even to lose one's temper. If we keep ourselves in the love of God, our spirits are lifted above irritations that proceed from awkward or evil men and their reasonings. A believer may find himself entangled in controversy with men who are far more than a match for him on the intellectual plane, but if he is himself well built up on

JUDE

the faith, and if praying in the Spirit, he keeps himself in the love of God, he will not come off second best in the conflict. He may not convince his opponents, but any bystanders will be aware that they have witnessed something greater than mere intellectualism.

In the fourth place, we are to be looking for the mercy of our Lord Jesus Christ unto eternal life. There is much that we have today, but there is more to follow. We are people with a prospect. The evil men may multiply around us and the full apostasy may approach, but we have a wonderful outlook and great expectations in the coming of the Lord. We look for His coming into the air, according to 1 Thessalonians iv. 15-17, when He will receive His saints to Himself. This great action of His is described as **mercy**. We do not deserve it, any more than we deserved to be forgiven or redeemed. But we are going to get it, simply on the ground of mercy. It will be an act of mercy, crowning all the other acts of mercy that have characterised His dealing with us. And it will land us unto eternal life in its fullest sense. We shall then not only have the life, but also be in the scenes where that life has its home and expands to the fullest extent.

But the exhortation is that we keep actively looking for this wonderful consummation. We are not to set our expectations upon improvement either in world or church. We are not even looking for revivals—though God may in His mercy grant something of that sort, and if He does we shall rejoice and thank Him. No, we are looking for the coming of the Lord; and the more brightly that hope burns within our breasts the more shall we rightly sustain the conflict for the faith.

Judes' four exhortations, then, concern respectively, the faith, the Holy Spirit, the love of God, and the coming mercy of our Lord Jesus Christ. In regard to these we are to be building up, praying, keeping ourselves, and looking. These exhortations are very personal, appealing to each who loves the Lord.

In verses 22 and 23 we get further exhortations as to our attitude towards two different classes of people; designated as "some" and "others." These are neither the evil man denounced in the Epistle, nor the God-fearing saints to whom the Epistle is addressed.

The "some" of verse 22 appear to be people who have to some extent been affected or ensnared by the evil men. Such must be carefully distinguished and treated with compassion. The "others" contemplated in verse 23, have evidently become more deeply involved in the evil and contaminated by it. Even these however are to be saved if possible, though the one who would rescue them must set about it in a spirit far removed from self-confidence. He must fear the fire that threatens to devour them, and hate the flesh that has defiled them. Only if he goes about it in that spirit will he escape being burnt or defiled himself, and so be able to rescue them.

JUDE

This is a very important word for us, for we are naturally very inclined to treat alike all who are in any way implicated in such ungodly things. We may discern the evil and feel most strongly against it and so be very ready to lump all together, the misled with the misleaders, leaving them in their defilement with nothing before them but the fire. This must not be. We must remember the word, "making a difference."

When we come to verses 24 and 25, how delightful is the contrast with all that has preceded! We come out from the darkness of human wickedness and apostasy, and even from the contentions and efforts of true saints in the presence of the evil, into the clear light of the power and glory of God. Our eyes are lifted to "Him that is able to keep you from falling." Here, and here only, is real rest for the heart.

We are to contend for the faith, building up ourselves on it, and we are to labour to rescue others from defilement and doom, but we can find no repose in ourselves or our efforts. We may have grace to keep ourselves in the love of God, at least in some degree, yet we can only find rest in the fact that He is able to keep us from falling, and present us faultless before the presence of His glory.

Since He is able, we have only ourselves to blame for any tumbles we get on the way. Yet though we may tumble we shall not ultimately fall. We shall be presented in the presence of His glory when forth it shines, and not even the light of that glory shall discover a fault in us. How amazing! How excellent! What a triumph for the grace and power of God!

Nothing remains but to bow in the presence of that Saviour-God, through the Lord Jesus, and ascribe to Him glory, majesty, dominion and power, both now and to all ages.   Amen.

THE REVELATION

Introduction

THE BOOK WHICH is now to occupy our thoughts has certain very definite characteristics. It is the one book of the New Testament which calls itself a "prophecy," and in which the final victory of the Divine will and purpose is clearly seen. The very word for victory, though more often translated by overcome or prevail, occurs in it nearly as often as in the rest of the New Testament put together. It was evidently written when the first century was drawing to a close; when, as the Gospel and Epistles of John show, false and even antichristian teachers were beginning to abound, and when as a consequence true-hearted saints might well have had dejection and a feeling of defeat creeping over them. How fitting then that a book portraying the final victory should be given to close the inspired record. Other distinctive features will come to light as we proceed.

Chapter 1

IT IS, "THE Revelation of Jesus Christ, which God gave unto Him," that is, the unveiling of things to come, for the simple meaning of revelation or apocalypse is unveiling. It is of course true that the unveiling of these future things all hinges on the unveiling or revelation of Jesus Christ in His glory, but the primary meaning is that God gave to Jesus this revelation of things to come that He might show it to His servants. Every clause of this first verse is worthy of careful notice.

It is remarkable, in the first place, that the revelation should be spoken of as **given to Jesus,** rather than as originated by Him. He is presented then as the servant of God's will and purpose just as He is in the Gospel of Mark, and it is in that Gospel that we find the passage in which He disowns knowledge of the day and hour of His advent. Here, too, He is the Servant of God to make known things to come as they had been given to Him. Moreover John, who received from Him the revelation, speaks of himself not as an Apostle but as a servant, and those to whom it is conveyed are not spoken of as saints but as servants. It was a day when defection was becoming pronounced, so while there are messages to churches—which reveal the defection—the revelation is given to those who really are servants of God, and who therefore will appreciate it. It is a fact that remains to this day that men who are but unconverted professors of Christ universally decry, if they do not ridicule it; and worldly-minded believers make nothing of it.

Another remarkable feature is the indirectness of the revelation. God gave it to Jesus, and Jesus signified it to John, not directly but by mediation of His angel. Moreover He did not declare it: He "signified" it. In the Gospel John uses the word "sign" for miracle. Here it is a verb formed from the same root. He signed these things to John; and this exactly gives us the character of the book. The prophecy is conveyed not in plain literal

THE REVELATION

speech as elsewhere, but in symbols or signs. Now all this is surely intended to make us feel that there is reserve and distance in the method of revelation, suited to the sad defection that had already begun in the church. How different the method of those revelations made earlier to Paul, as for instance Acts 26: 16-18; 2 Corinthians 12: 1-4; 1 Thessalonians 4: 15-17.

The things signified are such as "must shortly come to pass." This expression helps to establish the fact that the messages to the churches in chapters 2 and 3 have a prophetic bearing. What was signified by the church at Ephesus was beginning to come to pass when John received the prophecy, which carries us right on to the coming of the Lord, and even to the eternal state. The reader is also admonished by this expression that he must not adopt the attitude taken by the Jews when they received the prophecies of Ezekiel. Then they said, "The vision that he seeth is for many days to come, and he prophesieth of the times that are far off" (Ezek. 12: 27). It is an inveterate tendency of our hearts to avoid the force of the Word of God, not by denying it but by relegating it to so distant a future that it can conveniently be ignored.

Having received the revelation John bare record of it, and he describes it in a threefold way. It is "the word of God," and this fact at once invests the book with full authority and puts it on a par with the other Holy Writings. Then it is "the testimony of Jesus Christ," and later we are told that this testimony is "the spirit of prophecy" (19:10). This testimony declares that the Jesus, who suffered and was set at nought here, is the coming Lord of all things in heaven and on earth, and that all might and dominion, power and glory is in His hands. He will execute judgment and bring to pass all the counsel of God. Now this is the spirit of prophecy. As we survey the prophetic field a great drama unfolds before our eyes, and we see beasts and Babylon and other anti-christian forces, but if we do not see them in relation to the testimony of Jesus we shall miss their real instruction and power. In the third place he speaks of "all things that he saw." for the revelation reached him in the form of visions. The words, "And I saw," or "And I looked," occur very frequently in the book.

Then a special blessing is pronounced on the reader, the hearer and the keeper of the words of the prophecy. Let us particularly note that we are to keep—that is, observe—these things. This indicates that the prophecy is to exert a powerful influence upon us. It is to enlighten our minds and guide our footsteps. The main point is not that we should be able to explain with accuracy every symbol used, or identify with certainty every "beast" or "locust," but that we should realize how all these actors in the sad drama of man's rebellion and judgment are like a dark background for the glory of the coming Lord, and that all is to lead to the separation of our hearts from this present evil age. In this way we shall "keep" the things that are written.

John addresses the book to the seven churches in Asia, as verse 4 says. In these seven churches all church history was portrayed, as chapters 2 and

THE REVELATION

3 show; we may therefore accept the book as addressed to the whole church during the centuries of its sojourn in this world, and appropriate to the whole church the grace and peace of this opening salutation.

The grace and peace proceed from the three Persons of the Godhead, but each of the three is presented in a way that differs from the rest of the New Testament. First we have God in His unchanging greatness; eternally and immutably He IS, and therefore as regards the past, He was, and as regards the future, He is to come. He sits therefore above the storms that in this book we are to see raging on the earth, and even in the Heavens.

The second Person named here is the Holy Spirit. He is not presented as the one Spirit of the Epistles but as "the seven Spirits," an allusion, we suppose, to Isaiah 11: 2. In our verse they are "before His throne," as being ready to act in the government of the earth. The Spirit is one as to His Person, and this fact is greatly emphasized in connection with the formation of the church, and his activities therein, as we see in 1 Corinthians 12. Yet in His governmental activities He is viewed in a sevenfold way, and the final actions of Divine government are contemplated in this last book of the Bible.

In the third place grace and peace proceed from Jesus Christ, who is presented in a threefold way. He is the faithful Witness in contrast to all others who have borne witness of God. They have each and all failed somewhere. In Him God himself has been perfectly declared, and all truth maintained in full integrity. In considering Him thus, our thoughts have mainly to travel into the past.

But He is also the First Begotten of the dead, and it is this that characterizes Him at the present moment. The church is based upon Him as risen from the dead. Indeed, it was not until He was risen and ascended that the Holy Ghost was shed forth so that the church might be formed. Then thirdly, He is the Prince of the kings of the earth. He is this in title at the present moment, but He will not publicly assume that place until His second advent, so that considering Him thus our thoughts travel to the future. How comprehensively then—past, present and future—is He set before us. All this He is, and all this He would be, even if no soul of man had received salvation through Him.

But we have received eternal blessing through Him, and hence we know Him in a very intimate way which calls forth an outburst of praise. He loves us and has declared that abiding fact firstly in a work of purification, washing us from our sins in His own blood, and then in a work of exaltation, making us kings and priests to His God and Father. Only as washed from our sins could we be introduced into such a place as that, and it is worthy of note that directly we have **Christian blessings** mentioned we have God presented in **the light in which we know Him**—the God and Father of our Lord Jesus Christ—rather than as the eternal I AM, as in verse 4.

THE REVELATION

To such an One as this, known through grace, we heartily ascribe the glory and dominion for ever and ever. Glory and domination have ever been pursued by fallen men. Not one of them has been worthy to receive it, and if in any measure they have attained to it, nothing but oppression has resulted for the masses, and ultimately disaster for themselves. Here at last is One worthy to have it, and wield it to the glory of God and the blessing of men—worthy by reason of who He is as well as what He has done. It is remarkable that we have exactly the same words in 1 Peter 5: 11. What is there ascribed to "the God of all grace" is here ascribed to Jesus Christ: pretty clear proof, this, of WHO He really is.

Verse 7 gives us in very small compass the main theme of the book. The consummation is announced before we see the steps that lead up to it. The same feature characterizes many of the Psalms in the Old Testament. The public and glorious appearing of Christ will bring everything to a head. Every eye shall see Him in surroundings that indicate His Deity, for it is Jehovah, "who maketh the clouds His chariot: who walketh upon the wings of the wind" (Psa. 104: 3). Zechariah had declared, "They shall look upon Me whom they have pierced" (12: 10), and this shall be fulfilled. He had also declared that there should be those of Israel who should see then the enormity of their national sin in His rejection, and mourn for it in deep repentance. Our verse here announces that all kindreds of the earth shall wail because of Him; not in repentance evidently, but because it seals their doom, and they realize it. Plain proof, this that the world is not going to be converted as the preparation for His coming.

The correct reading in verse 8 appears to be "Lord God," and not "Lord" only. This being so, we hear in the verse the voice of the Lord God Almighty, the eternally existent One, who guarantees the fulfilment of the Advent in its appointed time. Jesus Christ is viewed, as we have pointed out, as the holy and perfect Servant of His glory; the exalted Man, by whom He will administer the world in righteousness. Nothing can possibly defeat One who is the Beginning and the End of all things.

Thus far we have had what we may call the preface. From verse 9 to the end of the chapter we have John's account of the vision of the Lord that was granted to him, out of which sprang the writing of this book. In recounting it, he does not present himself as an Apostle, but as a brother of those to whom he wrote and as a sharer in their present trials and future prospects. This is the time marked by tribulation for the saints below, and of patience for Christ glorified on high. He waits in patience for the hour to strike when the Kingdom will be His. We are called to enter into that same patience, as we shall see when we read verse 10 of chapter 3, and as the Apostle Paul indicated in 2 Thessalonians 3: 5.

At that time John was suffering the tribulation that is involved in isolation. Banished to Patmos, he was cut off from his fellow-believers, yet he was in no way isolated from His Lord. On a certain first day of the

THE REVELATION

week, which is the Lord's Day, he was carried outside himself by the special energy of the Holy Spirit of God, and so he was brought into a condition in which he was enabled to see and hear heavenly things. It is well for us to remember that though we have never needed, and therefore never come under such a special action of the Spirit, yet it is only by the ordinary action and energy of the Spirit that we discern and apprehend anything of the things of God.

He tells us first what he heard. A powerful voice of authority bade him write the things he was about to see in a book, and send it to seven selected churches in the Province of Asia. John was thus constituted a Seer. He was also told that it was the Divine intention that the revelation he was now to receive should be **enshrined in a Book.** In their eagerness to get rid of a written revelation from God, men decry the Scriptures and accuse of "Bibliolatry" those of us who accept the Bible and reverence it as the Word of God. They would like us to regard a book revelation as something quite beneath the Divine dignity. We, on the contrary, regard it as exactly suitable to His dealings with men whom He has endowed with powers of reading and writing, and who have learned to hand on knowledge from one generation to another by means of books. The seven churches were to have the book, and that which they symbolized—the whole church throughout the centuries until the Lord comes—was to have it too.

The seven churches, whether we view them historically or prophetically, differed widely in their character and state, yet the same revelation of things to come would be salutary for each. Let those who decry the study of prophecy note this! Whatever our spiritual state as individuals may be, it will be for our health and blessing if we gain a clear understanding of the solemn scenes of judgment by which God is going to bring earth's sad story to a triumphant conclusion.

Hearing this trumpet voice of authority, John turned to see the majestic Person who uttered it, and thus was he brought face to face with his Lord, and granted a sight of the One he had once known so well on earth, but now displayed in a character and amidst circumstances that to him were entirely new.

The Lord Jesus presented Himself to John as "like unto the Son of Man." This was not an unknown title to John, for Jesus in the days of His flesh spoke of Himself thus. What was new was the fact that the Son of Man had exchanged conditions of humiliation for surroundings of glory. John had just been instructed to write in a book what he saw, and this he faithfully carried out. In the course of this book he describes a great many things that passed before his vision, but all of them hinge on this first great vision of the Son of Man in His judicial glory. The Lord's own words were that the Father had given Him authority to execute judgment, "because He is the Son of Man" (John 5: 27).

THE REVELATION

The description given to us in verses 13-17 speaks entirely of judgment. John had once leant on Jesus' breast at supper, now that same breast is under restraint, girt about with a girdle of gold. The sight of His head was like unto that of "The Ancient of Days" of Daniel 7, in whose presence "the judgment was set, and the books were opened." The eye symbolizes intelligence and discernment, and His were as a flame of fire, not only discerning but also resolving all things into their first elements. So too, His feet, which contact the earth, and under which all things are put, were as fine brass glowing in a furnace, just as once the fine brass of the altar glowed beneath the fire of the sacrifices. His voice was full of authority and majesty, irresistible like the thunderous roar of the ocean.

The right hand too speaks of power. His tongue was like "a sharp two-edged sword:" that is, His verdicts had all the discerning and cutting power of the veritable word of God. Finally, His whole countenance was clothed with sun-like glory, too bright for mortal eyes. No wonder, that in the presence of such an One—the Son of Man, arising to judgment, invested with the insignia and glory of Deity—John fell at His feet as dead.

But though he was a servant, and therefore a subject of His judicial scrutiny, John was also a saint, and hence a subject of His grace. His grace is as great as His glory. His right hand, which held the seven stars, was laid upon John, so that he might be lifted up and strengthened to receive and record the visions in which the revelation was to be conveyed. "Fear not," was the assuring word.

The judicial glory of the Lord had been conveyed in the vision; now we have His glory declared in His own words, and that in a threefold way. First, **the glory of Deity.** He is "the First and the Last, and the Living One." Compare this with verse 8, where the Lord God, the Almighty, proclaims Himself the "Alpha and Omega, the Beginning and the Ending." No one but God can be, "the First" or "the Beginning," but being a Person in the unity of the Godhead, Jesus is God.

Secondly, **the glory of redemption,** of death and resurrection. He "was" or "became" dead, but now is "alive for evermore," or "living to the ages of ages." He, who is revealed as the universal Judge, has Himself tasted the judgment of death, and risen above its power into resurrection life.

Then, thirdly, **the glory of dominion.** Death and hell (**Hades**) are the great foes of sinful mankind, the symbols of the curse under which sin has brought them. Holding the keys, He is the complete Master of both. Thus Jesus presented Himself in His Deity; in His risen estate, redemption having been accomplished; and as the complete Master of man's ancient foes.

What an uplift this must have been to John! And what an uplift it should be to us! It prepared him to write as he was bidden in verse 19. It will prepare us to read and digest what he has written, and to face with undismayed hearts the searching unfoldings of the book.

THE REVELATION

Verse 19 should be carefully noted, as it contains the Lord's own division of the book. John was to write (1) the vision he had just seen. This he did in the few verses we have just considered. Then (2) he was to write "the things that are," and (3) "the things which shall be hereafter," or, "the things that are about to be after these." Now in verse 1 of chapter 4 the voice from heaven lifts John in spirit to heaven that he may be shown "things which must be hereafter," or, "things which must take place after these things;" so that as we pass into chapter 4 we begin the third section of the book. Clearly therefore chapters 2 and 3 comprise section 2. We believe this verse 19 is an important key to the right unfolding of Revelation, so we ask our readers to note it carefully. We have no hesitation in saying that any explanation of the visions of this book which violates this distinction, or does not observe it, is bound to be defective, if not positively erroneous.

The last verse of chapter 1 is introductory to "the things that are," given in chapters 2 and 3. In the vision the Son of Man was seen in the midst of seven golden candlesticks or lamps, and holding seven stars in His right hand. The meanings of these symbols are given to us. Each lamp is a "church" or "assembly." Each star is an "angel" or "messenger" or "representative" of an assembly. We have not here, then, the whole church in its place of privilege, as presented through Paul in Ephesians, Colossians and elsewhere, but each local church in its responsibility to be a light for Christ during the time of His absence as rejected from the earth. The whole church in its oneness men cannot see, but a local church they can, and the practical state and condition of such widely differs. The angel may signify one or more in each church who are representative of it and of its state. The Lord conveys His verdict in each case not to the church as a whole but to the angel, thus again showing the reserve that marked Him in His judgment of their state, and the sense of distance that had supervened. This sense of reserve and distance characterizes the whole book, as we have already observed.

Chapter 2

Chapters 2 and 3—"the things which are"—may be read in three ways. First, as a record of the state of seven churches in the Province of Asia as the first century drew to its close. By then all the Apostles, save the aged John, were gone, and their shepherd care no longer available. Various dangers were discerned and uncovered by the Lord, and various declensions, defections and defilements exposed. Of the seven only two churches, the first and the seventh, are alluded to elsewhere in Scripture. Ephesus was perhaps the crown of Paul's labours, and hence the Lord's verdict on it, 25 or 30 years after his death, is a searching lesson for our hearts.

We have two allusions to Laodicea in Paul's Epistle to the Colossians, but these are enough to show he had some anxiety as to their state even

THE REVELATION

then, and in that Epistle he ministered just the truth that might have preserved them. If the Laodicean saints had received the Colossian unfolding of the supreme excellence of Christ, the Head of His body, the church, He would have become "all, and in all" **to them.** Then Christ would not have represented Himself as standing **outside their door** and knocking, as in Revelation 3. Here again is something that should search us through and through.

But secondly, we may read the two chapters as giving us an exposure of conditions that may be found reproduced in local assemblies of saints that exist today. As we go through the seven addresses we may well see our own collective state as in a mirror, and learn our Lord's verdict as to it, and discover the corrective and remedy.

Then thirdly, since the whole of this book is a prophecy, as we saw in its opening verses, we have in the seven churches an unfolding of the historic course of the professing church, viewed as a body in which the light of God was to be maintained during the time of Christ's personal absence from the world. The church was to be the candlestick or light-bearer, till the moment when Christ should arise to execute judgment and assert the Divine authority in the earth. The number seven bears the significance of spiritual completeness, and in the seven addresses the complete history is surveyed. As we go through them let us consider them in all three ways.

To Ephesus the Lord presented Himself as the One who upholds the responsible angels, whilst critically surveying all the churches. Nothing escapes His eye. To Ephesus, as to each church, He says, "I know." Now in Ephesus He knew much that was good and commendable—works, labour, hatred of evil, careful testing of pretensions, endurance, care and zeal for the Lord's Name. But one great thing He had against them; they had left their first love. In our Authorized Version the insertion of "somewhat" weakens the sense. It is, "I have against thee that thou hast left thy first love." This fundamental defect quite spoilt the otherwise favourable picture.

For, what did it mean? This: that while the mechanism was still moving with fair regularity the mainspring was seriously weakened. It was with the church as it had been with Jerusalem, indicated in Jeremiah 2: 2. The church, too, had lost the love of her espousals, which had for a brief moment carried her even into a wilderness for love of her Lord. And if love for the great Head wanes the love that circulates amongst the members of His body cannot remain unimpaired. No outward zeal or activity or care can compensate for this inward loss. It is such a fall as jeopardizes everything, and demands nothing short of real and deep repentance, as verse 5 indicates.

If "first love" be recovered, the "first works" will naturally follow. These may look to human eyes exactly the same as the works mentioned in

THE REVELATION

verse 2, but to His eyes they are very different. He estimates everything according to the motive that lies behind. The mainspring is of all importance to Him. So much so, that if first love be permanently impaired the ability to shine departs and the candlestick is removed.

This is the state of things that was developing as the last of the Apostles departed. If present day assemblies of saints are judged thus, what candlesticks will remain? There are not too many characterized by even the outward zeal described in verses 2 and 3; but what is revealed if the mainspring be uncovered? A searching question indeed! Does not the word "Repent" sound loudly in our ears? It should do so, inasmuch as all who have ears to hear are called upon to hear the Spirit's messages to the churches. What is said particularly to one church through its angel is of importance to all true saints at any time.

It is worthy of note that the message, though spoken by "One like unto **the Son of Man,**" is also "what **the Spirit** saith." What the Lord says the Spirit says—the Lord **objectively to** John, and the Spirit **subjectively through** John, for he was "in the Spirit" (1:10) on this occasion. It was all "the word of God" (1:2). Thus the unity of the Divine Persons is manifest.

In verse 7 we have overcoming mentioned for the first time. The word thus translated occurs 17 times in the book. Even in the Ephesus condition of things overcoming was a necessity, and there is given the incentive of eating of the tree of life in the midst of the Paradise of God. Man never ate of the tree of life in Eden. The overcoming here must be the **retaining,** or the **returning to** "first love." As John's Epistle shows, there is the most intimate connection between love and life. Apart from the love of God we should have had no life at all. Having life, it manifests itself in love flowing from us both towards God and our brethren. To eat of the real Tree of life (22:2), of which Eden's tree was only a figure, is to be as filled with the life of Divine love as a creature can possibly be.

This overcoming was what was needed by saints at Ephesus as the first century closed. It was needed by saints generally in the earliest stages of church history. It is needed by us today.

The address to the angel of the church in Smyrna is the briefest of the seven. Four verses contain the whole of it. This is remarkable, since it shares with Philadelphia the distinction of receiving from the Lord no word of censure or blame. On the contrary, it receives a word of commendation.

Tribulation and even martyrdom characterized the outward circumstances of the church in Smyrna, and the Lord presented Himself to them in a character that exactly suited this. He is the first, and therefore none can forestall Him, so as to hinder. He is the last, and hence none but He can have the final word in any matter. Moreover He became dead and lived, and this guarantees that He wields the power of resurrection on behalf of those who belong to Him. If the Smyrnean saints apprehended

Him in this way, they must have been greatly fortified against their approaching tribulations.

Having presented Himself thus, the Lord again said, "I know." Tribulation and poverty marked them to the outward eye. They must therefore have been most unattractive to any who could not penetrate beneath the surface. To the all-seeing eye of the Lord it was far otherwise, and His surprising verdict was, "but thou art rich." So we have here the exact opposite of what presently He says to Laodicea, who claimed to be rich, and in His eyes was miserably poor. Thus it is that the Spirit speaks to the churches, and if we have an ear to hear we shall be profited. All through the church's history times of poverty and tribulation have been accompanied by spiritual enrichment: times of affluence and ease by spiritual impoverishment. Thus too it is today.

They had to face also opposition of a religious sort. There were those who falsely called themselves Jews; that is, claimed to have an earthly religious standing before God, as the people that He acknowledged in the world. Saying that they were this, they naturally assumed that worldly prosperity and possessions would be theirs, and they would repudiate those in poverty and trouble. Consequently they slandered and reviled—for this seems to be the force of "blasphemy" here — those who were true saints of God. The One who has eyes as a flame of fire discerns their true character and exposes them. They were not Jews, but they were a synagogue, a word which signifies "a bringing together" — a "synagogue of Satan." They were probably people of the Judaizing type that so persistently opposed the Apostle Paul, only now further advanced in their evil, coming together as a party, and wholly disowned by the Lord.

In Ephesus there were those that said they were apostles. Here we find those that said they were Jews. Before we finish the seven churches we shall find others who claim to be somewhat, but in each case we shall hear the Lord utterly disallow their claim. This making of claims is a natural proclivity of the flesh, so we may very easily be betrayed into it in our day. Let us carefully avoid it.

Verse 10 shows that behind the world that persecuted, and the self-assertive "Jews" that reviled them, lay the power of the devil. He is the great instigator of the opposition that comes from both the pagan world and the religious world, persecuting even to prison and to death. But the One who wields the power of resurrection places Himself behind these saints in their tribulation and poverty, exhorting them to faithfulness, even unto death, and holding before their eyes a crown of life. The power of death is the devil's great weapon: the power of resurrection life is in the hands of Christ.

The "ten days" of tribulation doubtless had reference to some definite but limited period of trial that lay before the church in Smyrna as the first century drew to its close. From the extended prophetic point of view the

THE REVELATION

reference would be to the successive outbursts of persecution during the first few centuries, which are said to have numbered ten, and ended under the Emperor Diocletian. These persecutions had the effect, under God's governmental hand, of checking the downward trend in the church and preventing the inrush of worldliness that later engulfed it, stimulating "first love" rather than extinguishing it. This accounts for no reproof being administered to the church in Smyrna. The much-needed lesson for us is that **tribulation** is the normal thing for Christians, if they are disentangled from the world, even as Paul states in 2 Timothy 3: 12. The "Great Tribulation" is another thing altogether.

The promise to the overcomer also has special reference to that which lay before them. Many of them might be hurt of the first death, the death of the body, but none of them would be touched of the second death, which would come in due season on their adversaries. This fact was to encourage the martyrs then, and doubtless has done so with the martyrs through the ages.

There is a tendency sometimes to regard the various promises to the overcomers as being special and exclusive to them. This promise in verse 11 would show that it is not so, for no true believer will be hurt of the second death. They are rather to be regarded as the Lord promising with special emphasis things calculated to act as an incentive and encouragement, though they may be shared wholly or in measure by all the saints.

To Pergamos the Lord presented Himself as the One who has the all-discerning, all-powerful word of God, that pierces and divides asunder all that is entangled and indistinguishable to the eyes of men. The church at Pergamos at that time, and the saints in the Pergamos stage of the church's history, needed to know Him in that light, since alliance with the world was being taught and consolidated in their midst. Nor do we need such knowledge less in our day, when alliance with the world is accepted as the proper thing with so large a part of Christendom.

All things at Pergamos were naked and open, and the sharp sword could divide and analyse, so again we have the words, "I know." The seat of Satan may have been an allusion to a particularly Satanic form of idolatry practised in ancient Pergamos, but viewing this church as prophetically indicating the third stage in the church's history, we see in it an allusion to the world system of which Satan is the god and prince. The church had begun to dwell in the world system; that is, to find its home there. This opened the door to the evils mentioned in verses 14 and 15.

Even so, the name and the faith of Christ had not been given up, but was still held fast, and there were some amongst them who were so true to both that they incurred the violent hostility of the world, even unto martyrdom. Antipas is named and designated, "faithful," which was high commendation indeed. His name is doubtless intended to speak to us, since translated into English it signifies, "against all." The saint who by reason of his faithfulness finds all the world against him is an Antipas indeed.

But while they had faithful witnesses among them, they also had, without definite repudiation, those who held the doctrine of Balaam, and of the Nicolaitans. We are given here a summary of Balaam's teaching, for the full details of which we have to turn to Numbers 25: 1-9; coupled with 31: 16. Balaam remained in the background but prompted Balac to cast the stumbling block, enticing to idolatry and fornication, two things that are always joined together in the heathen world. The former is the most fundamental of all sins against God; the latter is against mankind as well as God. Both sins are seen amongst the heathen in their grossest forms, but in a more spiritualized way flourish in Christendom.

In 2 Peter we read of "the way of Balaam . . . who loved the wages of unrighteousness." In Jude, of "the error of Balaam," and in this, as well as in his way, he set an example that has been followed by many to their destruction. But here we have his doctrine; that is, a system of teaching which maintains that **alliance with the world** is quite the proper thing for the people of God. There seems to be no certain knowledge as to the Nicolaitans, either as regards their deeds, denounced to Ephesus, or their doctrine, denounced here. Their name, however, is a compound of two Greek words, which translated mean, "Conquerors of the people"; so this may be intended to indicate that type of teaching which exalts a priestly caste, leading to that spiritual enslavement of the people which has risen to its heights in the Romish system. How bad priestly rule can become is borne witness to in Jeremiah 5: 31, and this when there **were** earthly priests, **instituted of God.** How much worse and hateful to God is it today!

In Pergamos neither of these evils were full blown in such fashion that the whole church was characterized by them. It was that they had in their midst those who **held** these things; it does not go so far as to say that they taught them. The Lord's words evidently imply that the church should not tolerate in its midst those who hold things so fundamentally evil as these. A solemn thought for us today. Again the word is "Repent," and if that word is not heeded the Lord will take action and use the sharp sword with two edges against the teachers of evil. He will deal with them if the church fails to deal with them. May we be among those who have ears to hear the Spirit's voice in this.

There will be found some who overcome in this state of things, and the promise to them makes reference first, to the Old Testament, and then to a custom common in those days. The hidden manna was that deposited in the ark and so hidden from human eyes. It was typical of the graces of the humbled Christ, so beautiful in the Divine estimation but hidden from the eyes of men. The overcomer should feed upon, and thus have communion in, that which is the very delight of God, whereas communion with the world was becoming characteristic of the church in Pergamos.

THE REVELATION

The white stone was given in those days as a token of acquittal. The overcomer should have not only this, but in it a new name, known only to himself and the One who gave it; a token therefore that the Lord owned them as His, in view of communion with Himself. So we may say that the overcomer is promised communion with both the Father and the Son.

Let us all accept the solemn fact that communion with God and communion with the world are antagonistic and mutually exclusive. We cannot have both. It must be one or the other.

To Thyatira the Lord presented Himself as **the Son of God,** who has eyes like a flame of fire and feet like fine brass. This is remarkable inasmuch as in the vision of chapter 1 John saw these features as characterizing One like **the Son of Man.** But if, as we believe, the church in Thyatira represents prophetically the period which witnessed the rise to power and ascendancy of the Romish hierarchy, how much to the point is this change of designation. Rome admits that He is the Son of God, yet lays all the emphasis on His being the Son of Mary, so much so that ultimately Mary becomes the more prominent. But no, the Son of God is He who has the eyes that penetrate and discern all things, and the feet that will crush all evil. And again we have that word, "I know."

He knew even in Thyatira things that were good; not only works but love, faith, service, patience. Moreover their last works were more than the first—they increased as time went on. Though things were very dark, as succeeding verses show, the eyes as a flame of fire discerned the good, where perhaps we should have seen none. An instructive thought for us today, for when things are really bad we are too apt to condemn wholesale without exception.

But on the other hand, having acknowledged the good, the Lord does unsparingly condemn the bad. In verse 20, the words, "a few things" should not be there. Their permitting the activities of Jezebel was a matter of great gravity. We have no doubt that the Thyatiran saints at the end of the first century would have at once known to what, or to whom, the Lord made allusion. Viewed prophetically, the symbolism exactly fits the Romish hierarchy. Note the four points following.

First, it is the **woman** Jezebel. Every attentive reader of Scripture knows that Jezebel was not a man. Then, why emphasize that she was a woman? Because in Scripture symbolism a woman is again and again used to represent a **system,** while a man may represent the energy that actuates it. As the Middle Ages drew on there was witnessed the development of the Romish system in all its enslaving power.

Second, the name **Jezebel** carries our thoughts back to the dark ages in Israel's history when Ahab ruled nominally, but sold himself to work wickedness under his wife's influence. Jezebel was a complete outsider who entrenched herself in Israel, and became the determined opponent and persecutor of the true saints of God.

THE REVELATION

Third, she called herself a **prophetess.** In Ahab's day she did it by taking hundreds of false prophets under her protection. Rome had done it by claiming to be the only authorized exponent of the word of God. Their slogan became, and still is, "Hear the Church," but for all practical purposes this has always meant, hear the college of cardinals with the Pope at their head; that is, hear the Romish hierarchy — hear Jezebel! They claim to be the only teaching authority.

Fourth, the whole drift of their teaching is in the direction of **spiritual fornication and idolatry,** which means utter worldliness. What was beginning in Pergamos became rampant, and acknowledged as the proper thing, in Thyatira. In the four or five centuries that preceded the Reformation the Popes and the whole papal system practised and gloried in worldly abominations of the most pronounced and outrageous sort. Repentance was necessary, and ample time for it was granted without avail. History records how many were the centuries during which Romish abominations increased. Time to repent was certainly given.

But judgment, though lingering for long, will not slumber for ever. It is not exactly the church in Thyatira that is threatened, but Jezebel, and also her children; that is, the lesser but similar systems that have sprung from her. Jezebel and her paramours shall be flung into great tribulation: her children smitten with spiritual death. It does not specifically say, **the** great tribulation, though we should judge that what Jezebel represents will develop into the mystical Babylon of chapter 17, and be destroyed during the great tribulation period. The judgment when it comes will be final.

But meanwhile the Lord so deals, both with the parent and the children, as to manifest to all the churches that He is the Searcher of all hearts. His governmental judgments take their course before He acts finally and for ever.

The closing words of verse 23 are really an encouragement. The evil system will be dealt with, yet each soul will be judged on an individual basis. According to their works will each be recompensed. The individual is not lost in the mass. In the case of Thyatira it leads to the discovery of a remnant that is for God, as the following verses reveal.

In the church at Thyatira there comes into view "the rest;" that is, a remnant who can be distinguished from the mass. The words, "unto you" in verse 24 lack authority and only obscure the sense. The Lord now addresses Himself directly to this remnant, who are marked by negative virtues rather than positive, rather like the seven thousand in Israel who had not bowed the knee to Baal. These had not endorsed Jezebel's doctrine and, being simple, had not known the depths of Satan that were in it.

So in this New Testament Jezebel, the counterpart of the woman with "painted . . . face and tired . . . head," of 2 Kings 9: 30, who mixed heathenism with Israel's pure religion, the depths of Satan were to be found! This need not surprise us, however, for at the end, when she changes her character somewhat, and in chapters 17 and 18 of our Book comes forth as the woman with Babylon on her forehead, the enormous evils that are in her come **to the surface.** In the days of Thyatira they were still **in the depths.** Though there were found God-fearing saints who had never seen these evil things, the eyes like a flame of fire searched all those depths. What a revelation it is!

It is lovely to see the Lord treating these true but undiscerning saints with a compassion far beyond anything that their better instructed brethren would be likely to show them. He only lays upon them this; that what they had they should hold fast till He comes. This is the first mention of His coming in these addresses to the churches, and it clearly indicates that viewed from the prophetic standpoint, that which Thyatira indicates goes on to the end.

If they held fast what they had till His coming, they would also keep His works "to the end," and thus be overcomers, as verse 26 says. The promise to such is very significant. An itching desire to obtain power over the nations has characterized the Romish system ever since it came into existence, and in the course of the centuries there have been times when it attained to a partial success, though never wholly achieving it. Now in this very thing the Thyatiran overcomer shall share in the coming day. The Lord will take this power from His Father, and He will delegate it to His saints, who are to judge the world, as we read in 1 Corinthians 6: 2. What Rome has tried to grab before the time for its own glory shall be theirs by the gift of God. And further, "the morning star" should be given to them, which we understand as an allusion to the first move which the Lord will make in connection with His second advent—His coming into the air for His own. That will be as the harbinger of the coming day.

In this fourth church, and in the remaining churches, the call to the one who has an ear to hear comes at the end, after the special word to the overcomer. Viewing things prophetically, this is significant. It indicates that from this point those who have ears to hear will only be found in the smaller circle of the overcomers. The enormities of the Jezebel system are so pronounced that the whole professing church is no longer addressed. The footing lost is not regained; not even when Philadelphia comes into review.

CHAPTER 3

TO SARDIS THE LORD presented Himself as the One who not only had the seven stars, as before mentioned, but also the seven Spirits of God. This is a fresh feature. In chapter 1: 4 they were said to be "before His throne," but now we learn they are in the possession of Christ. The fulness of spiritual power for the government of the earth, according to Isaiah 11: 2, is His. And not only power but vitality also; which was much to the point in dealing with this church which was dead, in spite of having a name to

THE REVELATION

live. Death characterized their general state, yet there were things amongst them not dead, though ready to die, and these could be strengthened if they were watchful.

We cannot doubt that here we have, from the prophetic view-point, a remarkable delineation of that political type of Protestantism that sprang out of the Reformation. That the Reformation was on the whole a powerful work of the Spirit of God we entirely believe, yet we cannot but recognize that from its beginning it was weakened by a large element of worldly politics entering into it, coupled with much reliance upon earthly potentates, and even the force of arms. In result the worldly element largely strangled the spiritual, and in result the works of Sardis were not found "perfect [or complete] before God." Earnest men of God laboured in it, but their works were arrested and never reached completeness. They had "received and heard" a good deal more than they ever translated into their works.

Sardis is called upon to remember these things that had been committed to them, to hold them fast, and to repent; that is, to judge themselves in the light of them, and this of course would lead to a fuller acknowledgement in their works of all they had received. If they did not thus wake up from among the dead and become watchful, they would have to face the coming of the Lord just as the world will. Sunk in spiritual death as the world, they would be treated like the world. But this remark shows that Sardis also will continue to the second coming.

Verse 4 indicates that alliance with the world means **defilement.** But there were a few in Sardis who had escaped this, and the promise to them seems to identify them with the overcomers of the next verse. Again here the virtue of the overcomer seems to be negative, but when the defilements of the world are the general thing it is no small thing to keep clear of it, and the Lord owns it. Their purity shall be manifested in a coming day; their names shall stand in the book of life, and be confessed before God the Father.

We do most certainly need an ear to hear these things, for a political Protestantism surrounds us and we are more likely to be affected by it than by the corrupt Romish system. Are we not conscious that, the flesh being in each of us, there is a continuous downward drag in favour of religion of a type that the world understands and even patronizes? To overcome in Sardis must mean spiritual vitality, and purity as well.

To Philadelphia the Lord presents Himself in characters which are new, as far as this book is concerned. He is marked by that intrinsic holiness which repudiates all evil, the truth that exposes all unreality, and He has the key that controls every door. The reference clearly is to Isaiah 22: 20-23, where Eliakim is in some sense a type of the coming Messiah. Like Smyrna the Philadelphian Church was faced by opposition, and to know the Lord in these ways would be at once a challenge and a support: a challenge as they thought on His holiness and truth; a support as they realized that all was under His control.

The Lord knew their works, and like all the rest Philadelphia is judged on that basis. Not the creed we profess but the works we do is the crucial point. Indeed the works we do give the best index to what we really believe. Knowing their works, the Lord credited them with a little strength, with the keeping of His word and non-denial of His name. We may remember that in the farewell discourse to His disciples (John 14) the Lord emphasized both His Name and His Word. They were left with access to the Father in His Name, and His commandments and His word were given them to be kept.

As the dispensation of law drew towards its close Malachi was inspired to call upon the godly in Israel to remember all the statutes and judgments given through Moses, and in Luke 1 we find a pious couple "walking in all the commandments and ordinances of the Lord blameless." As the prophetic view of the Church draws to its close similar things come into evidence. But even so, the Lord does not credit Philadelphia with strength that is great. He says, **"a little strength,"** which we do well to remember. To keep His word, as far as it is known, and not to deny His name is not the maximum but the minimum to be expected of those who really love Him.

We have before observed that Smyrna and Philadelphia are the two churches out of the seven to whom no word of rebuke is administered: we now notice that both had to face the same kind of religious opposition. Those who are the synagogue of Satan, falsely claiming to be Jews, reappear. In Paul's day Satan was transforming himself into an angel of light, so it is no new thing for him to assume a religious garb. Smyrna was fortified against the revilings of these people, and Philadelphia is encouraged by the assurance that a time of vindication will surely come when the love of the Lord will be manifested. The true Philadelphian can have the assurance and enjoyment of that love, while waiting for the day when it will come to light in a public way.

This leads to what we have in verse 10. The day of vindication and manifestation is future, both for the Lord and His saints. The present is the day of His patience and of theirs, for He is not publicly interfering at present with the course of man's days. For the moment He has accepted the rejection which was meted out to Him, and He sits at the Father's right hand in patience, till the hour strikes when He is to take the kingdom. The word of His patience has reached us, and we are to keep it by attuning our spirits and our whole manner of life to it. This the Philadelphian saints had done, and they are encouraged by the assurance that the Lord would differentiate between them and "them that dwell upon the earth," or "the earth-dwellers." These are a class of people that appear several times in this book—people akin to those who "mind earthly things," of whom

THE REVELATION

Paul warns the Philippian saints. The Christian is called to be a "heaven-dweller," the exact opposite of this.

These earth-dwellers are of the world, and so they will have to face the governmental wrath of God which is coming on the world. From that the Philadelphian is to be exempted altogether. He will be kept not only out of the tribulation, but even out of the hour of it; that is, out of the limited period of time in which it falls. The great event described in 1 Thessalonians 4: 16, 17 will take place—the first movement in connection with the Second Advent—and of that Advent verse 11 speaks.

The Lord acknowledges, then, that Philadelphia did have certain things in possession. His injunction to them is, Hold it fast! They were not a people of great strength, who might go from one conquest to another; or of great possessions, who might be steadily acquiring fresh stores of light and understanding. They were to hold fast what they had. No small task this! How frequently in the history of the church do we see Christians being robbed of what once they had under cover of the enticement to spend all their energies in the pursuit of new things. It was in this way that the earliest heresies were introduced, as we see in 2 John 9; where the true reading seems to be "goes forward," and not "transgresseth." Those Gnostics did not abide in the doctrine of Christ under pretence of going on to more developed understanding.

The promise to the overcomer is couched in figurative terms. A pillar speaks of support, and on pillars inscriptions were made. The overcomer who had but little strength here, and was outside the synagogue of those who said they were Jews, is to be a pillar of strength in the temple of God and go no more out. He is to be descriptive of God, of the city of God, and of Christ Himself. Not until we get to chapter 21 shall we find the city of God described, but it is evidently a symbol of the Church as the centre of heavenly administration. The fourfold repetition of "My God," in this verse is very striking. God is known to us as "the God of our Lord Jesus Christ," and He is "the Father of glory" (Eph. 1: 17). In our verse that glory is in view, and we are associated with Christ, and through Him with God.

It is evident from verse 11 that what Philadelphia represents from the prophetic point of view goes on to the coming of the Lord. We believe that since each of the last four churches run on to His coming, they represent four phases or states which have developed in the order given, and which persist to the end. The Thyatiran phase can be definitely located in the Romish system and the daughter systems springing out of it. Equally Sardis can be located in the political and national Protestantism that in later centuries was severed from the greater abominations of Rome. Philadelphia follows, but indicates a phase which cannot be located in just the same way. We cannot point to any body of believers, or group, which so displays the features we have been considering, that we can point to them and say, There is what Philadelphia represented. Many years ago now, certain believers did begin to think and say that they were Philadelphia, when one much wiser than themselves warned them that such claims would only eventuate in their becoming like Laodicea.

Equally of Laodicea we have to state that it does not describe some visible body that we can name, but rather it describes the sad phase or state which is to become very pronounced at the close of the story. During the past two hundred years there has been a gracious work of reviving in the professing church, which has brought to pass in not a few quarters such a measure of faithfulness and devotion as Philadelphia indicates, and God grant that we—writer and readers—may be amongst them. But within the last century this has been damaged by a stealthy counter-movement of the enemy, the feature of which has been the glorifying of man and the powers of his mind. It has blossomed forth in the so-called "higher criticism," which in its turn has led to that attitude to the whole faith of Christ which is summed up in the term "modernism." Men are so lifted up in their fancied sufficiency that they feel competent to criticise the Word of God rather than allow the Word to criticise them. They have a highly inflated opinion of themselves.

To Laodicea the Lord presents Himself in a threefold way. Not only are all the promises of God amen in Him; that is, they are steadfast and carried to their completion in Him; but He Himself is "the Amen." He takes it to Himself as a title, reminding us of the way in which Jehovah speaks of Himself twice in Isaiah 65:16, as "the God of truth," literally, "the God of Amen." The Jehovah, in whom all is made verity, is the Jesus of the New Testament; and significantly the word verity, so often upon His lips, is really the word, Amen.

Connected with this, He is the faithful and true Witness. What He is, that He declares. The Church has been left in the place of witness, as is shown by each church in these chapters being represented by a candlestick; but alas, the adjectives faithful and true cannot be applied here. That in which the churches have failed—which failure is most pronounced in Laodicea—is found in its perfection in Him.

Thirdly, He is the beginning of the creation of God. Apart from Him therefore nothing of that creation can be known, and, as we shall see, in Laodicea He is standing outside. What part can they have then in that creation?

They have no part, as is evident, and that because two things characterized them. They were indifferent as to Christ, and inflated by self-conceit as to themselves. These are two very ominous features which should occasion much heart-searching with all of us. They abound in Christendom as it exists today, and we may very easily catch the infection of them.

Neither hot nor cold, but lukewarm, is the verdict. Some centuries ago men felt deeply about the things of God. We cannot approve the violence both in speech and act that so often marked their controversies, yet we can admire their strong convictions. The present tendency is in exactly the opposite direction. Convictions are shallow. Everything can be tolerated; anything condoned. No heat is generated; no zeal displayed. Lukewarmness is fashionable. Men may teach what they please as to Christ, and it does not matter.

It is always the case that those who think much of Christ think little of themselves, while those who think little of Christ think much of themselves. Thus it was with Laodicea. They felt themselves to be rich, and making advances in wealth, and thus to be self-sufficient, having need of nothing. The wealth of which they boasted was not gold or silver but doubtless of a more intellectual sort. Modernism is the fashionable thing today, which claims to be the latest and most advanced thing in religious thought, and far in advance of the cruder notions of earlier days. The taint of this has crept into circles where in days gone by it would have been wholly refused.

Laodicea not only felt this and thought this of themselves, but they boldly said it. They claimed it and proclaimed it. This in its turn proclaimed their own folly and obtuseness, and their claim is decisively rejected by the One who knew all their works. Smyrna claimed nothing, but the Lord knew their poverty and yet declared them to be rich. Laodicea claimed to be rich and is told its poverty in scathing terms—wretched, miserable, poor, blind, naked. The language is most emphatic for the definite article precedes the adjectives—**the** wretched . . . That means that they were all these things in a pre-eminent sense.

Here is an illustration of that great word, "Not he that commendeth himself is approved, but whom the Lord commendeth" (2 Cor. 10: 18). Let us take good heed to it.

Though the claims of the Laodicean church are so decisively rejected, and its true state so unsparingly exposed, the grace of the Lord still lingers. In verses 18-20 it finds expression in a three-fold way.

First, there is the Lord's counsel to the church through the angel. There was still available for them "gold tried in the fire," "white raiment" and "eyesalve." They had been boasting in their riches, of which gold is the symbol, but their fancied wealth had not yet faced the fire. When their "goods" went up in smoke, their pretensions would perish. But fire only refines true gold, while it consumes all the gaudy human things that glitter. They needed a righteousness which was **divine** in its origin, when the vain things of their own imaginings would be seen by them in their worthlessness.

Later in this book "white linen" is used as the symbol of "the righteousnesses of saints." Only the saint, who stand in righteousness before God, as justified in Christ, can produce these acts of righteousness in daily life. The Laodiceans, pleased with themselves and their acts, might imagine themselves to be well clothed, but in reality they were naked. Raiment of a sort they might have: the white raiment they had not.

And, worst of all, they were so blind that they did not see their own desperate need. When on earth the Lord had said, "The light of the body is the eye . . . when thine eye is evil, thy body also is full of darkness. Take heed, therefore, that the light which is in thee be not darkness" (Luke 11: 34, 35). A sad illustration of that is before us. They doubtless boasted of being rich in "light" amongst their other possessions, but in reality they were full of darkness; blind as to themselves and as to the Lord, and thus needing the eyesalve.

The Lord's counsel is, "Buy of Me" these necessary things. He is the only Source of them, and in speaking thus He was using the figure which occurs in Isaiah 55, at the mouth of Jehovah, where every thirsty one is invited to buy without money or price. Absence of thirst was the trouble at Laodicea, yet that did not alter the fact that all they needed was to be obtained from the Lord on the same gracious terms. In the New Testament Jesus speaks in just the same absolute way as Jehovah did in the Old.

Second, the rebuking and chastenings of the Lord are an expression of His grace. This is a point which comes to light in Scripture from the early days of Job, yet it is one very easily overlooked, if we get infected by the spirit of self-satisfaction, such as characterized Laodicea. There was a minority who were like that "afflicted and poor people," of whom we read in Zephaniah 3: 12. These are in contrast with "them that rejoice in thy pride" and are "haughty," spoken of in the previous verse. The majority at Laodicea were of this haughty type, yet they did not come under the rebukings and chastenings as did the minority. It is thus in our day, which is very Laodicean in character.

Because of this the haughty majority may feel themselves greatly fortified in their position. They may point out that the minority never seem to prosper as they do, but always to be in trouble, and under the governmental hand of God. It looks therefore as if the minority is disapproved, and by contrast they are the approved ones. Did we ignore the uniform teaching of Scripture we might think so too. But the reverse is the fact. The discipline comes on "as many as I love," that it may stir them to zeal and repentance. A zealous man is one moved to warmth of desire, the very opposite of lukewarmness. Repentance is the opposite of the self-satisfaction, which characterizes the haughty. The spirit of Laodicea is very strong in this our day, so it behoves us to pay much attention to these solemn words of our Lord.

Verse 18, then, is counsel to the haughty majority; verse 19 is discipline for the poor minority. But between the two a certain number may be found that it would be difficult to classify. They are not rooted in pride as the former, nor can they be distinctly identified with those who are Christ's and loved by Him. So, third, there is for such this gracious invitation and offer. The Lord is outside the door but knocking. He is excluded from that which professes to be His own church! What a tragic situation, and what a descent from that departure from first love, which was seen in Ephesus! The final end of this will be utter repudiation. At His second Advent there will be a fulfilment of the word, "I will spue thee out of my mouth," for they will be wholly nauseous to Him. While He lingers, some may be found who have ears to hear His voice as He knocks and calls. For such there is hope in His grace.

The invitation is very inclusive. "If **any man:**" nothing could be wider than that. The only limitation is the having ears to hear His voice, and consequently a readiness to open the door to Him. This done, He will enter to commune with us in our small circumstances; and then lift us to commune with Him in His large circle of pleasure. This is a mighty privilege indeed! Let us be sure that we embrace His offer and enjoy it. It is also a strong evangelistic appeal for the last days, when so many are Christian as regards outward profession and yet lack all reality and life.

There will be those who overcome even in Laodicea. Repentance and reality will mark such, the result of hearing the Lord's voice, and they will be associated with Him in His throne. He overcame—in His case over all the power of evil that assailed Him from **without** — and is associated with His Father in His throne. Those who hear His voice, while He is in the outside place as regards a lukewarm church, will be associated with Him in the inside place in the day that is to come.

The last verse of the chapter must remind us once more that what the Spirit says to each church is not for that church alone, but for everyone who has an ear to hear. Judgment begins at the house of God, and the state of each church is severally scrutinized, yet the Lord's pronouncement as to each sheds valuable light which shines for all. What is necessary correction for one church is wholesome for all, if they have ears to hear. What is local is thus happily blended with what is universal.

Chapter 4

THE FIRST VERSE of chapter 4 is, we judge, a very important one. It introduces the unveiling of "the things which must be hereafter;" that is, according to chapter 1: 19, the third section of the book. The vision now takes a fresh departure, and John sees a door opened in heaven and hears an authoritative call to come up into heavenly scenes. Being, as he tells us, "in the Spirit," all that he experienced and saw had to him a vivid reality, and though a vision it conveys prophetic realities to us.

In the first place, then, John's own position was changed. He left earthly scenes for heavenly, so that he might view thence the Divine dealings with the earth in judgment. This change has symbolic significance, we believe. Chapter 3 ends with, "the churches," and these two words do not occur again until chapter 22: 16 is reached; that is, the

THE REVELATION

churches do not appear right through the unfolding of "the things which must be hereafter." The church as a whole is symbolized in chapter 19: 7, and again in 21: 9, as "the Lamb's wife," but she is then manifestly in her heavenly seat. The catching up of John into heaven is symbolic of the rapture of the church, as detailed in 1 Thessalonians 4: 17, and from this point begins the vision of things that take place on earth after the church is gone.

Next, we notice that before John is permitted to view the governmental judgments of God on the earth, he is shown the secret spring of all. In the coming day of the Lord, men cannot fail to see and feel the judgments, but they will be in the dark as to whence all proceeds. Now we are not to be ignorant of this, and so this chapter and the next are occupied with John's vision of the heavenly scenes and of the One in whom all judgment is vested. The record of what he saw furnishes us with a picture of the heavenly world in solemn session, preparatory to judicial action on earth.

John's attention was claimed first by the central throne and by Him that sat on it. He did not see heaven as "My Father's house" (John 14: 2), the eternal home of the saints, but as the seat of authority and rule, and the Divine glory appeared to him as the rays of precious stones. Such stones reflect the light—the glory of God, which in itself is a light too bright for mortal eyes. The throne of judgment was, however, encircled by a rainbow, showing that in judgment God remembers His promise of mercy, as in Genesis 9: 13. Yet the rainbow was of a super-natural sort, of one colour, and that a tint not seen in the rainbows of our present world.

Then twenty-four lesser thrones encircled the central throne, and on these sat elders in the white raiment of priests, but crowned as kings. At once we perceive a resemblance to what Daniel saw some six centuries before, when he says, "I beheld till the thrones were cast down," or rather, "were set, and the Ancient of days did sit" (Daniel 7: 9), and then not only did One like the Son of Man have the dominion but, "the saints of the Most High shall take the kingdom" (7: 18). So here there is a sight not only of God, the supreme Ruler, but of the complete kingdom of priests, who are to judge the world, according to 1 Corinthians 6: 2. We identify the elders with the saints raised at the first resurrection, and their number corresponds with the 24 courses into which David divided the descendants of Aaron—the priestly family under the law. Twelve is the number of administration, and so 24 suits the priestly company, composed of both Old Testament and New Testament saints, now glorified together.

Verse 5 declares that the throne is characterized not by grace but by judgment, yet judgment which is to be executed in the full light of the Spirit of God. In chapters 2 and 3 the churches were each a "candlestick," or "lampstand," and the Lord was He who had the seven Spirits of God. Now the seven Spirits of God burn as lamps before the throne, illuminating the course of the Divine judgments. The "sea" is there, not filled with water for cleansing, as once in front of the Temple, but of glass, speaking of a state of fixed purity, and "in the midst" and "round about" the throne, as supporting it, were four "beasts," or "living creatures." There are strong similarities to the living creatures of Ezekiel 1, who later in that book are called cherubim. There are differences also: for instance, there only four wings are mentioned, whereas here there are six wings, agreeing rather with the seraphim of Isaiah 6.

The first mention of cherubim, in Genesis 3: 24, certainly conveys the impression that they were some kind of angelic being. On the other hand Ezekiel 1 and Revelation 4 and 5 are records of visions granted to prophets, and the living creatures appear to be rather symbolic of God's governmental actions in the sphere of creation. God's ways have the strength of the lion, and endurance of the ox, the intelligence of a man, the swiftness and elevation of an eagle. The living creatures are also "full of eyes," not only before and behind, but also within—they scrutinize all the future, and all the past, and the deep internal secrets of the ways of God. Hence they contribute to His praise, giving glory and honour and thanks to Him continually, declaring Him to be the thrice Holy, who lives for ever and ever. **Thrice** Holy, notice! Father, Son and Holy Spirit, one Lord God Almighty, who was, and is, and is to come.

As the living creatures give thanks the elders fall in worship, casting their crowns before the throne. They ascribed all glory, honour and power to the Lord on the ground of His creatorial work and supremacy, and thus very suitably they discrowned themselves. Since all things came into being for His pleasure, His judgments must now operate to rescue for His pleasure all that had been marred by sin. But something more than creating power and cleansing judgment is needed. That something chapter 5 brings before us, even the redeeming blood of Christ.

Chapter 5

THE BOOK IN the hand of Him who sat on the throne, written on both sides and sealed with seven seals is evidently the book of judgment, now completed by man's sin. Men had filled to overflowing the cup of their iniquity, the record was complete, but as yet the seals restrained. Who was worthy to break the seals? This was the question now raised. The judgment is richly deserved, but who can execute it?

This was the question raised in the incident recorded in John 8: 1-11. The sinner was undeniably guilty and the law explicit. But who was there so clear of every charge under the law as to be worthy to execute this sentence? All the accusers slunk away, and the only worthy One declined the office at that time. His mission then was to save and not to judge. Now however the hour of judgment is come and He is about to act.

In the vision John wept much. He did not rejoice at the thought of judgment against evil failing by default of a worthy executioner. The very

THE REVELATION

reverse: it outraged his feelings to imagine that it should fail in this manner. We know that, "Because sentence against an evil work is not executed **speedily,** therefore the heart of the sons of men is fully set in them to do evil" (Eccles. 8: 11). It would be a crowning calamity if it were **never executed at all,** and John might well weep at the thought of this. The elders however, were in the secret of heaven and one of them gave John the key to all. It is by a Man that God is going to judge the world in righteousness, and that Man has prevailed and acquired the title to do it. He is the Lion of the tribe of Judah, an allusion to Genesis 49: 9, 10, and at the same time the Root of David—not merely the Offspring of David, but the Root, from whom sprang all David's authority and victory. The title to the crown was His to begin with. It is doubly His as the Overcomer. The closing verses of Psalm 78 indicate how definitely God's purposes for the government of the earth centre in David and Judah. All failed in David's immediate successors, for he had to lament, "Although my house be not so with God" (2 Sam. 23: 5) and yet all is accomplished in Christ. Nothing fails.

The Lion of Judah, then, has prevailed, and so is worthy to open the book of judgment. But how did He prevail? Verse 6 tells us. It was by dying as the Lamb of sacrifice.

The Lord Jesus is mentioned 28 times in the book of Revelation as the Lamb, and verse 6 is the first occurrence. It is worthy of note that here and all through the book a diminutive form of the word is used—"little Lamb" —emphasizing thus the fact that He, who now appears wielding omnipotence, was once the Lamb of sacrifice, minimized and depreciated by men. He now has sevenfold power—symbolized by horns and the sevenfold discernment of the Spirit of God, who as the seven Spirits of God is now sent forth into all the earth. Therefore no corner is hid from His penetrating gaze and intelligence, and nothing will escape His powerful hand.

The Lamb, in lion-like power, came forward to take the book and thus assume His rights and execute the judgments of God in the earth: an action which provoked an outburst of praise and worship, that reverberated to the utmost bounds of creation.

This outburst begins in the inner circle of the four living creatures and the twenty-four elders, who were involved in the earlier ascription of glory and honour and thanks to Him that sat on the throne, when creation was in question. Now redemption was in question, and consequently the Lamb is the Object of worship. All gladly honour the Son even as they honour the Father. Indeed the Father refuses honour professedly offered to Himself, if the Son be not honoured.

The elders had harps, golden vials of incense and a new song: symbols taken from the Old Testament. The temple worship as ordained through David was based on Asaph with his harpers, the priests with their censers of incense, and then also there was "the song of the Lord," as mentioned in 2 Chronicles 29: 27. So the elders are seen functioning as priests both in song and in prayer. The Psalmist said, "Let my prayer be set forth before Thee as incense" (141: 2), and here are prayers which arise as incense and song which is based on redemption. The song is new, since it is based on a redemption out of every nation, instead of having a national character as in Exodus 15; and also inasmuch as it celebrates His worthiness to judge rather than to save.

The worship of the elders is characterized by three things. First, by intelligence and personal directness. They understand that the basis of all God's purposes is the redeeming blood of the Lamb, and they address Him personally, saying, "Thou art worthy." They do not merely sing about Him in the third person—"Worthy is the Lamb." Second, they sing, whereas the angels of verse 11 and the creatures of verse 13 are marked by "saying" and not by singing. Song, as we have remarked, belongs to those who have been redeemed.

Third, though redeemed themselves, they celebrate in an abstract way the Lamb's work of redemption by blood, being carried in spirit far beyond themselves. They are occupied not so much with their part in it as with the supreme worth and excellence of the redemption in itself for the pleasure of "our God." This we say, because the better attested reading omits the "us" which occurs twice, and has, **"they** shall reign," rather than "we." The glorified, heavenly saints are lifted out of themselves to view things and worship from the Divine standpoint. This feature should surely be seen in the worship of the church today, though the reigning time is not yet come. In Revelation 5 we are on the threshold of the time when "the saints of the Most High shall take the kingdom, and possess the kingdom for ever, even for ever and ever" (Dan. 7: 18), and consequently it can be said, "they shall reign [on or **over**] the earth."

Now comes the voice of the innumerable angelic band, followed by the voices of all created things. In both these cases, as we have noted, they praise the Lamb without addressing Him personally. The ascription of praise is sevenfold on the part of the angels; fourfold on the part of every creature—four being the number indicating universality in creation. The angels declare that the Lamb, who was adjudged by men to be worthy of death, and who was led to the slaughter, is worthy of all glory in sevenfold completeness. Every creature sees the Lamb to be associated with Him who sits on the throne, and inheriting all blessing, honour, glory and power. To this the living creatures add their Amen. The elders are moved afresh to worship.

Before passing to chapter 6, we may again remind ourselves that John is recording for us a vision He was permitted thus to see and hear things heavenly and earthly, and so put on record in advance the ultimate outcome of the Lamb intervening in judgment. This particularly applies to **verse** 13. In subsequent chapters he records much evil and blasphemy,

THE REVELATION

rather than praise, from creatures on earth; but ultimately all creatures will have to declare His praise.

Chapter 6

CHAPTER 6 GIVES us the opening of the seals. Judgment dealings with the earth begin. The words, "and see" in verses 1, 3, 5, 7, are doubtful, and the "Come," uttered by the four living creatures, seems to be a call to the respective riders to come forth. The living creatures speak with a voice like thunder, which befits a call, which has governmental justice and judgment as its object. One after the other there appear four riders, mounted on horses, white, red, black and pale or sallow. Each has his own special feature, but all under the controlling hand of God, symbolized by the living creatures.

First in order, there is the going forth of a great conqueror—bloodless conquest apparently, since white is the colour. Second, an outbreak of war, especially civil war with its lawless horrors. Third, black famine and scarcity. Fourth, pestilence ending in death and Hades, but over a limited area—the fourth part of the earth. It is certainly remarkable how in recent times colours have come to be identified with human movements and confederations. We have heard of armies both white and red, and of blackshirts, etc.

All the activities indicated in these verses are oppressive and destructive: human activities, and yet called forth as retributive judgment under Divine control. They remind us of what the Lord Himself called, "the beginnings of sorrows" (Mark 13: 8). Then the next verse in Mark 13 speaks of the persecution of those who will be witnesses for God in those days; and similarly, the fifth seal follows here. It is opened by the Lamb as before, but no "Come" is uttered, for it only revealed to John the souls of those who had been slain for the word of God. The movements under the four seals, which meant oppression and misery for men generally, had meant persecution and death for these, and their souls cried out for vengeance. They had to wait, however. They had fallen under these beginnings of sorrows and other martyrs were to follow. Vengeance on their adversaries and the full vindication of themselves would not take place until the end of God's ways was reached. But meanwhile they were given a more secret token of approval, symbolized by the white robes.

The contrast between the cry of these martyred souls and the dying cry of Stephen is worthy of note. No request for vengeance came from his lips, but the very reverse—"Lord, lay not this sin to their charge." But he lived at the beginning of the present dispensation of grace, and the church is still here as the exponent of the grace of God. These souls under the altar belong to the age of judgment, that follows the calling out of the church. Their cry coincides with that which we so often find in those Psalms, which men have called, "imprecatory." What would not be suitable on

THE REVELATION

our lips is quite suitable on theirs, for when God is going to take up His "strange work" of judgment it is in order to ask Him to do it speedily. He is going to make it a short work in the earth, only what is short to Him may seem long to the creature.

So verses 10 and 11, we judge, confirm the thought that we have left the church dispensation behind; and the opening of the sixth seal makes this yet more plain. Again there is no "Come," for agencies that are superhuman, and more directly from the hand of God, come into play. There are great convulsions both terrestrial and celestial, which result in the overturning of all that had seemed firmly established. What more firm than sun, moon and stars in the heaven and mountains and islands on earth, though stormy seas surround the latter? They symbolize established authorities and powers, whether in the heavens or on earth, and all are involved in a catastrophic fall or at least thrown into a state of flux. Recent happenings among the shaken nations of Europe have shown how disconcerting it is when those who have been like established luminaries are cast down. The allusion to the fig tree, which is so often symbolic of the Jew, may indicate that this upheaval will specially affect that people, thus preparing the way for the acceptance of antichrist.

How all these upheavals will affect men, from the greatest to the least, is shown in the close of the chapter. Apparently they will discern that the hand of God is behind them, and the wrath of the Lamb will strike them as dreadful beyond words. Better be crushed out of existence on earth than face that! Psalm 2 had said, "Kiss the Son, lest He be angry, and ye perish from the way, when His wrath is kindled but a little;" and at this point there was only a little wrath, for we are at the beginning of sorrows, yet perishing from the way was plainly before them. Though the climax of "the great day of His wrath" was not yet, they had entered upon that day, for the day of God's grace in the Gospel was closed. Men may stand in God's grace but no one can stand before His wrath.

Chapter 7

The sixth seal had now been opened, and John does not see the opening of the seventh till chapter 8 is reached. Chapter 7 therefore presents us with a parenthetical interlude in which we have recorded Divine activities and their fruits before we see even more serious judgments falling on the earth. True to the order which runs consistently through the Scriptures, we have the Jew first and after that the Gentile.

There is a brief pause in the Divine dealings. The sixth seal had produced what is likened to a "mighty wind," but now the four winds of the earth are entirely restrained by angelic power. They were not to blow until the servants of God had been sealed in their foreheads—the most prominent part of their persons. These servants of God were found in the twelve tribes of Israel; but Levi coming into the reckoning and also both

THE REVELATION

the tribes that represented Joseph, the number twelve is maintained by the omission of Dan. It has been thought that the way Jacob prophetically referred to Dan in Genesis 49: 16-18, may throw some light on this. If the "serpent by the way," and the "adder in the path," are an allusion to the antichrist, instigated by Satan, rising out of the tribe of Dan, it may do so.

The numbers cited might of course be literal, but more probably are to be understood symbolically, especially as twelve and the square of twelve occur elsewhere in the book in a symbolic sense. The godly remnant of Israel are to have a place of administrative importance in the coming age, and twelve is the number of administrative completeness.

It is to be noted that at this point in the book angels again come into prominence. The Lord's parables in Matthew 13 have told us that they have a large part in the work of selective judgment at the end of the age. They "gather out of His kingdom all things that offend;" they "sever the wicked from among the just." What we see here is that they seal the just of Israel, so that they may be preserved and carried through. Until such are sealed the winds of judgment may not blow.

John **heard** the number that were sealed, and that recorded, he tells us the next vision that passed before his eyes. He **saw** a great multitude that came out of all nations, who appeared as standing before the throne and the Lamb. This was clearly a vision of a great host gathered from the Gentiles, as distinguished from the sealed remnant of Israel, that has just come before us. Another thing also differentiates the two companies. The elect of Israel are sealed, and thus marked for preservation, before the more direct judgments of God begin. The Gentile multitude is arrayed in the white robe of righteousness and holds the palms of victory as having come out of the great tribulation. The one case, therefore, shows that God knows how to secure those already in relation with Him, **before the judgment begins**: the other shows how God can overrule tribulation, even of the fiercest sort, to reach people not previously in relation with Him, bringing them into relationship with Himself, and carrying them victoriously **through the tribulation.**

In the vision this Gentile multitude acclaimed God and the Lamb as the Source of their salvation. They did so with a loud voice that all might hear, and it met with an immediate response from the angelic throng. The multitude was before the throne, whereas the angels encircled the throne and also the elders and living creatures, who formed an inner circle. The angels are moved to worship. They add their Amen to the ascription of salvation to God and the Lamb, though they do not themselves experience salvation, and consequently they do not name it in their own ascription of seven-fold praise, as given in verse 12. Though they do not share the salvation, they can see the excellence and glory of God in it. They ascribe honour and power unto eternal ages to Him who has wrought it.

THE REVELATION

It is remarkable that one of the elders should have raised with John the two questions that would naturally rise in all our minds. Who are these people in their multitudes, and whence did they come? John's response, "Sir, thou knowest," was justified in the result. The elder did know, and gave the information. Consistently through the book the elders are characterized by the spirit of worship and by a very full understanding of God and His ways. As representing the glorified saints, this is what we should expect of them, in keeping with the Apostle Paul's saying, "Now I know in part; but **then shall I know even as also I am known**" (1 Cor. 13: 12).

The elder's reply shows that this great company have a special place inasmuch as they have experienced special sorrows and tribulation. The whiteness of their robes was not produced by their own works, or even by their much suffering, but only by their having been washed in the blood of the Lamb; yet they have a recompense which is a suited answer to their sufferings, and for which their suffering had educated and qualified them.

Their place is "before the throne," a phrase which indicates, we believe, the place they have morally and spiritually: they are put into close touch with God. They have moreover a priestly place since they serve Him day and night in His temple. All the burden and oppression which they have suffered has ceased for ever, and on the contrary the Lamb Himself becomes the Minister of their joy and satisfaction, God having removed for ever anything and everything that causes a tear.

Thus it is a beautiful picture of millennial recompense and blessedness, which will be enjoyed by multitudes called out of the Gentile peoples and carried through the tribulation period. We have not yet reached the millennium in the orderly unfolding of the book, but in this parenthetical chapter we are permitted to have a glimpse of how God will preserve His people in view of it, whether they are Jews or Gentiles.

There will of course be other multitudes, born during the progress of the age to come, also enjoying its blessedness. They will not belong to this company, however, nor share its special nearness, not having had the spiritual training involved in passing through the special tribulation. For us the principle is stated in the words, "If we suffer, we shall also reign with Him" (2 Tim. 2: 12). The principle is the same for them, though the exact recompense may be different.

CHAPTER 8

THE OPENING OF the sixth seal (6: 12-17), produced great convulsions, affecting both the heavens and the earth, which brought terror into the hearts of all. Then came a pause; the winds of heaven being arrested until the servants of God were sealed. Chapter 8 brings us to the opening of the seventh seal and again there is a pause, described as "silence in **heaven** about the space of half an hour." What transpires on earth during that

THE REVELATION

time is not stated. Divine judgment, when it falls, is not only sure but **swift,** yet it is never **hurried.** During this interval of silence the seven angels "prepared themselves to sound" their trumpets. There is a calm serenity about the Divine action in judgment, and it is postponed to the last possible moment.

Angels now come into prominence. This is in keeping with the Lord's own words in Matthew 13: 39, 41, 49; and again in 24: 31. Angels of special importance are indicated here—"**the** seven angels which **stood before God.**" To Zacharias, the father of John the Baptist, the angel announced himself as "Gabriel, that stand in the presence of God" (Luke 1: 19). These seven angels had that peculiar privilege also. In the trumpets that were given to them we have a symbol that differs from the seals. The breaking of the seals not only set in motion the providential judgments that came on men, but also revealed their secret source. Such things, in a less intense form, had come to pass before. The hand of God in the judgments might not have been discerned, had not the seals been broken. The trumpet, on the other hand, is the symbol of what is clearly avowed, constituting an unmistakable call to all. The trumpet was commonly used in Israel, whether for calling an assembly or sounding an alarm. In our chapter the alarm is sounded with great emphasis.

But again, there took place during the half hour the action of "another angel," detailed in verses 3-5. This great Angel acted in high priestly capacity, adding the fragrance of His incense to the prayers of all saints. Many therefore see in Him a symbolic representation of Christ Himself, and we think they are right. His action was twofold. First, He acted on behalf of living saints, so that their prayers might ascend before God as "an odour of a sweet smell." There were still saints on earth, though many had been martyred as chapter 6: 9 showed. Those uttered their cry for vengeance but they did not need the action of the High Priest as these did.

In the second place, His action indicated the fire of judgment. The same censer, that was used for incense and fragrance, was now filled with fire from the altar, and flung to the earth as a signal for the trumpet judgments to begin. The censer was **golden** in keeping with the golden altar, symbolic of that which is divine in its intrinsic excellence. So whether it was the prayers of saints ascending in fragrance, or fire descending in judgment, all was executed in a righteousness which is divine.

In verses 7-13 we get the sounding of the first four trumpets and the results. The language continues to be highly symbolic, and a feature common to each is that the judgments only fall upon a third part of the things affected. This shows that for the moment the effects are not universal but limited. The phrase, "the third part," occurs again in chapter 12: 4, where the Roman Empire, energized by Satan, is in question. This leads to the conclusion that here it is used to indicate the Roman earth, which is practically to be identified with the western European powers, or perhaps we may say, **Christendom**.

Another thing we notice in these verses is that the judgments fall on things rather than men. Yet the things specified—earth, trees, grass, sea and creatures in it, ships, rivers, fountains, sun, moon, stars—are not themselves moral agents, and so accountable to God. Man is the rebel sinner who has to be dealt with. The things are symbols of man and of what is connected with him.

For instance, "earth" signifies the stable organized nations, in contrast with "sea"—the restless, disorganized peoples. "Trees" signify the great men of the earth, in contrast with "green grass," which indicates the common people, but in a prosperous state. "Ships" would be the symbol of commerce. "Rivers" and "Fountains" of the channels and sources of life and refreshment. The darkening of part of both day and night would indicate the disturbance of the whole course of nature to the blinding of men.

The judgment inflicted is symbolic in each case. "Hail and fire, mingled with blood," must signify judgment from heaven of a crushing and searching nature, bringing death in its train. "A great mountain burning with fire . . . cast into the sea"—some imposing and apparently stable institution crashing under divine judgment into the restless masses of humanity. A "great star" burning as a lamp and falling from heaven, speaks rather of some prominent individual, who had shone as a luminary utterly apostasizing, and spreading death-dealing poison of a spiritual sort. The smiting of the third part of sun, moon and stars indicates the partial putting out of the sources of light and direction for men.

It is of course quite possible that we may have here reference also to great sights and signs and catastrophes in the realm of nature. But such things are not, we judge, the main objects of the prophecy, which has to do with what is spiritual and moral rather than what is physical and material.

After the fourth trumpet a very grave warning was sounded. "Eagle" rather than "angel" is the better attested reading in verse 13, which is significant in view of the Lord's words in Matthew 24: 28. The state of "the inhabiters of the earth" is becoming like that of a putrid carcase, and hence the three following trumpets are to unleash judgments of threefold intensity. This phrase or the equivalent, "them that dwell on the earth," occurs a number of times in the book, and usually indicates a special class, whose interests and hopes are completely centred on the earth, and who have excluded all that is of heaven from their thoughts. As Christians we have a heavenly calling, and yet the present trend of religious thought is to concentrate exclusively on the earth, and to treat our hope of heaven with derision. When the church is gone, the earth-dwellers will be striving for their earthly paradise and expecting it as a result of their efforts. These apostates will specially come under the governmental wrath of God.

THE REVELATION

Chapter 9

THE FIFTH AND sixth trumpets follow in chapter 9; both of them are termed a "woe," so severe is the judgment they inflict. In general there is a resemblance between them, but the fifth brings torment so fierce that men will desire death and yet death will elude them. The sixth does bring death. In reading this chapter we need hardly remind ourselves that the descriptions are couched in symbolic language. If taken literally we should have to picture something very grotesque.

Under the fifth trumpet infernal influences are let loose upon the earth. The star that falls from heaven to earth indicates some person of eminence that apostasizes, and to him the key of the abyss was given. The personal pronoun, "him," certainly infers that a person is meant. In the light of what follows later in the book, this may well be the Antichrist himself. The immense cloud of smoke that arises from the opened pit, darkening the air, graphically figures the sending forth of dark and even demonic influences, which shut out from men the light of heaven. In our times we have witnessed something like a preliminary essay of Satan in this direction. About the middle of the nineteenth century a puff of smoke from the pit arose and shaped itself into the mystic word, "evolution." Think of the darkening influence that puff of smoke has thrown over the minds of millions! The light of God has been obscured in their minds by an imaginary ape-man, or even a mere speck of protoplasm. It is the god of this age who blinds the minds of them that believe not.

Out of this darkening influence comes the swarm of "locusts." Here is another graphic figure. The locust is an insignificant insect in itself, but terrifying when it arrives in countless hordes. These had the posion of scorpions, and unlike the natural locust that preys upon every green thing, these were only to afflict the unsealed of men. This refers us back to the opening verses of chapter 7, where we find that those sealed were the servants of God out of the tribes of Israel. We presume, therefore, that those **of Israel** who were not sealed are particularly in question here. If this inference is correct it would strengthen the thought that the fallen star is the Antichrist, for the darkening influence of his apostasy would specially affect the mass of Israel who are still in unbelief. The effect produced is described as the torment of a scorpion's sting, which is very acute but does not usually kill. There is a limit to the period of this infliction—5 months; that is, while the torment is so acute that men would prefer death, it is not prolonged.

The details given in verses 7-10 have a meaning which is not really obscure. Battle horses surely signify aggressive might. The crowns they wear are not the diadems of royalty but the wreaths of victory, which they have assumed. To the eye they looked like gold, but they were not really what they appeared to be, but only, "as it were." The face of a man speaks of intelligence: the hair of women of subjection: the teeth of lions of ferocious power. Breast plates of iron would indicate complete imperviousness to attack. Their sting being in their tails is reminiscent of Isaiah 9: 15, where we read, "The prophet that teacheth lies, he is the tail." Another reference this, which directs our minds to the Antichrist.

Finally, these symbolic locusts were under the direction of a king, whose name means "The Destroyer." He is described as "the angel of the bottomless pit." This indicates that these locusts are an organized force, and under the direction of a controlling destructive power, just as in nature the locust swarms of countless millions act like a well-directed army. Though under the direction of the destroyer, this woe falls upon man not unto death—for death flees from them—but into the destruction of all that makes life on earth worth living. Darkness and torment of a spiritual sort is what is indicated.

At the sounding of the sixth trumpet the golden altar is again mentioned. Not now the priestly offering of incense with the prayers of saints, but forth from it a voice of Divine authority, commanding the loosing of the four angels that had been bound in the Euphrates, who were prepared to bring death upon men—not torment now but **death.** Four speaks of universality, and the Euphrates was the great river that divided the lands of the east from the land of Israel. In chapter 16: 12, we find this great river mentioned again in connection with the sixth vial. It may well be that what happens here has a bearing upon the happening indicated then. This woe is strictly limited, not merely to the day but even to the **hour** of its execution.

The loosing of the four angels of death precipitates upon men the immense army of 200,000,000 horsemen, who were their instruments in this dreadful task. Verses 17-19, give us details of these horses and their riders, which are again symbolic and figurative. The "third part of men" appears again here, so we gather this woe from the east falls especially on what we have called the Roman earth. It is indeed a woe, for even the breastplates—normally a piece of armour wholly defensive are of fire and jacinth and brimstone, and therefore bear an offensive character. This time too the "power" is in the mouth as well as in the tail; but the tails were like serpents with heads dealing out "hurt," while the mouths cast forth fire and smoke and brimstone. All this is indicative surely of something that is very satanic on the one hand, and what is suffocating and death-dealing and full of judgment and pain on the other. If the earlier woe was more applicable to the unsealed apostates of Israel, this falls rather on the Gentile nations and the proud Roman Empire, which in its revived form will be the dominant political power in the earth in the last days.

The "death" spoken of here we understand to signify utter and irremediable apostasy which sinks a man into final alienation from God. Those smitten with this death would be past all feeling or judgment as to what is

THE REVELATION

right and what is wrong. We have recently had some striking examples of this kind of thing in those who fell under the Nazi delusion and became the instruments of its appalling cruelties. It may well be, of course, that literal death of the body follows in many cases, but it is not, we believe, the primary thought.

Verse 20 speaks of "the rest of the men" who were not smitten by death. They did feel the weight of the plagues but they did not repent. Here for the first time in Revelation we get this word, "plague." It at once turns our minds to the plagues in Egypt, recorded in the early chapters of Exodus; and this, we think, not without reason. God's judgments run a course which is consistent with Himself. Judgment is His "strange work;" He does not delight in it, and therefore He does not strike the final overwhelming blow without giving ample warning by preliminary blows of a lesser sort. He may well know that these lesser judgments will not produce repentance and so avert the final intervention, nevertheless He justifies His ways in judgment in the sight of all heavenly intelligences, and permits them to see how right He is when at last He strikes overwhelmingly. So in the case before us: men did not repent. We are permitted to see the depths to which men will have sunk in those days; worshipping demons on the one hand, and the insensible works of their own hands on the other.

Is it possible that men, who live in lands where the light of the Gospel once has shone, can sink to such a level? It certainly is. Millions of men and women were recently worshipping Hitler, who apparently was in touch with a demon by means of clairaudience—hearing voices from the unseen world. He would have been next to nothing without his "familiar spirit," and in worshipping him men were really worshipping the demon that inspired him. The worship too of the material grows apace, as more and more men are obsessed with their great discoveries, and the works of their own hands by which these discoveries are made available, whether for good or for ill. In worshipping these works of their hands, man really is worshipping himself. In those days then, men will worship themselves and demons. They are not very far away from it today.

The last verse of our chapter shows that along with this will go complete moral breakdown. Sorceries or witchcraft indicate traffic with demonic powers, in all its various forms; the other three things specified we are all acquainted with. When life is held cheaply, when personal purity is quite disregarded, when the rights of property are ignored, a state of things must be produced reminiscent of the state of the earth before the flood, or the degradation that prevailed in Sodom and Gomorrah at a later date.

Such is to be the state of things on earth when these "woe" judgments are unleashed. But we have heard the Lord's own words, "As it was in the days of Noe, so shall it be also in the days of the Son of Man . . . Likewise also as it was in the days of Lot . . . Even thus shall it be in the day when the Son of Man is revealed" (Luke 17: 26-30). So we are not surprised.

THE REVELATION

Chapter 10

The record of the things that come to pass, under the sixth trumpet and second woe, does not come to an end with chapter 9. We have to read on to chapter 11: 14 before we get the words, "the second woe is past." After the opening of the sixth seal and an account of the immediate results, we had the angelic action, recorded in chapter 7 and the early verses of chapter 8, as a kind of appendix to it. Now, after the sounding of the sixth trumpet, angelic action is recorded, and also the way in which a witness to God and His claims will be raised up on earth, as an appendix before the seventh and final trumpet sounds.

The close of chapter 9 showed us a state of affairs amongst rebellious men which could hardly be exceeded in its depravity and wilfulness. Chapter 10 opens with a vision of an Angel of peculiar majesty and glory, who announces a speedy ending of God's mysterious dealings with the earth. Thus the final blow that is to fall is preceded by solemn and ample warning in the mercy of God.

In this mighty Angel we see again the One who formerly acted as the Angel of Jehovah's presence—our Lord Jesus Christ. The description of Him in verse 1 agrees very much with that given in chapter 1: 14—16. None but He has a face like the sun. Cloud and rainbow and pillars of fire are also characteristic of Deity. His voice moreover was of highest power and majesty, which had as its echo or reverberations the seven thunders, which surely speak of further judgment actions. The seals, the trumpets, the vials are all made public but the thunders are unrecorded by express command. It is a solemn thought that though many details of the Divine judgments are revealed, there are to be judgments beyond anything made known to us.

The Angel stood with His right foot on the sea and His left on the earth: that is, the whole world is dominated by Him, whether the unstable, turbulent masses or more stable and organized kingdoms. This will be the true situation then—as seen by John and revealed to us—just before the time arrives when God will publicly put all things under His feet. Thus He is viewed as dominating the entire scene, though for a short time yet His supremacy is not manifested nor acknowledged by men.

There is, however, the solemn oath and proclamation, of which verses 5—7 speak. If we are right in identifying this "mighty Angel" with our Lord, in swearing "by Him that liveth for ever and ever," He was really swearing by Himself, as when the promise was made to Abraham (Heb. 6: 13). **That** was an oath for blessing: **this** an oath for judgment; but both are alike **immutable**. The word, "time," at the end of verse 6 should be, "delay." The full stroke of Divine judgment had been held back in the longsuffering and patience of God, but the atrocious nature of the evil, together with the utter lack of repentance, exposed at the end of chapter 9,

THE REVELATION

was now precipitating the climax, to be reached when the seventh trumpet sounded. At last the cup of man's iniquity was full.

"The mystery of God" (verse 7) is of course the mystery of His ways and dealings with men in relation to their sin. Contemplating more particularly God's ways and judgments with Israel as a nation, the Apostle Paul had to exclaim, "How unsearchable are His judgments, and His ways past finding out!" (Rom. 11: 33). What is this but a confession that to the most enlightened of the Lord's servants His ways and judgments are full of mystery. At present God is acting behind the scenes and we cannot penetrate the veil, but when He brings His judgments into the light of day, the mystery of it will vanish away and be finished. What the prophets have declared will be fulfilled, and the rightness of all His dealings through the ages will be seen, as well as of His final judgment at the Second Advent.

The episode, which John relates in verses 8—11, reminds us of the similar incident in the visions of Ezekiel, related in chapters 2 and 3 of his prophecy. Take note of the underlying thought that what the servant of God gives out in the way of prophecy or instruction must first be eaten, digested, assimilated by himself. Nothing is more ruinous spiritually than to proclaim and parade our knowledge of truth, which as yet we have not really made our own in meditation, in prayer, in experience. The acquisition of fresh truth is sweet and exhilarating as honey, but when inwardly digested and assimilated it ever displaces flesh and self and the world, and that is a bitter process. This is so, even if, as here, the little book is concerned with judgment which is to fall on others and not on oneself. Twice the book is spoken of as "open," so in this short chapter we get things that were uttered and yet sealed and not to be published, and also things which though open were to be eaten by the prophet before he conveyed them to others. Even in the solemn matter of judgment there is a time to keep silence and a time to speak.

Chapter 11

IN THE OPENING verses of chapter 11, John has not only to see and hear, but to act. He was to measure the temple, the altar and the worshippers with a divinely-given reed. Once again the language is symbolic, for though a measure of length may suit a temple or an altar, it is quite inapplicable to worshippers in a literal sense. The thought seems to be that these three come under divine scrutiny and are taken account of, whilst the outer court is ignored as being under Gentile feet. This indicates, we gather, that God is going to support what is of Himself in the midst of His earthly people, Israel, and also maintain a remnant according to His election, but the "court," the large outer circle, identified with "the holy city," is to be defiled for the stated period. We ourselves are now in the "times of the Gentiles," during which, "Jerusalem shall be trodden down of the Gentiles" (Luke 21: 24). This period has been running since the days of

THE REVELATION

Nebuchadnezzar, but there is to be a specially intense treading under foot of the holy city for these 42 months. The court is not measured so that the hostile powers are given full scope.

But though they act unhinderedly, they are not permitted to pollute without God raising up a witness against them, and verse 3 speaks of this. The witness lasts for 1,260 days, which according to Jewish computation is exactly the 42 months of the previous verse. As to external things, the witnesses were marked by deepest humiliation, expressed by being clothed in sackcloth, but from a spiritual standpoint marked by the shining of a light, which is divinely given and supported. The reference clearly is to Zechariah 4, only here each witness is symbolized by an olive tree and a candlestick. The olive tree supplies the oil, and the oil feeds the light. God is the God of the earth, and though the holy city is trodden down He has not relinquished His claim to the earth. So before He makes good His claim in irresistible power He maintains His witness in the face of the foe. So much so, that for the time of their testimony they are invulnerable. It is their assailants who die, not they.

Verse 6 shows that these two witnsses have the characteristics of both Elijah and Moses, so evidently they wield immense power. Yet it is not the kind of power we find characterizing believers of this dispensation, who are rather to be "strengthened with all might, according to His glorious **power,** unto all **patience** and **longsuffering** with joyfulness" (Col. 1: 11). In the earliest years, when apostles still wielded miraculous powers, none of them slew men, or shut heaven, or smote the earth with plagues. Such displays of power suit the Old Testament, but not the New. What then shall we deduce from verse 6? Simply that here we are no longer in the present dispensation of the grace of the Gospel and the calling out of the Church. We are again on the ground of **government** and not of **grace.** It confirms what has been advanced; namely, at this time the Church has been taken to heaven.

The witnesses are invulnerable only until their testimony is completed. Then they are slain under the beast that ascends from the abyss, of whom we get details in chapter 13. Their witness was centred in Jerusalem, and there their dead bodies lay. Jerusalem had been called the "holy city" in verse 2: it is that in the purpose of God. With the slain witnesses lying in its street it is called the "great city," which from a spiritual point of view is just "Sodom and Egypt." It is clearly identified by the statement, "where also our Lord was crucified."

Sodom has become symbolic of the world in its unbridled lust and wickedness, where man degrades himself below the level of the beasts, so that the cry of it arises for God's intervention in judgment. Egypt symbolizes the world with its magnificent exterior, the supplier of all that ministers to man's pleasures and fleshly gratification, but withal itself dominated by an idolatry that degrades, and which even enslaves the

THE REVELATION

people of God if they fall under its power. All this may be **great** in man's eyes but it certainly is not **holy**. This is what Jerusalem is to become by the treading under foot of the Gentiles and the domination of the beast from the abyss. In such a city the witnesses die, and the rejoicings over their end are to be great.

Verse 10 mentions, "they that dwell upon the earth,"—the earth-dwellers, of whom we have before spoken. The people generally, according to verse 9, will be glad, but these earth-dwellers rejoice exceedingly and hold high festivity, because the witness of the two prophets "tormented" them. We can quite understand this, for the same kind of thing can be seen today. True witness to Christ in the Gospel is opposed by the careless world, but it arouses specially fierce resentment and repudiation by present-day modernists, whose effort is to degrade the faith of Christ to a mere scheme for earthly improvements, denying its heavenly origin and the heavenly end to which it leads. Its truth they simply cannot abide; it torments them.

The jubilation of the earth-dwellers, and of the persecutors generally, is however to be short-lived. After $3\frac{1}{2}$ days they rise from death and ascend to heaven in a cloud. Their enemies behold it, so that their triumph is complete. They suffer under the beast, but are caught up to a heavenly portion, not an earthly one. Their **going-up** presaged the speedy **fall** of the beast and his satellites.

The question naturally arises: are we to understand these verses as predicting the rise of two actual men, or is it rather that God raises up and maintains, for as long as suits Him, a sufficient and powerful testimony having the characteristics of both Elijah and Moses? We incline to the latter view and that especially because of the symbolic character of the whole book. We think then that they indicate—not a large and abundant testimony; that would be indicated by 3 and not 2—a **sufficient** testimony, divinely, indeed miraculously, preserved and sustained at this epoch — the darkest in the world's history since the cross of our Lord. If we are right in this, the witnesses may be identified with, or at least included in, those "beheaded for the witness of Jesus," in chapter 20: 4, who "lived and reigned with Christ a thousand years." The great point of instruction for us today is the way in which God maintains His own testimony and yet terminates it as soon as its work is done. This instruction stands, whichever view of the two witnesses we take.

At the finish of their story the triumph of the two was complete, and this will be the finish of the story for all God's rejected and persecuted witnesses. They went to **heaven;** at the same time a great earthquake smote the **earth.** They **ascended;** a tenth part of the city that persecuted **fell.** The **Spirit of life** from God had entered into them; seven thousand of their foes were plunged into **death.** Those not slain were filled with fear and compelled to give glory to the God of heaven. It looked as if they were still reluctant to admit Him to be the God of the earth.

This episode concludes the second woe, which is the sixth trumpet, and we are told that the seventh trumpet and third woe follows quickly, for there is to be no longer delay, as we saw in chapter 10: 6. There is therefore hardly any interval between the resurrection and ascension of the witnesses and the final act, which brings man's day to a close and ushers in the kingdom.

The sounding of the seventh trumpet does not bring to pass some fresh infliction similar to the preceding trumpets. Great voices in heaven proclaim that which is the end of all God's judgments—the establishment of the kingdom "of our Lord and of His Christ," This phrase reminds us of Psalm 2: 2, where, "the kings of the earth set themselves, and the rulers take counsel together, against the Lord, and against His Anointed." This they have done all along, but here their proud opposition is quelled, and the reign of the Lord by His Anointed is established. Once established, His dominion abides. Other Scriptures inform us how the kingdom of a thousand years will end, and the eternal state begin. But the tragic rebellion which is to close the thousand years will not mean any interruption in the reign. Our verse says, "He shall reign for ever and ever." From this point of view the millennium and the eternal state are considered as one.

Verses 16—18 give us the reaction of the 24 elders—the heavenly saints —to this tremendous climax. The first thing is their **worship.** Today false professors of religion abound, whose reaction is **criticism,** when they hear of the kingdom of God, enforced by righteous judgment. They denounce the idea of a God who acts in righteous judgment. In heaven it will provoke not criticism but worship. This is a striking fact.

This merges into thanksgiving. They address God by the names in which He revealed Himself of old as the Governor of men and nations—Jehovah, Elohim, El Shaddai, the Eternal One—nothing before Him; nothing beyond Him, supreme and unchallengeable. He is known to us as the God and Father of our Lord Jesus Christ, but this name of love and near relationship would not come in suitably here, where His acts in judgment are being proclaimed. His reign in righteous authority, and not His saving grace, is what is now before us.

Verse 18 summarizes in a remarkable way the things that come to pass when God establishes His kingdom. They are not mentioned in chronological order, as we might have been inclined to place them. For instance, the judgment of the dead does not take place till the end of the thousand years, as chapter 20: 12 shows. Our verse states the results achieved, first in wrath, and then in discriminatory judgment, and not the order in which they will be achieved. Each statement is worthy of careful note.

When Jehovah and His Christ take the kingdom to reign for ever and ever, "the nations **were angry.**" This statement is sufficient to demolish altogether the false idea that the Gospel is going to convert the world, so that the kingdom will be established as the fruit of Gospel effort, and the nations **will be delighted to see it!** Again, the kingdom will be established as the result of the coming of God's **wrath.** This tells the same tale, and is in agreement with Psalm 2 also. When the age of the Gospel closes and wrath comes, bringing with it righteous judgment, it will extend over a long period, only ending in "the time of the dead that they should be judged"— the final scene of wrath, as we have just seen.

But then, as well as the outpouring of wrath on manifested evil, there will be a condition of mixture, where discrimination is necessary. This had been predicted by our Lord in Matthew 13: 41—43, and here it is fulfilled and accomplished. The prophets, the saints, the God-fearing will have their reward in the glory of the kingdom, whereas the destroyers of the earth will be themselves destroyed.

All sin is destructive in one way or another. As man has become increasingly inventive and wilful, his powers of destruction have increased. In Europe and elsewhere today we see a sample of what is coming. But underlying all these powers of physical and material destruction, now so manifest, there is the propaganda of the destroyer himself—the deceiver, the father of lies. The real root of the terrible mischief is here. The primary destructive force is found in the region of **mind,** not **matter:** in false religion, false philosophy, masquerading as science, but really, "science, falsely so called" (1 Tim. 6: 20). These false ideas reach into the moral, the political, even the material world, and today they are manifestly leading men, who are intoxicated with them, into uncontrollable violence. "Them that destroy the earth," under cover of improving conditions, whether materially, socially or religiously, are becoming more and more numerous and powerful.

The establishment of the glorious kingdom of our Lord will mean the destruction of all such. Then at last earth's golden age will begin.

The last verse of chapter 11 is evidently the preface to the visions that follow, marking a fresh division of the book. Chapters 4 and 5 are a magnificent preface to the visions recorded from 6: 1 to 11: 18. There the sign was the rainbow and the throne. Here it is the temple and the ark of His testament. In that the visions deal with God securing a remnant for Himself, whether of Israel or of the Gentiles, and at the same time breaking the pride and power of men in the earth, and finally establishing His kingdom, and what is involved in this is stated succinctly in 11: 18. In this fresh section we are now to cover part of the same ground, but from another view-point.

The ark had been the throne of God in the midst of Israel, and the temple was the shrine for it in the days of the kingdom established through David. All had been desecrated and destroyed on earth, but we are permitted to see that the real things, of which the others were only the shadows, were secured in heaven. David's greater Son is to be the supreme Ruler, exerting His authority through Israel on earth, and yet more widely through the church, as we shall presently see. God will fulfil and establish His covenant through judgment, hence the opening of the temple is accompanied by judgment, whether directly inflicted from heaven, or generated on earth—lightning, hail, etc., indicates the one; an earthquake indicates the other.

The point in this fresh section seems to be, not so much the establishing of the throne, as the question—Who is going to ascend the throne and thus dominate the earth? There is "that Man whom He hath ordained" (Acts 17: 31). But there is also a rival, as we are quickly notified—Satan, represented as a dragon. We shall also see his three chief agents—the two beasts of chapter 13, and the harlot of chapter 17. We are now to see these rival powers one by one disposed of, and thus the way cleared for Christ to ascend the throne.

Chapter 12

IN VERSES 1 and 3 of chapter 12 we should substitute "sign" for "wonder." Two signs appeared in heaven, but that which they signified transpired on earth. The woman we judge to be Israel. She is invested with sun, moon and twelve stars, symbols of authority, for it is through Israel that the Divine authority will at last be made effective on earth. Clearly then we view Israel ideally, according to that which is in the purpose of God, and therefore in a light which up to the present has only been realized in that small part of the nation that we speak of as the godly remnant, and even there only imperfectly. Out of that godly remnant the Man-child sprang.

The second sign was that of the great red dragon. The woman had the symbols of heavenly authority: he had not that, but he was invested with heads and horns and crowns — really "diadems," the symbols of royal estate—which indicated the wielding of immense power in the earth. Here, then, we have Satan, but clothing himself in the pomp and greatness of the fourth great world-empire of Daniel 7; that is, the Roman. There is, however, the further feature that his tail drew the third part of the stars of heaven; an allusion, it would appear, to Isaiah 9: 15. We have "the prophet that speaketh lies" in the latter part of chapter 13, and he seduces and draws after him a third part of the lesser luminaries, who should shed light on the earth, and in result they apostatize from the position in which originally they were set.

Who shall occupy the throne? Judging as the world does, there would seem to be only one answer. What more helpless than a man-child newly born? What more vigorous and powerful than a great red dragon? Yet ultimately it is the Child who is to rule all nations with a rod of iron. The devil is set to frustrate if possible the purpose of God; and hence through the dragon he was prepared to devour the Child as soon as born.

THE REVELATION

The sign appeared in heaven before the gaze of John, but historically the thing signified took place at Bethlehem soon after our Lord was born. Divine action frustrated the dragon's design. The action is described here as, "her Child was caught up unto God, and to His throne." The life of our Lord, His death and resurrection are passed over in silence. There may also be here an allusion to Micah 5: 3, where Israel travails and brings forth Christ in a mystical sense—Christ at last recognized and acknowledged in the hearts of the remnant—only one could hardly speak of that being followed by the catching up to God and His throne, but rather by Christ seating Himself on His own throne of glory. The design of Satan as the devourer of the Man-Child is defeated.

This being so, the dragon turns his attention to the woman, and in this the sign carried us on to things yet to come at the extreme end of the times of the Gentiles. The true Israel of God will not be called upon to resist the dragon but to flee to a place of no human resources where she will be under Divine protection and care for the stated period. Elijah, we may remember, fled into the wilderness to a place ordained of God, and later to Zarephath, and in both places was miraculously fed, and the time of trial for him lasted three and a half years. Now the 1,260 days of our verse is exactly $3\frac{1}{2}$ years, according to Jewish reckoning. This same period appears again as "a time, and times, and half a time," in verse 14, and we have had it already in chapter 11, as 42 months as well as 1,260 days. It is doubtless the fateful latter half of Daniel's 70th week (see Dan. 9: 27).

We have had signs in heaven; now in verse 7 we have "war in heaven." To some it may be a strange thought that the heavens, in part at least, have been polluted by the presence and action of Satan, but the first chapter of Job should have prepared us for this. Then again, Daniel 10: 10—21, gives us a glimpse of angelic powers in the heavens acting both for and against saints of God on earth. In that passage we have mentioned, "Michael, one of the chief princes," spoken of elsewhere as the Archangel, and in Daniel 12: 1 he is spoken of as "the great prince which standeth for the children of thy people." Here again, where the Israel of God are in question, Michael appears with his angels, and Satan and his angels are cast out of heaven to the earth. Their place in heaven is finally lost, as verse 8 indicates.

Verse 9 is very striking. The great dragon, though externally bearing marks which identify him with the Roman Empire, yet personally is Satan. This terrible spirit of evil, like so many human criminals, has several aliases: he is the devil, and also the old serpent of the Garden of Eden. He is also the deceiver of mankind, either directly or through his agents—in this book he is spoken of in this character seven times, the first occurrence being in this verse. In deception he is a practised hand. He deceives the whole world, and Matthew 27: 63 shows how effectively he did it with some of the most religious men the world has ever seen. He deceived them into regarding the One who was the truth as "that deceiver."

THE REVELATION

In Luke 10: 18, the Lord Jesus used the past tense, "I **beheld,**" in announcing prophetically this great event, yet future; just as Daniel said, "I **beheld** till . . . the Ancient of days did sit," and other prophets spoke similarly, using the past tense in describing things to come. It is an event of far-reaching import, as verse 10 indicates. Heaven sees in it the presage of the complete establishment of the kingdom and power of Christ, and the complete overthrow of the adversary. Moreover it will bring to an end an evil work in which he delights at the present moment; that of accusing the saints before God, as also is illustrated in the first chapter of Job. His work in this is incessant—day and night. Those whom he accused heaven acknowledge as "our brethren." There is no need for saints to accuse each other before God. This is done most efficiently and incessantly by Satan.

But here certain "brethren" are specially in view. They overcame him and his accusations, firstly by the blood of the Lamb. In a judicial sense nothing but that could meet the accusations, as we all know right well. But secondly, on practical lines they overcame by adhering to the word of their testimony, even unto death. Like their Master, only in a lesser sense, their death was not their defeat but their victory.

The heavens rejoice at the ejection of the devil, but his fall means woe to the earth and the sea; that is, as we understand it, to men generally, whether in nations of comparative stability or in restless, unsettled communities. The devil will realize that since he could not maintain his footing in heaven, he will not be able to maintain it upon earth. His time is short and this stirs him up to great wrath, which, as he cannot vent it directly upon God, he will upon all that represents Him on earth. The godly remnant, symbolized by the woman, become the special object of his persecuting hatred.

Let us not fail to notice, and put together, the four characters in which the devil appears in this chapter—verses 4, 9, 10, 13. As regards Christ, he was the devourer: as regards the world, the deceiver: as regards the brethren, the accuser: as regards saints in testimony on earth, the persecutor. Before he is dealt with in unsparing judgment his malign character is fully revealed.

His persecution of the woman is going to fail. That the woman had a place of refuge, prepared of God, was mentioned in verse 6: we now find that by means of an extraordinary sort she will be enabled to flee, as verse 14 indicates. The effort of the devil to hinder her is frustrated by more ordinary means, according to verse 16. It would appear from verse 17 that while the majority of the God-fearing will be thus miraculously protected, there will be others who do not flee and so are specially a target for his animosity. They are marked by obedience, and they have "the testimony of Jesus." They are called to a special place of testimony, whilst the mass are to flee, as indeed the Lord Himself had indicated in Matthew 24: 15—21.

THE REVELATION

Chapter 13

THERE CAN BE no doubt, we think, that the $3\frac{1}{2}$ year period, mentioned in several different ways in this passage, is the time of the great tribulation. It will be a time when the devil is excluded from heaven and consequently concentrating his wrath upon earth, and, as we shall see presently, the time when the vials of the wrath of God are poured out on the earth: a much more serious matter. It will also be the time when human lawlessness and iniquity rise to mountainous heights, and as a result the most fearful oppressions are instituted and wrongs are perpetrated. Chapter 13 now brings to our notice the two chief human instruments of Satan's power, by whom these evils are brought to pass.

John is now transported in his spirit to the sand of the sea, and out of the sea a wild beast arises. This beast has features which clearly connect him with the fourth beast seen in vision by Daniel, and described in his seventh chapter, and also with the red dragon we have just been considering. The symbolism is not obscure. Out of the restless, surging sea of nations the Roman Empire in its closing form will emerge. For the significance of the seven heads and the ten horns we may consult chapter 17: 8—13; a passage we must deal with later. It will suffice here to notice that in the case of the dragon the diadems are on the heads: in the case of the beast they are on the horns. The heads signify the varied forms which the ruling power has assumed through the years, and whatever they have been the devil has claimed to wear the diadem; and has, in fact, dominated the scene. When the Roman power reappears in the last days, it will be in a ten-kingdom form, and each king will claim a diadem under the beast.

Verse 2 indicates that this beast of the last days embraces within himself the characteristic features of the first three empires mentioned in Daniel 7. The Babylonian was like a lion: the Medo-Persian like a bear: the Grecian (or Macedonian) like a leopard. This beast had the features of all three. All their forms of beastly violence will be incorporated here, and even worse features of its own added. Here is blasphemy, a form of sin directed specially and definitely against God. Moreover the power that is wielded is directly Satanic, for "power and his seat and great authority," was delegated by the dragon. Evidently when the Roman dominion reappears it will be a distinctly Satanic production.

In these early verses we pass almost insensibly from the kingdom to the remarkable man in whom the dominion is to be headed up. When we read of one of the heads of the beast being wounded "as it were" to death, we think of it as figuring the empire. The deadly wound is healed in the surprising uprising of the beast energized by the devil; and now the beast figures the imposing individual, who will wield the power of the Empire in the last days. The word, "seat," in verse 2 is really "throne." Solomon, we may remember, inherited from David a throne that came from the hand of

God, and there was added to him riches and power from the same hand. This individual will accept all from the hand of the devil.

Let us recollect also that Satan approached our Lord in the temptation in the wilderness with an offer of all the kingdoms of the world, if only He would worship him. The Lord's answer was, "Get thee behind Me, Satan.". He utterly refused it. But the offer which the Lord in His perfection refused, will appeal to this man, who is called, "the beast," and he will do homage to the devil and get the kingdom for a brief spell. For that same brief spell Satan will be publicly acknowledged as "god," and thus seem to achieve what he has coveted from the beginning. We find a prophetic reference to it in Isaiah 14: 12-14. "I will ascend . . . I will be like the Most High." Yet in result, "How art thou fallen from heaven, O Lucifer, son of the morning!" The achievement of his darling desire is the prelude to his fall.

As the chief political agent of the dragon, the beast will be a very powerful and imposing personage; so much so that men will worship him, and regard his power as irresistible. Men will feel that here at last is the superman and the super-kingdom, which can effectively impose its will and subdue all opposition. This it is, we judge, that will induce men to say, "Peace and safety," as foretold in 1 Thessalonians 5: 3, but which leads to "sudden destruction."

We have recently had striking and terrible proof of the superhuman influence and power that can be exerted by a man of the basest description, if he traffics with demons, as the late ruler of Germany did. In what we are considering not a mere demon is at work but Satan himself. In all the greatest crises that Scripture records it would appear that Satan employs no inferior agency but acts himself. This is so, for instance in the fall of man; in the temptation in the wilderness, when the Deliverer came forth; in encompassing the death of Christ through Judas Iscariot; and here, where the final bid is made to completely dominate the earth.

Inspired by Satan, the beast acts as Satan; his mouth is filled with promises and boastings on a great scale, coupled with blasphemy against God and depreciation of everything divine. Not only the Name and dwelling of God but also those who have their dwelling or tabernacle in heaven, come under the lash of his tongue. Satan has just been cast out of heaven, and previously to that, saints have been caught up into heaven. They are therefore beyond Satan's power, but the more therefore the objects of his hate.

There will be saints still on earth and on these he will make war successfully. His rage is against everything of God. Those that dwell in heaven he can only speak against. Those on earth get different treatment. Some, represented by the woman in the previous chapter, flee and are protected from his animosity. Some are overcome, presumably by death. Some, represented by the two witnesses of chapter 12, have a special place

THE REVELATION

of testimony, and are only overcome for a moment, and just before the end.

As to men generally, he completely captures their imagination. They will see in him all that they desire. Only the elect, whose names from the foundation of the world have been in the book of life of the slain Lamb, will fail to worship him. It will be a time of intense testing and patience, and faith will be tried to the uttermost.

And for ourselves, the revelation of these things is a test, and if we have not "ears to hear," we shall not profit. It is a revelation that runs counter to every thought of the natural man.

Another beast now engages the attention of John, the seer. If the first holds a dominating position in the government of the world, the second is equally dominating in the sphere of religion. The government of God in relation to the earth is largely the theme of the Old Testament, whereas the New Testament unfolds the grace of God in Christ and brings heaven within our view. The devil will introduce his counterfeits, acting in both directions, and when men are brought under the power of both his grip upon them will be complete. They will be held by "totalitarianism" as in a vice. Our chapter predicts this, long before the word "totalitarian" had been coined.

The second beast rises not from the sea, but from the earth; that is, from a settled state of things. The rise of the first beast will have quelled the surging sea of nations, and prepared his way. He impersonates a lamb, but his true character is revealed by his speech. Jesus came as THE LAMB of God, as John 1 shows, and chapter 10 of the same gospel shows that as the true Shepherd of the sheep He was recognised by His voice. Here the false "lamb" proves himself to be no true shepherd but a slave-driver, speaking with the voice of the dragon.

Tyrannous power marks him, power derived through, and exercised in favour of, the first beast, who supports him. This interplay of forces has always been sought through the centuries by the civil rulers on the one hand and the religious leaders on the other—particularly by the Roman hierarchy. It will be attained in very full measure at the end of the age. We do not forget that there will be the apostate "church," symbolized by the harlot in chapter 17, but this is to be destroyed by the ten kings under the first beast, whereas the second beast continues to the end and meets his doom together with the first beast. He is supported by the worldly power of the first beast, whom he supports religiously by displays of supernatural power, even to the extent of bringing fire down from heaven, thus claiming Heaven's approval.

In 2 Thessalonians 2, we read of the coming lawless one, "whose coming is after the working of Satan with all power and signs and lying wonders, and with all deceivableness of unrighteousness in them that perish." Here

THE REVELATION

John sees him deceiving the nations, and particularly "them that dwell on the earth." These earth-dwellers will doubtless feel that their dreams are to be realized in these "super-men;" that here at last has been organized the ideal condition of things, wherein great MAN may display himself in all his glory. It will be the apotheosis of Humanism; that is, of religion which finds its centre in man and not in God. Hence the suggestion to set up some great image of the super-man will be a very natural one.

It is remarkable that at the beginning of the times of the Gentiles, Nebuchadnezzar, the first head, arrogated to himself almost divine honours and made a great image, the worship of which was to institute a kind of super-religion, thus unifying the diverse religions that prevailed in his wide dominions. Thus he glorified himself; but he was defied by a mere handful of godly Jews, defeated when he attempted to exterminate them, and soon after was debased below the level of the beasts and made to appear one of the greatest fools that ever crawled on the earth, by the mighty hand of God upon him. He learned a salutary lesson, as the end of Daniel 4 shows. Our chapter is showing us that the times of the Gentiles will end just as they began and with apparently greater success, for those who refuse to worship the image of the beast will be killed. This time God will not intervene to frustrate the intentions of these wicked men as He once did with Nebuchadnezzar. Their judgment will fall on them in one overwhelming blow at the finish, as we see in chapter 19.

The lying wonders performed are evidently Satanic in origin, and their effect is to subjugate the minds of men and make them completely subservient to the designs of the devil. The system instituted being totalitarian, its tentacles are spread over matters of a commercial nature as well as religious. Every man will have to bear a mark. Just as the ancient slave-owners used to brand their slaves, so men will carry a mark which will brand them as slaves of the devil through the puppets of his creation. The brand employed will apparently have three forms; either "the mark," whatever that may exactly mean, or "the name of the beast," or, "the number of his name."

As to the last we are informed that it is 666. Verse 18 has intrigued many minds and led to much speculation as to its significance; and hitherto all to no purpose. Nearly sixty years have passed since we ourselves first heard confident solutions put forth, all to be falsified by subsequent events, as many since have been. We believe that when the time arrives, and those who fear God need a distinguishing mark, this point will be illuminated by the Spirit of God and so all will be clear. For us let it suffice that just as seven is the number of completeness and perfection, so six is the number of human incompleteness and imperfection. It is significant that six is a number stamped upon the Philistine giants—see 1 Samuel 17: 4—7; 2 Samuel 21: 20. Goliath's height was six cubits and a span; six pieces of his armour are specified; his spear's head weighed six hundred shekels.

THE REVELATION

His brother had six fingers on each hand, six toes on each foot. Yet the giants fell like ninepins before David and his warriors. The imposing beast, whose number is six thrice over, will similarly fall before the presence of the Lord.

With steady gaze John had observed the scenes unrolling before him. He had looked at the sea and seen a beast rise therefrom; then at the earth and seen a second beast arise. But now chapter 14 opens and his gaze is directed to Mount Zion, and there he sees the Lamb, whom he had previously seen in chapter 5. What a delightful change! No longer is it a beast of grotesque and frightful appearance, or a pseudo-lamb that is a dragon at heart, but the true Lamb, who is indeed the Son of the Father, and He stands on Mount Zion, which is symbolic of that royal grace which is the only hope for any man. That being so, we are permitted to see others associated with Him.

CHAPTER 14

CHAPTER 14 GIVES us a series of visions, all of which set before us in various ways God's thoughts and actions from heaven during the period when the two beasts are dominating the earth, persecuting and even slaying the saints. In the first of these visions we see how God will preserve for Himself faithful souls who will be true to the Lamb and free from the corruptions that the beast is enforcing on all under his power. The number given is symbolic. Twelve is the number of complete administration, and here we have the square of it multiplied by a thousand. We have had it before in the number sealed of the tribes of Israel in chapter 7, but we must not infer from this that the two companies are identical. There it was a question of securing the elect of Israel before the judgments were permitted to burst forth. Here we have a company redeemed from among men as firstfruits for the millennial earth, who have been preserved in virginal purity, and who have "His name and the name of His Father"—as it should read—written on their foreheads, instead of the name or mark of the beast. As a result of their unique experiences they sing a new song which is peculiarly their own. The tried saint of today may well take courage from the fact that, if special trials are endured with God, we are thereby qualified to sound His praise in a special song. When the heavens and the earth join in the great orchestra of praise in the millennial age, what a variety of tone and utterance there will be! Yet all will be in harmony.

The better attested reading in verse 5 is, "and in their mouths was no lie found; for they are blameless." The propaganda of the two beasts of chapter 13 was one huge lie, just as Paul indicated in 2 Thessalonians 2. The miracles wrought by the beast he characterizes as "lying wonders," and he tells us that God will send men a strong delusion "that they should believe a lie." These saints were wholly separate from all this. They were

THE REVELATION

true followers of their Master, who would not take up the names of evil into His lips, as Psalm 16 prophetically puts it. Hence they were without blame in a course of practical righteousness. The words, "before the throne of God," lack authority; so it is evidently not the point that they were judicially righteous by the blood of the Lamb, but practically right in their course below.

The second vision of the chapter is in verses 6 and 7. In that very dark hour in earth's story there will be rendered to all men everywhere a clear testimony to God in His creatorial greatness, which demands that He be feared and glorified, especially in view of the fact that the hour of His judgment is come. Two things may be noticed. First, it is called "the **everlasting** gospel . . . unto them that dwell on the earth." The presentation of God in the glory of creation is always "glad tidings," no matter what the age or dispensation. We have lived to a day when the earth-dwellers have been grievously deceived by the devil's lie of evolution, so we can appreciate how glad is the tidings of a Creator-God. The word "everlasting" may also carry back our thoughts to the "everlasting covenant" of Genesis 9: 16.

Second, this gospel is committed to **an angel,** flying in the midst of heaven. We often say, rightly enough, that no angel can preach the gospel which speaks of the redeeming blood of Christ, inasmuch as no angel has any experimental knowledge of redemption. But when creation is in question angels can speak in a way that men cannot. Angels saw its wonders and shouted for joy. Men only know of it by revelation. By angelic ministration this testimony will be diffused through the earth in that solemn hour.

Verse 8 gives us a third vision of a second angel. The fall of Babylon is briefly announced; full details of which are given to us in chapters 17 and 18. The wording of our verse suggests first a city and then a corrupt woman, just as we find Babylon portrayed in those chapters. It clearly symbolizes the corrupt ecclesiastical system, headed up in the papacy, which will rise to great heights of splendour and influence after the true church is gone, and which will for a brief moment dominate and seduce all the nations. So in the second vision we have the proclamation of the true Creator-God, just when men are deifying a man in the person of the beast; in the third vision the judgment of the false religious system, which was aiding and abetting this evil.

In the fourth vision a third angel appears—verses 9-13. On God's behalf he utters the sternest possible warning of the judgment that will fall on all who accept the mark of the beast and worship him. It will indeed be a solemn hour when men have to face such alternatives. If they do not worship the beast death is the penalty before them, as we saw in chapter 13: 15. If they do, the far more awful penalty will certainly come upon them, as verses 10 and 11 of our chapter state. If we were asked what two

THE REVELATION

verses in the whole Bible present us with the darkest and most terrible picture, we should select these. We may well ask. Why language of such tremendous intensity here?

The answer we believe to be, that here we have the climax of all the preceding ages. Mankind started on its fallen and lawless career fascinated by the lie of the devil, "Ye shall be as gods" (Gen. 3: 5). Under the same evil leadership and through the two beasts, mankind will make its supreme and last bid to reach the goal of its desire. At this point then human sin reaches its climax and rises to its highest expression. Is it not fitting that the most bitter judgment is to fall on the highest sin? Testimony to the eternity of punishment is quite uniform throughout the New Testament, but at the same time the Lord's own words — Luke 12: 47, 48, for instance — have indicated that with God, as with men, there are degrees in the severity of judgment. Here, then, we have eternal judgment of the utmost severity which will lie on those who will have carried sin to its most outrageous lenghts; the very reading of which fills the soul with horror. Those who fall under it will have "no rest," and they will stand as an eternal witness to the severity of God's judgment against sin. The "smoke of their torment" will be something for every eye to see.

Verses 12 and 13 speak of the saints who will not bow to the beast. It will be a supreme test of patience and endurance. When men generally are being forced to comply with the demands and commandments of the beasts, these will keep the commandments of God; and this they will do because they cling to "the faith of Jesus." They may not know Him in that full way, which is the portion of the Christian today, but they will know that Jesus, who once came and was despised and rejected, is the true Christ of God, and the faith of this will possess them in spite of everything, and they will brave the wrath of the devil.

Some of them will escape his power, but many of them will fall as victims before the beasts, and a peculiar blessedness is the portion of such. The beast-worshippers will pass out of this life into eternal damnation of special intensity—out of apparent glory into the torment. Saints with the faith of Jesus may be martyred in circumstances of utmost distress and apparent defeat, but "henceforth", from that very moment, their blessedness begins. Great emphasis is added to this by the way the whole Godhead is introduced here. These saints keep the commandments of **God**; also the faith of **Jesus**; they die in the **Lord**; that is, because owning His authority; the **Spirit** endorses their blessedness. We have just seen that the damned have no rest, but these "rest from their labours; and their works do follow them" into the eternal world, that they may receive their due reward.

The chapter closes with a vision which comprises two sections—the reaping of the harvest, and the gathering in of the vine of the earth. John beheld a white cloud. The cloud indicated the presence of God: its whiteness, the pure and spotless character of the judgment which the presence of

THE REVELATION

God must now involve. One like the Son of Man sat **on** that cloud—not **in** it, as though concealed by it, but fully manifested—crowned and with the sickle of judgment in His hand. All judgment is committed to the Son of Man, as we know. He acts mediatorially, and therefore thrusts in His sickle when the word of direction reaches Him from the inner shrine through an angel, and the earth is reaped.

The figure of a harvest is used in connection with judgment in both Old and New Testaments—Joel 3: 13; Matthew 13: 38—43. It is more particularly a figure of discriminatory judgment, as Matthew shows. The wheat will be reaped as well as the tares. In the final result there is the shining forth as the sun for these, and the furnace of fire for those.

But another angel comes forth; this time not from the sanctuary but from the altar where the fire of judgment burned, and over that fire he had power. The instruction now is to cut down the clusters of the vine of the earth, which were fully ripe. The grapes were gathered and cast into the great winepress of the wrath of God. This indicates overwhelming judgment falling upon that which is so wholly evil that no discrimination is necessary. It is remarkable that Joel 3: 13, which predicts the harvest, also predicts the winepress judgment. It is of this terrible moment that Isaiah 63: 1-6 speaks also. It is, "the day of vengeance," according to verse 4 of that passage, but also, "the year of My redeemed," inasmuch as the total crushing of the adversaries will mean a final redemption of the godly, just as it happened when Israel was redeemed at the Red Sea and the Egyptians crushed. It is "the day of vengeance of our God," the words which the Lord **did** NOT **read** in the synagogue at Nazareth.

The last verse of our chapter gives us in symbolic language an idea of the devastating and widespread effect of this judgment. Jerusalem is, of course, indicated by "the city," and 1,600 furlongs is about the whole length of Palestine. There will be a complete and crushing sweeping away of all the adversaries who will at that time gather themselves together against God—see again Joel 3: 9-16.

The Lord Jesus is not treading the winepress today, nor is He reaping the harvest of **the earth.** He is sowing the seed through His servants, and fruit therefrom is being reaped. But it is **for heaven,** and not earth.

Chapter 15

CHAPTER 15 BEGINS another sub-section of the book. Chapter 14 gave a series of visions, in which things were presented to us in brief summary. In verses 9 and 10 the wrath of God against the beast-worshippers was announced. We now learn in much more detail how that wrath will be poured out.

The seven angels having the seven last plagues are introduced to us as "another sign in heaven." This expression has occurred twice before at the

THE REVELATION

beginning of chapter 12, though our Authorized translators used the word "wonder" instead of "sign." The three signs in heaven are, then, first, that of the elect Israel, out of whom Christ sprang; second, that of the dragon, the great opponent of the Man Child, operating by means of the two beasts; third, that of the angels to whom it is given to pour out the vials filled with the wrath of God, which wrath is specially directed against the beasts and all who own their authority. The wrath of the dragon and the beasts is against the Man Child and all who own Him. The wrath of God is against the dragon and all who own him.

It is evident, then, that chapter 15 does not follow chapter 14 chronologically, but rather breaks back to a time preceding the execution of the harvest and vintage judgments by the Son of Man; just as we find the wrath of God against Babylon announced under the seventh vial at the end of chapter 16, and then full details of Babylon's fall given in chapters 17 and 18. Its fall indeed had been briefly announced in verse 8 of chapter 14.

But before John had to contemplate the outpouring of the vials in detail he was given a vision of those who will be carried in triumph as overcomers through that terrible period and then ascribe the glory of their victory to God. The mingling of fire with the sea of glass would indicate that these victors had been subjected to the fiery trial of death but from their martyrdom had stepped into victory. Consequently their song is not only that of Moses but of the Lamb. The first song recorded in Scripture is that of Moses in Exodus 15, celebrating Jehovah's victory in crushing the might of Egypt and redeeming His people. Our verse gives us the last record of a song in Scripture, and again the song of Moses appears for once more and finally God is crushing the adversary and redeeming His people. But coupled with that is the song of the once suffering but now triumphant Lamb, for in their suffering they had trodden in His steps; and it is never to be forgotten that He triumphed in and through His suffering and apparent defeat.

The song celebrated God's works and ways in judgment. They may be full of mystery while in process of accomplishment, but once completed they are seen to be great and marvellous, righteous and true. The names by which He is addressed are not those indicating the peculiar relationship in which He stands to the church, but those relating to Israel and the nations —the Jehovah, Elohim, Shaddai, of the Old Testament. And then again, the correct reading here is evidently, "King of nations," and not "King of saints." There is a strong resemblance here to Jeremiah 10: 6, 7, where the wrath of God against the nations is prophetically announced. The King of nations will subdue all nations in His wrath, and vindicate and glorify His elect.

The song closes in giving three reasons why God should be feared and glorified. First, because of what He is in His gracious holiness; second, because of His supremacy, which will ultimately command the homage of

THE REVELATION

all nations; third, because the rightness of His judgments is now being made manifest. The word here is literally, "righteousnesses," the same word as is used for the righteous acts of the saints in verse 8 of chapter 19. God's judgments are so righteous that the prophet could say, "When Thy judgments are in the earth, the inhabitants of the world will learn righteousness" (Isa. 26: 9). In contrast to this, Israel will at last have to confess, as we do today. "All our righteousnesses are as filthy rags" (Isa. 64: 6).

Having been granted the vision of these, who though victims under the beast were nevertheless victors over his power, a wholly new scene unrolled itself before John's eyes. He saw the seven angels with the seven last plagues come out of "the temple of the tabernacle of the testimony in heaven." This is a remarkable phrase. In the Old Testament we read of "the tabernacle of testimony" in the wilderness and also of the "temple" when the people were in the land; both of them figures of the true. Here both figures are coalesced. Out from the inner shrine of the Divine presence, where the testimony to all His purposes had been preserved, came the seven angels, empowered to deliver the final strokes of judgment, previous to the manifestation of His purpose for the earth by the appearing of Christ.

The two verses which close chapter 15, emphasize the exceeding solemnity of this moment. The vials handed to the angels were full of the wrath of God, who lives to the ages of ages—the eternity of His Being adding an infinitude of weight to His wrath. They were handed to them by one of the Living Creatures, that we saw in chapter 4, symbolizing the power, endurance, intelligence and swiftness of the Creator's ways in dealing with a rebellious earth. And again, the temple was filled with smoke from the glory of God. We had smoke from the pit in chapter 9, symbolic of Satanic influences which excluded all that is Divine. Here we have the Divine glory excluding all men and all that is merely human, while these last plagues were in process. There is an analogy between the plagues of Egypt, preceding the death of the firstborn, and these seven plagues, which will precede the revelation of God's Firstborn from heaven.

CHAPTER 16

As we read chapter 16, we shall notice that these last plagues are very specially God's answer in judgment to the enormous evil which reaches its climax in the beast and his followers. This is mentioned specifically in verses 2, 10, 13, but it is also inferred, we think, in other details that are mentioned. The first plague will affect the more stable and ordered peoples, the masses of whom will have received the mark of the beast. Upon these God puts His mark in the form of "a noisome and grievous sore." The sixth plague in Egypt was of this sort, but bearing in mind the symbolic character of the Revelation, we regard this as indicating a fretting evil in the region of mind and spirit, while not denying that it may also

THE REVELATION

have a more material application. Their lives will be made a misery to them under the mighty hand of God.

The second vial affects the sea; that is, the less formed and stable masses of mankind. They too come under judgment for though the beast specially dominates the ten kingdoms, power is also given him "over all kindreds, and tongues and nations" (13: 7). The second plague means spiritual death to all who come under it. The figure is very graphic. The sea became dead blood, bringing death on all within its compass.

The third vial affected rivers and fountains in the same way. These are symbolic of the sources and channels of spiritual life, just as are literal fountains and rivers as regards our natural lives. The sources being corrupted, apostate, dead, all hope of a revivifying is gone, and men are hopelessly shut up to their doom. It will be with them even as it was with Pharaoh, when the Lord hardened his heart. Are men today inclined to cavil at this, even as they do regarding Pharaoh? It is just at this point that there comes in a two-fold angelic testimony to the rightness of this stroke of judgment; and angels have powers of observation, and opportunity for observing, far exceeding that of the greatest and wisest of men. Those smitten had themselves been smiters of saints and prophets, and this of course would be specially true of the beast and his followers. Jehovah, Elohim, Shadai, by His angel, is acting and they are simply getting what they richly deserve.

The fourth vial affects the sun; the symbol of supreme authority. Here, however, it is clearly the symbol not of anything Divine but of the supreme power in this lower scheme of created things. The power of evil, vested for the time in the beasts, becomes oppressive and intolerable like burning heat. When their power was assumed men accepted it as great and wonderful (see 13: 4, 14), but now it becomes under the Divine judgment a terrible infliction. Yet such is the moral and spiritual death into which men are plunged, as seen in the third vial, that instead of humbling themselves in any way they only blaspheme the God of heaven: in other words, like Pharaoh, they only harden their hearts.

The similarity that exists between the objects of judgment under the first four vials and those under the first four trumpets is too clear to be missed; only in chapter 8 the sphere is limited to a third part. Here the judgments are more complete and more intense, and appear to be on God's part an answer to the defiant and persecuting actions of the beast and his followers.

This is seen more particularly in the outpouring of the fifth vial. A concentrated judgment falls upon the seat of the beast, and it presents us with a terrible picture. In Egypt the last plague before the death of the firstborn was "a thick darkness," even "darkness which may be felt" so dark that it stopped all movement. But it is even more terrible when a thick darkness descends upon the minds of men, blacking out from them every ray of light from God. There are heathen today still in very dense darkness, but it is even worse when atheists or agnostics, living in Christendom, have to say—as sometimes they do—to some simple believer that they envy him his faith, and wish they could believe but they cannot. Their experience is, they confess, a painful one. Here apostasy is complete, and their darkness painful to the last degree. Their pains and sores only provoke them to blasphemy, and they are far from repentance, which is the only door into recovery and blessing.

The sixth vial also has a resemblance to the sixth trumpet. Again the Euphrates is affected, which is one of the great natural barriers between the East and the West. Under this plague the barrier between the great masses of Asiatic peoples and the nations of Europe is removed and the assembling of both East and West becomes possible. The door is thus opened for the gathering of all the nations, as predicted in Joel 3. They little realize that they assemble for Jehovah to "roar out of Zion," and "to sit to judge all the heathen round about." But such is the case, as Joel says.

To begin with, it does not look like it, for verses 13 and 14 of our chapter show that the power of the devil will be exerted to gather the nations together. The unclean spirits that go forth to influence men in this direction go forth from the trinity of evil—the dragon, the beast and the false prophet—and they wield superhuman powers to sway the minds of men in the desired direction. But in all this, unconsciously to themselves, they do what God in His ways of wisdom and judgment has determined before to be done. They are simply preparing themselves for the last stroke of overwhelming judgment—that treading of the winepress of the wrath of God that has already been mentioned. It is spoken of here as, "the battle of that great day of God Almighty."

Verse 15 is clearly a parenthesis. It is as if the voice of the Lord Himself breaks in at this point, announcing His appearing when He will come as a thief on the nations wrapped in their darkness. In contrast to this, His coming for His saints is spoken of as the coming of the Bridegroom. Still there will be a remnant of Israel who will be carried through this terrible time without falling as martyrs, as well as some from among the Gentiles, represented by "the sheep" in Matthew 25: 33. These will be marked by watching and keeping themselves clear of defilement. But the reality of this will be tested, and apart from it a moment must come when all pretence will be stripped off and the nakedness and shame of the unreal and the untrue will be exposed.

Verse 16 picks up the thread from verse 14, though we might have expected it to read, "**they** gathered," since the three unclean spirits went forth to do the gathering. It appears, however, that our thoughts are directed away from the Satanic agents employed to the Almighty God, who overruled their actions for His own purpose and glory. To Armageddon, meaning the Hill of Megiddo, were the multitudes called. In the valley of

THE REVELATION

Megiddo the last godly king of David's line fell before the advancing nations. At last on that very spot the far greater Son of David will deal the swift death blow to all the proud might of the Gentiles. The incitement to gather together for their destruction takes place, however, as an act of Divine judgment under the sixth vial. We do not get details of what takes place when they are gathered together until we reach chapter 19, though we do get the fact of all nations being gathered predicted in verse 2 of Zechariah 14. There, too, it is God who does it, though as our chapter shows, He makes the power of the adversary serve His purpose.

The pouring out of the seventh vial completes these terrible strokes of wrath. This was declared by a voice from the inner shrine in heaven. The vial was poured into the air, which had been the seat of Satan's power, but from which he had been dislodged. Air is the life element for man, and now destruction begins to fall on him out of that very element. Thunders and lightnings are entirely beyond man's control, but there were voices controlling them. Moreover the earth was affected as well as the air.

Literal earthquakes there will doubtless be, but the earthquake of colossal magnitude here predicted signifies, we think, the complete shattering of all man's organized systems. Verse 19 speaks of "the great city," of "the cities of the nations," and of "great Babylon." We understand by these the break up and collapse of the imposing civil system or empire which will find its centre in Rome, and also of similar systems, but subsidiary, which will be found among the more distant nations; and thirdly, of the great system of religious craft and deceit, which Babylon represents. The special **fierceness** of the Divine wrath is fittingly reserved for this last. Moreover, every island and mountain disappeared in the convulsion. Things that are detached from the mass like islands will not escape, and all that is lofty will go.

Verse 21 seems to connect itself with the thunders and lightnings of verse 18. Hail is symbolic of sharp, crushing judgment, inflicted directly from heaven, so direct that men cannot possibly attribute it to any other than God. Every stone is said to have the weight of a talent; that is, about 125lb. We believe that in historic times storms of exceptional violence have been recorded in which stones weighing 1 lb., or even a little more, have fallen with terrible effect, similar to that recorded in Exodus 9. We are clearly intended to understand by stones weighing over 1 cwt. each, a judgment from God of a supernatural and crushing kind.

And what is the effect of all this? Simply additional blasphemy hurled against God. As in Egypt the heart of Pharaoh was hardened, so in this day the hearts and consciences of men will be hardened beyond any possible point of recovery. They are no longer atheists, even if once they were. There is a God, and they know it to their cost by these crushing judgments, but they defy Him. When the creature reaches such a pitch of defiant hardness as here indicated, what can be expected but the delivery

THE REVELATION

of the final stroke? Two parenthetical chapters intervene, however, before we have the record of that stroke in chapter 19.

CHAPTER 17

CHAPTERS 17 AND 18 give us with full details the judgment of Babylon. We shall find it helpful to read chapter 21: 9—22: 5, by way of contrast. Having done this, we shall note that in both cases, the vision is introduced by one of the angels who had the vials, and that what is seen is figured as a woman and as a city. The similarity ceases with this: all else is in sharpest contrast. There we view "the bride, the Lamb's wife;" here, "the great whore." There we have the true church, loved by Christ, redeemed and cleansed by Him, under the symbol of a city. Here we have the false religious system, which claims to be the church, also under the symbol of a city.

Babylon played a considerable part in Old Testament history. It was founded in defiance of God, as Genesis 11 shows; and the beginning of Nimrod's kingdom was there. It was also the fountain head of the idolatry that overspread the earth after the flood. This is indicated in such a verse as Jeremiah 51: 7, and historical records seem to corroborate it. Very appropriately therefore the mystical Babylon of our chapter symbolizes the harlot "church" centred in Rome, which has been in the present age "a golden cup . . . that made all the earth drunken." After the true church is gone all that is Laodicean, and spued out of Christ's mouth, will gravitate to Rome, we believe, so that the mystical Babylon will represent the sum total of apostate Christendom.

John is called by the angel to see the judgment of the great whore "that sitteth upon many waters." In the Old Testament Israel in her apostasy is treated as an adulterous wife, because she had been brought nationally into an established relationship with Jehovah. The Church is espoused to Christ "as a chaste virgin" (2 Cor. 11: 2), with the marriage day still in the future; hence the false church, wholly allied with the world, is with accuracy called not an adulteress, but a whore. She "sitteth upon," that is, dominates "many waters," which in verse 15 is explained as "peoples, and multitudes, and nations, and tongues." She practices unbridled worldliness in order to become the mistress of the masses of mankind. In keeping with this, verse 2 shows the kings of the earth seduced by her, and the inhabitants of the earth intoxicated by her wiles.

John is carried in spirit into a wilderness to see this great sight of the woman, riding the beast that he had previously seen in the vision of chapter 13. No colour is mentioned in that chapter, but in chapter 12 the dragon who gives his power to the beast is spoken of as red. Here we find the colour, which denotes the glory of this world, characterizing not only Satan but the revived Roman Empire, and apostate Christendom, which for the moment is exercising control over the empire.

THE REVELATION

Of the three, the woman presents the most gorgeous spectacle. She has in addition the imperial purple, since for this brief moment she seems to have attained the object for which she has always striven—recognized sovereignty over the nations. Gold, precious stones and pearls are elsewhere symbolic of all that is beautiful and of God, but here she is "decked," or "gilded" with them. All is superficial, and these things, excellent in themselves, are perverted to base uses. Similarly the cup in her hand is golden, as may be seen viewing it externally, but internally full of filthiness. The sin of the Pharisee was similar, as we see in Luke 11: 39, but here it is carried to its highest pitch of iniquity.

Her name, however, was carried on her forehead so as to be visible to every eye. The first word, "Mystery," instructs us that "Babylon the Great" is not to be understood in a literal, but in a mystical or symbolic sense. All the principles of evil that first sprang up in the literal Babylon of ancient days are found in their most virulent form in this abominable system. It has been said very truly that in Scripture symbolism a system is represented by a woman, whilst the power or energy marking a system is represented by a man.

The Romish system, enlarged by the inclusion in it of all that is corrupt in Christendom after the church is gone, is represented by the woman here. She has become "the mother of harlots and abominations;" that is, the source of lesser yet similar systems of corruption, when she should have been the "chaste virgin" for Christ. How fearful is this charge laid against her! Notice too how the word "earth" occurs frequently here. We have had it twice in verse 2. It occurs again in verses 8 and 18, and also several times in the next chapter. Earthly religion is her stock in trade.

In Philippians 3, Paul reveals how he entered experimentally into the heavenly calling made known in Christ, but before the chapter closes he mentions certain "enemies of the cross of Christ," and he states of these, "whose god is their belly, whose glory is in their shame, who mind earthly things." The system that the woman represents may boast of "apostolic succession:" they have succession indeed, but not apostolic. It proceeds rather from these whom Paul had to denounce—a succession of self-gratification and earthly-mindedness. In its final development it has come to this.

Then again, the adjective, "great," is applied to her, and this is a feature that appeals very much to the world. Earthly greatness and abominable corruption reach a climax in her, whereas the true church is to have on her the stamp of heaven and holiness, as we see in chapter 21: 10, where the adjective, "great," as applying to the holy Jerusalem, ought not to appear.

Verse 6 adds another sinister feature. The system that the woman symbolizes is a great persecutor of the true followers of Jesus, and is so full of their blood that she is intoxicated therewith. All down the centuries their blood has flowed at the hands of the Romish church and her harlot

THE REVELATION

offspring, but at the close this feature too will reach a climax. The sight of all this, even in symbol, so filled John with wonderment that the angel offered an explanation of the mystery, or inner meaning, both of the woman and of the beast. This explanation follows in the rest of the chapter; yet it is to be noted that it nearly all concerns the beast. That concerning the woman is only given in the last verse.

In the light of the explanation, the beast is evidently to be identified with the one described in the early part of chap. 13. Additional features, however, appear here. The empire that it symbolizes had an early existence, then it became extinct—to outward appearances at least—and then it is to reappear. It "shall ascend out of the bottomless pit;" that abyss into which Satan shall be cast for 1,000 years, as we are told in chapter 20. This means that it will be revived in a very evil form under Satanic influence, and be of so remarkable and sensational a character that all the earth-dwellers, who had no part in the book of life, will be filled with wonder, and fall easy victims to its enslaving power. That the empire in its revived form would be Satanically **supported** and **directed,** chapter 13 showed us. Here we discover that it will be Satanically **produced,** and that in such a way as to enslave the minds of all those false religionists, who have debased the faith of Christ to a mere religion of earthly things. We think there must be a definite connection between this and that of which 2 Thessalonians speaks—the "strong delusion, that they should believe a lie."

The seven heads of the beast have a twofold meaning. They represent firstly, seven mountains on which the woman sits, and this helps to identify with Rome both the beast and the woman; that is, both the empire and the religious system. In John's day Rome was without doubt the city of the seven hills.

But seven kings are also signified, and these distinct from the ten kings signified by the horns. The ten are kings who rise up in the last days, when the beast will represent not only the empire but also the empire's last and imposing head. In verse 10 the kings are clearly different, and represent successive heads of the empire, or rather successive forms of despotic government, and not individuals. Emperors held the power when our Lord was crucified and when John wrote, and they continued to do so until the empire broke up, but they had been preceded by five other forms of rule. A seventh was to come, that would continue but a short time and then be replaced by the eighth, who would be "of the seven;" that is, not entirely new but a reproduction of one of the earlier seven—of the imperial form.

This eighth, then, we should identify with the beast of chapter 13: 4-8, and again with the "little horn" of Daniel 7: 8. If this be so, we may understand the seventh head, who continues for a short time only, to be a personage of importance and in control when first the empire reappears, but

THE REVELATION

to be replaced by the "little horn" — Satan's nominee — when he rises up with a "look . . . more stout than his fellows," and three kings fall before him, as Daniel 7: 20 predicts. But the eighth, in spite of his dazzling splendour, is not permitted a long course. God intervenes and he "goeth into perdition."

The ten horns, according to verse 12, are the actual individuals who attain to kingly power for the brief spell during which the beast wields supreme authority. They are his willing vassals and support his Satanic schemes, even to the point of madness in making war with the Lamb. Men are going to reach such a pitch of mental inflation and self-confidence and arrogance, that they will actually fling themselves against the mighty power of God. We may say—borrowing the language of 1 Corinthians 8: 5 — that however many lords and kings there may be in heaven and on earth, the Lamb is Lord and King of them all, the beast and his satellites included. They inevitably fall before Him; and He has His associates, called, chosen and faithful. They too were rejected by men but are chosen of Him.

Verse 15 mentions the woman, but only to emphasize how complete her dominating power had been. It is remarkable that in this chapter she is seen sitting on the waters, on the beast, and on the seven mountains. Putting the three together, we are helped to identify her, and conducted to the last verse of our chapter. Two verses, however, intervene, in which we are shown her miserable end.

The ten kings, represented by the horns, are to be distinguished not only from the seven kings of verse 10, but also from "the kings of the earth," spoken of in verse 2, and who reappear in the next chapter. These kings of the earth are seduced by her, have illicit commerce with her—the "fornication" that is spoken of—and they greatly lament her destruction. They are doubtless the kings or leaders of many peoples who are outside the revived Western empire. The ten kings are leaders within the empire, who favour her at first and help to support her, but finally find her yoke intolerable, hate her and fall upon her with such fury as to destroy her.

When the corrupt religious system, symbolized by the woman, shall have reached the height of its influence, its apparent success and glory, it will be completely overthrown by the worldly powers that have been its main support. It is God's way to permit each successive form of evil to come to a head in fullest manifestation and apparent success before His judgment falls upon it. Here the judgment falls mediately through the ten kings and not immediately from the hand of God. The two beasts are to be dealt with immediately, by the Lord Jesus in person, as we shall see in chapter 19, for in them the **violence** of sin reaches its climax. In the harlot the **corruption** of sin reaches its most horrible expression. God does not put His hand upon the filthy thing but uses the violent to destroy the corrupt.

THE REVELATION

That God lies behind the violence of the ten horns is made quite clear in verse 17. The horns act with an agreement and unanimity which is very rarely found amongst men. Usually there are dissentient voices, and the majority prevails over the minority. Here all act together as with one mind under the guidance of the beast, and as a result vengeance falls in a stroke of swiftness and completeness.

The completeness of her judgment is expressed in four ways in the latter part of verse 16. Bearing in mind that she symbolizes a religious system, the significance of each item becomes clear. She is made desolate; that is, forsaken by all who formerly were friends and supporters. She is made naked; that is, stripped of everything that had formerly hid her true character. They eat her flesh; that is, appropriate to themselves all her wealth and luxuries. They burn her with fire; that is, utterly destroy the whole framework of her system. A clean sweep is made of the whole accursed thing. Little as they may realize it, the kings are acting as the executors of God's vengeance.

The identification of the woman and the great city, which is Rome, is made quite clear in the last verse of the chapter; and following this, in chapter 18, the city aspect becomes much the more prominent.

Chapter 18

ANOTHER ANGEL OF special power and glory now appears, coming down from heaven and announcing Babylon's fall. In chapter 14: 8, John saw an angel who made this announcement, but here it is given with greater impressiveness and with more detail. The evil system which is thus represented had long been fallen **morally,** now it is fallen **under Divine judgment.** Yet it is acknowledged as "great" even by this angel, who himself had "great power." Men are naturally inclined to worship what is great, especially if it is something produced by themselves, though this had really been Satan's masterpiece.

When God judges any system or individual their real character is made wholly manifest. This feature is seen here. Babylon had become infested with evils of the most virulent type. Demons had made it their habitation or dwelling place, and not merely a spot that they visited occasionally. Moreover every foul or unclean spirit was there. Demons **are** spirits but men **have** spirits that sin has made utterly unclean, and every kind of spirit is included in this statement. Thirdly, there are hateful birds. We may remember that in the parable of the sower the Lord used the birds as figures of agents that Satan uses in the world of men. So Babylon had become a place where demons were perfectly at home, and where every kind of evil spirit and evil man had been held as in a cage or prison. A fearful and crushing indictment indeed!

Verse 3 again emphasizes what had been stated in the previous chapter. This abominable system by her very corruption had exercised a controlling fascination over the kings of the earth—the leaders of earth's politics. And her wealth and luxury had equally fascinated and controlled the merchants of the earth—the leaders of earth's commerce. So in the last days religion, politics and commerce will find for a brief moment in Babylon a centre that unifies. And the religion will be as **earthly** as the politics and the commerce.

A voice from heaven gives the final cry, "Come out of her, My people." One can hardly imagine that many of those, who can be owned as God's people, will be in any sense inside such a system as it faces its final overthrow, yet doubtless there will be some like Lot, who was only dragged out of Sodom at the last moment. It is ever God's way to give such a final warning. Another illustration of it is seen in the Epistle to the Hebrews, written a short time before the destruction of Jerusalem, and calling upon Jewish Christians to go forth to the rejected Christ without the camp, and reminding them that they had no continuing city on earth.

Those who in the last days might remain in Babylon would run the risk of partaking of her sins and of the plagues visited upon her sins. This also is vividly illustrated by the case of Lot, his wife and daughters. But do not let us miss the application of all this to ourselves. Verse 4 plainly declares that association with evil has a defiling effect. By remaining in an evil and defiling system we become a partaker of its sins, and eventually of the governmental judgments of God that fall upon it.

In our day religious evil and sin is not yet headed up in one great system, but is surrounding us in many lesser and apparently conflicting systems. There are many traps for our feet, though smaller ones. The situation is more confused, but no less seductive. Let us be careful to obey this injunction to come out; cutting our links with associations that defile. And having **come out,** let us **keep out.**

It is God's way to sever His people from the ungodly, and take them out of their midst, before His judgment falls. He acted thus before the flood, and again in Egypt, as well as in the case of Sodom, and with His people before the destruction of Jerusalem in A.D. 70. Thus it will be with the Church before the vials of wrath are poured out, and with earthly saints who may be entangled in Babylon before it is judged. This is shown in verse 4.

Verse 5 shows that judgment only falls when the cup of iniquity is full to the brim; or, as it is stated, "her sins have **reached unto heaven.**" This is striking language, for the ancient city, Babylon, started when men began to federate, with the idea of self-aggrandizement and influence by the building of a city and tower, "whose top may **reach unto heaven**" (Gen. 11:4). The ancient Babylon reached the height of its splendour under the famous Nebuchadnezzar, who wielded the widest influence and reached the top-stone of self-aggrandizement. Shortly after this, the city lost its supremacy and descended into ruin. The principles for which it stood

THE REVELATION

were, however, perpetuated in Rome; first in the imperial, and then in the papal form.

In this mystical Babylon, then, we see all the old evils displayed in their intensest and most virulent form, and at last the "tower" of man's iniquity does indeed attain such dimensions that it has "reached unto heaven." In drastic fashion the well-merited judgment then falls and the hateful thing sinks out of sight for ever.

Verses 6 and 7 emphasize how apposite are God's judgments. They fit the case exactly. The same thing may be noticed in the enactments of the law of Moses, which brought upon the offender the very penalty he had inflicted on another, and relieved the offended party. Babylon is to get her exact "double" or equivalent, and her torment and sorrow is to be the counterpart of her previous self-glorification and luxury.

There is an allusion in verses 7 and 8 to Isaiah 47: 8 and 9. What was said, in predicting the fall of the literal Babylon by the Euphrates, is duplicated in the judgment of the mystical Babylon, but with one addition. It is the mystical Babylon who says, "I sit **a queen.**" This again is striking, for here we have the full-blown result in display of the apostate "church." The true church is the bride of Christ, and destined to be His partner in the day of the glory of the kingdom. The apostate church is "no widow," though her Lord has been slain upon the earth, and she claims to be "queen", though He is absent, and the day of His power not yet come. She aims at queenly influence and a life of delicious self-indulgence and self-glorification, while He is still absent and rejected.

But judgment is to fall upon her "in one day." A stroke of terrible severity and swiftness falls upon her; described as plagues, death, mourning, famine. Nothing mitigates the stroke; no time for a parley to avert it. The overwhelming stroke is administered by the ten kings, as the end of chapter 17 showed, but behind their action is the hand of God. The Lord God who judges her is strong, and all her tinsel glory vanishes beneath His avenging hand.

Verses 9 to 19 indicate how the kings of the earth, the merchants of the earth, and the shipmasters of the sea will react to her judgment. The ten kings, who had been dominated by her, rise up and destroy her, but outside the ten-kingdom empire are many kings who had profited by their connection with her, and they lament. By "kings" we understand national leaders: by "merchants of the earth" leaders of trade and commerce: by "shipmaster and all the company in ships" leaders in transport. For all these her destruction is a disaster, for she was the great trafficker in all earth's luxuries. The list of verses 12 and 13 begins with gold. It ends with the bodies and souls of men.

Even today there is no sadder scandal than Rome's traffic in the bodies and souls of men—more particularly in their souls. Souls become most

THE REVELATION

profitable "merchandise," when it is a question of extricating them from an imaginary "purgatory;" merchandise which has brought into her coffers more gold and silver and precious stones than all the trading in other objects of luxury put together.

The lament of verse 16 has a familiar sound to those who know Rome's ways in lands where her sway is nearly absolute. Many years ago we stood in the great Cathedral of "Our Lady of the Pillar," in Saragossa, Spain, and watched some kind of "mass" being performed by ecclesiastics, gorgeous in "fine linen, and purple, and scarlet." Then some visitors were being shown the great collection of gifts, left by deluded votaries, housed in a kind of side chapel. We slipped in with them, and beheld enormous cases reaching up the walls, which, when the lights were turned on, sparkled with "gold and precious stones, and pearls" in dazzling variety.

And just when all this greatness and costliness and outward glory reaches its finest display, her outrageous sin reaches its climax, and the judgment of God falls. The action of the mighty angel, recorded in verse 21, gives us an idea of the violence of the overthrow from the hand of God.

How great is the contrast between earth and heaven! Their respective reactions could not be more opposite. The casting of dust upon the head, weeping and wailing, on the one hand; rejoicings, on the other. Holy apostles and prophets are now avenged on her: further proof, if it be needed, that mystical Babylon represents the great system of false and corrupted religion, which from the outset has persecuted the servants of God. This interpretation is further reinforced by the last verse of the chapter. The day of reckoning had now come. Individual sinners have an eternity to spend. Evil systems do not pass into eternity. Their judgment in its full weight falls upon them in this world.

Chapter 19

How DELIGHTFUL IS the contrast as we pass into chapter 19! As before remarked, a word that characterizes chapters 17 and 18 is "earth." The Christian faith, which is centred in a **heavenly** Christ, has been debased into an **earthly** religion—a scheme for producing an **earthly** paradise where men may have their fill of **earthly** joys. That kind of religion very well suits "the kings of the earth," and "the inhabitants of the earth," and "the great men of the earth," and "the merchants of the earth;" though it may involve "abominations of the earth," and lead to saints being "slain upon the earth." Now, "after these things," says John, "I heard a great voice of much people **in heaven.**" Consequently we step into a scene of purity and praise. The characteristic word is "Alleluia."

Let us note that while Babylon is being judged on earth there is "much people," or, a "crowd," in heaven. All the saints, who gathered to Christ at the rapture, are there. They understand the significance of what has taken place. They see that, God having dealt with the seat of earthly corruption, He will swiftly deal with earth's violence. They ascribe the salvation to God, and give Him the glory, the honour and the power. However evil men may be in this day of salvation, it hardly becomes the saint to shout "Alleluia" if he sees judgment fall upon any. But here we are contemplating the day of judgment, and God's acts of judgment are to be praised **then** as much as His acts of grace **now.**

Men's judgments are never absolutely true and intrinsically righteous, for selfish elements can never be wholly excluded from them. What men's judgments are **not,** God's judgments are. The great whore had corrupted the earth, and heaven's pure and holy judgment had fallen upon her. The smoke of it should rise up for ever and ever. A memorial this of God's judgment against corruption, which should utter its warning voice to the ages of eternity.

Heavenly scenes again being before us, the twenty-four elders and the four living creatures appear once more. God is on the throne in judgment, and in the light of this they fall down in worship. They say "Amen" to His destruction of Babylon, and join in the "Alleluia" of praise. The praise and worship described in chapter 5, started with the elders and the living creatures, and spread out to angels and all creation. Similarly here, their praise being uttered, a voice from the throne calls upon all the servants of God to follow suit, and the thunders of praise reverberate through heaven. God is manifestly on the throne in His omnipotence. God is equally on the throne today, but it is to us a matter of faith. We can sing,

> "God is still on the throne,
> And He will remember His own."

though the fact is not displayed at present as it will be then.

The false, harlot "church" being judged and destroyed on earth, the moment has come for the true church to be acknowledged as the "wife" of the Lamb in heaven. There is a peculiar majesty about the language of verses 6 and 7. A terrible drama of unspeakable corruption and violent judgment has passed before us, and far above the evil and turmoil the Lord God omnipotent has sat upon the throne. All things have served His might and nothing has diverted Him from His purpose. He has been working behind the scenes that the One, who here is called the Lamb, may see fully the fruit of the travail of His soul, and secure for Himself the "bride," for whom He died. His purpose as to this is now accomplished, the saints are in glory, and moreover, "His wife hath made herself ready."

Our meetness for glory is of course altogether the fruit of Divine workmanship; but there is also a readiness of an experimental and practical nature, and it is this which is mentioned here. On the day when the church is acknowledged as the wife of the Lamb, she will be arrayed in the "fine linen, clean and white," which is interpreted for us as "the righteousnesses of the saints" (New Trans.). Every act of righteousness, wrought out in the lives of saints composing the church, will be woven, as it were into the robe, which will adorn the wife of the Lamb in that day.

In this there is immense encouragement for us today. If we look around us at that which professes to be the church, there is nothing but discouragement. Nor are we much relieved if we confine our attention to those we can recognize as true Christians—**including ourselves.** We might easily become obsessed with the delinquencies of saints—their worldliness, their follies, their errors. But all the time there has been the working of the Spirit of God in them and amongst them; there have been all those right things, often unnoticed by man but ever before the eye of God, and these things will be brought to light at the judgment seat of Christ, and be for the adorning of the church when her relationship to the Lamb is publicly acknowledged in heaven. If our eyes were as quick to discern the right as to detect the wrong, we should get the encouragement of this today.

The elders together with the living creatures appear for the last time in verse 4. They were first mentioned in chapter 4: 4. In chapters 2 and 3 we have the seven churches of Asia—local churches—and they are mentioned once more in chapter 22: 16. The word, "church," is not used in the Revelation as referring to the whole body of Christians. Immediately we commence "the things which shall be hereafter," in chapter 4, the churches disappear, and the elders in heaven take their place. But in our chapter the church is acknowledged as the wife of the Lamb, and in the glory of this relationship the "elders" disappear. Henceforward it is "the Bride, the Lamb's wife," and only when at the end we are brought down again to the testimony to be rendered on earth, while we wait for the Lord, do the "churches" again appear. Observing these changes, we find confirmation of the thought that the elders represent the saints raptured to glory.

But besides the Lamb's wife, there are "they which are called unto the marriage supper of the Lamb." These, we judge, are the glorified saints of Old Testament days. Though these were never baptized by the one Spirit into the one body, which is the church, they were raised at the same time as the saints composing the church, for they were Christ's, purchased by His blood, and the Scripture says, "they that are Christ's at His coming" (1 Cor. 15: 23). Risen and glorified, they enjoy a rich heavenly portion, far beyond the blessedness that may be enjoyed upon the millennial earth. They are called in their heavenly seats to participate in the joys of the marriage supper of the Lamb. In them too the Lamb will see some of the fruits of the travail of His soul. So great is the blessing they enjoy that John is particularly instructed to write it down. It is delightful to us to know how rich is the reward of the beloved servants of God of whom we get a glimpse in Hebrews 11, and of many less known saints like them.

In a small way we have surveyed and contemplated these things. We have seen the false and corrupt church system judged and destroyed. We have seen the true church acknowledged in heaven, and the once suffering

Lamb thus finding His abundant recompense in having the object of His love with Himself for ever. We have heard all heaven filled with praise and worship like the voice of mighty thunderings. What has been the effect upon our spirits? Are we not all saying in our hearts—This is wonderful, wonderful, wonderful! But is it not too good to be true? This was doubtless the effect upon John; so the angel assured him, "These are the true sayings of God." We may rest assured that **all is true,** and to come to pass in its season.

Assured of its truth, John was moved to worship, though his worship was misplaced, since he fell at the feet of the angel who was showing him these things. Being a holy angel, he repudiated it instantly. Only the fallen angel, Satan, aspires to divine honours, indeed it was in aspiring to such that he fell. The angel acknowledged himself to be but a servant, or "bondman," and therefore a fellow to John, and a fellow to all John's brethren who had the testimony of Jesus. As originally created man belongs to an order in creation a little lower than the angels, yet both men and angels are but servants, and thus fellows in that respect. God alone is worthy of worship. The fact that our Lord Jesus accepted the worship of men is a tribute to His Deity.

In his closing words the angel gave the key that unlocks all the prophetic scriptures. It is, **"the testimony of Jesus."** All Old Testament prophecy looked forward to the coming of Jesus—Jehovah, appearing as Saviour. All New Testament prophecy is the testimony of Jesus, coming in power and glory, that His work of redemption by blood may be crowned by His work of redemption in power. This **key** to prophecy is also the **test** of men's prophetic systems. Any system which makes prophecy a testimony to Israel or to the British people, imagined to be Israel, or to millennial conditions on earth and schemes for attaining to them, stands condemned.

Everything in heaven has now reached a climax of Divine order, and nothing remains but to deal with the rebellious earth. So in verse 11 the heavens are opened for the appearing of the glory of our great God and Saviour Jesus Christ. We know it to be He, though symbolic language is still used. Judgment will be in absolute righteousness at last, and His name—Faithful and True—is the guarantee of this. At last the long period of man's unrighteousness and sin is to reach its end.

All the symbols used speak of purity, of searching discernment, of all authority and power being vested in Him, yet of there being that in Him that defies all creature investigation. He has a name that no man knows but He Himself. In His manifestation all other power, all the might and majesty of the creature, shrivels into nothingness.

The Divine Names are full of significance. In His glorious appearing the Lord Jesus is presented to us with a fourfold Name. Seeing that He appears for judgment, His Name as "Faithful and True" stands first, securing the absolute rectitude of His every judgment act. Next comes the

THE REVELATION

Name that no man knows but Himself. This Name, though unknown to us, signifies that there is in Him — true God and yet perfect Man — that which surpasses all creature apprehension. That being so, we are not surprised to read, "How **unsearchable** are His judgments" (Rom. 11: 33).

Thirdly, "His Name is called, The Word of God." This is most significant. We read, "The Word was God . . . All things were made by Him" (John 1: 1-3); so God has been expressed very really in **creation.** Again, in the same chapter, "And the Word was made flesh, and dwelt among us," so that there might be a full declaration of the Father in grace and truth to us. But now neither creation nor **redemption** is involved but rather judgment. That in judging His Name should be called "The Word of God," signifies that God will also be declared and made known in **judgment** — particularly in His righteousness and holiness, without a doubt. Thought is expressed in word. The Lord Jesus is the expression of the Divine thought in all three connections.

Lastly, His Name, "King of kings and Lord of lords," is written on His vesture; that is, externally, where every eye may see it. It is also on His thigh; internally, in the place of His secret strength. It is hardly an eternal designation like the others, for it could hardly be assumed until kings and lords came into existence as created by Him. Still it will be of the first importance in His glorious appearing. Kings are earthly potentates, whereas "lords," we think, would cover heavenly as well as earthly dignitaries. In His appearing the Lord Jesus comes forth "to subdue all things unto Himself" (Phil. 3: 21). The many crowns, of which verse 12 speaks, being kingly diadems, are in keeping with this.

We have before us, then, "the coming of our Lord Jesus Christ with all His saints" (1 Thess. 3: 13). In our passage we have "the armies which were in heaven," representing the saints in a symbolic way. They ride upon white horses too, for the time is being ushered in when "the saints shall judge the world." Their "fine linen" raiment, "white and clean," identifies them with "the wife" of the Lamb, who was similarly adorned. The righteousnesses of the saints will be their adorning in the inside place when the marriage of the Lamb is celebrated. It will adorn them in the outside place also, when they are displayed to a wondering world with Christ in His glory.

It will be good at this point to read again chapter 16: 13-16. At Armageddon the kings of the earth and of the whole world are gathered together to the battle of that great day of God Almighty. The armies of the earth gather to battle, but the armies of heaven have not to inflict one stroke. The decisive blow proceeds out of the mouth of their glorious Leader, like the stroke of a sharp sword. No man can stand before the incisive word that proceeds from the mouth of the Word of God. By the might of His word all creation came into being. By the might of His word this warrior judgment will be inflicted. But redemption, which lies between

THE REVELATION

these two, was not thus accomplished. No wonder-working word brought this to pass; nothing short of His own death and resurrection achieved it.

He was clothed in a vesture dipped in blood. But this, we judge, does not allude to the blood of His cross, but rather to what is predicted in Isaiah 63: 1-6, where His work of judgment is foreseen. When reading in the synagogue at Nazareth, the Lord Jesus closed the book before reaching "the day of vengeance of our God." In chapter 63 we have the words, "the day of vengeance is in Mine heart," and blood — that of His foes — is sprinkled upon His garments, when He treads the winepress alone. This is a work of judgment, as we saw when considering the end of chapter 16. The overthrow of men in their pride is to inaugurate a period when the nations are to be ruled with a rod of iron.

The eyes of John are now directed to an angel, who stands in the sun, a symbol setting forth supreme power. The clash between the might of proud men and the Christ, appearing in His glory, is about to take place. There is no doubt as to the issue. The call of the angel to the fowls of heaven declares it in no uncertain terms. There may be kings and captains and mighty men and horses, but all of them will be but food for vultures. We may adopt the words of one of our poets, and give them a meaning beyond his thoughts.

"The tumult and the shouting dies,
The captains and the kings depart."

Human pride and violence rise to their climax and are brought low. The leaders, who looked so imposing, depart to their doom.

In vision John sees the kings of the earth and their armies gathered together under the beast for the express purpose of making war against God, as represented by the heavenly Christ and His army. That mortal men, even in combination, should for one moment contemplate fighting against God might have seemed to us incredible not so long ago. We have lived however to see a day when the marvellous discoveries and inventions of men have so inflated them and turned their heads that not a few are imbued with just that spirit. Some years ago a Russian revolutionary leader boasted that, having disposed of Tsar and earthly authorities, they would deal with the Lord God in due time. So far had he travelled on the mental road which belittles God and glorifies man.

Verse 19, then, gives us the climax of this spirit. Verses 20 and 21 indicate the completeness of its overthrow. The two men in whom it had found its fullest expression are singled out for condign punishment of a most extraordinary kind. In the "Babylon" of chapters 17 and 18 full-blown corruption was seen. In the beast, described in chapter 13, violence comes to a head. The "times of the Gentiles" finish with him, even as they began with the tyrant, Nebuchadnezzar. The false prophet we identify with the one our Lord predicted, saying, "I am come in My Father's Name, and

THE REVELATION

ye receive Me not: if another shall come in his own name, him ye shall receive" (John 5: 43). He is the false Messiah, the "idol" or "worthless" shepherd, who will be raised up "in the land," of whom Zechariah 11: 15-17 speaks. An apostate Jew himself, he will be eagerly received by apostate Jews. On the political plane he will find it a paying proposition to play a secondary part to the great Gentile monarch, following the example of the Herodians, of whom we read in the Gospels.

Both these men are seized by the irresistible power of the Lord. No future day of judgment awaits them. Taken red-handed as leaders of the most violent, God-defying enterprise ever undertaken, they do not first pass into death — the dissolution of soul and body — but are flung direct into the burning lake. The language here, as throughout the book, is symbolic, no doubt, but it is terribly expressive of God's judgment in its searching power. The very word translated "brimstone," has in it the thought of "divine fire." In Old Testament history two men were taken to heaven without passing through death. Here two men pass alive into hot damnation.

The mighty hosts, that follow the two, are men that have received the mark of the beast and supported his enormous wickedness. They do not immediately share his fate. They die, smitten by the all-conquering word of Him who is the Word of God, that they may await their judgment in the great day of which the next chapter speaks. Their cases will be tried in solemn session. The sin of the two leaders is so outrageous and open that summary judgment can righteously be inflicted. The principle of it is seen in 1 Timothy 5: 24.

Chapter 20

IT IS REMARKABLE that while our Lord will deal personally with men, it is an angel, a spirit being, who will deal with the great spirit being, who is the originator of all the evil. He is described in a fourfold way so as to identify him without a doubt. As Satan he is the adversary. As the devil he is the accuser. He is the old serpent of the opening book of the Bible, and the dragon of the closing book. All through the ages his aim has been to "deceive the nations," as verse 3 of chapter 20 shows us. How effectively he has done so all history bears witness, and coming days will show even more disastrously.

His activities will reach their climax in provoking this climax of human corruption and violence, but only to fail ignominiously before the might of the Lord. He is to find himself bound and a prisoner in the abyss for a thousand years. The "great chain" necessary to bind him is in the angel's hand — symbolic language again, for no literal chain could bind a spirit being. The "bottomless pit" is not the lake of fire but the dungeon in which he is confined while the millennial age runs its course. The seal of God is put upon him there by the angel's hand. It was an angel who broke the seal which men put on the sepulchre of the Lord Jesus.

The author of all the evil being dealt with, John turns to contemplate those who are blessed in association with Christ. Three distinct groups are mentioned. First comes those who are enthroned and to whom judgment is given. Daniel the prophet foresaw this great day, as he records in his seventh chapter. When the Ancient of days did sit, then the thrones were "cast down," or "set." But there is no mention of any who sat on them. In our passage the enthroned ones appear and are described by the simple pronoun "they." To whom does the pronoun apply? Where is the noun? We answer unhesitatingly it applies to "the armies in heaven," of the previous chapter, which were composed of "much people in heaven," covering both the wife of the Lamb — the Church — and those called to the marriage supper — the Old Testament saints.

The pronoun "they" covers, then, the saints who were raised and changed at the rapture, as to whom Paul asked the Corinthians, "Do ye not know that the saints shall judge the world?" But another and much smaller class follows. There were those who, subsequent to the removal of the church, had suffered death for the testimony of Jesus and the word of God. Again, there were those who were martyred under the beast because they would not receive his mark. We have read of these two groups before. The former in chapter 6: 9-11; the latter in chapter 13: 15. Both are now seen as living and reigning with Christ in the day of His glory.

Verse 4 indicates, then, that all the saints who suffer death between the coming of the Lord for His saints and His coming with them will be raised when He does come in His glory. In that risen life they will reign with Him, while those who did receive the mark of the beast and worship him will suffer the dreadful penalties described in chapter 14: 9-11.

There is a sharp line of demarcation between verses 4 and 5. The one gives us the saints in risen life and power. The other speaks of "the rest of the dead," who remain in their graves during the thousand years. Then, referring back again to verse 4, comes the remark, "This is the first resurrection." This is corroboration of the fact that the "they," at the opening of verse 4, indicated the saints raised, as prophesied in 1 Thessalonians 4: 15-17. It also establishes quite clearly that "the resurrection of life" and "the resurrection of damnation" (John 5: 29), are separated by a thousand years.

Verse 6 also makes it abundantly clear that only those who are blessed and holy have part in the first resurrection. The second death has no power over them, though it has over those who are left for the second resurrection. Their blessedness is described in a twofold way. It is not that they enter into things entirely new in their character, for even **now** Christ has "made us kings and priests unto God and His Father" (chap. 1: 6), and in chapter 5 the twenty-four elders were presented in those characters.

THE REVELATION

Here, however, what the saints have been made, and which is known now to our faith, comes into full display in the millenial age.

Still, there is one new feature here. They are "priests ... of Christ;" it is really "of **the** Christ." Nowhere else does this expression occur, and it reminds us of Aaron and his sons in Exodus 29, who, when together, typified the saints as a priestly company. The sons of Aaron were priests of God and of Aaron — if we may so say. The risen saints will be manifested as priests of God and of the Christ, as taking their character and place entirely from Him. And they will share in His kingly reign.

Verse 6 gives us in brief summary the power and blessedness of the millenial age on its heavenly side. More instruction is granted us when we come to the latter part of chapter 21, but still it is as to the heavenly side of it, just mentioning "the nations of them that are saved," and "the kings of the earth," but giving us no details as to the earthly blessings enjoyed in that delightful age. Such details were not needed here as they had been fully given in Old Testament scripture.

We know that the earth will rejoice and prosper under the benificent reign of Christ; that it will be full of the knowledge of God as the waters cover the sea. Let Psalm 72 be considered for there we see Christ as the priestly King, absolute in His rule but sustaining the poor and needy. In Revelation we are let into the secret of how He will dispense His power and goodness through His heavenly saints — even such as ourselves.

Do we really believe it? If we do it will take the shine out of the present age through which we pass, and out of all its achievements.

The Millennial age will be characterized by righteous yet beneficent rule. At the end of the ages of sinful misrule by men, with all their attendant miseries, there is to be displayed the excellence and glory of Divine rule, under Christ as Son of Man and King of Israel. Yet sin will not be entirely absent, as Isaiah 65:20 shows.

Moreover, during the thousand years human life on earth will continue as at present and multitudes will be born as the years pass, and the Lord's words, "That which is born of the flesh is flesh," will be as true then as now. If a work of grace does not take place in the hearts of such, all the old fleshly tendencies will be there, repressed only by Divine rule from without; Satan, the instigator of evil, not being there to work upon them. This accounts for the solemn facts of verse 8, which otherwise might seem inexplicable.

At the end of the millennium Satan is to be released from his prison and allowed to work his will. He has learned nothing and received no correction. He is absolutely unchanged. Out he goes at once, again to deceive the nations. Men of Adam's race, apart from the new birth, are unchanged also, in spite of having lived for centuries under a regime of absolute righteousness. In the Gospel we have learned that, "the carnal mind is enmity against God; for it is not subject to the law of God, neither indeed can be. So then they that are in the flesh cannot please God" (Rom. 8: 7, 8). Hence nothing but a new birth will do. This will again be shown in striking fashion at the close of the millennium. Men in the flesh cannot please God, and God and His righteous rule does not please them. So at the first opportunity, when instigated, they rebel.

Out of all nations the rebels come, though "Gog and Magog" are specially designated. Ezekiel 38 and 39 predict the destruction of this great northern power as the millennial age begins — the last stroke, it would appear, of the great Armageddon conflict. A thousand years have passed, but again we find the representatives of that power taking a leading part in the anti-God movement. The great Russian territories are pretty clearly indicated in the chapters in Ezekiel, and even in our day the anti-God spirit seems to have come to a head there. Their objective is the camp of the saints and the beloved city, in the centre of which will stand the Temple of God, whence will proceed both the authority and the blessing of the millennial age. It is unadulterated rebellion against God. It merits condign punishment, and it gets it.

Fire from heaven devours them, and this dreadful episode brings to a close the millennial age and all the ages of time, so that we stand on the threshold of the eternal state. Our chapter goes on to relate God's acts in the judgment of sin, both governmental and eternal. There is no mention of what happens to the material earth (save that "earth and the heaven fled away"), until the first verse of the next chapter is reached, and then we are only told that the first heaven and earth have "passed away." We have to refer to 2 Peter 3: 7, 10, for more precise details, and then we discover that fire is to be the agent used for that. So it may very well be that this falling of fire from heaven to devour the rebels is also the act of God which releases the atomic forces which will produce what Peter predicts.

The last six verses of our chapter give us the results of God's last judgments; not the material side of them but the moral and spiritual. The fountain-head of all evil is first dealt with. In all the wide universe, that the Scriptures reveal to us, Satan was the original rebel. Into this world he introduced sin by way of deceit. His name, **devil,** means **accuser, calumniator,** and by his calumnies against God and His word he deceived Eve, as Genesis 3 bears witness. As a mighty spiritual being, possessing powers of intelligence vastly beyond anything human, he has no difficulty in deceiving fallen men. He is doing it today, and will do it to the end. But the limit determined by Omnipotence is now reached, and he is cast into that "everlasting fire, prepared for the devil and his angels," of which the Lord spoke in Matthew 25: 41. Here the fire is spoken of as a lake, which gives the idea of a place circumscribed and confined. Into it the beast and the false prophet were cast as the millennial age began, and now at the end of that age we read that there they still **"are,"** and not that they **were.** The fire had not destroyed them.

THE REVELATION

We are well acquainted with fire and its effects in material objects; but, as far as we know, it has no effects on spiritual beings. We judge therefore the phrase to be symbolic, as so much else in this book, but it stands as the symbol of the hot displeasure, the scorching judgment of God, which even for the devil will mean that he "shall be tormented day and night for ever and ever."

The originator of sin and his two chief lieutenants being disposed of, the great mass of sinful mankind, who have fallen a prey to his deceits, now appear at the final assize. The language is deeply solemn and impressive. John sees the throne of judgment, which he describes as great and white. The second resurrection, that of damnation, has taken place, and the earth has fled away. This earth is but a tiny spot in God's great universe and all the limitations which it would impose upon this scene are gone. In result, "the dead, small and great, stand before God." They have been raised and reclothed in bodies, as verse 13 clearly indicates, but they are still the dead in a spiritual sense — dead towards God.

The One who will sit on that throne, from whose face the very earth and heaven will flee, inasmuch as they have been defiled by sin, must be our Lord Jesus Christ, since, "the Father judgeth no man, but hath committed all judgment unto the Son" (John 5: 22). His face was **once** marred more than that of any man. In it **now** there shines the glory of God. **Then** it will be characterized by the penetrating understanding of omniscience, and the severity of a judgment which springs from righteousness and holiness, of which the whiteness of the throne is a symbol.

Yet the judgment will not be apart from the divine records, nor apart from their works. It will be based not on what God knew them to be but on what they had manifested themselves to be in their outward actions. Of those actions a record had been kept before God. It is remarkable that the Old Testament as it closes should speak of "a book of remembrance" written before the Lord in favour of **the godly**: the New Testament at the close speaking of "the things written in the books," on which **the ungodly** are condemned. In recent years men have discovered how to record human speech and actions in such a way as to preserve them for future generations. What they are learning to do imperfectly God has done in perfection through the ages. A terrifying thought for the sinful sons of men!

About three-quarters of the earth's surface is sea. If any of the dead could be overlooked in that hour, it would be some who found their burial in its wide expanse and its immense depths. But the sea will give them up. Death is viewed as having held men's bodies and "hell" or "hades," had held their souls. Both yield up their prey that soul and body may be reunited. They had sinned in their bodies, and in their bodies they will be condemned. Again it is emphasized — "every man according to their works."

THE REVELATION

At that time death and hades will contain only the unsaved, so that verse 14 records the solemn fact that all that they contain will find their place in the lake of fire, and thus death and hell will disappear. Neither of these two were marked by finality: each was a provisional arrangement, and now they come to an end. Verse 15 states the same terrible fact in another way. If the record of "the books" condemned men in a positive way, the "book of life" did so in a negative way. If their names were **not** there, it sealed their doom.

Chapter 21

FROM THESE DREADFUL scenes John lifts his eyes to behold scenes of everlasting felicity in a new heaven and a new earth. In our present earth the sea is the great dividing element, and into its salt water flow the impurities created by man in his sinful state, and they are rendered harmless. It will not be needed in that blissful day when the impurities and the divisions are no more. The first eight verses of chapter 21 give us, then, the eternal state, which will succeed the millennial age, and abide.

Its chief feature will be God dwelling with men in His tabernacle, which is identified with the holy city the new Jerusalem, which city is likened to "a bride prepared for her husband." This might seem a strange mixture of symbols did we not remember that we have already, in chapters 17 and 18, seen that which falsely claims to be the church represented as great Babylon and as a seducing woman — a harlot. In this new Jerusalem we have in symbol the church of God, which is the bride of Christ. It descends "from God," since it is altogether His workmanship, and it comes "out of heaven," for its calling was from heaven, and to heaven it had gone at the coming of the Lord Jesus for all His saints.

In that eternal order of things the prominent thoughts are GOD and MEN. The Persons of the Godhead are not thrown into prominence, though of course they are there, just as They were enfolded in the **Elohim**, translated God, in Genesis 1: 1. Distinctions amongst men, such as nations, only came in as the result of sin, so here they disappear. It was ever in the purpose of God to dwell with men; an indication of this being found in Proverbs 8: 31. When man was created in innocence the Divine approach did not go further than a visitation, "in the cool of the day" (Gen. 3: 8). When in type Israel was redeemed from Egypt, God took up His abode on the tabernacle in their midst. Now by the Spirit the church is His habitation. In the eternal state His desire to dwell will be finally accomplished; and it will be in fullest measure — **the dwelling of "God Himself."**

The holy city is called "the **tabernacle** of God," thus directing our thoughts to the earliest type of God dwelling amongst His people. Two words in the New Testament are translated "temple." One signifies the

THE REVELATION

whole of the sacred buildings and the other the inner sanctuary only. The first word is never used in the Revelation; always the second. So in chapter 15: 5, we get, "the temple of the tabernacle;" that is, the inner sanctuary of the tabernacle. Again later in our chapter we read that there is no inner sanctuary in the heavenly city, for the Lord God Almighty and the Lamb are the inner sanctuary of it. This may help us to understand why tabernacle rather than temple is the suitable word in the verse we are considering, though in Paul's epistles the church is called the temple (inner sanctuary) of God.

All God's redeeming activities have been in view of His dwelling, and then, having taken up His abode, He exerts His power in blessing. Very little is said, however, as to the positive side of this. It seems to be summed up in two facts. First, that men will dwell in the presence of God. Second, that they will be in relationship with Him as sons, and thus as overcomers inherit all things. But how much is involved in these simple facts! To know God and dwell before Him in a near relationship must exceed in its blessedness even the inheriting of all things.

Verse 4 gives us the blessing on its negative side, and this we can understand more easily. The things that will never enter those blissful scenes are all painfully familiar to us at present. We know them only too well! We may remark that the "crying" is not the same as the "tears." It means "outcry," and the world is full of that today. Cries of dissatisfaction, resentment and threatening fill the air. All the five things mentioned are the fruits of sin. As men multiply on the face of the earth the volume of them increases. The advent of Christ and the establishment of His kingdom will largely assuage them, but they will never be wholly and for ever abolished until the eternal state is reached. And then, God himself will do it. His hand it will be — sweet thought! — that wipes the tear from every eye.

In the eternal state everything will be new in the fullest sense of the word. The material heavens and earth will be new, and "all things" found therein will be new according to verse 5. All those things that we know at present, spoken of as "the former things" will have passed away. He who acts, to produce these new creation things, is "He that sat upon the throne," — our Lord Jesus Christ. He acted to bring into existence the old creation, according to Genesis 1. He acts again to bring into existence the new. As before, so here, the word of His power is sufficient. Formerly, "He spake, and **it was done**" (Psa. 33: 9). Now again He speaks and His words are, "**It is done.**" Both are accomplished with equal ease.

But we must never forget what lay between these two points. Redemption had to be accomplished, and far more than His word was needed for that. Apart from redemption and its wonderful fruits the new creation scenes and blessings would lack a solid foundation.

THE REVELATION

He who sits upon the throne asserts the fulness of His Deity, for no one but God can be the A and the Z — as we should speak — the beginning and end of all things. In this light He presented Himself to John, speaking as One who dwells in the eternal present, above and beyond all questions of time. But at the end of the verse He again speaks in view of time conditions, for thirst is not something that characterizes the eternal state. Thirst is a symbol of unsatisfied desire, and that eminently marks the present time. For the thirsty there is still the water of life, which springs up like a fountain and is freely given. Such is the grace of our God, persisting to the end.

From the grace of verse 6 we pass to the overcoming of verse 7. At first sight it looks like a complete change, but after all, no one does overcome save those who have received the grace. This is the last mention of overcoming, or victory, in the book, which, as we before remarked, is the book of victory. The victorious saint will enter into full possession of the inheritance, but no saint at all would overcome had not the Lamb prevailed (same word), as we see in chapter 5.

The terrible import of verse 8 is apparent. It stands in contrast to the victors in verse 7, and in both verses we are carried outside the bounds of time and into the endless expanse of eternity. There is that confined region, burning with the holy judgment of God, which will be the second death to those that are cast there. The first death is not annihilation. If it were, there could be no second. It is dissolution of soul and body. The second death will be the complete and absolute dissolution of every link that connects with God; complete severance from all that is summed up in the words, **life** and **light** and **love**. There will be existence but not life in the full and proper sense of the word.

The list of those on whom this doom falls is sadly instructive. It begins with the fearful and unbelieving. Being without faith, they feared man and did not confess Jesus as their Lord. Those who bore the character of the devil, who is a murderer, and were marked by lust and traffic with the powers of darkness, come next. The list finishes with "all liars," for lying is another characteristic of the devil, and deceit takes a variety of subtle forms. The overcomers of verse 7 are sons of God. The damned of verse 8 proclaim themselves as sons of the evil one. They share his doom.

Beyond the point we have reached, the Scripture does not carry us. An eternal state is something which lies beyond the compass of our minds. God then will be all in all, but no description of it in detail is given. Were it given it would be unintelligible to us in our present state. We may gather this from what Paul tells us in 2 Corinthians 12: 4. We may find however deep instruction in what we are told.

John is now granted a fresh vision, the description of which begins in verse 9. Two remarks of a general nature may be made as to it. First, it stands in very definite contrast with the vision he was given of Babylon, the great whore, in chapters 17 and 18. In both cases the vision is introduced by one of the angels who had the seven vials, but to see Babylon John was carried in spirit into the wilderness, while to see the holy Jerusalem he is carried into a great and high mountain. A wilderness is a region where is specially seen the curse that rests upon creation because of man's sin, according to Genesis 3: 18. In ascending a high mountain a man travels as far as his feet can carry him towards heaven, and away from the mists and defilements of earth.

Second, in this vision John sees the holy city, the bride, the Lamb's wife, not as it will be in the eternal state, as in verses 2 and 3 of our chapter, but as it will be in connection with the millennial scene. The fact that we read of the twelve tribes of Israel, the nations who are to be healed and saved, and the kings of the earth, make this manifest. So when John sees the city descending out of heaven from God, in verse 10, he is viewing it coming down to take up its connection with the millennial earth at the beginning of that epoch. When he saw it coming down, in verse 2, it was at the beginning of the eternal state, the millennium being over. The recognition of this fact enhances the value of the words in verse 2, "prepared as a bride adorned for her husband." A thousand years have rolled, yet her bridal beauty for the heart of Christ is untarnished and as fresh as ever.

As with Babylon so here we have brought together the two symbols of a woman and a city. They appear, on the surface, to be quite incongruous, but not so when we come to their significance. The one sets forth what the church will be **to** Christ; the other what it will be **for** Him: as the bride, the object of His love; as the city, the centre from which His powerful administration will proceed.

The adjective, "great," in verse 10 lacks authority and should be omitted. The harlot city, Babylon, was characterized by greatness, the bridal city, New Jerusalem, is characterized by being from God, and hence it is holy and heavenly and has the glory of God — not the glory of man. This being so, it descends over the earth as a luminary, and "her light" is likened to "a jasper stone clear as crystal." Jasper indeed is mentioned three times in the description of the city, and the only other occurrence of the word in the book is in the description of the One who sits on the throne in chapter 4: 3. That which is descriptive of God is descriptive of the city.

Verses 12 to 21 are occupied with the wall, the gates, the foundations, and the city itself. We may consider them in that order. The wall is described as great and high. No adverse power could force an entrance. Evil is totally excluded. Its measure was 144 cubits, the square of 12, which is the number of administration. Here at last then is administration in such perfection as to shut out all that is wrong.

The wall, however, was not absolutely continuous: there were twelve gates, three on each of its four sides. Now gates are made in order that

THE REVELATION

there may be going out and coming in, so that the city, though amply protected by its wall, is not a self-contained and isolated unit. There is to be happy intercourse between it and the millennial earth. He who approaches it finds an angel at each gate, so that all come under inspection. Moreover each gate is a pearl; a reminder this, we should say, to all who approach, that the city itself as "the bride" represents that "pearl of great price" for which the Saviour "sold all that He had." Those who go out find on the gates the names of the tribes of Israel, as indicating the route by which one travels to the happy earth beneath. All the administration of that day will proceed from the throne in the heavenly metropolis, and reach the earth by way of Israel.

Here too is a city which has foundations, and God is the Builder and Maker of it. Twelve again appears, as the number of the foundations, and on each the name of one of the apostles of the Lamb. The church is built upon the foundation of the apostles and prophets, according to Ephesians 2: 20, so this confirms us in thinking that in symbolic way the city sets forth the church. Again the foundations are garnished with precious stones; a stone to each foundation. The first has jasper, which, as we have just seen, is peculiarly descriptive of God Himself. That which speaks of God lies at the very foundation of everything here, but each stone in one way or another acts as a prism, reflecting the various hues that go to make up light. The very foundations of the city sparkle with the light of God, but so reflected that men may appreciate its colourful details.

The city itself as well as its gates and wall is measured by the angel, using a golden reed. Thus the measuring standard was divine, and it was found to be a perfect cube of immense dimensions. A furlong (or stadium, as the word is) was about 200 yards, so 12,000 would equal about 1,375 miles. The fact that its height was this as well as its length and breadth, helps to confirm the thought that we are dealing not with literal language but symbolic. In this measurement we again meet with twelve, the number of administration, and the very street of the city is gold like transparent glass. In earth's cities the street is the place where dirt accumulates. There all is divine purity and transparency, and as is the city so is the government that proceeds from it.

Verses 22 and 23 unfold to us that wherein the glory of the city consists. The earthly Jerusalem of the millennial age will have the Temple of Jehovah as its crowning glory. Ezekiel sees this in vision, and records it and the measurements of it in his chapters 40 to 48. The glory of the heavenly Jerusalem is that it has no temple for the Lord God Almighty and the Lamb are the Temple of it; that is, there They shine in Their glory without the necessity of a covering or screen. In "Lord God Almighty" we have reference to the three names under which God was revealed in Old Testament times, and with Him is coupled on equal terms the once humbled Lamb, depreciated and set at nought by men. There is no mention of God as Father here, but that is, we judge, because the emphasis is not

THE REVELATION

on the **relationship,** in which the church is set, but on the **administration,** which is committed to it.

Amongst men administration is so often a failure by reason of unrighteousness or ignorance. Here all is marked by the perfect light of God. The glory of God illuminates the city, and the "light," or more accurately "lamp" of it is the Lamb. In Him the light will be concentrated and made available for the city. All natural light is superseded and no longer needed there. Verse 24 shows that though the light has its seat in the city it is diffused upon earth so that the saved nations enjoy it. All their activities will be governed by it, and thus we see how at last heaven and earth shall be brought into sweet accord, as was hinted in Hosea 2: 21, 22.

But just as the light of God streams out of the heavenly city so into it shall flow the glory and honour of the kings of the earth and of the nations. In chapter 17: 2, we saw the kings of the earth trafficking with the false Babylon before the advent of Christ. They have now departed to their doom, as also the nations who forgot God. The kings and nations of our chapter are those who have passed into millennial blessedness in happy subjection to the Lord. Heavenly light shines forth upon them and glory and honour streams back into the city from them on earth. Here is a scene portrayed which may well enrapture every heart; only to be exceeded by the joys of the city itself.

This delightful intercourse is uninterrupted as far as the city is concerned. Its gates are never shut, for within it is continuous day. If we compare this with Isaiah 60: 11, we find an instructive contrast. In that glad day the gates of the earthly Jerusalem will be open continually. There will be night there for it says, "they shall not be shut day nor night." Into that city, the "forces" or "wealth" of the Gentiles, and their kings, will be brought. Thus on earth things will be on a lower footing, though there is some similarity with the heavenly city, which will be more clearly seen if all the latter part of that chapter be read.

From the heavenly city every form of evil and defilement and untruth will be wholly excluded, and only those written in the Lamb's book of life will enter it. This could hardly be said of the earthly Jerusalem, even in the millennial age.

Chapter 22

WE HAVE ALREADY seen that there is no temple in the heavenly city inasmuch as God and the Lamb are the Temple of it. The opening verse of chapter 22 shows that the throne of God and the Lamb is there, and this is again stated even more definitely in verse 3. Out of the throne proceeds the water of life like a flowing river. No earthly throne — not even the best of them — has proved itself to be a fountain of life. Their rule has been too oppressive or too weak, or their decisions before reaching the people have

THE REVELATION

been too polluted in passing through lesser human channels. Here at last is a throne of absolute righteousness, which is exerted in beneficence, and life is the outcome. Moreover the city from which it flows out to men, is protected from every kind of defilement, and therefore no pollution reaches it as it flows. It is "pure" and "clear as crystal." We read of Zion on earth as the spot where, "the Lord commanded the blessing, even life for evermore" (Psa. 133: 3). We are now contemplating the heavenly source whence all flows.

The river of life nourishes and supports the tree of life, and that tree is in the midst of the golden street of the city. Our thoughts are carried back at once to Genesis 2 and 3. In his condition of innocence Adam had two trees within his reach. The tree of life was not forbidden him: the tree of knowledge of good and evil was. The one open to him he passed by: the one forbidden he took. As a fallen man the tree of life was placed beyond his reach by angelic action, never to be reached by anything that any man can do. There was no solution of the fearful problem raised until the Son of God appeared to put away sin by the sacrifice of Himself. Then, and only then, the responsibilities incurred by the knowledge of good and evil were met, and the risen Christ becomes the true Tree of Life for men. It is as true today as it will be then, that "the tree of life . . . is in the midst of the paradise of God" (Rev. 2: 7).

On this glorious tree the number twelve again is stamped. Its fruit is in twelve-fold diversity, and yielded twelve times a year. The fruits are apparently for the heavenly city, but its very leaves are to bring healing to the nations. The mention of months, of nations and of healing, show that the whole scene is concerned with the millennium and not with the eternal state.

When considering the eternal state, at the beginning of chapter 21, we saw that much of the detail given is of a negative order — the mention of what will **not** be there. We find the same feature here. The city has no temple, no need of sun and moon, and no possibility of pollution. Now we find that there is no more curse, and it is repeated that there is no night there. Directly sin entered a curse entered, as Genesis 3 bears witness. The entrance of the law only made the curse more emphatic, and Malachi, the last prophetic word to the people under the law, uses the word freely: it is indeed the last word of the Old Testament.

The disobedience of the first man brought in the curse. The obedience of the Second, even unto death, laid the basis for its removal. When the throne of God and of the Lamb is established in the city then the curse goes out for ever. All disobedience will have disappeared. The Divine authority will be fully acknowledged, and righteousness, having nothing to challenge it, will be exercised purely in blessing.

Therefore it is that we read, "His servants shall serve Him." But, if they were His servants, did they not always serve Him? — we may ask. The

THE REVELATION

answer would have to be — only in part. So often, alas! selfish motives were mixed in with their service to Him, and the more spiritually minded they were the more they were conscious of it. Now at last the flesh in them has been eliminated and they really do serve Him. All that is entrusted to them, in carrying out the will of God and the Lamb, will be perfectly accomplished.

Then comes that glorious statement, "they shall see His face." His face is connected with His glory in the revelation of Himself. When the law was given, and broken, Moses found **grace** in God's sight, and thus emboldened he said, "I beseech Thee, shew me Thy **glory**." The answer was, "Thou canst not see My face: for there shall no man see Me, and live." Under grace the contrast is great. We can say, "God . . . hath shined in our hearts, to give the light of the knowledge of the glory of God in the face of Jesus Christ." But what we have here far exceeds that. Brought into favour, we shall dwell in the full light of the knowledge of God, perfectly revealed in Christ. The prayer of our Lord will be fulfilled, "that they also, whom Thou hast given Me, be with Me where I am; that they may behold My glory." We shall see the face of God for ever, **in beholding Him.**

Out of this, surely, springs the next statement, "His name shall be in their foreheads." In chapter 13, we learned that the followers of the beast had to have the mark or the name in their foreheads, thus declaring their allegiance to him, and that they represented him. Such come, as we have seen, under the wrath of God. We shall bear the name of God and the Lamb in the most prominent place, declaring our everlasting allegiance to Him, and reflecting His likeness as His representatives.

It would be difficult to conceive of anything more blessed than this — dwelling in His light, and reflecting His likeness for ever. Note the striking fact of "His" thrice repeated — not "Their." God and the Lamb are both brought together under a pronoun in the singular. They are clearly distinguished; but They are **one.** Another indication this of the Deity of Christ.

Brought thus into this blaze of living light, all the darkness of night is for ever gone, and no feeble candle of man's making is needed. Our chapter began with life and has proceeded to light. Love is not mentioned, it is only inferred, inasmuch as the city is the bride, the Lamb's wife. That doubtless is because it is the city which is dwelt upon, and that sets forth not love but a centre of Divine administration.

So the closing words of the description are, "they shall reign for ever and ever." As we learned at the opening of the book, the saints are made a kingdom of priests to God; that is, they are priestly kings. Further, as Paul told the Corinthians, "the saints shall judge the world." And again, "we shall judge angels." This is the thought of God, long purposed. Now we find it brought to accomplishment.

THE REVELATION

Here, then, are things that rise far above our feeble powers of apprehension at present. Nevertheless they are, blessed be God, profoundly real and, accomplished in their season, to be established for ever.

In verse 5 we have read the last utterance of prophetic revelation, and in it we were conducted to a condition of blessedness far beyond our highest thoughts. In Genesis 3 we have seen man departing from the light of God — such as was vouchsafed to him — plunging into spiritual night and becoming a slave of sin. Here we see redeemed men, who have received "abundance of grace and of the gift of righteousness," established in everlasting light, and they "reign in life by One, Jesus Christ," as the Apostle Paul had written in Romans 5: 17.

We are not surprised therefore that verse 6 gives us a solemn affirmation of the truth of the wonderful prospect unfolded. The Apostles made known the power and coming of the Lord, and Peter assures us that they had not followed cunningly devised fables in so doing (see, 2 Peter 1: 16). Here we are contemplating glories which stretch out into eternity and which would be beyond belief were they not guaranteed to us as "faithful and true."

Moreover they are "things which must shortly be done." This statement surely is intended to intimate to us that we must reckon time according to the Divine estimation and not according to ours. The word translated "shortly" is almost the same as that translated "quickly" in the next verse, where we have the first of the three declarations, "I come quickly," that occur in these closing verses. Our centuries are but so many minutes in God's great clock! We incline to think however that this word is also intended to signify that when the Divine action takes place it is marked by swiftness, as it says in Romans 9: 28, "A short work will the Lord make upon the earth." When Jesus comes it will be no slow and long drawn out manifestation but rather like the lightning's flash.

While we wait for His coming our blessedness lies in keeping the sayings of the prophecy we have been considering. We shall "keep" them if we bear them in mind so effectually that they govern our lives. We have heard the study of prophecy decried on the ground that it is but an intellectual exercise. It may be merely that of course, but it is not intended to be. If we keep the sayings of the prophecy we shall be enriched by the understanding of God's purpose, of the objectives He has before Him, and of the way in which He will reach them. We shall also be blessed by the assurance of the complete victory that will crown all His judgments and His ways.

The effect of all this upon John was very great, as indeed it should be upon us who read it. The impulse to worship was doubtless right, though falling at the feet of the angelic messenger was wrong. This was instantly repudiated by the angel for he took the place merely of a servant, and in that respect on a par with John or the prophets, or indeed with all who

THE REVELATION

take the place of obedience to the word of God. God alone is to be worshipped. No holy angel will accept it, though it is the dearest desire of Satan, the great fallen angel, as is shown in Matthew 4: 9.

Verses 8 and 9 are parenthetical in their nature. We must link verses 10 and 11 with verse 7. These sayings of the prophecy which are so profitable to the one who keeps them, are not to be sealed but kept open for any to inspect. The contrast to the close of Daniel's prophecy strikes one at once. He was to "shut up the words, and seal the book, even to the time of the end." The epoch in which we live — the Christian dispensation, we may call it — is "the time of the end," or as John calls it in his epistle "the last time" (2: 18). The Holy Ghost is come and that which formerly was sealed is open, and that now revealed is not to be sealed. No doubt it is also true that we are now in the last days of the last time, so that all this unsealed prophecy should have a special interest for us.

Verse 11 also is connected with the "Behold I come quickly" of verse 7, as also with the same announcement at the beginning of verse 12. The coming of the Lord will give fixity to the state of all, whether good or bad. Today there are the unjust and the filthy; the righteous and the holy. But today the unjust may be justified and the filthy may be born again and enter the ranks of the holy. The Lord having come, the state of each is unalterably fixed. May this tremendously solemn thought weigh heavily with us all!

Moreover, as verse 12 shows, the coming of the Lord will mean the judgment seat, where every man will have his work valued and rewarded according to its deserts. This is a very solemn thought for each believer. After the rapture of the saints comes the judgment seat of Christ.

It would seem as if, having uttered what is recorded in verse 11, the angel disappears, and the voice of Christ, the coming One, is heard alone. He is the Alpha and the Omega, the beginning and the end, the first and the last. There could hardly be a stronger affiirmation of His essential Deity than this. Obviously no created being, however exalted, could speak thus. It guarantees the rectitude of all His judgments, and that every reward He bestows will be in exact keeping with deserts.

Again we find the two classes in verses 14 and 15 — the holy and the filthy. In verse 14 the better attested reading seems to be, "Blessed are they that wash their robes;" that is, once they were filthy but they have been cleansed. Only thus can anyone have right to the tree of life or be given access to the heavenly city. Those washed are within. Those characterised by the evils of verse 15 are without. The Apostle Paul had issued the warning, "Beware of dogs, beware of evil workers" (Phil. 3: 2), and here we find such excluded for ever. Moreover he had plainly indicated that today in the assembly of God there is a divinely recognized "within," and there is the world "without" (1 Cor. 5: 12, 13), so here we find the same separation maintained and carried into eternity.

THE REVELATION

Verse 16 has in it an element of contrast if compared with the first verse of the book. The prophetic unveilings, given by God to Jesus Christ, and conveyed to us by His angel through John, are now completed. The angel through whom they were communicated has disappeared. Jesus Himself remains, and in this verse and those succeeding it His voice only is heard. In the first place He endorses all that had been conveyed by the ministry of the angel, who had been sent by Him. We are not to think that the prophetic witness was anything less than Divine, though it has reached us in this way, The testimony was given in the seven churches which are in Asia, as stated in chapter 1: 4, but through them is intended for the enlightenment of the whole church until He comes.

Having thus endorsed the whole book, the Lord Jesus, using only His personal Name, presents Himself to us in a twofold way. First, as the root and the offspring of David, which gives us His title in Manhood to the kingdom and all dominance on the earth. Let Psalm 78: 65-72 be read, and then 2 Samuel 23: 1-5. These passages show that by a special intervention of Divine Power David was raised up to kingly estate, and how he was but an imperfect forecast of the infinitely greater One who was to spring from him after the flesh. Hence, in Isaiah 11: 1, Christ is spoken of as a "rod" or "shoot" out of the stem of Jesse, and as a branch who is fruitful out of his roots. Here He is clearly presented to us as the "Offspring" of David.

But in the same chapter in Isaiah, verse 10, He is presented as "a root of Jesse" which shall be "in that day," which answers also to what we have in our chapter. He is both "shoot" and "root" in Isaiah; both "offspring" and "root" in Revelation. In the former words His Manhood is the prominent thought; in the latter words, His Deity. And then — again reverting to 2 Samuel 23 — when at last He rules over men in justice and in the fear of God, He will be "as the light of the morning, when the sun riseth, even a morning without clouds." In this striking and poetic imagery is set forth the opening of earth's bright millennial day, when He comes.

But as the Revelation closes He presents Himself to us, not only in a way that refers us back to the Old Testament predictions of the rising of the Sun of righteousness, but in a second way more distinctly connected with New Testament hopes. He had been predicted as coming "a Star out of Jacob" (Num. 24: 17), without any reference to the morning. As the bright Morning Star, Jesus presents Himself as the Forerunner and Pledge of the uprising day. Now Israel does not know Him thus, for it has rejected Him and treated Him as an imposter. The Church, and the Church alone, knows Him in this character, and is authorized to entertain those heavenly hopes, centred in Him, which are to be realized before the day of glory breaks for Israel and the earth.

So in verse 16 the Lord Jesus addresses us personally as the One in whom all hope is centred both for the heavens and for the earth and He

THE REVELATION

strips Himself, if we may so say, of all His titles and honours that more simply and effectively He may present HIMSELF. It is this that most directly appeals to the hearts of His own. Consequently there is an immediate response.

We may find encouragement in the fact that at the end of this book, and indeed of the New Testament as a whole, the Spirit is discovered as still remaining and the bride as a still existing entity on the earth. The failure which has so grievously marked the professing church, as indicated prophetically in chapters 2 and 3, has not grieved away the One nor destroyed the other. The Spirit indwells the bride, and hence as with one voice the response, "Come," is uttered. Such is the fact; but we may well challenge ourselves whether we are altogether in harmony with this cry. It is to be feared that all too many Christians are still looking for improvement on the earth, or at all events to an ideal condition of things being produced by the preaching of the Gospel, laying great stress on its social implications, and hence hardly joining in the cry.

This is it, we believe, which accounts for the next sentence, which contemplates some who hear, but who so far have not joined in the cry. Is any reader one of these? If so, you are invited to fall into line with the Spirit and the bride and add your "Come" to theirs. The more we realize our part in the Church and the place which the Church has as the bride of Christ the more ardently we shall desire the coming of the Bridegroom.

The third and fourth sentences comprised in verse 17 give us the happy assurance that until He comes the living water that the Gospel bestows is available for every thirsty soul. If our Lord speaks, as He does here, we who are His humble servants may boldly address men in the same confident terms. It is a joy to know that just as we may turn to Him who is the bright Morning Star and say, "Come," so we may turn to men generally, and to the thirsting and the willing in particular, and bid them come to take of the water of life freely. Until this era of grace is replaced by an era of judgment the Gospel invitation is to go forth. It is for "whosoever will" and we may be sure that to the end there will be found some who by the working of God's Spirit will be willing to take.

There is great solemnity about verses 18 and 19. To tamper with the Word of God is a great sin of which it is assumed no true believer will be guilty. Be it noted that the sin may be committed by adding to the words as well as subtracting from them. In olden days the former sin was that of the Pharisees, the latter that of the Sadducees. The one added their tradition, which had the effect of neutralizing the true word of God. The other adopted rationalist views and refused to believe in resurrection or in angel or spirit, and so took away much from the Divine word. Though the names are obsolete the spirit of both is very much alive today and this warning is greatly needed. The threatening at the end of verse 19 is perhaps

THE REVELATION

the graver of the two. The taking away of his part from the tree of life, as the margin reads, seems to be correct.

Be it noted also that it is tampering with the "words" that is forbidden. At the very close we have a final intimation that the words of the Divine Writings are inspired. **Verbal** inspiration is claimed right up to the finish. If we have no **verbal** inspiration we have no inspiration at all. It is easy to see this if we transfer our thoughts to mundane affairs. The laws of our land are certainly not inspired but they are authoritative, and they have been enacted by Parliament in written form, sentence by sentence and word by word. In our Law Courts appeal is frequently made to the very words of our laws, knowing that they are valid and cannot successfully be impeached or altered. If counsel in some legal action waived the **words** of the law aside and pretended to interpret what he called "the spirit of the law" apart from the words, he would be quickly shown the emptiness of his contention and that the **words** had the authority and governed the case. Let us reverence the WORDS of this prophecy and of every other part of the Divine Writings.

In verse 20 we have what we may regard as the closing utterance of our blessed Lord in the Holy Scriptures — His last inspired word to His Church. He had just testified to the integrity and authority of His holy word, but in saying "these things," we believe He referred to all contained in this wonderful book; indeed to all that we have in the Scriptures. And His last word of testimony is, "Surely I come quickly." Thus for the third time in this closing chapter He announces His coming. In view of this how extraordinary it is that the very thought of His coming should have so largely slipped out of the mind of the church for ages, and even have been denied or explained away.

The explanation doubtless lies in the fact that the church slipped into the world and set its mind on the earth, as was indicated in the addresses to Pergamos and Thyatira in chapter 2. Enticed by earthly allurements, the coming of the heavenly Christ lost its attraction. Let us see to it that the same process does not take place in our own hearts and lives. If we know what our portion and prospect really is we shall find His coming to be attractive beyond words, and our response will surely be, as indicated here, "Amen. Even so, come, Lord Jesus." We cannot desire delay and we add our hearty "So be it" — Come quickly, as Thou hast said, Lord Jesus. God grant that this may be the true response of all our hearts.

We have had in verse 20 the closing affiirmation and promise of our Lord, and the closing response from the hearts and lips of His saints. Now finally in verse 21 we have the closing benediction from the Lord through the Apostle John, who was the vessel of these communications. The better attested reading is, "The grace of the Lord Jesus Christ be with all the saints." His full title is used here, and the closing note that is struck is that of His well known **grace**. This grace is to rest on ALL the saints and not

THE REVELATION

on a few only, who may be specially faithful. And it will rest upon them ALL the time while we wait for Him.

The last word of the Old Testament is "curse." That is because its main theme is the government of God and His law, ministered through Moses. And we read, "As many as are of the works of the law are under the curse" (Gal. 3: 10). The New Testament introduces that "grace and truth" which "came by Jesus Christ" (John 1: 17). Hence the great contrast furnished by the closing words of the New Testament.

We may well bless God that the grace of the Lord Jesus Christ shines like the sun upon every saint, while we all wait for the coming of our Lord.

www.ingramcontent.com/pod-product-compliance
Lightning Source LLC
Chambersburg PA
CBHW020745160426
43192CB00006B/249